Praise for *New World Witchery*

"Filled with hundreds of examples of American folk magic and folklore, no better word than 'trove' would describe such a book as this, as it's truly filled with valuable information on the magical heritage of North America."

—Jake Richards, author of *Backwoods Witchcraft*

"A wonderful combination of culture, history, and ethnography culminates in a valuable guide to the world of healers, spirits, and magical approaches to living."

—Tony Kail, anthropologist and author of *A Secret History of Memphis Hoodoo*

"Deep and extremely thorough, *New World Witchery* encapsulates the diversity of American folk magic as a distinct multifaceted contribution to the history and execution of witchcraft."

—Christopher Orapello, cohost of the *Down at the Crossroads* podcast and coauthor of *Besom, Stang & Sword*

"[This book] provides just the right blend of magic and folklore that we need to navigate the complex streams of modern Witchcraft."

—Lilith Dorsey, author of *Water Magic* and *Orishas, Goddesses, and Voodoo Queens*

"A veritable goldmine of history, folk magic and occultism, *New World Witchery* is the finest contribution to the study of witchcraft in the United States yet."

—Via Hedera, author of *Folkloric Witchcraft and the Multicultural Experience*

"Overflowing with hundreds of pieces of folkloric knowledge, it is an unparalleled resource for traditional witches seeking to ground their practices in New World lore."

—Christine Grace, cohost of the *Betwixt and Between* podcast

"A whimsical and extensively researched journey into the lore and folk practices of the New World... This is, in every way, a love letter to lore and easily one of the most fun and fascinating books about witchcraft I've ever read."

—Josh "Bones" McWilliams, host of the *Cursed!* and *Hex-Files* podcasts

"This is an exceptional book. Well written, readable at a number of educational levels, and I like the organization of topics … I predict that this will become a classic in the genre."

—Jack Montgomery, author of *American Shamans: Journeys with Traditional Healers*

"Hutcheson has given us a perfect compendium for the time: well-organized and beautifully written … [This book] is filled with history and strange delights and invites the curious mind to go both farther afield and deeper."

—H. Byron Ballard, author of *Roots, Branches, and Spirits*

"[Hutcheson] lays a sumptuous banquet of folktales and witchlore before us, collected carefully over years of respectful research and written for this modern age, combined with page after page of lord-get-your-hands-dirty practical workings."

—Tara-Love Maguire, coauthor of *Besom, Stang, and Sword* and cohost of *Down at the Crossroads* podcast

"Hutcheson has crafted a definitive, yet accessible, book exploring the history and practices of North American witchcraft and magic. Trust me, you need this book on your bookshelf."

—Judika Illes, author of *Encyclopedia of 5000 Spells*

"Cory Hutcheson has gifted us with a wide-ranging and in-depth look at the witchcraft and magical traditions of North America … The book is a dream and a charm all of its own."

—Aidan Wachter, author of *Six Ways: Approaches and Entries for Practical Magic*

"[Hutcheson's] gentle, magical voice takes the reader through one of the most expansive and thorough examinations of North American folk magic I've ever seen. It is a masterwork."

—Fire Lyte, host of the *Inciting a Riot* podcast

"A perfect blend of history, folklore, practice, and path-crafting that any magical practitioner can benefit from. Cory writes with a warm and conversational voice that is a pure joy to read."

—Laura Tempest Zakroff, author of *Weave the Liminal*

NEW WORLD WITCHERY

About the Author

Cory Thomas Hutcheson is the cohost of the popular podcast *New World Witchery*. He has a doctorate in American Studies with specializations in folklore, religion, and ethnicity from Penn State. He is a contributor to the *Oxford Handbook of American Folklore and Folklife Studies* and *American Myths, Legends, & Tall Tales*, and he has written for popular occult publications, including *Witches & Pagans*.

Llewellyn Publications
Woodbury, Minnesota

First Edition
First Printing, 2021

Book design by Donna Burch-Brown
Cover design by Shannon McKuhen
Editing by Marjorie Otto
Interior art by Cory Thomas Hutcheson

Library of Congress Cataloging-in-Publication Data
Names: Hutcheson, Cory Thomas, author.
Title: New world witchery : a trove of North American folk magic / Cory Thomas Hutcheson.
Description: Frist edition. | Woodbury, Minnesota : Llewellyn Publications, [2021] | Includes bibliographical references and index. | Summary: "A collection of stories, rituals, exercises and beliefs, this book looks at folklore and folk magic in North America"— Provided by publisher.
Identifiers: LCCN 2021004742 (print) | LCCN 2021004743 (ebook) | ISBN 9780738762128 (paperback) | ISBN 9780738762227 (ebook)
Subjects: LCSH: Witchcraft—North America. | Magic—North America. | North America—Folklore.
Classification: LCC BF1584.N58 H87 2021 (print) | LCC BF1584.N58 (ebook) | DDC 133.43097—dc23
LC record available at https://lccn.loc.gov/2021004742
LC ebook record available at https://lccn.loc.gov/2021004743

Llewellyn Publications
A Division of Llewellyn Worldwide Ltd.
2143 Wooddale Drive
Woodbury, MN 55125-2989
www.llewellyn.com

Printed in the United States of America

Other Books by Cory Thomas Hutcheson

54 Devils: The Art and Folklore of Fortune-Telling with Playing Cards
(CreateSpace)

Dedication

This book is dedicated to those who, like enchanted magpies, have shown me the shiny bits of magic in my world, little by little, every day.

To my magical partner, the friend and co-witch who has made this entire project possible, Laine.

To my mother, Sue Zack, who opened the doors of riddles and lore to me.

And to my children, Jack and Poppy, whose imaginations provide more magic than I could ever hope to use.

Thank you, all. I hope this book adds a little magic back into your world.

Acknowledgments

A book like this absolutely cannot exist without an enormous number of people providing support, guidance, care, admonition, sympathy, criticism, love, and no small amount of their own enchantment. Inevitably, I will falter here in remembering them all, and for that I beg forgiveness in advance, and ask that you do not send curses at me. My intentions are good, and my failures—I think—mostly harmless.

Enormous thanks to my patient family: Kate, Jack, and Poppy (and Baudelaire the greyhound), who have all put up with my strange obsessions and weird tendencies with unflappable good humor. For the same reasons, I must thank my mother, Suzanne Elizabeth Zack, as she not only supported but actively encouraged my oddity in the best possible ways.

I also could not do this without my friends, the people who have frequently fuelled my quirky passions. I am grateful to Laine, of course, a partner in both magic and crime without whom none of this would have happened. Thanks also to my dear friends Justin and Bob, who have frequently been the ones to inspire me and have the deep conversations that challenge me in the best possible ways. I am deeply thankful for my magical community, who have offered their feedback, lore, enthusiasm, and kindness at so many turns: Vic, Heather, AthenaBeth, Fire Lyte, Chris Orapello, Tara-Love Maguire, Velma Nightshade, Kathleen Borealis, Via Hedera, and Jen Rue.

Special thanks as well to my early readers for this book, whose feedback has been immensely valuable to me in making it what it is today: Jonathan D. Clayton, Xamonster, Tarsha Gragsone, Astara Dragonheart, Mari Lee Ray, Victoria S., Wisdomqueen, Montine Rummel, Signy Hege Myrsdottir, Catriona McDonald, and Rosalie.

I know this book is not explicitly an academic one, but so much of my work is built upon the foundations of my folklore and history peers and mentors, and to all of them I am profoundly grateful for their contributions and guidance: Simon Bronner, Anthony Bak Buccitelli, John Ernest, Jenn Lewin, Mary Sellers, Kate Anderson Holmes, John Price, Annamarie O'Brien, Jeanna Jorgenson, Morgan Daimler, Andrea Kitta, Lynne McNeill, Semontee Mitra, Kay Turner, Marc Norman, Lilith Dorsey, Tony Kail, and Patrick Donmoyer.

And to the many witches, conjurers, cunning folk, root doctors, Hoodoo men and women, curanderas, yarb doctors, Pow-wows and brauchers, and all other magical folk who have lived on this land and left a legacy of enchantment; truly, a deep and abiding thanks. I also could hardly have come so far in my study and practice without those who have been magical teachers and guides to me directly and indirectly: Atticus Hob, Robert Schreiwer, Rob Phoenix, Starr Casas, Jack Montgomery, Stephanie Palm, Sarah Anne Lawless, Juniper Birch, Concha Ruiz, Peter Paddon, Michael Howard, Benebell Wen, and Laura Tempest Zakroff (without whom this book would not exist, as she very much threw me over her broomstick and flew down the chimney of my editor to introduce us).

To that end, I must also offer deep thanks to my editors at Llewellyn, Elysia Gallo, Marjorie Otto, and Lynne Menturweck, as well as to Judika Illes at Weiser, who have all been phenomenal guides and resources in the world of witchy publishing (as well as delightful human beings all around).

And finally, my thanks to frankly every author I cite in my bibliography, because I am standing on the shoulders of an entire army of giants. But especially to Zora Neale Hurston, whose legacy of folklore, magic, literature, and life have spoken to me since I first read her words many years ago.

Contents

Exercises/Practical Work

Chapter 2

Chapter 3

Chapter 4

Chapter 5

Chapter 6

Chapter 7

Chapter 8

Chapter 9

Chapter 10

Chapter 11

Chapter 12

Chapter 13

Chapter 14

Chapter 15

Chapter 16

Chapter 17

Chapter 18

Chapter 19

Chapter 20

Chapter 21

Chapter 22

CHAPTER ONE

The Crossroads—An Introduction and Guide to This Book

It is probably useless to attempt to convince you, the reader, that a "witch" is something you do not already understand. Whatever image pops into your head when that word passes by in conversation—whether whispered reverently or barked in anger—that will be the definitive image for you. Perhaps your image has shifted, but most likely that shift occurred gradually, over time, and there is still a very good chance that if someone showed you a picture of Margaret Hamilton from *The Wizard of Oz* you would at least get a flicker of the word "witch" in your brain. Similarly, seeing a Waterhouse painting of a faery woman drawing a circle in the sand around a burning pot emitting fumes is likely to conjure—forgive the pun—the word "witch" to mind. For many, a "witch" may also be an ornery older woman who lives alone in a house that is a bit overgrown, or maybe a word that people around you use to talk about spiteful ghosts that linger in the shadows. Those suffering from "hag riding" syndrome may perceive a "witch" as a presence, heavy and ominous, that holds them down in bed at night.

In fairy tales, popular culture, and literature, we conceive of witches everywhere and give them numerous forms. In our everyday lives, we may not think much about witches, or we may think about them a great deal in a romantic or symbolic way. We all know, though, what a witch *is*, don't we? Yet for all the images we can summon when we hear the word "witch," we must also admit that if one fits, they all do, which hints at how hard it is to capture a witch in one place and hold her still, on film or in one's cellar where the good wine is kept. Why then can we instantly understand the word "witch" when we hear it spoken?

The simple reason is that witches are creatures of story, and we all love a good story. Those can be fairy tales, yes, but they can also be "true" stories told about our neighbors, our friends, women we have known and loved, or women we have feared and reviled. Witches excite our collective imagination, a point that will be even more cogent when we consider just how creative the magic of witchery can be. We understand witches, even if we all conceive of them a little differently. Through all the trappings and trivia and tinsel that we use to cobble together something resembling a "witch" when we make our pictures and films and sculptures, we understand the underlying characteristic of the witch: she has magic, and she uses it.[1]

I have always been a little bit obsessed with witches. More specifically, I have always been a little bit obsessed with what witches *do*: magic. For me, the defining characteristic of witches is that they cast spells, they bottle potions, they transform those who wrong or offend them into various denizens of swamp and field. When I was in elementary school, I spent an inordinate amount of time scouring our small-town school library for anything remotely magical. At first, I was interested in the sword and sorcery I had seen in films and television shows, but very quickly I found there were people who used magic not for zapping lightning bolts from their fingers, but for ever-so-slightly nudging Fate in their favor. Sometimes, that nudge wound up causing problems for other people, and sometimes it was simply a twist of luck for the better. What I noticed with many of the spells I found was that they would be gathered alongside things like nursery rhymes, fairy tales, and descriptions of holi-

1. I have been saying "she" and "her" quite a lot, and this is not by accident. A great many witches in the stories we tell are women—perhaps one of the very few places where the primary characters are women more often than men without emphasizing a motherly or purely sexual role. I will most certainly be sharing a number of stories in which men play a part, even as witches, but in general I use the feminine pronouns not to cast aspersions at feminine gender or sexuality; witches *do* come from all genders, and in the cases where the witch in question is not identified in strictly feminine terms I will use the most appropriate pronoun I can find. Since, however, so rarely are feminine pronouns the *preferred* pronoun in writing, I have chosen to lean into the trope a bit and follow the lead of the stories I share by defaulting to "she" and "her" in most cases.

days and festivals from around the world. The magic was part of something called "folklore," and, reader, I was hooked.

Coming to the Crossroads—Finding New World Witchery

The combination of folklore and magic has been my passion and my focus for nearly two and a half decades. I began collecting spells and tidbits of folk magic on index cards, in journals, on sticky notes and scraps tucked into books of folktales. My search for magic led me to pick up spells like a magpie, trying them out, seeing what worked, and putting down what didn't. It led me to the strange sections of libraries and odd monsters in the shadows of old stories. It led me to try to learn new languages, dozens of them, just to understand some of the spells I found in their original words. (I am by no means a polyglot, but I have a somewhat unhealthy obsession with picking up phrase books and using language-learning software or taking classes in half a dozen languages in college, and thus knowing just enough to be dangerous when I try to ask where the bathroom is in a number of countries.) I have pursued advanced degrees, eventually taking a doctorate with a focus on folklore studies, specifically because of my interest in folk magic. With my long-time magical partner, I have created and hosted a long-running podcast about folk magic in North America, a project that has afforded me the opportunity to interview dozens of magical practitioners and scholars from a wide variety of backgrounds. That same project connects me with thousands of listeners, many of whom also are eager to share their experiences of magic or to ask questions that prompt me to look more deeply at certain parts of North American folklore and magical work than I might have otherwise. In this regard, I have been incredibly lucky and privileged to pursue this passion. I have also worked very hard to pull all these disparate strands together for myself and others, and to identify what I would call "New World Witchery."[2]

Why the "New World" part? Well, one thing I found very early and often in my studies was how closely magic linked to location. There is a strong sense that the

2. I will note here that while I use the term "New World," I am really referring to North America. This was sort of an early flub on my part in equating the two terms. The New World (from a European perspective) actually includes North America, South America, and even Oceania (especially Australia and New Zealand) as well. I am not an expert on most of the magical traditions of South America or Oceania, however, so I will leave it to a better-equipped writer to discuss those lands and their magic (and eagerly encourage them to point out my shortcomings here as a part of their work).

place of magic shapes the *form* of magic. Huge amounts of magical lore from Europe have found their way into print through brilliant (sometimes nefariously brilliant) authors. In my "collecting" days, before I started the podcast or pursued my degrees, I moved overseas to live in Prague, the capital of the Czech Republic, in order to teach English. While there, I experienced a lot of enchantment, and all of it seemed extremely particular to the Slavic people who lived there. Stories abounded of alchemists living in tiny rowhouses near the palace, a king with a love of the occult and esoteric, saints' bodies with magical healing properties, or even a clock charting the movement of the spheres in the heavens on the public square (a clock still operating today and which inspired the clock on Cinderella's castle in Disney World). The enchantment permeated everything, and all the places I walked and wandered seemed touched by that Slavic magic.

When I returned to the United States, I experienced a brief moment of dejection, because I thought that the magic was still "over there." I began looking for other sources, and studied with the Outer Court of a Gardnerian coven while also looking into other forms of British Traditional Witchcraft such as the Robert Cochrane–derived 1734 tradition. I began listening to Trad Crafter and mage extraordinaire Peter Paddon and his *Crooked Path* podcast, then devouring his books as well.[3] All of those sources, though, emphasized distinctly British and European roots, even as they focused on connecting with local spirits and a magical landscape around you. The magic still felt like it was coming from somewhere else.

It wasn't until I was reading some books of folktales from the southern United States that I noticed something: there was magic here, too. Stories like those of Brer Rabbit or "Sop Paw" (about a group of witches who turn into cats to harangue a weary traveler) all contained little bits of magic—spells or ingredients or simple rituals. I read a story about a pair of "greasy witches" in the Smoky Mountains and immediately noticed parallels with some Irish folktales I had read previously, and realized that both stories contained information on magical flying ointments in coded ways, but also offered a distinct "flavor" of magic depending on where they were told. That got me thinking about something I should have seen so much earlier (but we can't always see what is right in front of us, can we?).

3. Sadly, we lost Peter in 2014. I was lucky enough to interact with him several times both online and in person, and he was infinitely kind, astoundingly wise, and full of magic. He is dearly missed.

Magic is everywhere. Which means, magic is *here.*

I had been living with magic all along. Not only that, the magic around me was robust, alive, growing, and active. It stretched out across North America in all directions, leading me to encounter magical paths and traditions that I had been bumping into for years, but putting aside because they weren't the same kind of "over there" magic I thought I was looking for. I had been treating the journey into folk magic like a road I could walk backward in time, finding some "original" source for it. Instead, I found a crossroads, a place where vast varieties of folk magic intersected and grew. Those who read much folklore know that a crossroads is one of the most powerful places for witchcraft and sorcery—it is a place to meet ghosts or devils and work spells and gather strange magical ingredients. North America crossed cultures—sometimes in horrifying and brutal ways—bringing together influences from West Africa, a plethora of Native Nations, sundry European cultures, and numerous other lands. Systems of magic developed in response to the peoples and their places, with Pennsylvania German-speakers creating healing systems like *bracherei* (also called "Pow-wow"), Scots-Irish and German settlers in the Appalachians generating folk magical "conjure" practices, African and African American enslaved and free peoples brilliantly crafting methods like Rootwork and Hoodoo as a way of coping with or combatting the oppressive systems around them. The more I looked, the more I saw that what I had before me was something like a buried treasure, only it wasn't even buried!

I had grown up with magic. It was in the things I did every day, from picking up lucky pennies to eating black-eyed peas and greens on New Year's Day for luck. It was in the prayers to St. Anthony I learned from my Catholic mother as a way to find lost things, or in the way my friends dangled a wedding ring over a pregnant woman's belly to guess the sex of her baby. It was in the stories of crossing water to keep ghosts from following you home, or in the "haint blue" paint on so many porches that kept specters (and wasps) away. All of that experience, all of that study, leads me to the text you hold in your hands. The purpose of this book is not to make you an expert in any particular magical tradition or tell you it's okay to take anything you like from the traditions here. I simply cannot do that. Instead, this book should help you to see that everyone has magic in their folk communities (which are many and varied, and you likely belong to several without even knowing it), and you can seek that magic out for yourself. Seeing parallel magics in other traditions can help you to understand, identify, and create your own map to a folk magical landscape you already inhabit. If that happens for you, I will consider this book a success.

At the crossroads, my journey began. This book, then, is also a crossroads. In the pages that follow, I lay out a series of points that comprise North American witchcraft based on the *practice* of folk magic, or as I term it, New World Witchery. I will explore different aspects of magical practice based on extensive research, including contemporary interviews and literature, to offer an interested reader an outline of what a New World Witch's practice might be like. This practice-based approach will guide anyone interested in this subject through the specific spells, magical objects, and rituals found in North America, while also giving those actions some context. I intend to give a reader a closely guided tour of New World Witchery, and I hope that my reader—you—will see what I see: a landscape that is and always has been enchanted (and haunted) by magic.

Un-"Grim"-ing the Grimoire: How to Read This Book

I have divided this book, somewhat ostentatiously, into a series of "Rites" corresponding to the practices and activities of North American folk magic. Each section, with the exception of this initial introduction and the final "Rite," will contain one or more chapters that reveal the practice of New World Witchery in specific settings, times, or traditions. You will encounter nineteenth-century magical treasure hunters and see how their practice relates to the rural farming practice of "planting by the signs." You will see witches engaged in life-or-death battles with those who hunt them in the mid-Atlantic region, the Appalachian Mountains, and the "El Norte" region of the American Southwest. Each of these sections is a meditation and a compendium of practices, with a handful of spells highlighted to enhance the narrative, rather than chaining them together in recipe-book format. There are nearly five hundred bits of folklore gathered from all over North America and peppered throughout this tome. In some ways, I am hoping that picking up this book will be like unearthing a box buried at the crossroads for you and finding it stuffed full of folkloric odds and ends—a veritable treasure trove of witchery, if you will. Each little piece will tell you something about magic, and let you put together your own picture of folkloric witchcraft here and now. Through seeing the stories, beliefs, rituals, language, and artifacts that exist here, I am hoping you will come to appreciate just what a rich treasure we have as a magical legacy in North America.

That being said, I also believe that witchcraft is best understood not only *as* a practice, but *through* practice, and so I have included a series of potential folk magical experiments along the way for you, the reader, to try if you wish. I am immensely fond of what folk magical author Aidan Wachter calls "dirt sorcery," the sort of practical, messy, active magic I see in all forms of folk magic, and so in a nod to him I have named my own experimental sections "Dirt Under the Nails."[4] I also include a section at the end of each chapter entitled "The Work" that focuses on more reflective experiments in witchery. Those works are designed to help you observe and integrate the folk magic all around you into your life, or discover where witchcraft is tucked away in the world you already inhabit.

Additionally, I see value in both history and folklore, especially intertwined together. In particular, I want to make sure that I put a human face on what can feel like somewhat abstract magical concepts, and I want to honor those witches and magical workers who have laid all the groundwork for me to build upon now. To that end, I have also included a series of occasional sections titled "Singing Bones" (after a folkloric motif of bones that reveal a secret). These sections will be short biographies or sketches of the lives of particular folk magicians, healers, seers, and witches that resurrect them—even if only for a moment—in the minds of those who read about them. Some are very much historical, others less so, and still others largely the creations of folkloric fictions, but in gathering this little coven (I have selected thirteen, because I cannot help myself), I hope to offer you some insight into the people who have made magic in North America for so many years. My selection process was entirely biased and unscientific, and there are literally dozens of other figures I

4. Wachter, *Six Ways*, 155–57.

could have chosen, but in the end I hope that you, the reader, will meet these baker's dozen and seek out the many I have omitted.

I should also note that each chapter after this one concludes with a short list of two to five reading suggestions that expand on the chapter's themes. Some of the suggestions are collections of folklore, some more experience-oriented, and some are denser scholarly tomes. In all cases, they are simply there as additional roads that you might explore (and roads into texts that I have found immensely helpful in my own studies). In this case, I am hoping that these reading lists will be like finding new treasure maps among the doubloons in my already overstuffed chest of folkloric goodies, pointing you to the next trove waiting for you to find it.

The book is not necessarily one you need to read straight through and cover-to-cover. Once you've passed through the first "Rite" of Naming, you should be able to go to other sections and chapters as you see fit and as your interest dictates. In the Second Rite, I will explore the concepts of initiation and magical heritage, including the ways in which magical knowledge gets transmitted from one generation to the next. The Third Rite delves into the various types of spells we find in North America, including spells of healing and spells of harm. The Fourth Rite turns to the unseen, calling upon powers of divination for insight and treasure. The Fifth Rite is the witch's flight, and I turn to that subject with an eye to understanding just why and how flight can be understood in historical and contemporary witchcraft. In the Sixth Rite, I unpack the witch's tool kit, examining the Bible on her bookshelf and peeking through her spice cabinet, as well as the bottle full of pins and other nefarious ingredients buried by her doorstep.

The Seventh Rite examines the relationship between a witch and her allies, including animal companions and various devils. In the Eighth Rite, I look at countermagic, magical protection of self and home, and the places of North American enchantment. The Ninth Rite explores the times when witches do the work they do. The Tenth Rite looks at that bookshelf again, to the types of magical texts and written charms that might be present in a witch's life, as well as the earlier Colonial concept of the "Devil's Book" and what that might mean for a contemporary practicing witch. In the Eleventh Rite, I look to the relationship between witches and the dead, including what happens when a dead witch won't stay dead. In the Twelfth and Thirteenth Rites (because of course I had to end up with thirteen sections, and am utterly incorrigible), I look to two sides of the same coin: witchcraft in the public eye. The incredible and powerful response that popular culture has to witchcraft has shaped North American identity for centuries, and has become especially acute in the past one hundred years or so. Yet at the same time, that attention has allowed for renewed attacks on witchcraft and witches in various forms and for a surprising number of reasons. Seeing the witch as a glamorous figure may do her some good, but it also singles her out as a target, too, as the final chapters illustrate.

My hope is that you can return to this chapter as you might a crossroads guidepost, full of various arrow signs giving you all sorts of potential directions to go. I have only just begun to explore the ways witches engage with the world around them here. The problems they face, they face with practical—if not necessarily logical—approaches, using magic as a specialized tool for overcoming barriers, including poverty or injustice (as well as exacting personal vendettas sometimes). They understand the world to be a wonderful one—not necessarily a "good" one, but a world inhabited by the uncanny and awe-inspiring. Witches engage with that wonder, form bonds with it and with the world it shows them. Witches go beyond wonder and belief, transforming their ideas into concrete reality through spells and charms, knotted cords, bones and skins from animals, and handfuls of gathered plants. They acquire their power and knowledge through struggle and effort, often developing it over a lifetime and passing it on to others sometime before they die. They do magic, cast spells, deal with curses, provide blessings, bewitch guns and cattle, find missing animals, brew love potions, get blamed when things go wrong (sometimes because they did, indeed, have something to do with it), transform into animals, suffer for their work, and often pay very high prices for the magic they do.

The life of a New World Witch, then, is one of action. Witches do work. Witches solve problems. Witches learn and grow. Witches make things. Witches talk to things that others don't or won't talk to. Witches see the world differently, and it changes them. Then, they change the world.

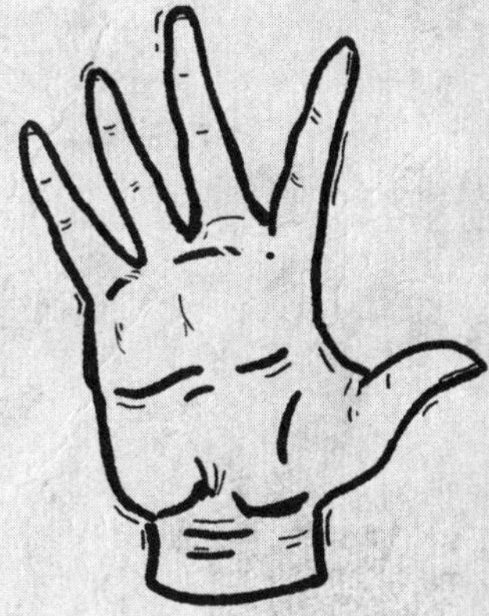

FIRST RITE: NAMING

Or, Defining Witchcraft and a Sampler of the Magical Practices Found Herein

"[O]rdinary people had more sympathy for ideas originating in the occult sciences. Many of the almanacs that every household used contained bits and pieces of astrology. Some people practiced magic to defend themselves from witchcraft, and some consulted fortune-tellers [...] No war broke out between magic and religion, in part because the clergy also were attracted to occult ideas; it was they who wrote most of the almanacs, and in their response to the 'wonder' they relied on older lore as much as any layman."*

* Hall, *Worlds of Wonder*, 7.

CHAPTER TWO

Are You a Good Witch?— Defining and Categorizing New World Witchery

What do you do when a witch comes knocking? Do you let her in, or offer her a cup of tea? In many tales from Appalachia and New England, that would be an invitation to disaster. At the same time, denying a witch a request could be just as risky, and you might wake up the next day to find your hogs all mysteriously ill—or dead. Worse, a member of your household may report being attacked in the night by unseen forces, or begin developing inexplicable illnesses that grow worse and worse for weeks to come. Then what do you do? In folklore, once all the mundane explanations were cast aside (a process that happens rather quickly in some cases, although it may take months of visits to "city" doctors first), you turn—of course—to witchcraft. Or rather, someone who knows about it, and maybe knows a bit of how to use it.

Such is the case in the Franklin County, Virginia, story of Mont and Duck Moore, a married couple that specialized in treating magical afflictions. The twist, of course, is that they also *caused* those afflictions. Duck, the wife, was thought to have a strong and powerful magical ability and would curse livestock or crops in nearby farms. Husband Mont would then show up and offer to remove said curses—for a fee. Mont knew all about countercharms and "witch doctoring," and between the two of them, they had quite the successful magical racketeering operation, at least until they died (within a few days of one another). After that, their little cabin became the locus of fearsome haunting legends.[5]

Tales such as those of Mont and Duck show the very complicated nature of witchcraft and witches in North America. The practice of New World Witchery is not a one-size-fits-all approach, nor can it be simplified down into categories of "good" and "evil" witchcraft, as even the most nefarious curses often have connections to larger social issues in a community (for more on that, see chapters six and nine on curses and witch flight, respectively). At no point is someone going to show up, *Wizard of Oz*–style, and ask "Are you a good witch, or a bad one?" Figuring out just what we mean when we talk about witchcraft and magic is complicated, and in North America no one witch will tick every box of "witchcraft" perfectly by someone else's definition. Yet we see over and over again in folklore—both historical and contemporary—that *magic* underlies virtually all that witches do, for better or worse, and so it is from those roots that I intend to follow witchcraft where it grows.

Defining Witches and Witchcraft in America

We still need to have a clear sense of who the witch is, though, especially in North America, or this book is not going to be of much use to you. In the most scholarly of modes, I might turn to a definition put forth by historian Ronald Hutton in his 2017 work *The Witch: A History of Fear from Ancient Times to the Present*. Building upon a series of historical accounts and folding in a selected number of anthropological comparisons, Hutton arrives at this definition: "an alleged worker of [...] destructive magic."[6] This definition will rub right up against anyone whose definition includes only the types of witches found in contemporary Neopagan religions, where the emphasis is often on the *non*-destructive nature of magic among practitioners of *religious* Witchcraft. Many adherents of this latter definition would point to the Wiccan Rede, a poetically rendered ethical code first fully articulated in the 1970s by Neopagan poet Lady Gwen Thompson, although it is likely derived from con-

5. Davis, *The Silver Bullet*, 214–15.

6. I am playing a little fast and loose with Hutton's efforts here, as he outlines a total of four potential definitions and selects the one focused on destructive magic solely as a convention for his specific investigations. I highly recommend reading his book, as well as many of his other works on British religious and magical history.

cepts and language from Aleister Crowley and Doreen Valiente.[7] The Rede emphasizes the idea that "Witches" should "harm none" in their practice of religious magic, although it does include a caveat excusing acts of self-defense in some forms. These versions may seem to be at odds, but I believe I know why. They are, as the proverbial expression goes, putting the cart before the horse (or the broom before the flying ointment, possibly?). Both visions of the witch start with a fully fleshed-out figure, a "witch," and apply their own definitions to her. Hutton's vision, thankfully, also focuses clearly on her actions, although in his particular case he is unpacking a particular form of "witch" and must, by necessity, discard variations that don't completely fit that form based on their practices. The more contemporary vision is a bit more centered on the belief structure, although it, too, emphasizes that a witch should be a creature of action and "do what [she] will" so long as she obeys the other moral dictum of the Rede.

I will point out that both of these definitions can be right in a certain context, and both can be wrong. Many magical practitioners reject the term "witch" either because of its negative or its religious connotations. Others embrace it while rejecting the moral codification connected to others who use it, as many Neopagan Wiccans do. In my own efforts to secure a definition, however, I will take a slightly different approach. Instead of looking at people labeled by outsiders for their wicked doings as definitive witches, as Hutton does, or assuming that the self-defined "witch" of Neopaganism is the only suitable definition, I want to embrace *both* insider and outsider perspectives. To do that, I have chosen to identify witches through what they do: witchcraft.

But what is witchcraft, then? When we look at stories of witches in North America—whether derived from European, African/African American, Native, or other sources—we see witches doing magical things in one way or another. Fortune-telling by cards and other means seems to appear nearly universally. Zora Neale Hurston recorded tales of African American conjure women and men rifling playing cards and seeing the future.[8] Some of the accounts of Salem's tumultuous sorceries involved sensational tales of divination by "Venus glass," or through the use of a special cake baked from urine and fed to a dog, or even some evidence that accused

7. See Hutton, *The Triumph of the Moon.*

8. See Hurston, *Mules and Men.*

persons, such as Dorcas Hoar, owned divination manuals and had practiced fortune-telling for years before the trial outbreak. Other tools, like the dowsing rod or the use of geomantic shells or coins, appear in other areas, and every cultural group in American history has had some means of divination or augury. Even in contemporary times, the Ouija board has become a popular trope of adolescent divinatory rites and remains a popular "game" among American youth.[9]

Witches also made use of prayers and psalms, sometimes in holy and sometimes in profane ways. Tales of Appalachian witch initiation rites discuss the use of prayers that reverse one's baptism. In many European-derived traditions, the recitation in reverse of whatever charm had been used to blight someone would remove that curse. In tales where witches work with spirits, they may make contact with faery creatures (see Emma Wilby's 2006 book *Cunning Folk & Familiar Spirits* for a truly excellent rundown of that subject), or they may keep a wee bug in a bottle to talk to (as in one Appalachian story).[10] While we get a sense of their spiritual worldview—which is heavily populated and constantly interacting with the mundane world—we seldom get a sense that witches are denominational. They might act in non-Christian or even anti-Christian ways, up to and including signing pacts with the Devil, but just as often they make use of Christian prayers and charms, and may even be very religious—if a bit unorthodox. Having a rich spiritual life certainly seems to be found in most tales of folkloric witches, but there's very little definition around that spiritual worldview. Instead, witchcraft in North America seems to be—from the perspective of history and folklore—less about gods and goddesses and much more about muttering under one's breath in a time of need, or knowing not to burn sassafras wood. It's a practice and a way of acting that is shaped by spiritual understanding, but not completely defined by it. Instead, it is informed by the immediate regional world of the witch, including her environment, her neighbors, and her cultural background. There's much more to say on what New World Witches do, based on folklore and history, and that is what this book is truly about.

9. Ellis, *Lucifer Ascending*, 174–96; Horowitz, *Occult America*, 66–79.

10. Davis, *The Silver Bullet*, 16–19.

What Is "New World Witchery"?

You may be imagining that I'm about to lay out a complete definition of "New World Witchery," one that locks down the complex web of various meanings into one single, unified explanation of North American magical practice. Or you may be thinking nothing of the sort, and instead be waiting to pounce on any proposed definition I give and point out its glaring (and inevitable) flaws. I think, then, that I am bound to disappoint all expectations, because attempting to cage "New World Witchery" in one place, form, or time will never work—it seems that so long as there is still a "New World" with practicing witches in it, that definition is going to have to remain somewhat flexible and fluid.

Through the process of attempting any kind of definition, however, I have managed to cobble together a set of *characteristics* that I feel reflect the identity of most witches within the North American magical context. Simply put, New World Witches are: practical (although not entirely logical), wondrous (in the sense that the world is full of strange, marvelous, and sometimes terrifying things), and traditional (as they pass their power or knowledge to others in service, teaching, or even curses!). What do I mean by using these words? Let me take just a moment to clarify using a few examples.

Witches Are Practical

In many historical and folkloric cases, witchcraft seemed to be less about a formal religion than about getting results. What I see repeated over and over again in witch tales is a deeply pragmatic approach to problems. I see this in the pay-the-bills fortune-telling of accused witches from Salem right into the twentieth century,[11] and in the words of one correspondent who wrote to me, saying: "My mom said that if someone wants to touch/hold your baby and you don't let them then there is a chance that person will leave casting 'mal de ojo' (evil eye) on your baby, causing them a lifetime of bad luck; conversely, she said that letting others hold your baby is good luck."[12] Integrating the baby into the community is important, and the folk belief reflects that, even if in a roundabout way. Witchcraft doesn't have to be logical, just effective.

11. Karlsen, *Devil in the Shape of a Woman*, 126–29; Davies, *America Bewitched*, 128–29, 216–17.

12. O, "Lore Contest," email message to author, January 30, 2013.

Witches Are Wondrous

The New World Witch has friends everywhere, because the world is imbued with life and magic. That sometimes means she has enemies everywhere, too. Witches in the New World, like Mont and Duck, operate largely in an amoral (although not necessarily immoral) framework—they have deep relationships with spirits, landscapes, and people, and those relationships can be both positive and negative. In the New World, relationships with spiritual folk from other realms have almost always been suspect, even diabolical. A New World Witch is accountable to herself, and answers to her own sense of morality. Some stories demonstrate a witch paying a price exacted later by a Devil, but for the most part any suffering they find is at the hands of those who work countermagic against them—for example in tales where a hexed butter churn is used to reverse harm upon the witch who cast the curse in the first place. That give-and-take is part of the wonder that makes the world an enchanted—if sometimes terrifying—place.

Witches Are Traditional

New World folk magicians inherit methods and tools, share their secrets with apprentices (as happens in the tale of one Virginia witch who offers a young preacher's son a chance to learn witchcraft),[13] and initiate others into witchcraft. There is a deep materiality to witchcraft, and so the objects witches make are imbued with power, a power that passes to all who connect with them. One of the most readily apparent examples is the humble broom. Whether the broom is used for sealing a marriage ("jumping the broom," a common form of matrimonial ritual in nineteenth-century African American culture) or sweeping luck around the room, it functions as both a mundane tool and a magical one (see chapter ten for more on brooms). I will note that "traditional" does not mean "unchanging." Witches adapt and change and grow their practices all the time, whether that involves incorporating new technologies such as railroad spikes (new to witches in the 1800s) or iPads (for more contemporary practitioners). The important thing is that tradition—which has its roots in the Latin words *trans* and *dare* meaning "to hand over," whence we also get the word "traitor"—gets *shared*. Traditional witches share their power, their knowledge, their magic, and pass it to those who can next use it best.

13. Davis, *The Silver Bullet*, 20–25.

Throughout this book, I will be drawing upon the treasure trove of witchery in North America to help pack flesh onto the bones of the characteristics I've outlined. These ideas will form a sort of backbone to the remaining book, although I cannot claim that all the anatomical pieces of my Frankenstein monster of assembled traits will be completely logical. This book will unfold each of these points further, demonstrating that witchcraft is much easier to understand through action and practice than through definition. I will also note that while I am drawing on sources from history and folklore, I will not only be turning to the past. Witchcraft is alive and well today, so I'm inclined to pull from contemporary sources, too. Your mileage with those sources may vary.

I Put a Spell on You—What Witches Do

Whatever the case, we understand that witches do a lot of different things, even while we also understand that many of the things we see witches doing seem to be part of a spectrum of behaviors we identify as "witchcraft" or "magic." In stories, witches do things like pass on secret magical artifacts or turn people into animals. In history, we find people called witches who told fortunes (like Dorcas Hoar in Salem, see chapter seven), healed their neighbors (as in the case of Grace Sherwood of Virginia, see chapter twenty-two), or even seemed to have no direct connection to magic at all until their death (as in the case of Tennessee's Bell Witch, see chapter twenty-one). Trying to pin down every single talent we see in narratives about witchcraft would generate a list that grinds even the sharpest of pencils into a worn nub, while still leaving copious room at the bottom of the page for all that I've missed. Still, I can assemble a broadly inclusive set of practices that I have seen repeated in my research that might at least put a pin in key locations throughout the spectrum of witchy doings. So just what is a North American witch capable of?

1. **Casting spells**: This may seem obvious, but it really shouldn't. Whether it's the act of burning candles, rubbing someone with eggs, or even "fixing" a luck charm of some kind for someone else's use, witches often work magic through specific spells (and as I've noted, those spells often involve "things" as well). Why spells? Because often magic is the one area in which a witch has power. In social structures where poverty and womanhood carried little or no weight, including legally, magic remained within the purview of the witch. Casting a

spell is active, and while it may seem impossible or unbelievable to some, taking action that appears to meet practical needs is exactly why people do other strange things like secretly writing test answers on the bottom of one's shoe or begging a deity to help heal a sick loved one. There are several examples, of course, where the active casting of spells has not been a main characteristic in a witch story (for example, in the Salem trials testimony focused mostly on demonic and spectral visitations that tormented victims, and so the accused "witches" were seen less as spellcasters than as nightwraiths). Given those few exceptions, however, we do see the active use of intentional magic (a definition I will return to later) in myriad tales, legends, and accounts of witchcraft.

2. **Witch flight**: The use of the word "flight" is also tricky and will require further exploration, but taking it to mean any form of travel through the air, whether in body or spirit, we do see a lot of witches participating in this kind of magic. That flight is part of a much bigger web of powers and prohibitions that I explore extensively in chapter nine, and the witch is sometimes punished for her flights. Just as often, she uses her flying as a way to punish others, too. Interestingly, lots of stories involve other non-witches gaining the power of flight by following the rituals of the witches they observe, only to find themselves in hot water when the effects wear off and they don't know what to do (or how to get out of the wine cellar they're suddenly trapped in). Again, not all witches in not all stories share this characteristic, but enough do in one way or another that I feel compelled to include it here.
3. **Using magical objects**: I mentioned earlier that witches in stories often express "tradition" by imbuing objects with power. The physical "things" of witchcraft are sometimes all we have left of a particular tradition, and I will discuss the nature of magical objects in the everyday world quite a lot as well. Creating or empowering talismans or charms, using cards or coins or bones to read a future, or tying up someone's good luck (or reproductive functions) with a bit of cord all feature in multiple narratives of witchcraft, so it's worth repeating: the "stuff" matters. Magical objects are often crafted, of course, in every sense of the word, but a number of witches also repurpose the objects around them or even purchase magical artifacts and tools for their use, none of which makes them any less of a witch.

4. **Harming and cursing**: If we are to listen to the stories and not simply dismiss them out of hand, a great number of witches are engaged in the practice of cursing, hexing, and magical theft. Crucially, they often have very good reasons for acting the way they do, including responding to a community's failure to treat its members equitably or fairly, making witchcraft an informal method of "justice." This is a complex topic, and one that I cover from a few different angles throughout the book (especially in chapter six). You may not always agree with my interpretations, and I am by no means insisting that you must be creeping into children's bedrooms to hex them while they sleep to be a "real" witch, but I also refuse to ignore such a key component of witch lore, either.
5. **Healing and blessing**: We have simply massive quantities of stories in which witches do their worst to those who earn their ire, but we also have more stories than you can shake a black cat at featuring a witch doing something helpful or kind for someone (even if it is done in a somewhat grudging way). Witches may execute justice on behalf of someone left out of the community, or offer a healing ointment, or even remove curses placed by other witches. One of the most common talents of those practicing magic is finding lost objects or even treasure, for example, which is a service rather than a curse. The New World Witch has complex motivations and her actions require a lot of context, it seems.
6. **Suffering**: If you think of the stereotypical folktale featuring a witch, she often winds up getting the bum end of the deal. She gets shoved into an oven, hung on an old tree, burned in the town square, or swallowed up by the forces of Hell. She loses a hand while transformed into a cat, or gets tortured because she has a pet rat and people don't understand that choice, or she gets scalded with hot liquid because she happened to be siphoning off some milk from a nearby farmstead (okay, that last one may be more about the repercussions of theft than any particular act of cruelty by the neighboring farmers). Witches, however, seem to take the brunt of abuse in the stories where they are present. Their spells get reversed or undone, and they wind up the worse for casting them, even to the point of (frequent) death.
7. **Surviving**: Even in death, however, witches carry on. They may engage with the dead and the spirit world their whole lives only to become one of those

> spirits in the beyond. Tales of witches returning from the grave to seek revenge are many, and I devote a good bit of chapter twenty-one to that topic. Witches don't go away easily, and almost never go down without a fight. They crucially spend a lot of time hiding in plain sight, even today, and witchcraft can be found in the most unexpected places, such as on the internet and in children's games, too (see chapter twenty-two).

As I stated earlier, this is hardly an exhaustive or even particularly detailed list, but it does provide some ideas about the ways we perceive witches in stories and the ways we understand what they do. A witch is likely to engage in an act of magical theft as a response to poverty, then be caught and punished for her spells, and finally return from the grave for vengeance. Or, she might quietly cast spells and divine fortunes with cards, finding lost goods and livestock as a nervous client sits in front of her. Our understanding of witches is shaped by their actions and behaviors far more than by the pointy hat or the bubbly cauldron, even though we often signal the idea of "witch" with those sorts of symbolic cues. Seeing these behaviors in combination helps us to see the emerging "witch" of legend and history as an active participant in her own story rather than just a victim of mislabeling by the ignorant around her (although there are certainly plenty of cases of that happening, too).

The remainder of this book will expand upon these talents, definitions, and the other key characteristics I've outlined in this initial chapter. Before we fly up the chimney and away, however, we should make one more stop at the card reader's table, because there are a lot of varieties of witchcraft in North America. It might help to introduce you to a few of the traditions that will get the most discussion in this book a bit more closely.

Pointy Hat Optional—A Sampler of Magical Traditions

There are literally dozens upon dozens of magical traditions present on North American soil (and quite likely hundreds, depending on where we draw our boundary lines around what is represented in each tradition). As you move through this book, however, it may help for you to know what I mean when I'm speaking of certain key traditions of magic that come up again and again and which also form the bones of many variants of witchery. Here I've included a very quick rundown of some of the traditions of magic that I turn to the most often within these pages.

New England Witchery (or New England Cunning Folk)

These are traditions largely inherited from early Colonial settlers (or invaders, depending on your point of view). Most came from the British Isles (itself a complicated term, as the boundaries of groups within those isles shifted over time). Generally speaking, when I discuss New England Witchery, I mean a set of practices affiliated with traditions of English folk magic and the "cunning folk" of that region, many of which were transplanted into New England in the sixteenth and seventeenth centuries.

Pow-wow and Braucherei

Largely rooted in Pennsylvania but also found throughout the Appalachian Mountains and the frontier zone of Ohio as well, the healing magic of pow-wow practitioners (also known as *brauchers*, or "those who work/try") represents a distinctly German American form of magic. This work is frequently couched in Christian spirituality, although it has roots in some older pre-Christian traditions, too. The Pennsylvania Germans (or "Dutch" as they are sometimes known, likely due to their German *deitsch* dialect) have practiced this since the 1700s, with a larger influx in the 1800s. One variety of this magic, known as *hexerei*, involves countermagic against curses more than the direct faith healing of *braucherei*.

Mountain Magic

This is often thought of as Appalachian folk magic, but it is essentially found throughout the mountain regions of the eastern half of North America, from the Ozarks eastward. It is also found in some rural locations outside of the mountains, and is deeply associated with practices such as herbal healing, midwifery, fortune-telling (usually through reading signs or natural objects like bones or skin markings), and faith-based healing. It sometimes gets called "Granny Magic," but that term seems to miss a number of practitioners, and so I will mostly use the broader "Mountain Magic" term.

Southern Conjure

Outside of the healing-oriented Mountain Magic and slightly akimbo from Hoodoo, Southern Conjure pulls from a few different systems to create a flexible practice of spellwork. It is sometimes also called "power doctoring" or "fairy doctoring" as well as the easily confusing "witch doctoring." This practice emphasizes countermagic, protection, divination, work with specific spirits, and the creation of spells like "packets" and witch bottles. It frequently also uses a loosely Protestant-derived magical framework and can involve fragments of Pentecostalism (such as faith healing or speaking in tongues) and even doing some hexing or cursing work. It is sometimes used interchangeably with Hoodoo, but in this book I consider Hoodoo to be firmly African American in origin and general practice, while Southern Conjure is practiced by people from both Black and white backgrounds much more widely.

Hoodoo

Essentially an African American folk magic (although there are some non-African Americans who practice it), Hoodoo is a name that seems to have been derivatively applied to a mélange of imported African practices. Things like foot track magic, the use of personal objects and bodily elements in spells, and the creation of "mojos" for spells all come through Hoodoo. Some practitioners in North America also link a specific New Orleans variant of Voodoo with this practice, although in general most workers of Hoodoo emphatically point out that Voodoo (or more properly Vodoun or Vodun) is a religion and Hoodoo is a magical practice.

Rootwork

This is often lumped in with Hoodoo, but I like to separate it out because some of the elements of Rootwork are very distinctive. Like Hoodoo, this derives from African American folk magic, but seems to be more rooted (pardon the pun) in the coastal regions of the Carolinas and Georgia, as well as a few other areas like Florida or Maryland. Rootwork is often very focused on natural elements such as—of course—roots from particular plants (as well as their leaves, fruits, or flowers) and animal bones (such as the raccoon's penis bone, also used in other magical traditions). It can be used for helping or hurting a person, and rootworkers are known for their ability to help in cases of legal trouble or interpersonal conflict as much as removing or casting curses.

Curanderismo and Brujeria

Broadly, this encompasses several traditions of Mexican American and Latinx folk magic, most of which are focused on healing physical or spiritual ailments. *Curanderos* and *curanderas* (the men or women who do this magic, respectively) treat things like *susto* (a deep "soul fright" that can leave a victim catatonic) or the *mal de ojo* (evil eye). Frequently practitioners mix herbal remedies with techniques like massage or cupping, while also incorporating things like ritual prayer into practices like the *limpia* (spiritual cleansing). They can also be called upon to combat *brujos*, or bad witches who use *brujeria* (evil witchcraft), although a number of current practitioners are increasingly embracing the title of *bruja* in their practices.

Native American Witch Beliefs

It is *highly* reductive to lump all Native groups together for any reason, so here I wish to note that in general I will be speaking of particular tribes, nations, groups, and their practices and beliefs rather than any unified and whitewashed "Native" magic. At the same time, I do wish to acknowledge that the beliefs of different Indigenous groups about witches varied greatly, but almost all had *some* belief in a witch-like figure, and these tales and beliefs dramatically influence much of the magic on the North American continent. Muskogee and Cherokee herbal ingredients show up in Hoodoo and other systems, for example, and the skinwalker tales of the American Southwest intersect Pueblo beliefs and the beliefs of Latinx cultural groups (who may also be pulling from Nahuatl folklore). In the end, I hope that someone much better qualified to write about these systems than I am will do so, but I couldn't ignore the enormous impact of Native herbal and magical practices on the North American magical landscape, either.

Neopagan Magical Practices

Neopaganism is still a relatively young religion, but it incorporates a wide variety of magical methods taken (sometimes rather appropriatively) from numerous magical systems. Many Neopagans mix in things like deities or spirits and derive the core elements of their practices from European-based systems such as British Traditional Wicca or Greco-Roman historical and mythological materials (such as the famed Greek Magical Papyri). Some Neopagans also build upon medieval grimoire (magical textbook) traditions or incorporate mythologies from places like Ireland, Scotland, Slavic lands, or Italy as a part of their work. Rituals are frequently linked to things like seasons and lunar cycles and can be used for anything from healing to love to luck to binding an enemy (although many traditions frown upon anything close to a curse).

European Traditional Witchcraft

This variety of witchcraft is somewhat linked to New England Witchery and Neopagan magic, as it is pulling from many of the same roots. However, many who practice it would draw sharp lines of distinction between their practices, insisting that the traditional lines of witchcraft are not about agricultural cycles, but rather focus on the *genius loci*—the spirit of place and the interactions with the Otherworld. These are frequently practitioners who use trances or out-of-body experiences and ritualized magic built upon folklore to accomplish their aims, although a number of practitioners also pull from grimoires as well.

Religious Folk Magic

Just about any religion can have a folk magical side, so this is a nebulous and overly broad category, but it still has its uses here. Each religious group generates individual variations on practice, and some of those will inevitably turn into folk magic. Catholicism has a number of "folk saints" and rituals not officially sanctioned by the Church but regularly used by lay-practitioners (we see this frequently in varieties of Hoodoo, Italian American folk practices, and *curanderismo*). Similarly, Mormon roots in folk magic are often tucked away in the official histories, but traditions of visions and prophetic dreams still linger on among everyday believers. Jewish American practitioners often incorporate not only the religious background, but ethnic and cultural ones as well, with Polish American Jews using specific house-blessing rituals performed in Yiddish, for example.

Contemporary Feminist Witchcraft

A new wave (the "witch wave" as described by author Pam Grossman) has surged in North America over the past few decades.[14] "Witch" is a word that many people—especially those marginalized by mainstream culture such as people of color, women, non-binary folx, and those with disabilities—embrace as a form of power. Religion and overt spirituality are sometimes downplayed, as rituals and magic are

14. See Grossman, *Waking the Witch.*

used in rhetorical ways to effect social change. This is not entirely new, as varieties of feminist-centered witchcraft have been a key part of the magical landscape in North America since the 1950s and 1960s, but the current wave is certainly incredibly strong and diverse. Latinx practitioners, for example, are rapidly reclaiming the title of *bruja* as a positive one, and women often embrace witch archetypes as empowering figures that break centuries-old cycles of patriarchal control.

This is not by any means the final word in all the forms of witchery you can find on North American soil, but it should at least offer a window into the vastness and depth of folk magic that appears here. Of course, there are a number of traditions that I'm missing in this. For example, the big tent of Asian American folk sorcery has had some significant impacts on the broader magical landscape of North America, particularly around the West Coast and in cosmopolitan cities like New Orleans. While I occasionally bring in a brief mention of some Asian American traditions, my sources on those topics are more limited (although I would eagerly welcome texts on such magics). Similarly, narrow and particular accounts of Slavic or Italian or Irish American witchery are all handled very lightly here by muddling them under a "European" heading, even though each group has had its own role in shaping North American folk magic. Some forms are addressed through combinations or overlapping categories, but inevitably I have missed *someone*'s favorite brand of folk magic. At some point, I had to focus on what I know best, and so I have mostly shared materials from the handful of traditions I just listed, and even among those I have tried to be judicious about just what to share.

Of course, any attempt to make these sorts of categories about witches overlooks a crucial point: many witches are not so easily categorized. Witches are creatures of liminal spaces, the spaces between things, and as such they are able to draw upon more than one tradition at a time. A witch may be pulling from traditions of *curanderismo* and Pow-wow in her own practice, particularly if she has social or familial ties to both cultures. There's absolutely no rule book for witches that requires them all to stick to their particular lane or only be a part of one given tradition. Most North American practitioners of magic are, at some level, always pulling on multiple strands of witchcraft at any given time to meet their magical needs (again, because of their pragmatism and the need to get things done).

That does open up an important question, and one I will be attempting to address throughout the book: what if you want to "borrow" some magic from one of these traditions, but it is not your own? What do we do about cultural appropriation in the world of witchcraft, especially given the long and rather frustrating history of certain cultures (especially white, Western European ones) riding roughshod over the traditions of others only to pick up pieces and claim them afterwards? Cultural appropriation is a heinous creature, and it is a very real phenomenon. The information I present here is not designed to be anyone's gateway into borrowing (or stealing) someone else's culture, magical or otherwise. Just because you read about a *braucherei* method or an Asian American spiritual belief doesn't mean it is suddenly yours. You cannot try to make a mojo hand a few times and suddenly be a "Hoodoo practitioner" or rootworker, because there is a depth of cultural background that goes with those terms.

On the other hand, what you read here *is* designed to offer you experiments to try from a variety of magical backgrounds, information that might serve as a springboard into learning about those other cultural depths (which are all absolutely worth learning about). None of the information here will make you an authority or an initiate or a practitioner of any one of these systems of magic. What might happen is that you discover the shared DNA of magical practices, particularly those that have grown so fruitfully in North America, and begin to see what sorts of magic have always been available right at your fingertips. You don't need to steal a *curandera*'s *limpia* to see how an egg-based cleansing and divination method appears in multiple systems and recognize that you can do such a cleansing yourself (importantly, without suddenly calling yourself a *curandera* for doing it). Learning from other traditions—respectfully—is part of what makes magic such a massively imaginative and exciting experience. My hope is that by sampling these traditions, it will become increasingly apparent that folk magic is everywhere, and you—my reader—will start to see patterns and connections that also relate to your own experiences. Be a magical magpie if you wish, and gather the shiny and beautiful things you like, but acknowledge that you are a magpie and not a bluebird or a cardinal, even if you add a few of their twigs or feathers to your nest. Be grateful and humble toward the magic and the people behind that magic, and you will find that magic opens up all sorts of new possibilities for you.

FIG 2-1: Being a magical magpie is fine, but acknowledge you are a magpie with a bluebird's feather in your beak, rather than a bluebird itself.

THE WORK—Folk Magician's Notebook

Often, I see people work very hard to cultivate and craft intricate illustrated volumes of their magical knowledge. A number of Wiccans I've known, for example, invest a great deal of time and effort into their Books of Shadows, binding them in leather, illustrating pages of holidays, and so forth. A number of folk charmers and healers, however, take a very different approach. For example, take Joshua Gordon's *Commonplace Book*, housed in the archives of the University of South Carolina. This text from 1784 contains a whole host of magical cures and spells scrawled in about fifteen handwritten pages. Or the diary of Martha Ballard, a midwife working from the 1780s to the early 1800s, who interspersed cures and remedies with local news, birth and death records, and weather information. John George Hohman's famed *Long-Lost Friend* has plenty of spells and healing charms, of course, but also a recipe for molasses! Many curers used a Bible in their work, and would simply add notes to the pages with important verses on them.

That's not to say you can't make a beautiful spellbook if you want, but why not start where you are first? Make a simple household notebook that inventories what you know, what you have available right now. Think of this as a sort of diary based on your own traditions and life (you could even use your diary this way). Write down favorite recipes you know by heart. Add in a list of places you've traveled or a list of your family tree as far as you can remember it. Do you have a cure you use for hiccups or colds? Write that down as well. Glue or tape in newspaper articles you find that relate to your town's history, or foods you like to eat, festivals you've attended. Add spells, but don't just copy them out of books. Instead, try to add only ones you've done enough times that you can write them down by heart. Imagine someone—a grandchild or distant relative or maybe even a high school kid doing some digging for a project in a local library—discovering this and suddenly seeing the world through your eyes.

Over time, you'll see you're putting together your own commonplace book, a record of your life and the world you inhabit, and you'll see the spells and magic of your world emerging in all sorts of places. Even that favorite comfort food will be a sort of spell, and your honey-and-lemon-and-whiskey cure for a sore throat will be an enchantment on par with your best protective charm. This is the kind of book that will become a personal legacy, a love letter to the future about just how magical your life was.

As you take this book in your hands, you are—I hope—asking questions about magic and seeking to learn something about it. What will you do with that information, though? Are you going to put on the ruby slippers and follow the yellow brick road to see where it leads? Or are you going to rush straight to the west and storm the Wicked Witch's castle and demand she teach you what she knows (and throw in one of those flying monkeys to boot)? Perhaps you're a Munchkin or a Winkie, already living in the land of magic and familiar with all the witchcraft around you, but not sure if it is there to hurt you or help you, and this book is your way of finding out more. Just don't be like the residents of the Emerald City, who don their green-tinted glasses to be able to enjoy the beauty of the world around them (even if it also means putting up with a fictitious "wizard" who demands all the magic for himself).[15]

Do not take what I write here at pure face value. While I have put a great deal of effort into this book and gaining the knowledge I needed to write it, anything I say here should be open to scrutiny and investigation. I recommend getting a notebook and keeping notes as you read here (or at least putting a mental pin into certain pages or dog-earing their corners, which should tell you just what sort of monster I

15. I know I am mixing the 1939 MGM film starring Judy Garland and the classic American fairy tale written in 1900 by L. Frank Baum here, but since I've already said witches live in the liminal, you will just have to put up with my mixed, liminal metaphor here.

am). Find the points that intrigue you and investigate further. If you discover a spell you like but don't feel comfortable with it as written, look deeper into where it comes from and how it might make more sense in a different framework for you. When you find places where you disagree with me, point those out and follow the paths down which they lead you. For all you know, I may well be writing at a crossroads that has alternative ways to travel and you may be discovering one I have never thought to explore. If you are practicing folk magic in North America, you are a New World Witch. Use this book as a way to travel around the landscape, exploring more, and adding to your magical stores along the way. Peek behind the curtain and see me spinning wheels and pulling levers from time to time, and remember I am only one man, and that all of magical North America awaits you, whether you stay on my yellow brick road or not.

Recommended Reading

Witchcraft in Early North America, by Alison Games. This is essentially a wide-ranging historical overview of witchcraft in North America from around the fifteenth century to the eighteenth century. As such, it misses many of the more contemporary elements (which is why I recommend Adler's book below), but it does provide a great deal of information on just how much magic was practiced on the continent in those three centuries. It is more of a history book than anything else, and so may be a bit drier than others I recommend, but the information in it is invaluable.

Drawing Down the Moon: Witches, Druids, Goddess Worshipers, and Other Pagans in North America, by Margot Adler. Adler's work is considered definitive in its scope, covering the early history of North American magical spirituality and then digging into the social landscape around a number of magical communities. It is more focused on the religious experience of magic in the land rather than the folk magical side of things, but it does offer a lot of historical context and more recent editions have revisions and expansions delving into a number of branches of magical practice mentioned here.

The Wizard of Oz (Illustrated First Edition: 100th Anniversary Collection), by L. Frank Baum. I cannot help but recommend this book, given that I spent a good bit of time drawing metaphorical parallels in this chapter. Plus, it is an excellent example of a distinctly American fairy tale, born as it was from the author's social activism, imaginative interpretation of the 1893 Chicago World's Fair, and the recognition that witches can be both good and bad in North America. If you haven't read it and seen William W. Denslow's beautiful illustrations that accompany the older text, you are very much in for a treat.

SECOND RITE: INITIATION

Or, Finding Your Way into Witchcraft through Body, Mind, and Ritual

"'Wall, Jonas, I cain't make you a witch myself; hit's the Devil's work,' Liz explained. 'But mebbe sence I've served him nigh on to forty years, I could argue him to make you into a conjure man.'"*

* Davis, *The Silver Bullet*, 23.

CHAPTER THREE

Seventh Son of a Seventh Son— The Call to Witchcraft and Magic

Where does witchcraft begin? This is a tough, complex, crunchy question that can get into mythological origin stories, murky tales of dark doings across many ages, and whispered lore of secret initiation rituals. One particular idea that we find in North American witch lore is the concept of a witch being "called" to her work. Often this calling is not unlike the reported priestly calling experienced by clergy in a variety of religions. Stories of being tapped to a witch's life are often remarkably similar. Several accounts describe the pull to witch work as coming through one of three categories: those physically marked as witches, often by a birthmark or a "deformity" of some kind; by lineage or heritage, coming from a family line of witchcraft that would often be passed down across generations; and by study, usually a close apprenticeship with an existing witch or magical worker or a spirit helper (frequently the Devil in folktales). Once the call came, the witch would be on her way to magical work, although she might have many other steps on her way toward a full membership in the community of witches.

This chapter looks to the circumstances that made the crooked path of witchcraft so much easier to walk. Discussions of initiatory lore, through which a witch takes the next step into her power, will follow in chapter four. A witch's "call" is a fundamental thing, and often sets her on a lifelong path, one which will demand as much from her as it gives to her. That call, however, is very hard to ignore.

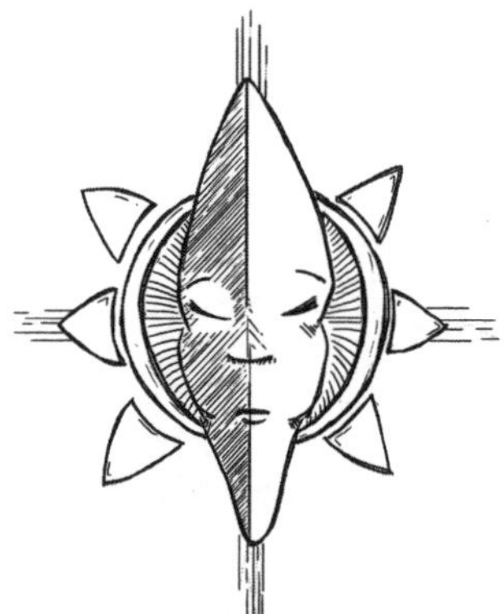

FIG 3-1: Paiute seer Wovoka's vision during the 1889 New Year's Day solar eclipse lead to the creation of the Ghost Dance.

SINGING BONES
Wovoka and the Ghost Dance

On New Year's Day in 1889, a Paiute prophet named Quoitze Ow (Anglicized to Jack Wilson) received a vision of not just his tribe, but all Indigenous Nations rising up in peace and unity to expel white invaders from their lands. As a part of this process, he took the name Wovoka, meaning "wood cutter," and learned a powerful ceremonial dance known as the Ghost Dance. By combining this dance with spiritual lessons, Wovoka was called to bring his message to the Indigenous peoples of North America. Initially, he was successful and managed to teach his dance to a number of tribes. Crucially, he reached the Lakota Sioux under the guidance of Kicking Bear and Sitting Bull. As the Ghost Dance spread, it took on the shape of a nonviolent religion, but it made local white settlers and military very nervous. They arranged for the assassination of Chief Sitting Bull, then removed all of his followers to Wounded Knee Creek. The Native people were ordered to cease the Ghost Dance, but many believed it to be the only way to bring peace and safety to their people, especially after the murder of their chief. The soldiers, in response to this defiance, disarmed the Sioux, and in the process began firing upon them. The Wounded Knee Massacre ended with the deaths of nearly three hundred Sioux, including many women and children on December 29, 1890, two years after Wovoka's calling.[16]

16. Dee, *Bury My Heart at Wounded Knee*, 431–45.

The Witch's Mark, or Physical Evidence of the Witch's Call

How do you know she's a witch? As Eric Idle so glibly puts it in the classic comedy *Monty Python and the Holy Grail*, "because she looks like one." Those marked as "different" by their skin or other physical features have a lot to say about the history of North America. You need only think of the cruel and hateful eras of slavery and Jim Crow to remember that the vast majority of United States history featured subjugation based solely on the color of one's skin. The skin we live in tells a lot about us, and we carry the maps of our lives in scars, wrinkles, laugh lines, freckles, liver spots, bruises, tans, burns, grafts, moles, tumors, birthmarks, and so many other visible markings. We may choose to hide those maps and stories under clothing, or flaunt them proudly, or both, or neither, but our skins say something about us.

Imagine, then, your skin betraying you. Imagine the birthmark you've had on your leg all your life or a more recent skin tag in your armpit suddenly being turned into evidence that you are not, in fact, part of the society around you. Imagine your skin saying "this one's a witch," especially in a time or place where those words weren't affirming, but condemning.

Being called to be a witch often involves bearing a mark of some kind, and the idea of a marked body as a magical body is hardly new. The biblical figure of Cain was supposedly marked by his god as a way of setting him apart from other people while simultaneously offering him a charm of protection from retribution in the wake of his brother's murder.[17] In terms of North American witchcraft, the skin of a witch provided a testimony against her when she was accused, since any unusual marking or growth could be considered a potential "witch mark" and used as evidence of her sorcery. William Perkins, a Puritan theologian, mentioned the presence of a witch mark as sufficient to inspire further inquiry into an accused witch's character, although Perkins did at least insist that the mark be found only "by some casual means" rather than the popular strip search that other, more aggressive witch-hunters favored.[18] The witch mark was far more prevalent in English legal proceedings, but still impacted the way people in the New World thought about witches. A person with a physical marking of

17. I would also note that there were many not-so-subtly racist ideas circulating right up to the twentieth century claiming that the "Mark of Cain" was the black skin of the African or African American, and thus the subjugation of dark-skinned peoples was falsely justified in light of the sins of the alleged mythic forebearer of their race.

18. Perkins, "On the Identification of a Witch," in *Witches of the Atlantic World*, 370.

any kind, especially from birth, could be considered a potential witch. This becomes even more complicated when you consider that in a lot of lore from southern states, a birthmark would have been caused by the child's mother having a craving that she did not fulfill during the pregnancy—a strawberry-shaped birthmark might indicate the mother's intense desire for strawberries, for example.[19]

Marks could also be broader, lumped into the category of "deformity," or a physical handicap of some kind such as a club foot, cleft palate, or extra digit. Even heterochromia—having eyes of different colors—could be seen as a mark of enchantment. Not every such mark was negative, however. The fine line between being marked as someone with "gifts" versus someone who would *become* a witch was blurry and people traversed it frequently in lore. One of the prime examples of this sort of marking was the caul—a lingering amniotic membrane that would often surround part or all of a person's head during childbirth. That caul would mark the child as someone with "second sight" in Appalachian communities, and in the seaside villages of New England, a dried and preserved caul might be bought by a sailor for protection from drowning.[20] Julius Caesar was sometimes said to have been born with a caul, which marked him for greatness.

Such birth-oriented mark finding, however, still has serious consequences today. While those born with cauls might be considered potential seers or have unique healing abilities, individuals with other birth differences often suffered—and still suffer—because of their bodily distinctions. Even in the twenty-first century, some witch hunters in places like Tanzania seek out children born with albinism specifically to remove hands or feet, which are believed to have magical qualities or to break the power of witchcraft.[21]

The belief in witch markings as a form of calling to magical work also has direct correlation to the phenomenon of initiation. Variant folklore in North America tells of initiatory experiences that permanently alter the physical form or abilities of an individual. For example, during initiations in New England lore, the witch would often receive the witch mark as a way to suckle a familiar or imp as part of her bargain with the Devil. This belief persisted well into the twentieth century, with one

19. Duncan, "Superstitions and Sayings," 234; Gainer, *Witches, Ghosts, & Signs*, 133; Roberts, "Louisiana Superstitions," 150.

20. Gainer, *Witches, Ghosts, & Signs*, 133; Randolph, *Ozark Magic*, 203; see also the Pitt Rivers Museum collection, "Caul: A Sailor's Charm."

21. "History of Attacks against Persons with Albinism," *Under the Same Sun*, 3–4.

story about a Virginia witch named Rindy Sue Gose claiming that the Devil bit her on the left shoulder to mark her and give her a place to nourish her familiar animal, a beetle she kept in a small bottle.[22] Initiation marks left on the skin would serve as a powerful reminder of belonging within a community of witches, even if those marks could potentially be turned against the bearer.

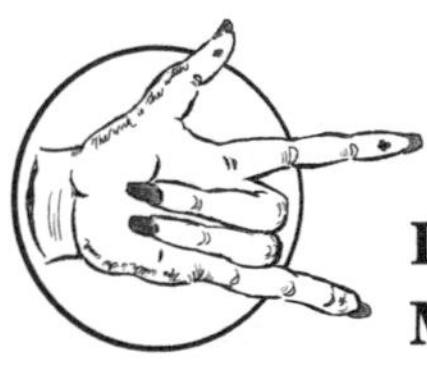

DIRT UNDER THE NAILS
Making Your Mark

Witch's marks are often thought of as a way of falsely accusing and scapegoating anyone with a physical abnormality, especially when it comes to witch trials. While that view is essentially sound in terms of historical accuracy, we can also use the idea of being "marked" to help us find others like us. Here are two short rituals you can try to get others to see you as a witch or magical worker (if you want them to see you), without drawing excessive attention from those who are not magically inclined:

1. Pick out a piece of jewelry that seems witchy or magical to you. This can be a stone talisman or amulet, a pendant with a moon on it, a tie clip with a little skull (something I received as a gift from a friend), or a little ring with a pentagram on it (which my longtime magical partner uses). Take the item into your hands and treat it like a living thing. Give it a name and whisper your request to it. Ask it to help others like you to see you, and to keep you from the sight of those who mean you harm. Feed it with a bit of magically infused oil, water, or incense smoke (whatever won't damage the material), and then wear it out in the world. See who comments and compliments your "mark," and use that as an opportunity to open doorways of discussion.
2. Pick a symbol or sigil that means something to you, something that would speak of witchcraft and magic if you saw it somewhere outside of yourself and in the wider world. Pick a spot on your body that is not too obvious and draw the symbol there using something like a makeup pencil, henna, or even a Sharpie marker (make sure it can be washed off

22. Davis, *The Silver Bullet*, 16–19.

if you need to and that you don't use anything toxic on your skin). Wear the mark around and see if it calls out to anyone around you, attracts a glance here or there, or maybe even sparks recognition in someone else's eyes. Try different symbols, too, and see if you find one "mark" that works better than all the rest. You may even consider getting it as a permanent tattoo at some point, if you find it particularly powerful.

The Witch's Line, or the Relationships that Define Witchcraft

If you want to start a fight among contemporary witches, one surefire way to get dander up is to talk about "lineage." Since the introduction of Wicca as a religious construction of witchcraft by Gerald Gardner in the mid-twentieth century, the fight over whether or not a witch can lay claim to an ancestral or initiatory line of magical predecessors has boiled over a number of times. Some practitioners claim that they trace their magical line through people like twentieth-century Wiccan founders Gardner or Alex and Maxine Sanders or Traditional Witchcraft progenitor Robert Cochrane but go no further. Some argue that those lines are connected to a magical heritage that runs back centuries or even millennia. A significant number of witches bypass any connection to Wicca and talk about family lines of witchcraft, the so-called "granny traditions" (not to be confused with "Granny Magic," the colloquial name for certain types of Appalachian folk magic).

Family connections play a significant role in a variety of stories of North American witchcraft. One of the first ways a family can "mark" a person as a potential witch—or in many cases a "witch master" or "witch doctor," as someone who works magic to fend off harmful witchcraft might be called—is simply by giving birth to enough children to make it possible for one of them to take on a magical mantle. For example, one of the best ways to know someone will become a witch or possess magical powers in the mid-Atlantic, Appalachian, and Ozark mountain regions of the United States is to be the seventh son of a seventh son.[23] Even simply being the seventh child often marked a person as special, as the number seven has strong magical connotations, especially in regions that prioritize biblical numerology, which set seven aside as a number of completion or holiness (seven days to create the world,

23. Thomas, *Kentucky Superstitions*, 128, 236; Randolph, *Ozark Magic*, 207; Wigginton, *The Foxfire Book*, 359.

for example). A seventh son of a seventh son, however, would be exponentially more likely to possess powers such as "water witching" (dowsing), fortune-telling or clairvoyance, and the power to "buy warts" by rubbing them with a penny or giving a coin to someone troubled with them. Other birth orders could also hold special power, with combinations of threes, sevens, and thirteens being potent, and youngest children often exhibiting special favor as well.

Having a relative with witchy powers also indicated that a person could take on the mantle of witch. An aunt or grandmother with a particular knack for reading cards or curing ailments would be an indication that you might be able to pick up a magical talent of your own. Often, that talent is not directly related to the one your relative has, so a family that has one witch gifted in herbal remedies might have a later witch more able to discern the future through second sight. Sometimes, your family history could work against you if you wanted to become a witch, though. One story of a witch named Liz Goins tells of a boy named Jonas who desperately wanted to learn witchcraft, but who had extra trials to prove himself to her (and the Devil) because he came from a long line of preachers![24]

A key caveat of magical family lore is that it often is not presented as "magical," but simply as a way of doing things, a simple belief, a "cure" or "wonder," or some other such epithet. Frequently these bits of homegrown and rooted spells and workings are also attached to belief systems like Christianity, and the power used is seen to be derived from the Christian God or one of his affiliated subordinates (such as angels, saints, etc.). On occasion, even positive magical work is seen as diabolical however, and lore varies from family to family. One contemporary magical worker told me that her "biggest regret in life" was not paying more attention to her grandmother—or "Mammaw" as she was known—while she was alive. She still remembered several good pieces of lore from Mammaw's storehouse of knowledge though:

- Never show your teeth to a "writing spider" (better known as the yellow garden spider, *Argiope aurantia*, which builds large webs with intricate designs that can look like writing). If you show your teeth and then the spider writes your name, you will die.

24. Davis, *The Silver Bullet*, 20–27.

- If a bird flies into the house, do not touch it, but try to get it out of the house quickly. It's a bad luck omen, and often foretells of an impending death.[25]

Mammaw's magical lore here is specific to her cultural situation, of course (she was located in the mountains of eastern Tennessee), but it was shared with her granddaughter as a part of regular family storytelling. She learned about the mountain spiders from encountering them with her Mammaw in childhood, and the bird lore came from an incident where Mammaw and her sisters were frightened by a bird getting into the house.

In the farmlands and the mountain spaces inhabited by the Pennsylvania Dutch, the transmission of power came through family connections as well, and a person could easily develop a magical calling by having a near relative with some gift or power. Crucially, one of the key factors in receiving the call to magical work was the direct passage of magical gifts from one relative to another. A person with a particular ability to heal—called a *braucher* or "Pow-wow," among other names—would have the ability to pass on her power through the laying on of hands or by whispering certain words and methods to a chosen heir. Sometimes this passage would happen only once (frequently on the deathbed of the magical worker), and sometimes it was allowed up to three times within the life of the *braucher*, after which she would lose her ability (hence the deathbed passage). The rite of passing power occasionally gets connected to gender, with women only able to pass to men and vice versa, but such rules are not universal or even particularly strictly observed.[26] Someone who wanted to pass the methods of healing without passing the power could also work around the rules by simply explaining their magical rites, incantations, or charms to an inanimate object like a lamp or a stove, while the person who wanted to learn the magic would hide just out of sight. These methods for passing power still exist even in the twenty-first century. One Pow-wow practitioner, Anita Rahn, planned to share her power and secrets with her nearly forty-year-old son in 1999, and a number of practitioners have even begun sharing their methods with unrelated students.[27]

Instruction in magical arts seems to work just as well as a family connection in North American lore. You can pick up witchcraft (or counter-witchcraft, as a lot of

25. Cootie, email communication, January 7, 2013.

26. Milnes, *Signs, Cures, & Witchery*, 102–03; Randolph, *Ozark Magic*, 265–66.

27. Kreibel, *Powwowing Among the Pennsylvania Dutch*, 148–49, 175.

magical training leans in that direction) through the instruction of a relative as mentioned above, or through finding a teacher and offering yourself as an apprentice, or even by devoting yourself to studying magic on your own.

The Witch's Question—Learning Witchcraft as a Calling

Picking up witchcraft, or any sort of magical practice, through listening to family stories is a rewarding process, but it is also a piecemeal one. You often get the sense that there's more behind each practice, spell, charm, prayer, or talisman you discover, but getting at that material can take time—years, in some cases. You may never really gather the knowledge you seek if your family isn't forthcoming or if you suffer the loss of key tradition-bearers (a fancy term we folklorists use to talk about people who *know things*).

Fortunately, we live in an age where a vast amount of folklore, history, and communities of tradition-bearers is at our fingertips, and we can often supplement our knowledge through research. That approach, picking up witchcraft through self-instruction, is not particularly novel even if our methods have changed with the boom in technology during the twentieth and twenty-first centuries. People have turned to magical instruction from teachers or books for centuries, and there's nothing wrong with either approach.

For many people, myself included, the draw to magic comes from a deep intellectual curiosity. We are fascinated by the possibilities that magic offers, and we seek out and sample bits and pieces of magical lore like magpies building an enchanted nest. While I had a good deal of magic in the cultural lore around me growing up, I often think of my "starting point" in magical exploration as one connected with a book. When I was eleven years old, my mother—an ostensibly Catholic woman who was also a teacher and had a deep interest in myths and folklore as well—took me to a bookstore. I browsed for a while, then bumped into a large, yellow-bound book called *The Encyclopedia of White Magic*, by Paddy Slade.[28] This book had folklore about seasonal rites, albeit ones slightly different from the ones I would later discover in Wicca, as well as charms and spells woven into the story of the year. I begged my mother for the book, and while she was initially hesitant, she finally agreed. From

28. The book as I first found it is sadly out of print, but a version of it is still available as a paperback called *Seasonal Magic: Diary of a Village Witch*, by Paddy Slade (Milverton, UK: Capall Bann Pub., 2001).

that point, I began devouring any and all bits of magical lore I could from a wide variety of sources. I found books of folklore and mythology in the library, but I even found valuable material in unexpected places. My school had a collection of books that were guides to the *Universal Monsters* films: *Dracula*, *Frankenstein*, *The Wolf Man*, and their ilk. In the book on the Wolf Man, I found a spell taken from a medieval text that described a diabolical pact that would transform the user into a werewolf. Not a bad discovery for an elementary school library!

Historically, learning witchcraft from books meant that you were able to keep your practices fairly secret in most cases, as no one needed to know about the tomes you hid away in your house. In some cases, however, owning such books would be cause for immediate concern and might even confirm charges of witchcraft against you, as happened in several New England witch trial cases in the seventeenth century. While the types of books a particular witch might turn to for magical knowledge varied—and are discussed in much greater detail in chapter nineteen—the mere presence of those books might be enough to convey power to an individual who possessed them. A person didn't even have to be able to read them to gain something from them magically, as the symbols inside grimoires like the *Egyptian Secrets of Albertus Magnus* or *The Black Pullet* were thought to have power in and of themselves. Learning to draw those symbols and phonetically pronounce key words might be enough to start one on the road to witchery. Even the books themselves were often thought to contain immense magical power, and ownership of books like *Egyptian Secrets* or "black bibles" warranted intense suspicion in places like Pennsylvania Dutch country, the Appalachians, and the Ozarks.[29]

Even the best of books, however, often did little to replace a powerful or knowledgeable teacher, and those conjurers who had access to training seldom passed up the opportunity. Zora Neale Hurston noted that in the Hoodoo practices she observed, almost all people became "Hoodoo doctors" by following one of three paths:

- The hereditary path we've already explored, in which a person's kinship to a noted Hoodoo worker offered the opportunity to train.
- A "call" or natural gift of power, similar to being marked from birth but also involving the revelation of talents or powers throughout a person's life (more on that below).

29. Milnes, *Signs, Cures, & Witchery*, 161–62; Gainer, *Witches, Ghosts, & Signs*, 135–39; Randolph, *Ozark Magic*, 287–88.

- By serving in an apprenticeship with a known and powerful Hoodoo doctor, who would teach the student all the ceremonies, rites, rituals, spells, charms, and formulae necessary to go out on her own (which is essentially what Hurston did).

Hurston describes in detail the apprenticeships she had with several well-established and well-known Hoodoo practitioners, but also makes a point that in many cases a combination of these three paths would be present. For example, when she studied with Luke Turner, he took great pains to establish that he had a family connection to the renowned Marie Laveau of New Orleans, as that helped guarantee his power and reputation.[30]

One major problem with the apprenticeship approach, however, is finding a good teacher. This has become increasingly frustrating as many stories of abuse, coercion, and violations of trust emerged from survivors of cult-like leaders. As a rule, a good teacher might push you in ways that feel uncomfortable because they ask you to go outside of your comfort zone for *your* growth, but they will not ask you to violate any personal ethical standards or trade favors for initiations. Anyone clearly seeking to abuse their power in that way should be reported to authorities if possible, and avoided at all costs otherwise.

Hurston also mentioned the idea of the natural "call," which as discussed above might literally be a marking of some kind, like being born with a caul around your head. However, there are a lot of other ways to interpret the idea of the natural call, including the exhibition of unique talents and abilities. Lee Gandee was a famed *hexenmeister* (witch master, a concept similar to a "witch doctor" among Pennsylvania Dutch practitioners). Gandee claimed that a childhood incident and subsequent frequent psychic episodes left him called to the work of countering witchcraft and offering magical solutions to those who sought him out.[31]

A natural call needn't be as dramatic as Gandee's, nor must it always be purely psychical or magical. What if we treated childhood obsessions and interests as a sort of marker of magical talents? One old ritual tells of how to determine a child's future occupation by laying a variety of objects in a circle around a one-year-old infant on her birthday. Things such as scissors, coins, a Bible, or a knife might be used (although

30. Hurston, "Hoodoo in America," 362, 381, 390–91; Hurston, *Mules and Men*, 198–201, 207–09, 215–17.

31. Gandee, *Strange Experience*, 23–26.

those specific choices would be frowned upon today). If the child reached for one object, that indicated the future trajectory for her life: coins might mean wealth or work in banking, a Bible a religious life or one in law, scissors an artistic temperament or a job as a hair dresser, and a knife work as a cook or even a life as a criminal. Looking to a child's interest in bugs or the way they gleefully embrace macabre subjects like death or ghosts or a love of gardens and plants all might be read in much the same way. That interest might be the "call" of witchcraft, which has many callings within it.

FIG 3-2: Objects for the Calling Circle.

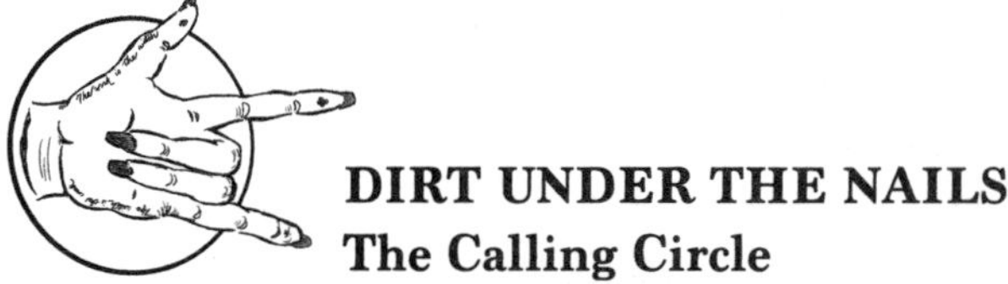

DIRT UNDER THE NAILS
The Calling Circle

Even if you're not an infant (which is likely given the book you are reading, although if you are an infant reading this book I applaud you heartily!), you can still try out the "selection" ritual to see what sort of work or goal you should be pursuing. You'll need some help for this one, though.

Have a trusted friend (or several) gather a group of objects for you. Preferably have them be a number with magical significance to you, such as seven or thirteen. Do not let them tell you what the objects are or how they interpret them, but simply let them bring them to a space where you can move around a bit. Draw a circle of space at least nine feet in diameter using chalk, flour, or something similar (this often works best outside). Sit in the center of the circle, and let your friend or friends blindfold you. Then, have your friends place the objects around the perimeter of the circle. When they are done, one friend should stand you up, hold you close and ask if you're ready. Let her spin you around a few times (another opportunity to use magical numbers if you like), then stop and stand for a moment. Collect yourself and breathe in. Extend your hands. Turn in a circle. Wait and see if you feel a pull in any one direction or another. Follow your impulse and go where the pull is strongest. When you think you are close, you can reach down and feel for the object. Whichever object you touch first is the one that "called" you.

Take off the blindfold and examine the object. Think about what it means *to you.* It's fine to discuss the object's meaning with your friend if you like, but it will be most crucial how you interpret its meaning. Does it give you an idea of what comes next for you? Does it open up possibilities you hadn't considered? What does it say to you, and what will you need to do to take the next step on your way?

The Witch's Ear— Discovering Witchcraft in the Community Around You

As many of the practical examples in this chapter have focused on the idea of being "marked" personally for witchcraft, I offer the last bit of this chapter to something more communal. I have been told on numerous occasions by numerous different people that they love hearing about folk magic and the family lore of others, but that they don't have any family lore of their own. They lament the lack of connection to their families or their inability to get a grandmother or great-aunt to divulge magical family secrets. They worry that any discussion of magic will instantly get them ostracized or worse by their relations.

While there are absolutely situations in which people have deeply toxic family situations and cannot do much to remedy those without extensive psychological scarring,

I also think that almost all of us do have more access to "family lore" than we think we do.[32] Here are a few suggestions that might make recovering lore—including magical lore but not limited to it—a little easier.

1. **Ask for stories.** Not magical stories, mind you. But stories from a person's life. In particular, you might try spending time with elders from your family or your community, and seeing what stories they have to tell. Get them to tell you about what life was like when they were growing up. Ask about their time at school, and what they remember about friends and neighbors growing up. Get them talking and truly listen to what they have to say. Write it down if you can (record it if they'll let you, and donate that to a local archive!). Make it a habit to ask questions and take an interest in them and their life.[33] Even if they say things you don't always agree with, try to be generous in your listening and pay attention to what emerges from these conversations. Over time, you're going to find that there are stories that involve "a way of doing things" that doesn't follow any rational structure. Make notes on these stories and see if you recognize something of the magical in them. Some of the subjects most likely to spark magical lore without mentioning magic: holiday traditions, wedding customs, pregnancy and birthing customs, discussions of weather events, major religious experiences like a baptism, and funeral or death customs.
2. **Tell your own story.** Get someone to interview you. Don't think about the magical side of it or even focus on that part. Just let them ask questions about your life and the world you grew up in, and see what you say. Get them to record you, and listen back to your words later (I know, no one likes hearing themselves played back, so pretend it's someone else if you must). Use the

32. Here I use the word "family," but as I often tell my folklore students, families are not just blood relations. They are often deeply entwined networks of close relationships that can involve friends (think how many people have an "aunt" or "uncle" not directly related to the family), neighbors, and even coworkers and teachers. If you have a deep enough relationship with someone, they are a part of your family, whether or not they share genetic code with you. We wouldn't negate someone's identification as a part of a family if they were adopted or part of a "step" relationship, would we? So don't let a narrow idea of what "family" is block your way here, either.
33. One of the great places to try this exercise is in nursing homes or care communities. Many people in those communities are eager to have company and would love the chance to play a game and tell a story or two, and you will likely make some good friends in the process.

same prompts in the previous suggestion and see just where your stories lead. You'll likely surprise yourself with how many little bits of magic, superstition, and folk belief you uncover with this process.

3. **Pay attention to how people in your community respond to issues of stress.** While major life events are great fonts of lore for general customs and beliefs, the way people deal with problems often involves a weaving together of rational and non-rational responses. When we get injured, even something as small as a scrape on the sidewalk, we often see magic suddenly pop out in the form of a kiss or a gentle blow on the wound after the bandage is applied. How does the community or family around you respond when someone loses a job or faces a sudden loss? Are they turning to prayer? Are those around them doing so? Are they adding them to prayer lists, or giving them foods or objects of comfort? Do people trying to get a job have a lucky token they take with them to interviews? Offering succor in times of strain is valuable, so if you can do so I encourage it, but also keep your eyes and mind open to what you can learn about the cosmology and enchantment in the world around you in those moments.
4. **Finally, visit your local library!** Libraries, and by extension local historical archives, often have absolute scads of records, documents, diaries, and books of lore tied to the community around you. Remember, your magical practices are not solely about kinship, but community, and your teachers and magical heritage come from the places and people surrounding you. Dig into local lore and legends, and see what they tell you about the landscape you see every day. Are there places reputed to be haunted or cursed? Spots where wonders have been observed, or local legends of people who might have had magical powers? Check into the folklore collections housed at your library, and look for local lore in particular. Does the library have genealogical records you can look into to find more information? Can you visit the places you read about, or even leave some flowers on the grave of an accused witch? Learn all you can, and you will find that the "call" to magic may be all around you.

THE WORK–The Witch's Mark

Think about the problem of the "witch mark" in history and folklore. For a long time, those marks might have shown a particular calling to magical work, but they also put the bearer in harm's way if they were discovered. Now, we have fewer risks of witch trials in which an errant mole or patch of parti-colored skin might be turned into evidence that gets us hung, but there are still stigmas around our skins and our bodies, and stigmas usually mean people are afraid of something. The witch, of course, to paraphrase fantasy author Terry Pratchett, should be the scariest thing in the woods, so perhaps it's time to reclaim marks of difference borne on our flesh.

In the contemporary age, what can we do with these sorts of marks? Many of us bear some sort of physical mark on our bodies, and we are all too often made to feel embarrassed or ashamed of such differences. If we see these differences with eyes attuned to magical possibilities, however, would we start to think of the lines, dots, spots, and bumps on our bodies as something to embrace? I know several witches who have taken this idea even further, getting tattoos that intentionally mark their skin to affiliate themselves with other witches or specific magical practices, such as protective charms or a beautiful sleeve tattoo of spiritually-linked herbs and flowers.

Stand in front of a mirror, especially a full-body one if you can. Look yourself over, and drink in the sight of your entire body. Do not be ashamed or abashed about any of it. Seek out its imperfections and unique qualities, and imagine them as the places where you "feed" your magic (like you might an imp). Look for any one spot on your body that particularly calls to you and feels most magical. Then take your finger, kiss the tip of it, and draw a symbol of power (such as a pentagram or a cross inscribed in a circle) over the spot in the mirror. Enchant it. Make it your witch's mark. Ask it to tell you when others like you are close by. Then, when you are out and about, pay attention to any sensation or feeling that arises unbidden in that spot. What does it call you to do, to be aware of, to feel? Trust it like a friend, like something familiar. Embrace your mark.

Recommended Reading

Seasonal Magic: Diary of a Village Witch, by Paddy Slade. I can't pass up the chance to offer my own "call" to witch work and the study of magical lore to you here. Slade's book is both a diary and a working "calendar" of magic. It's solely rooted in British lore and traditions, but it differs somewhat from Wiccan structures in its "wheel" and offers an immense amount of folk magic in the mix along with the seasonal rites.

Your local library! Seriously, make a trip and see what they have to offer. Check especially the areas under Dewey Decimal numbers 306 (Culture and Institutions), 390 (Customs, Etiquette, and Folklore), and anything the library puts in its "regional" or "local" sections.

CHAPTER FOUR

Killing the Moon—Initiation Rituals

Tales and legends from the American South inevitably contain magic, sometimes in trace amounts and frequently in copious quantities. In the mountains of Appalachia, the Otherworldly is not just a trope, but an expression of how people understand the universe in which they live. A central figure in this mythos is the witch, a dangerous component of any Appalachian community, yet one tolerated to a very high degree, even when the spells worked are killing local livestock or bringing sickness to the door of a farmer. Witches—and their counterparts, sometimes called "witch doctors," "power doctors," "fairy doctors," and the like—appear with only slightly less frequency than ghosts in supernatural mountain tales. Where do these witches come from, and how do they acquire their powers?

In this chapter, I hope to unpack some of the tales of becoming a witch from North American folklore and look at how witches become witches on their own terms.[34] That means dealing with a lightning-rod of a word: initiation. More than enough ink and electrons have been spilled over what makes for a "valid" initiation and I am not about to tell you definitively there is one right answer to that argument. I can say that there is no shortage of folklore about witches initiating into their practice, and that lore includes witches initiating alone, in groups, with only

34. Note: A version of this chapter previously appeared in *Hands of Apostasy: Essays on Traditional Witchcraft*, Three Hands Press, 2014.

a single other participant, or (as already discussed in chapter three) simply through their existing family connections. However we think about initiations today, in the stories I pull from here, it seems important, but it is also not the sole defining quality of a witch. So we will see just how and why mountain folklore talks about these initiations, and what we can learn from those stories. We shall also compare the lore of witch initiations with lore found in the Ozark Mountains to the west of the Mississippi River, tales of initiations imported from European sources, and examples of lore generated on American soil following colonial expansion. These rites, practices, oaths, and sacrifices comprise a body of lore previously only addressed as a tangent to the spells wrought by witches on their communities.[35] By understanding the way one becomes a witch, however, we are better able to understand a witch as more than a stock character of folklore. Instead, she is the power that comes with a price.

The Witch's Routine—Elements of the Initiation

There are several different ways a person becomes a witch, according to traditional lore. The act of initiation usually involves a pledge of some kind to a dark figure—often the Devil, though I would argue that this "Devil" is something other than satanic. An Ozark tale recorded by folklorist Vance Randolph outlines how mountain folk during the mid-twentieth century thought a witch was initiated. He notes that a woman (and he largely includes only cases of women becoming witches) recites a reversed version of the Lord's Prayer, then goes to her family plot in the local churchyard, strips naked (or "nekkid" if you're Southern and up to no good) and leaves her clothes on an infidel's grave, and has sexual relations with the Devil. The rite is done under the watchful eyes of imps and at least two other nude witchy witnesses, and occurs over at least three nights, after which time she is officially a witch for life, and obligated to serve her diabolical master.[36]

Randolph's description gives nearly every sensational trope associated with the witch and found in medieval and early modern witchcraft trial records. Yet even within the riotous passage, slivers of subtle and significant material manage to push through. For instance, the point that the clothing must be hung on an "infidel's

35. See Burns, *Witch Hunts in Europe & America*, 157; and Breslaw, *Witches of the Atlantic World*, 77–88, 322–29.

36. Randolph, *Ozark Magic*, 266–67.

tombstone" becomes more relevant when connected to "the family buryin' ground." After all, if the family controls who is buried in their hallowed ground, the presence of a non-believer or spiritual rebel indicates that perhaps the family has a history of witchery (and truly, who among us hasn't occasionally been a bit of an infidel when it comes to our families?). Could such a statement be a hint about the passage of magical lore, which might be kept within certain family traditions?

Speculation aside, the case outlined by Randolph in the Ozarks is quite similar to tales found in the Appalachians as well. Hubert J. Davis, in his astoundingly good compilation of American witch lore entitled *The Silver Bullet*, outlines another method of becoming a witch:

> 'Fust, he'd [the potential witch] have to climb to the top of the highest knob on Witch Mountain and tote either a black cat or a black hen. Then, he'd have to find the Indian graveyard at the place nigh where two Indian trails cross. There, he'd have to draw a big ring in the dust 'bout fifteen feet acrost, and dance in this circle each morning at break of day for eight mornings in a row. Then, on the ninth morning, he'd have to put one hand on the top of his head and 'tother on the sole of his foot and say 'I give all betwixt my two hands to the Devil ... Then the Devil comes ... and nips him on the shoulder so hit bleeds. Then, the Devil tells him to wet his finger in the blood and sign an X to this pact ... the Devil will say some magic words over the cat or the hen and change hit into an imp [another name for a familiar].[37]

This story resembles the Randolph example in many ways: the remote location, the graveyard—notably an "Indian" one, which would have hinted at non-Christian alliances, the Devil's pledge. Then there's the bodily offering—sexualized in the Ozark version and symbolic in the Appalachian one. Key differences also appear—the importance of crossroads, the use of magic circles, and the written nature of the pact are all elements absent from Randolph's account. There are a number of regional components that influence these differences. The strong Germanic influence in the Appalachians, for example, would have provided witches there with greater access to European grimoires (sometimes written in German) containing the magic circles referenced in the story from *The Silver Bullet*. Focusing on the similarities, however,

37. Davis, *The Silver Bullet*, 14–15.

allows us to see the mechanics of initiatory witchcraft rituals across several cultures. In general, witch initiations in North American folklore share a few commonalities:

- The renunciation of Christianity, often through a ritual like repeating the Lord's Prayer backward or a ritual immersion in water to reverse baptism
- The giving of oneself, physically or symbolically, to an Otherworldly entity, such as the Devil or a "Man in Black" in exchange for magical powers
- An act of exposure, such as being naked or sexual union of some kind
- A sign or omen of the candidate's acceptance as a witch, such as a witch's mark
- The transmission of magical knowledge in a ceremonial way, usually with very strict rules regarding who can initiate or teach another witchcraft
- The presentation of a familiar spirit, and/or specialized magical tools

For the most part, these elements are similar to the lore of Europe, but with some significant local color added in, such as an emphasis on the water source used in a reversal of baptism or the sign of acceptance following the initiation in the form of a bloody moon. Not all of these components are found in every case and the nature of the witch may be such that they are not an "initiated" practitioner, but merely someone who has picked up magic throughout his or her life. This last circumstance is occasionally found in places where magic is prevalently mixed with Christian practice, such as in the Appalachians (where it has recently been described as Granny Magic, although that nominative term was used no more frequently than other familial appellations like "Auntie" or "Mother") or among the Pennsylvania Dutch as *hexerei*, and sometimes confused with the folk healing practices of *braucherei*. Of course, in these cases, a magical worker is seldom called a "witch," though sometimes the term "witch doctor" is used. Even in contexts where the Christian elements subdue the most extreme aspects of witchcraft initiation, the lore still demonstrates that trials or ritual transmission of knowledge remain key elements of magical practice.

FIG 4-1: Zora Neale Hurston was one of the first and most prolific folklorists in North America, focusing on largely African American communities in the South and on the islands of Haiti and Jamaica.

SINGING BONES
Zora Neale Hurston

Folklorist, adventurer, writer, actress, Hoodoo woman. Zora Neale Hurston's life seems like the stuff of storybooks and legend, but she truly sought out what she called "the boiled-down juice" of human experience and life wherever she went. Born in the late nineteenth century, Hurston went on to receive her education at the famed Columbia University in New York, where she studied under anthropologist and folklorist Frans Boaz. Boaz encouraged her to distill her experiences and seek out stories and insights from her community, which she did with remarkable skill and style. Her book *Tell My Horse* chronicles her experiences of Vodoun and Obeah in Haiti and Jamaica, while *Mules and Men* opens up her native Florida and other parts of the African American South and all of its magical practices, especially Hoodoo. Her research went beyond chronicling what she saw, and she underwent multiple initiations and trainings to learn more about folk magic and religion from those she met, participating in ceremonies and spells along the way. Hurston was part of the Harlem Renaissance as well, and collaborated with writers like Langston Hughes, eventually producing her own masterpiece, *Their Eyes Were Watching God*. By the 1950s, however, she was virtually unknown, and only after her rediscovery by author Alice Walker in the 1970s was her reputation restored. She had unfortunately died in 1960, however, and did not live to see her return to the spotlight. Subsequent scholars have questioned some of her research, particularly her methods, although her imagination and authorial skill remain as bright as ever.[38]

Black Bibles and Reading Free—Changing the Path

So what did one do if one was eager to become a witch, but still had all that pesky, normal religious pietism clinging to one's shoes? The pages of history and story contain numerous accounts of how witches were and are initiated according to specific folkloric examples. From German Appalachian lore, there are stories of witches being initiated by obtaining a "Black Bible." Scholar Gerald C. Milnes links this tome to the *Key of Solomon*, a grimoire with many reputed magical properties and a host of instructions on how to accomplish various magical tasks. He describes a ritual in which an eager acolyte acquires such a Black Bible and goes into a spring flowing "away from the sun." They strip their clothes and bathe in the water while holding their book and calling out that they are free from the Christian God and his baptism.[39] This is inverted orthodoxy via the use of a profane "Bible" and the act of exposure by bathing in the stream, which also performs the function of a de-baptism. In almost all cases, some sort of renunciation of Christianity or abuse of scripture or prayer accompanied physically obscene acts. The recitation of a reversed Lord's Prayer, which appears in sources on modern interpretive currents of witchcraft—the most widely distributed likely being Paul Huson's *Mastering Witchcraft*—would act as both a casting-off of the formerly Christian life and an embracing of a subverted order in which occult forces would be at the behest of the witch through the use of speech or action.

The reversed prayer has its origins in a number of heretical activities recorded in European witch trial records, and the recitation of the prayer in perfect orthodox form was considered a test for accused witches on both sides of the Atlantic.[40] Language matters here, for while there were many mountain folk who could read, literacy was far from universal and the use of oral charms was standard in the performance of witchcraft (and this may explain why there's a strong horror movie

38. See Hurston, *Dust Tracks on a Road: An Autobiography.*

39. Milnes, *Signs, Cures, & Witchery*, 162.

40. Calef, *More Wonders of the Invisible World*, 198; Burns, *Witch Hunts in Europe & America*, 260.

trope of people "accidentally" reading forbidden magical passages and unleashing all kinds of damned mayhem around them). The very act of reading was occasionally suspect, and could accidentally entangle an unwitting person in witchcraft. Richard Dorson recounts a tale of mountain witchcraft in which a man had a Black Bible—in this case likely a grimoire like the *Key*—and after he meets with an untimely and mysterious demise, his son discovers the book and becomes entranced by the Devil, unable to eat or sleep and becoming very ill. A witch doctor comes and "reads him free," then destroys the nefarious book.[41]

This "reading free" practice means to expertly read a text in reverse to undo its hypnotic power and release someone bewitched by a magical tome. The remedy for being read into witchcraft is an inversion of the text to break the charm, showing the power of words and implying the need to read them aloud for full effect. Some mountain dwellers firmly believed that witchcraft came fully equipped with its own language, which was cobbled together out of twisted and inverted Christian liturgical elements. Vance Randolph, for example, recorded that widows were the most likely to become witches, for all they had to do was "learn the Devil's language."[42] A widow—who had an intimate contact beyond the grave already—would only have needed to learn the right words to conjure him to perform acts of witchcraft. While I will explore the idea of the familiar spirit more in chapters thirteen and fourteen, for now it should suffice that the purgatory nature of a witch's initiation is reflected both bodily and linguistically. In another example, Milnes also describes a rite similar to the "Black Bible"—one which involves taking dirt and shaking it off of a plate or dish while stating aloud that you are as clear of Jesus Christ as the dish is of dirt, combining the physical and verbal elements of the purge. Something more is added to this folklore:

> If, through a pact, the Devil is granted your soul in exchange for some talent, gift, or magical power, it is thought that he then receives some gift of the body in return. This could be a fingernail or even a withered finger.[43]

41. Dorson, *Buying the Wind*, 113.

42. Randolph, *Ozark Magic*, 267.

43. Milnes, *Signs, Cures, & Witchery*, 164.

Such a "sacrifice" is not uncommon in witch-lore. The physical offering could be anything from a bit of blood to sign a pact to a body part like a finger or toe to—at the extreme end—the death of a loved one. The sign of acceptance through the sacrifice and the bodily sealing of a pact with an Otherworldly power resembles mythological examples such as that of Norse god Odin, as well, who gave up his eye to gain magical knowledge. Randolph describes such an extreme sacrifice and goes on to say that the transformation of a person into a witch was a moving one with a morbid downside: the death of a close kinsperson, which causes a crisis of the spirit more powerful than any Christian conversion they have experienced. In this case, the lost loved one is called by some a "witch's sixpence," and is the "price" paid for the witch's powers. This is not a universal belief, however, as many witches do not lose anyone close to them, and instead gain a new friend: the familiar, fetch, or imp—another key element of the initiatory process (see chapter thirteen).[44]

In the earlier example involving the devilish love bite on the shoulder, the witch's personal sacrifice is a type of blood offering in exchange for the presentation of a magical imp. In another account from Virginia, the initiate goes to a high mountain, throws rocks at the moon, and curses God. They then find a spring running east and wash a brand-new knife in it as the sun rises, all the time saying they wish their "soul to be as free from the [saving blood] of Jesus Christ as this knife is of sin." After a period of thirteen days, they watch to see if the moon turns red, or is "drippin' blud [blood]" as a sign they have been accepted as a witch.[45]

This variant is distinguished by a few unique elements. First, in this initiation, the spring must flow east (or towards the rising sun, though against the natural path of the sun), which seems to be different than in the Milnes version. In this initiation, too, the witch isn't naked, but has a new knife (thus a "virgin" one, in a state of innocence often symbolized by nakedness). That "naked" knife is washed in the stream while a renunciation is made. One of Milnes's informants, Dovie, insists that initiatory streams must flow towards the rising sun, a concept that Milnes links with the esoteric practices of Swedenborgian Christianity—a sect with very divergent views from other denominations, including transcendental spirituality and the concept of

44. Randolph, *Ozark Magic,* 268.

45. Davis, *The Silver Bullet,* 11.

a heavenly sex life after death.[46] The tension between the orthodox Christianity of some mountain groups and the mystical variations practiced by others likely exacerbated accusations of witchcraft. It is quite likely that a Swedenborgian baptism, which may have been performed in an east-bound stream, would be perceived as a witchcraft initiation of sorts by non-Swedenborgians. Locations touched by such mystical acts could gradually acquire a certain magic of their own, adding to the perceptions of witchery. Culture scholar Katrina Hazzard-Donald notes a similar phenomenon in Southern African American communities, where river-immersion baptisms performed by magically-affiliated sects such as the Sanctified or Spiritualist Churches would leave eddying pools of water wherein locals said no one should fear a snake bite, due to the holiness of the site.[47] Such sanctity within a Christian context denoted a blessed site to some groups, a cursed one to others, but in either case was a sign of the enchantment wrought by the water-initiation.

Signs and omens play a crucial role in almost every mountain witchcraft induction but also create a paradox. In the above example from Davis, the bloody sunrise is a sign to the witch indicating acceptance or denial of the initiation—this feature is common in several variations of the rite. This final element appears often and with great emphasis in the traditions of a number of Appalachian and Ozark witch tales. The act of doing violence against the sun or moon becomes a key element of the initiatory rite. In fact, "killing the moon" appears in lore ranging from the German-influenced areas of the Appalachians down through Kentucky, Tennessee, the Carolinas, and Georgia, and makes its way all the way over to the Ozark Mountains in Missouri and Arkansas. The shot must frequently be made using a silver bullet, which also was the weapon of choice for killing a witch in many mountain stories. The act of celestial violence would often be paired with another element or elements of initiation—nudity and exposure, defamation of Christian icons, blasphemy, or an encounter with the Devil. The bleeding sun or moon would act as a sign that the witch's initiation had been successful, and that she was now free to call upon Otherworldly forces to do her bidding.

What can we make of this act? A witch clearly does not "kill" anything with the act of killing the sun or moon (although if she shoots straight up there's a good

46. Milnes, *Signs, Cures, & Witchery*, 162.

47. Hazzard-Donald, *Mojo Workin'*, 125.

chance that bullet is coming down somewhere in a dangerous way—don't do that!). Considering the tremendous body of lore—American, European, and otherwise—which surrounds the role of the moon in witchcraft, why would a witch be required to perform any such violence against one of her closest allies?

In light of the idea of an offering as a way to gain power, this act makes more sense. The act of killing the moon using a weapon designed to kill a witch is an act of self-sacrifice, as well as a method for murdering the Mother of Witchcraft in the case of the moon (or the Father, in the case of the sun). Witchcraft initiations that involve visitations from initiatory spirits, devils, and imps are often rather bloodthirsty affairs, with the initiate being torn apart in dreams and reassembled with new power and identity in tow or scratched, bitten, and otherwise "marked" by the entity performing the initiation. Shooting the sun and the moon, paired with other debasements of former identity such as the cursing of the Christian God or repetition of the Lord's Prayer backwards, performs a similar function. The witch removes the self that existed prior to witchcraft and becomes a new person with an identity forged in the crucible of witchcraft. Such a rite links the witch to a concept of an "Old Faith," which exists outside of and beyond Christianity (although not necessarily *before* it, despite the name). Milnes specifically makes a point of saying that the initiation described by Dovie is linked to a quasi-heretical mysticism, and that her "example may come from even older pagan sun worship beliefs, which pervade European witchcraft traditions."[48] Blood binds the pact of self and also becomes the token of acceptance within the initiatory rite, and the gates between the heavens and earth are opened to the newly-formed witch.

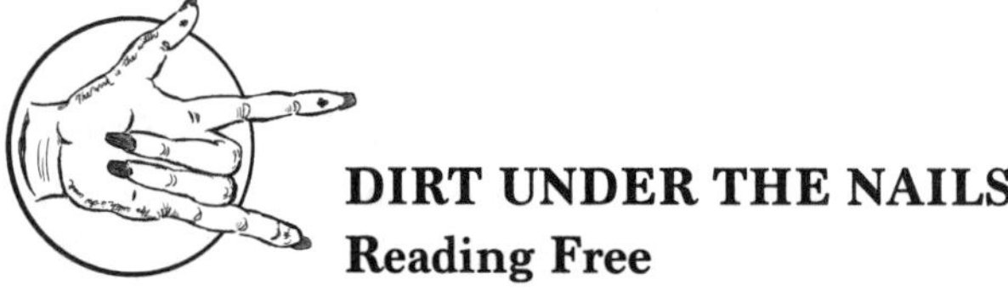

DIRT UNDER THE NAILS
Reading Free

In traditional folk magical practice, "reading free" is a way of enacting a countercurse or a defense against any witchcraft done from a specific book or spell. The victim or a proxy must read the passage that caused the sorcery to take root in the first place, but they do so backwards. This has a cou-

48. Milnes, *Signs, Cures, & Witchery*, 162.

ple of potential meanings, including reading it word for word backwards, as in, "Ghost Holy the and, Son the, Father the of name the in." Alternatively, the words could be phonetically read backwards by the letters or syllables, as happens when reading free using the Lord's Prayer: "Nema. Reverof ylorg eht dna, rewop eht, modgnik eht," as an inversion of "The kingdom, the power, and the glory forever. Amen."

If you are bespelled by someone and know what they did to enchant you, reading free can be incredibly useful as a defense mechanism. On the other hand, very few targets are able to pinpoint spells with that kind of precision, so reading free can also be useful as an initiatory rite. To use it, you would simply need to figure out a particular passage of text that represents an old part of your life you are ready to give up (or, as is appropriate in initiations, sacrifice) and read that passage backwards as you dedicate yourself to a new path. That might well be something associated with a childhood religion, such as the Lord's Prayer or a passage of Torah, but it could even be a piece of poetry you read or wrote at a point in your life you're ready to leave behind. Read yourself free from that past, and then put one hand upon your head and another under the sole of your foot (if you are physically able, modifying as best you can if your body has different abilities than those described here). Pledge yourself to your new path, and then wash yourself or a symbolic object in water to remove any lingering remnants of that past version of you.

The Apprentice and the Devil—Who Initiates the Witch?

The acts of exposure, renunciation, and the sacrificial sign all act as steps toward initiation, a set of prerequisites for the act of the witch's transformation from mundane person into something much different—a creature set aside from mortality and marked by her power. The transference of that power has several strict regulations that determine just who can initiate a witch and how it must be done. Of course, in several of the above examples, the witch commits all the acts necessary for initiation entirely on her own, or so it would seem. Behind the façade of solitary action, though, the Appalachian mind understands a cosmology that makes a witch a decidedly unsolitary creature. They gain the company of numerous spirits—sometimes in the form of the dead, with whom the witch holds necromantic discourse—and more often in the form of devils and other witches. These spirits may be "gifts" provided by the initiator, who is often seen in diabolical terms. In fact, many examples of initiatory lore show a witch undergoing her transformation not alone, but specifically aided by the Devil and sometimes even other witches. One such example from the eastern mountains of Kentucky demonstrates a rite that echoes previous examples and includes the witch's Master as a key component of the ritual:

> To become a witch: the candidate goes with the Devil to the top of the highest hill at sunrise nine successive days and curses God; the Devil then places one hand on the candidate's head and one on his feet, and receives the promise that all between his hands shall be devoted to his service.[49]

This initiation shows the hallmarks of other Southern mountain witch-makings, including renunciation and the exposure at the top of a high hill (while nudity is not explicitly mentioned in this example, the mountain-top location frequently appears in European witch lore in which assembled witches cavorted in the buff, and it's not a stretch that to those hearing the tale, some sort of bodily exposure might have been imagined). The Devil in this example claims his witch's body, although not explicitly her soul as medieval and early modern church writings would have claimed (the Devil as a figure of North American witchery is discussed more at length in chapter fourteen).

Importantly, a witch did not come into her power capable of performing all the acts of an alleged witch. As mentioned above, the witch received instruction as a portion of the initiation, and often tools or gifts of her trade as well. An induction ritual from the southern Appalachians describes an older witch taking on an apprentice, a young woman who came knocking at her door at midnight.[50] In this and similar stories, the initiate is taken to a mountain spring where she helps the girl knot a handkerchief in three corners while renouncing the Father, Son, and Holy Ghost, then summoning the Devil and signing a pact. The young witch in this case learns an element of magical practice as well as the method for contacting her Master from an experienced witch as part of her adoption rite.

49. Thomas, *Kentucky Superstitions*, 278.

50. Davis, *The Silver Bullet*, 11.

A final and divergent point on the topic of Southern mountain witchcraft initiations is the idea of coercive or nonconsensual induction. While accounts of initiations occurring against the will of the initiate are rare, they do crop up in the lore of Appalachia or the Ozarks from time to time. In some accounts, a parent or relative who practices witchcraft bespells a daughter or niece and forces her through some of the ordeals of initiation. Examples found in Patrick Gainer's *Witches, Ghosts, & Signs* as well as *The Silver Bullet* show that a seduction or entrapment into witchcraft often appear as part of a person's "salvation" story, in which the one being initiated manages to escape a lifetime of diabolic servitude and witchcraft at the last moment due to a force of Christian faith. Since these stories strongly resemble the sorts of recanting done in medieval witch trial records, it is possible they share some literary and folkloric heritage in the way Appalachian "Jack" tales resemble faery stories from European lore.[51] Richard Dorson's sweeping account of American folklife notes that among the Pennsylvania Dutch, possession and use of forbidden texts, such as the *Sixth & Seventh Books of Moses*, in and of itself could cause a good person to slip into witchcraft.[52] One informant from the Georgia Appalachian region points out that a witch initiation is an exercise in consent and intention, saying, "You just had t'pay no 'tention t'witches. They can put a spell on you, but they can't turn you into a witch if you pay them no mind."[53] The point seems to be that a witch's *spells* might target anyone but that an *initiation* was an affair for the willing, which seems to be the standard found in mountain lore.

Each of the stories mentioned here contains fragmentary pieces of initiatory lore, but always with a layer of sensationalism on top. These folktales were intended to amuse and spark curiosity, after all, so it should come as no surprise that a small offering of blood, say on a new witch's ritual cord (sometimes called a "cingulum") or a few drops in a cup of wine poured out to the god, gods, or spirits to which the witch is binding herself, has become exaggerated into the death of a family member or the withering of a limb. Initiations have a profound impact on those that undergo them, and that many of the common elements (the renunciation, the vow to serve a

51. The Jack Tales are also found throughout the British- and Scottish-influence Appalachians, and feature variations of such stories as "Jack and the Beanstalk" or "Jack the Giant Killer," among others.

52. Dorson, *Buying the Wind*, 111–14.

53. Wigginton, *The Foxfire Book*, 355.

witch-god/goddess/devil/etc., and the granting of magical gifts like certain charms or familiar spirits) are profound acts that may well belong in an initiation ceremony. Many of these features are also found in other initiation ceremonies and modern works on witchcraft, such as Paul Huson's *Mastering Witchcraft* or Nigel Jackson's *Call of the Horned Piper*. Some elements are overlooked in these sorts of folkloric imaginings of "witch-making." For instance, witchcraft writer Sarah Lawless notes that in some Traditional Witchcraft initiations, once one becomes a witch (or takes initiation), one finds "growth and strength of abilities and experiences the more one practices and keeps their promises."[54] Most stories about witches seem to either end at the oaths taken upon becoming a witch, or to start in medias res of a witch's career, showing a witch operating in one way, unchanging, until she is (inevitably) defeated. That makes for good storytelling, but perhaps not for so much good practical witchery. Instead, the process of initiation in the mountains of southern North America is full of sensational elements hiding certain key themes. A renunciation of Christianity acts to break ties with the mundane life of a witch but becomes exaggerated into blasphemous acts and congress with devils. A certain fearlessness shown by the witch's act of exposure becomes vaguely sexualized nudity. The peculiar act of killing the moon becomes the symbolic self-sacrifice and adoption into the "bloodline" of witchcraft. The imps of the Old World become ghosts or "haints" of dead family members in the New World. The skills a witch acquires are learned through an incredibly powerful initiatory process which rivals adoption into a new family in its significance, and often the skills are learned through contact with other witches (living or dead). The rite of initiation encapsulates the tightly bound lineage and heritage of Southern mountain witchcraft and demonstrates the tremendously rigorous requirements of a Craft that forever changes the life of the initiate witch.

54. See Lawless, "What Makes One a Witch."

FIG 4-2: Signing the "Devil's Book" was one way of securing your initiation into witchcraft in many folktales.

THE WORK—Signing the Devil's Book/ The Contract/Self-Initiation

It is sometimes said only a witch can initiate another witch, but we also see through the lore explored in this chapter that many witches undertake rituals of initiation themselves. While I cannot recommend that you undergo any of the trials or rites outlined in Appalachian lore here for yourself (especially if that is not the tradition whence you come, since that would be appropriative and, frankly, a little messy), if you look at the "bones" of these ceremonies you might see some things worth doing in your own life. For example, you may wish to incorporate the idea of a ritual renunciation of past influences and a dedication of yourself to a new path or direction. To that end, I offer the following questions to guide you as you consider how to apply what you've read here to your own life.

Are you willing to or able to separate yourself from a previous spiritual identity (or a lack of one)? Will a ritual help you to make the most of that separation? Do you need anyone to witness it, or will it be enough to do it on your own?

How important are written words to your selection of a path? Would you write in the "Devil's Book," so to speak, to commit yourself to a practice (especially if you know there are loopholes everywhere)? What about a contract with yourself? Could you draft such a contract and commit to it ritually? Is there a magical book that you feel particularly close to that you could use as a framework for your study and your commitment?

Note, a book or contract like this does not have to be patterned explicitly after the ones I've described. You have the freedom to choose. My long-time magical partner, for example, has a deep affinity with Frances Hodgson Burnett's *The Secret Garden*, and has even drawn magic from that work, so it would be conceivable that she could use that book as her "contract" text because of its emotional connection to her.

Finally, could you be "naked" in your practice? This doesn't have to mean physically naked, but vulnerable. Can you read omens, and accept when they say "no" to you? That is sometimes the hardest part of initiation, because the risk of being rejected is a powerful fear. Facing that fear makes you more naked than stripping on top of any old mountain could do, so spend some time looking for signs (or divining for them) and remaining open to the "tough love" messages you get. They are part of your nakedness.

Recommended Reading

Besom, Stang, & Sword: A Guide to Traditional Witchcraft, the Six-Fold Path, and the Hidden Landscape, by Chris Orapello and Tara-Love Maguire. This book is not connected to Appalachian lore, but, like Huson's work, presents a folklore-derived and very accessible approach to traditional witchcraft of the practical sort. There are several rites here that work as potential initiatory portals for a budding witch.

Signs, Cures, & Witchery, by Gerald C. Milnes. Many of the initiatory practices in this chapter are at least loosely explored in Milnes's work. It's a scholarly read, but also pulls heavily from first-hand accounts and interviews, which makes it a little like sitting at the feet of an old storyteller while a thoughtful professor offers some color commentary on the magical practices you're reading about.

Southern Cunning: Folkloric Witchcraft in the American South, by Aaron Oberon. In his updated take on Hubert J. Davis's book *The Silver Bullet* (which offered much of the lore in my own chapter here), Oberon looks at the rituals of Southern and Appalachian witchcraft with an eye to holding onto traditions without being stifled by them. His section on initiation will seem very familiar to you if you've read this chapter, but will offer you some new insights as well.

Weave the Liminal: Living Modern Traditional Witchcraft, by Laura Tempest Zakroff. Zakroff's book thoughtfully revisits the idea of "tradition" from her own contemporary perspective. She absorbs aspects of myth, legend, magic, and ritual, then reinterprets them from her own point of view. Her chapter on defining your own path rings many of the bells you find in the initiatory rites described in this chapter, too.

THIRD RITE: CASTING THE SPELL

Or, Magic Beneficial and Baneful through Herbs, Healing, Hair-Theft, and Hexes

"I grew up hearing how there were people who inflicted evil on others. That evil could be obtained by going to a person who was the mediator (whether folk healer or not). If someone wanted to inflict harm on another person because of revenge or something like that, he or she would ask the folk healer or the mediator for help. The mediator, by virtue of a special ritual, would ask…for the victim to receive a certain punishment. I heard this many times, ever since I was a little girl. To get out of that situation, the person who was considered the victim would go to another mediator or folk healer so that with her rituals she could have the opposite effect—that is to say, to extract the evil from the victim."*

* López, "Santa Fe, New Mexico," 114–15.

CHAPTER FIVE

The Ladyhearted Worker—Magic for Healing and Love

A young man lies in bed, writhing in pain as he clutches his arm, only recently freed from the clutches of a hay baler and sporting a nasty gash. His family has gathered around, save for his little sister who was sent out the moment the boy was carried into the house. He's wailing, his skin pale and sticky with sweat, and already his mother is praying with tears on her cheeks for the grace of Mary to save her boy. Her prayer is peppered with bits of Creole and sobs, and the boy's father is standing behind her with his hay-dusted hands upon her shoulders, looking down into the face of his agonized child.

Just as the wailing, praying, and sobbing hits a fever pitch, the little sister returns, a short, broad-faced older woman behind her. People clear a path for Miss Thibodeaux, the local *traiteuse*, a woman said to be given the power of healing from God. She sees immediately the seriousness of the situation but takes a moment to pause and put her hand on the mother's head, praying the divine love of Mary and the Saints on her, and the mother's sobs soften, then stop. Miss Thibodeaux walks over to the boy, still heaving in pain, and puts her hand on his head, too. She begins murmuring softly, snatches of her words all that anyone can hear, a mixture of Creole and French and English and Latin. Her eyes are fluttering, and everyone is watching her intently, even the injured boy as he looks into her face with a raptured expression. He is quiet now, no trace of pain on his face.

Her hands float down over his bleeding arm, her murmuring prayers continuing. Her words are still mostly inaudible, although the word "Live!" seems to rise up from her throat from someplace deeper than her short frame would allow.

Then, quietly, slowly, the blood in the wound stops flowing. The wound begins to close up right before their eyes, becoming not a gash, but a narrow slit. Miss Thibodeaux continues praying until it is a thin, angry red line that needs dressing, but which no longer poses a threat to the young man's life. As her words stop, her eyes open, and she smiles sweetly into the boy's face, brushing his hair away with her hand and whispering one more prayer. He drifts off to sleep.

She gathers her things, the grateful family piling around her to press hands, the boy's mother holding her tightly, staining the shoulder of her dress with tears, but everyone resists the temptation to say their thanks aloud, knowing that may undo all she has done. She leaves a few instructions on cleaning the wound and wrapping it, telling them to continue their prayers and that she will do the same. A few days later, the boy and his father drop by her house to visit, bringing with them a dozen eggs and a smoked ham, the first of several such visits. Before they leave, she asks to see his arm, where a thin red line is all that remains of the once-threatening wound.[55]

"Ladyhearted" vs. "Two-Headed" Workers

When it comes to folk magic, everyone wants miracles. They want someone who can wave a wand and cure cancer, or stir a magic cauldron and have it bubble over with an unlimited supply of soup, or pasta,[56] or meat. As most spellcasters, conjurers, and magically-inclined folk will tell you, however, in general that's not how magic works. It functions in subtler ways, making changes in the tides of events around us to guide us to uncannily good (or bad) results.

Yet there are occasionally miraculous or unexplainable things we find in the annals of North American folk magic. Ethnographer Jack Montgomery describes a folk healing by a *braucher* very similar to the one at the beginning of the chap-

55. This story is based on several accounts of Louisiana *traiteurs* found in Richard Dorson's *Buying the Wind*; Ellen Daigle's "Traiteurs and their Power of Healing: The Story of Doris Bergeron"; editor Wayland D. Hand's "Folk Medicine in French Louisiana."

56. If you've never read Tomie DePaola's *Strega Nona* books, I highly recommend them. The overfilling pasta pot features in the first one, and there is a lot of Italian folk magic woven into the stories, which are usually based on folklore.

ter.[57] I have seen the "bloodstopper" charm work like this for myself as well, and it truly is unbelievable until you see it happen. At the same time, just because someone can heal a cut or gash with a Bible verse and some focused "hands-on" magic doesn't mean they can also cure cancer or stop a stroke in its path. There seem to be some real limits to what folk healing can and can't do, and those boundaries are well understood by those who use folk healing magic.

Most folk communities have some kind of folk healing tradition. Often, those who practice magical healing are seen as different from the rest of the community—gifted by God or blessed with their power. They are almost always needed. They fill in where medical practices seem to "miss," whether that is a particular bedside manner, a placebo effect, or just a long-standing relationship with the patient. Some communities, such as Latinx ones that call upon *curanderos*, may have a variety of illnesses that are not strictly medical in nature, but which affect the spirit and whole being of a person in ways that only the folk healers can deal with. They are usually not regarded as "witches" in the most negative light of that term, although in some cases their magical healing may be treated as a form of witchcraft by members of the community. Folk healers often distinguish themselves from any stereotypes of witches casting curses, or actively work *against* the harm of witchcraft in their practices. For example, in traditions of Hoodoo, Rootwork, and Southern Conjure, the terminology for those who practice healing magic and those who practice other forms of spellwork specifically set them apart. A healer may be called "ladyhearted," meaning someone who does only folk healing, love work, and gentler forms of magic, such as finding lost things or divination. A "two-headed" worker is one that can usually do some of the magic a folk healer does, but who focuses more on hex-breaking (or hex-making), gambling or money charm-making, or even rooting out community witches.

This division between magical workers is not unique to Hoodoo, however, and we find those same divisions in most communities with traditions of witchcraft and magical healing. Even when all magic is somewhat suspect in certain communities, healing magic seems to get much more of a pass than anything else, largely because those who do folk healing will generally say their power is not their own, but divinely supplied. Thus, the magic is also a miracle, proof of a religious framework that the

57. Montgomery, *American Shamans*, xxx-xxxi.

community already has. Below are some (but certainly not all) of the different terms used in various North American folk communities to describe their folk healers, as well as some of the maladies they are most often called upon to treat.

- **Braucher/Pow-wow**—These are healers in the Pennsylvania Dutch (and affiliated or derived Appalachian German) communities. They can treat "wildfire" (a type of skin rash), bleeding, being "liver-grown" (a folk illness that could be a few different problems, all resulting in abdominal pain), or wart removal. They also provide other magico-medical services such as dowsing/divination, home blessings, and the concoction of herbal remedies. A number of *brauchers* also specialize in the removal of supernatural illnesses, a practice sometimes known as *hexerei* (or "witchcraft treatment"). The term "Pow-wow" was apparently an English term applied to these practitioners from outside the *Deitsch*-speaking communities, and is similar to the term "power doctor" found in other places.[58]
- **Cunning Folk**—This term sometimes shows up in the British-dominated communities of New England, the mid-Atlantic states, parts of Canada, and even some Appalachian zones. They treated folk ailments of "falling" (a term for epilepsy or any fainting disorder), being "elf-shot" (suddenly struck by an illness, sometimes after being hit with "elf arrows" that left red marks on the skin), or suffering from "bewitchment" (harmful magic that could take the form of headaches and ailments or bad luck). Largely, the work of the cunning folk—also called "fairy doctors," "wise women/men," or "conjurers"—involved divination and diagnosis, with treatments focusing on removing magical harm from a client.[59]
- **Curanderos/Curanderas**—These are the healers of Latinx communities specializing in spiritual and magico-medical cures involving everything from rituals to herbal treatments to "cupping," a practice that uses glass bowls to provide deep tissue massage for clients. While a number of physical ailments are treated, a *curandera* can also deal with spiritual problems such as *susto* (a type of "soul fright" that leaves the person in a mentally debilitated state), bad *aires*

58. Dorson, *Buying the Wind*, 107–117; Donmoyer, *Pow-wowing in Pennsylvania*, 3–4; Milnes, *Signs, Cures, & Witchery*, 39; Schreiwer, "Requirement for Butzemann Construction."

59. See Davies, *Popular Magic: Cunning-folk in English History*: and Wilby, *Cunning Folk & Familiar Spirits*.

(airs or winds that can cause a person to fall ill), *chipileza* (a nursing sickness thought to be caused by imbalanced heat and cold), or *mal de ojo* (the evil eye, which could make a target sick or even cause them to die).[60]

- **"Granny" Women**—This is an Appalachian term that represents a number of practices, but could be used to indicate women healers in a community. They treat lots of "blood" illnesses using things like tonics and herbal preparations, as well as providing spiritual prayers and healing for fevers, sprains, and burns. Granny Women can also serve as midwives and frequently deal with issues of women's health including birth control, menstruation, and childbirth. They sometimes practice bloodstopping and a few heal solely by using faith healing and the "laying on of hands" to transmit divine treatment.[61]
- **"Medicine Men"**—This is a generically applied outsider term for a variety of Native American practitioners of a variety of Native American healing practices.[62] It's a frustrating term because it is deeply Colonial and reduces cultural distinctions. At the same time, many people understand the term to mean "folk healer" even within Native communities. More specific terms like *leku* (Cherokee, meaning something like "ceremonial guide"), *pejula wacasa* (Lakota, essentially a "doctor of spiritual healing"), or *hatáli* (Diné/Navajo, meaning "singer") vary among tribes, and not all carry the same significance, although in most cases there is at least some connection between the spirit world, healing, and ceremony. These leaders can treat medical illnesses using traditional remedies or more deeply spiritual problems, including issues of mental health or social ostracism, but everything depends very much on context.
- **Root Doctor/Ladyhearted Worker**—A term used in African American Hoodoo and Rootwork (and some Southern Conjure). Ailments include wasting sicknesses (sometimes called "fading"), a feeling of "live things" inside a person, runs of bad luck (being "crossed," "jinxed," or "goophered"), or having "roots

60. See Torres, *Curadero: A Life in Mexican Folk Healing*; Ingham, "On Mexican Folk Medicine"; Curious Curandera, "Spiritual Cleansing Six-Week Course."

61. Milnes, *Signs, Cures, & Witchery*, ch. 13; Montgomery, *American Shamans*, ch. 10–12.

62. Jones & Molyneaux, *Mythology of the American Nations*, 53.

put on" a person to give them poor health, mental disorder, or severe misfortune.[63]

- **Traiteur/Traiteuse**—These terms for a male and female folk healer, respectively, appear in Louisiana Creole and Acadian communities, as well as very occasionally in the Canadian Acadian communities whence they came. Strictly speaking, a *traiteur* or *traiteuse* will deal with spiritual causes of common ailments like fever or "wasting" sicknesses, while a *remedé* worker will employ herbs, animal dung, knotted cords, or even ice packs and store-bought pharmacy drugs to heal those illnesses. They may also treat sprains, cuts (using the bloodstopper charm mentioned at the beginning of the chapter), or other physical ailments.[64]
- **Yarb Doctors/Power Doctors**—These terms are mostly found in the Appalachians and Ozarks, and are essentially something of a cross between the Granny Women's healing, treatments found among cunning folk, and a bit of magic from Irish, German, and African American sources as well. They treat many of the same ailments Granny Women do, minus those specifically connected with women's health, and also take off witchcraft and spirit ailments. In Irish-influenced areas they may be called "fairy doctors" who cure conditions like being "elf-shot."[65]

This list is by no means complete, because for any community, the terminology and treatment regimens and even diseases can vary. These are only some of the better-known and more widely studied examples of folk healing visible to us in North America, but there are truly dozens more—such as the Hmong Too Tse Neng healers or even Chinese American traditional medicine practitioners—that exist to provide magical and spiritual healing to the communities around them.

63. Hurston, "Hoodoo in America," 317–320; Chireau, *Black Magic*, chapter 1.

64. Dorson, *Buying the Wind*, 261–66; Roberts, "Louisiana Superstitions," 147–48.

65. Milnes, *Signs, Cures, & Witchery*, 39; Randolph, *Ozark Magic*, chapters 6 and 7.

FIG 5-1: Lee R. Gandee believed that the Pennsylvania German barn sign designs were useful for creating magical charms that could be drawn or painted to offer their benefits.

SINGING BONES
Lee R. Gandee

Lee Gandee, known as the "Hexenmeister of Dutch Fork," was hardly a conventional person. They kept a coffin from the local Odd Fellows Lodge in their living room, frequently saw and interacted with spirits that they called their "boys," and practiced folk healing based in Lee's Pennsylvania Dutch roots. They also modified much of that practice to fit their own life, adding in elements of folk magic they found throughout their tenure as a history professor and practicing folk magician, including modifying "hex signs" from Pennsylvania barn patterns for magical purposes. Lee's relocation to South Carolina saw them moving into the house of a woman who had been executed for witchcraft two centuries earlier, which was a major selling point for Lee. They also struggled with a number of issues in their personal life, including a divorce as they began to experience the surfacing of a "Queen" persona within their male-assigned body (they did not refer to themselves as transgender, but that language may not have been available to them during their lifetime; I have chosen to use the singular "they" in deference to that possibility in this mini-biography, but that is solely my own interpretation). The Queen also made much of Lee's power available to them, giving them a "second sight" or psychic clairvoyance and visions. Lee passed away in 1998, leaving a legacy chronicled in their autobiography, *Strange Experience: The Secrets of a Hexenmeister*.[66]

66. Gandee, *Strange Experience*; Montgomery, *American Shamans*, chapters 3–9.

Babies Marked and Veiled—Midwives and Folk Magic

One group that crosses a number of cultures and carries significant healing lore is midwives. Women who cared for other women during childbearing and childbirth maintained an expansive body of knowledge that incorporated herbal remedies, divination practices, medical manipulation of the body of mother or child, diagnostic techniques, pain relief methods, proverbial wisdom, and even things like beauty regimens. With the expansion of the male-dominated field of professional medicine in the eighteenth and nineteenth centuries, midwives often became marginalized in North America (they had been experiencing marginalization for years in Europe and areas of Catholic-dominated New Spain). Suspicions of witchcraft cropped up from time to time against midwives, especially in the event of a mother or child's death, but in some communities, midwives could skirt the accusations of witchcraft because of local dependence on their skills. Additionally, communities like those in the Appalachians and Ozarks—intentionally very self-isolating groups in some cases—had serious suspicions of professional doctors, and midwives had their implicit and embedded trust.

An entire body of lore developed through midwifery practice, much of it associated with divination or protection of the mother and child. For example, the sex of a baby could be determined by using the woman's wedding ring as a pendulum, suspending it from one of her hairs over her pregnant belly. If it moved in a circle, it would be a girl. If it moved side to side or back and forth, it was a boy. Iron could be put under or near the bed to help protect mother and child during delivery. Similarly, a knife or ax might be placed under the bed to "cut" labor pains. As soon as the mother started going into labor, the midwife might untie all knots in the room, including letting the mother's hair down. Knots are thought to magically interfere with the ease of the birth, so removing them helped provide a smooth delivery. Midwives might also save the caul (or veil, a membrane from the amniotic sac) or the placenta for later use in bolstering the health or magical powers of mother and child (although in some cases cauls were sold as magic charms to sailors to ward off drowning, as well).

Midwives also knew some of the best abortifacients, including the use of herbs, such as pennyroyal, as a way of preventing or terminating an early pregnancy. While these services were not always explicitly offered, midwives often understood the need for safe birth control in communities where women had little power over their sexual experiences. The midwife also frequently operated as a record-keeper of sorts, and might note down crucial information about births, deaths, marital relationships, patterns of illness, and even things like weather and agriculture in the community. This makes the diaries of midwives extremely valuable historical resources.[67]

Sympathetic, Contagious, Preventative, Curative—The Types of Folk Medicine

To deal with illness and maintain health, a number of cultures have developed systems of medicine and magic that rely more on a worldview than a specific and empirical data set. That's not to say that all folk medicine (or folk magic for that matter) lacks method or reason, but rather that the reasons are frequently tied to a complex and interlinked web where pulling on any one thread can change things for anything the web is touching. In the nineteenth century, author James Frazer categorized pieces of these webs, noting that magic was either *sympathetic* (meaning that the magic effectively worked because two like things have a relationship with each other, so a doll that looks like someone can be used to hurt or help them) or *contagious* (magic spreads by contact, the way that rubbing a lucky rabbit's foot is thought to give the person rubbing it luck).[68] These classifications are highly oversimplified, but they to seem to capture at least a very general sense of the way that magic and healing is thought about in Western-derived systems. Other magico-medical systems look at illness and health as something *holistic*, rooted in balances and imbalances in the body. For example, a person might be carrying too much "heat" in themselves, leading to things like anger or headaches, and need to take cooling herbs to readjust their nature. We see these systems in Ayurvedic medicine, *curanderismo* from Mexican-derived healing traditions, and even somewhat in the "four humors" system inherited from Ancient Greece.

Additionally, plenty of magical medicine focused not on healing a particular disease, but on keeping the body healthy in general, staving off any potential illness. The philosophy behind the "spring tonics" of Appalachia seems to be that during

67. I highly recommend reading *A Midwife's Tale: The Life of Martha Ballard*, edited by Harvard historian Laurel Thatcher Ulrich. Taken from the diary of an eighteenth- and nineteenth-century midwife, it provides a lot of insight into all aspects of life over a thirty-year period in North American history.

68. See Frazer, *The Golden Bough*.

the winter, a person's blood begins to lose its potency and strength, and a strong herbal dose of something like sassafras, willow leaves or bark, or tansy steeped in water (or whiskey) would "tone" the blood back to healthy levels. The famed Four Thieves Vinegar was also used as a tonic, and we still see plenty of tonics that call for using apple cider vinegar infused with various ingredients as a daily dose of health. My Pennsylvania German and Appalachian friends often use elderberry syrup as a preventative during cold and flu season, and echinacea is sometimes thought to have preventative properties for illness. This line of thinking is hardly gone from us even in more mainstream society—go to any grocery store or pharmacy and you'll find lots of vitamin C-based daily dose tablets that make general claims about their effectiveness in helping keep colds at bay. These aren't a huge leap away from folk cures like mustard plasters on the chest, a hot toddy, or wearing socks stuffed with onions to "sweat" out a fever or cold.

In addition to these magical structures, much folk healing depends upon following the *doctrine of signatures*. This concept appears in multiple folk magical systems, and at its core assumes that in a universe ordered in such a way as to allow magic and spiritual healing, everything must also be connected in some way and a gifted person will be able to see "cues" that reveal those connections. For example, if a person is looking for an herb that will treat heart problems, they might first look at herbs with heart-shaped leaves or flowers, since the "heart" is a key. Similarly, the aphrodisiac qualities of something like ginseng are revealed in the way it resembles certain body parts (or whole naked bodies in some cases). A plant like raspberry, with its prickly, hairy brambles and leaves, is thought to help ease menstruation because the hairs act like a comb and help smoothly remove uterine lining material (and the red berries may also play a part in this association). Whether the doctrine of signatures is effective or not is largely a case of personal opinion. It could be that those who follow it are able to see the signatures clearly before they use a new cure (or an old cure in a new way), or they may simply notice the "signature" after they've already determined a cure is effective (the "retroactive" approach).

Of course, staying healthy never really means avoiding health problems altogether, because accidents are inevitable. This is where healers often come in, and where magic flourishes.

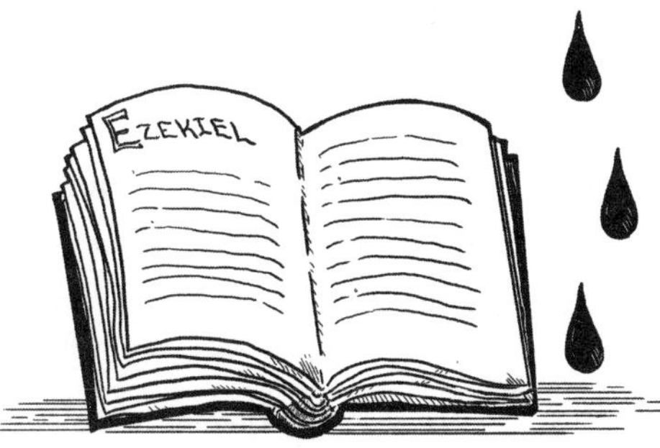

FIG 5-2: The "blood verse" of Ezekiel 16:6 is believed by some to have the power to staunch minor bleeding and wounds.

DIRT UNDER THE NAILS
The Bloodstopper's Charm

The so-called "blood verse" is a well-known charm found in several magical traditions, including various Southern mountain healing practices, Pow-wow/braucherei in Pennsylvania German areas, and among Louisiana *traiteur* traditions. While generally these cures and spells are highly secretive about spoken formulae and often only someone who has been passed "the power" can use them anyway, this is one verse that seems to be available to most people, even if it is not as effective as it might be when used by a healer. All the traditions insist that the healer and the person being healed should be believers in a higher power (some go so far as to say "a believer in God" but that shifts a little bit among traditions, and so long as there is *some* belief present it seems to be considered enough).

The spell involves simply speaking the biblical passage of Ezekiel 16:6 while passing a hand over the wound to make the blood stop flowing so it can be bound up and heal:

"And when I passed by you and saw you polluted in your blood, I said unto you while you were in your blood: Live. Yea, I said unto you while you were in your blood: Live!"

Many folk accounts tell of healers whose power actually does the binding and healing, as in the tale at the beginning of the chapter. Often the

> healer will make the sign of the cross three times over the wound and conclude the healing by saying "In the name of the Father, the Son, and the Holy Spirit (or Ghost). Amen."
>
> **Note:** This is NOT intended as medical advice, but as an example of a common folkloric charm found among multiple traditions. Please do NOT depend on this charm for first aid or medical treatment.

Healing Herbs, and Who Uses Them

Plenty of people use herbal remedies, even if they don't know it. They may have a cup of peppermint tea when their stomach is upset. They might take an aspirin when they have a headache. Possibly they eat a high-bran food when they are constipated in order to get past their problem. These are all rooted, pardon the pun, in herbal formulae or treatments: mint is good for digestive relief, aspirin comes from the same willow bark used to treat headaches, and bran is a plant product loaded with fiber that can help with bowel regularity. Herbal remedies represent one of the first lines of medicine human beings developed, and the ability to carefully manipulate the body using herbs in order to heal it has been both a common skill and one requiring specialization and training. Many people use general home remedies including herbal ones without any detailed knowledge (such as in the mint tea example). Other forms of herbal medicine, such as using foxglove to treat heart disease symptoms, can be lethally dangerous if misused, and so training and expertise is required.

Often those who learned herbal folk remedies in the past did so by studying with an experienced herbalist or healer, such as often happened with midwives or even a number of country "doctors" who might lack a formal medical degree in times gone by. Studying the herbs that were available in the immediate landscape—as well as few imported ones that might prove useful at times—was a prerequisite to being a good healer. A folk healer often learned a few magical charms but relied heavily on her herbal knowledge, including her knowledge of where herbs grew in her region, when to harvest them, and how to recognize dangerous "look-alikes."

Below I list some of the commonly found and used herbs from the two key "regions" of North America (the Rocky Mountains form something of a dividing line for the native plant species). These are the herbs that have been used by indigenous peoples and colonizers for centuries, and many of which are still in use today. There are no dosages listed, nor am I recommending the use of any of these, as I am not a medical professional. Please consult with a physician, midwife, or other knowledgeable medical source before using any herbs or remedies.

Eastern Herbs

- Alder—Used to treat skull ailments, blood issues, and mouth sores or infections.
- Black Cohosh—Often used for treating women's reproductive medical complaints, such as menstrual cramps or menopause symptoms.
- Black Snakeroot—Used to treat liver issues and made into a wash for smallpox sores.
- Boneset—Brewed into a medicine used to treat chest colds.
- Echinacea—Long thought to stave off colds and flu when taken daily, although recent medical research has called its efficacy into question.
- Elder—The berries are made into a syrup used to treat throat complaints and colds, and sometimes taken as a preventative against colds and fevers.
- Ginseng—Widely used as an energy-boosting treatment and a male aphrodisiac.
- Juniper—Used to treat whooping cough and lung disorders.
- Mulberry—The bark was brewed into a tea to help remove worms from a person's body.
- Mullein—Used along with herbs like boneset or wild cherry for respiratory problems and colds.
- Sassafras—Brewed into a tea to help treat fevers and influenza. The twigs were chewed and used as toothbrushes, and also thought to ease toothaches.
- Spicebush—Made into treatments to sweat out fevers as well as washes to help with measles or chicken pox.
- Tobacco—Used widely for drawing out illnesses as a poultice (for animal bites or stings) and to bring boils to a head. Tobacco smoke was sometimes blown into the ear to cure earaches.
- Wild Cherry bark—Boiled to make a syrup to ease coughing and cold symptoms.
- Witch Hazel—Decocted into a liquid that treats skin ailments, burns, and blemishes.

Western Herbs

- Agave—Probably most famous as a tequila and mescal ingredient, agave also has laxative properties. It may be used to ease menstrual cramps as well.
- Cascara Sagrada—Used as a laxative and for digestive health.
- Cat's Claw—This is made into a strong brew that soothes coughs and can also be used to treat rashes.
- Chicory—A European import that grows throughout North America, the bitter root is roasted as a coffee substitute (famously blended with coffee in New Orleans), and used as a gastric stimulant.
- Licorice—Wild licorice is used to treat sore throats and to boost immune health.
- Mallow—The sticky mucus-like sap is used to treat skin irritations, bug bites, and even snake bites.
- Mormon Tea—A bitter herb used treat respiratory ailments and help with allergies, as well as to treat urinary tract infections.
- Poppy—The California Poppy is used as a lactation stimulant and sometimes to help with toothaches.
- Sweet Cicely/Sweetroot—The North American species has been used as a poultice for boils and wounds, as well as a tea to soothe upset stomachs.
- White Sage—Used for purification rituals and also to treat sinus infections. A tea can be made from it that is thought to purge fevers and colds.
- Yarrow—This widely-found plant is used to treat fevers, and has also been used to ease cramps and abdominal pain.
- Yucca—Used as a food source by some, yucca can also help with heartburn and is thought to relieve arthritis.

DIRT UNDER THE NAILS

Spring Tonic—Fire Cider

One popular spring tonic involves making a potent but-not-entirely-unpleasant concoction called "fire cider." I've used a version of this before (essentially a doctored Four Thieves Vinegar) and at the very least you *feel* a good bit more bulletproof after taking this every day. Again, this is NOT medical advice (but does make a tasty recipe that does no harm to most people, although you should consult with your doctor before doing any daily regimen of any kind).

Ingredients:

- Ginger root (wild if possible)
- Sassafras root
- Hot peppers (whatever you prefer, at least jalapeño levels of heat if possible)
- Cayenne pepper
- Spicebush bark or wood
- Ginseng root (if available, but do *not* pick endangered ginseng!)
- A lemon or other citrus fruit
- Organic apple cider vinegar
- Honey to taste (local is best)

Chop all ingredients (except honey and vinegar) and place in a mason jar. Cover with the vinegar and shake hard. Leave in a cool, dark place (like a pantry) for two weeks or up to a month, shaking daily. You can start this on a new moon and work until full if you want to give it an extra kick of energy. Strain the liquid, then warm gently and add the honey until you can handle the taste. Take one big spoonful every day as a tonic for good health, two if you're feeling a bit weak or like a cold might be coming on.

Digging a Little Deeper—Mental Health and Witchcraft

When we talk about folk healers and curers, we're often talking about the way they treat a particular ailment or offer long-term preventative tonics. One thing that I think we often miss, however, is that in some communities the local "witchy woman" with her bag of bones or tarot cards has another health function: listening. In a number of stories about witches, healers, and curers of various stripes, I see over and over again that while they do magical work, some of the most important work they do is simply sitting down with their client or patient and truly listening to them. In a way, a tarot reader or bone-thrower can act as a kind of therapist (although I will very concretely note that professional therapy is complex and crucial, and will address the mental health needs of most people far better than getting a card reading ever will). In communities where visiting a licensed therapist is not an option, either due to money or availability or even the stigma attached to mental health, magical workers might fill in that gap in ways that are accepted by local communities, or at least tolerated in some way.

Additionally, folk magicians often offer real, concrete steps that those who come to them can take to improve conditions. Lighting a candle or carrying a talisman may seem strange, but that can be a benefit since they shake up the normal flow of daily life a little in ways that take a person's problems seriously. If someone is a little less anxious carrying a mojo bag, or sleeps a little better after saying a small charm and making a few hand motions, that can be immensely beneficial. Similarly, if a person feels isolated or alone, feeling that spirits are there to help them, or that they have a guardian angel looking out for them, might offer comfort and reassurance in darker moments (although again, professional therapy is a wonderful thing and I highly recommend you consult with a pro rather than placing all your mental health eggs in one enchanted basket). Just the time a diviner spends listening to a client's problems, that simple act of unburdening and offering some sort of commentary and comfort, some hope for the future—that is powerful. It is also easy to abuse, and many people who need the mental health benefits that some get through magical workers have been taken in by scams that empty their pockets. Preying on the emotionally hurt and vulnerable is a disgusting abuse of "magic," and so I can only say that for anyone who has been a victim of such scams, my heart goes out to you. There are magical workers out there who are better than that.

Being seen and heard and feeling that spiritual forces are available to you—that is a kind of magic all its own. Witchcraft is a nuanced craft, and magical healing can go well beyond easing the symptoms of a cold or buying away a wart. It can reach into the very heart of us and work its transformations there as well.

THE WORK–Working with Plants

Magical work sometimes gets a bad reputation because of the way it oversimplifies very complex concepts, or because its results aren't laboratory-ready and reproducible (and I am not knocking good science here, as I am quite happy to have wonderful things like the computer upon which I am typing and the vaccines that keep my kids healthy!). Sometimes I see complaints that too many magic books are simply long lists of correspondences, saying "this stone is good for this" and "that herb is good for that."

What I think gets missed in that complaint is the amount of effort expended to develop those correspondences in the first place. If a person is solely going to depend upon a table listed in a book that says cinnamon is good for money magic and that sends them running to their spice cabinet, that might eventually be a problem. Why? Because the knowledge coming from the book lacks context. Each herb on someone's list of correspondences has a history, a reason it has been associated with a particular ability or quality. Much like saints and spirits, herbs have narratives and stories of their own, and knowing those stories makes the relationship with those herbs much deeper. Memorizing a list of correspondences (and yes, I certainly have made my own such list in this chapter, I know) is all well and good, but really getting to know a plant or two with some depth speaks to the kinds of folkways and magical knowledge that I think so many of us crave.

For me, rosemary was a revelation. My mother always grew it and it wound up in all sorts of food for us, and I have always had a positive association with it. Then I found it has connections in some Catholic lore to Mary (which makes sense, given its name). Once, at a craft fair, I was given just a few little cuttings of rosemary branches a couple of inches long when I purchased a small pot from a craftsperson. It was a tiny bonus gift, but I took it home and rooted it, and within a few years, those finger-length cuttings were a four-foot tall bush that guarded the front corner entrance of my home. Rosemary found its way into my herbal smoke preparations for rituals and magic. It was in my sauces for supper. I held it to remember my mother, and I still light a bit of it when I talk to her sometimes.

The depth of that relationship with rosemary was organic, but there's no reason you cannot set out to develop that kind of connection with a few plants as well. It takes time, energy, and patience, so my recommendation is to find a few plants—no more than two or three at a time—that will grow in your area (or which grow natively, even better!). Plant them. Take care of them. Look for local lore about them. Learn their stories. You may find you do not need the shelves full of exotic herbs we sometimes fetishize in our magical fantasies, but only a half dozen or so sister herbs that will work with you readily and happily because you have taken care of them so well. Make yourself part of their story, and see what magic they can help you with in your own lifelong tale.

Recommended Reading

A Midwife's Tale: The Life of Martha Ballard, Based on Her Diary, 1785–1812, by Laurel Thatcher Ulrich. This account of a late seventeenth-century midwife's daily routines is a splendid read. It offers numerous insights into the culture of the era, but also shows how integrated a healer was in everyday life. Mentions of herbs and treatments mingle with stories of families, weather, and religion in powerful ways.

Jude's Herbal Home Remedies: Natural Health, Beauty, & Home-Care Secrets, by Jude Todd (updated edition). When I started working with herbal and holistic remedies for my own use, this book was the cornerstone for me. The material here is usually not very magically-inclined, but more focused on learning how to brew tinctures and tisanes at home for therapeutic use. It covers everything from cold and fever remedies to beauty tips based on botanical ingredients.

Curandero: A Life in Mexican Folk Healing, by Eliseo "Cheo" Torres and Timothy L. Sawyer, Jr. This book provides a lot of insight into the branch of magical curing known as *curanderismo*. Torres' work documents not only the practices found among contemporary and historical Latinx healers, but also highlights some of the cultural heroes who were *curanderas/curanderos* as well.

Powwowing Among the Pennsylvania Dutch: A Traditional Medical Practice in a Modern World, by David W. Kriebel. Kreibel's work focuses on Pennsylvania Dutch healing practices as a medical alternative and cultural heritage. While he is not always sympathetic to his subjects, he does provide a lot of good information about both the cultural context and the practical everyday uses of *braucherei.*

Hoodoo Medicine: Gullah Herbal Remedies, by Faith Mitchell. Mitchell looks in detail at the magico-medical remedies of rootworkers in the Sea Islands of South Carolina. The perspectives are specific to the Gullah people of that region, but provide a wonderful snapshot of the mixture of practical herbal and esoteric methods used to deal with illness, misfortune, and community health.

CHAPTER SIX

Hair, Milk, and Blood—Cursing Magics

When we hear a fairy tale about a witch, we always seem to be waiting for the "wicked" thing to happen. The witch will poison fruit or a comb to kill a princess, or she might be fattening up children for a feast at which they will be—well, the feast. There are plenty of stories, of course, where the witch is a positive and helpful figure. Baba Yaga appears in a number of Slavic tales in which she aids the protagonist by providing a helpful hint or a magical tool such as a golden ball that shows them the way, for example.

Still, no matter how you slice the poisoned apple of folklore, the witch often has a fairly fearsome reputation for doing "bad things" to "good people." Witches steal and curse and kill, and North American folklore doesn't give them a pass on these tropes. At the same time, we should be at least a little suspicious of folktales about witches' hexes as purely malevolent for the sake of chaos and evil. There are certainly stories like that, but most accounts of hurtful magic by witches are more subtly woven, and the witch often has very good reasons to do what she does.

So just *why* do witches in stories do such heinous deeds? In North American witch stories, we see them doing everything from stealing a bit of milk and confounding her neighbors' butter churning process to the outright magical murder of children. In the Maryland folktale of Moll DeGrow a witch gets a wretched reputation among her neighbors for cursing them at any perceived slight. When one neighbor insults her, she turns their milk sour. People who go so far as to openly accuse her of witchcraft find their dogs turning against them. One family angers her so much with their gossip that she begins haunting them with spectral hellhounds and eventually causes the death of the family's infant daughter. When she is confronted, Moll laughs about her deeds. The townsfolk eventually gather a mob to come kill her, only to find she is already dead, her corpse grinning at them and mocking them, and her ghost lingering in the area to haunt them all.[69]

On the surface, DeGrow seems like a stereotypical wicked witch, sowing calamity and chaos for the sake of villainy. Historian Keith Thomas makes a strong case that in most accusations of witchcraft, the alleged witch almost always acted in a roundabout form of self-defense, taking justice into her own hands when necessary and using one of the few tools at her disposal—magic—to effect real change on her own behalf. "Contemporaries were horrified by the witch's activities," Thomas says, "but they seldom denied that she had genuine reason for wishing ill upon her victim."[70] Thomas then goes on to point out that in many cases, the "witch" in question was known to her accusers, and her persecutors frequently had turned away a request for aid in a time when the interdependence of a community was a nearly sacred bond. These calls for aid were not usually trivial, but instead associated with necessities like food or drink, and Thomas warns that this is not just "simple begging."[71] Instead, the informal agreement among local communities that mutual help and aid should be available to all for the greater good is shattered by the inhospitable attitudes of neighbors toward an alleged witch. Why would they treat her badly? Because, in most cases, she is part of a marginal world that the locals do not want to think about: an older widow with no one to help care for her, or a woman who has turned to sexual work or selling vices like alcohol to make ends meet. In the context provided by Thomas, a witch was a victim—even a begrudgingly acknowledged one—within the social rules of her community. With that in mind, let's look at the story of Moll DeGrow again.

69. Schlosser, *Spooky New Jersey*, 191–96; and Carey, *Maryland Folklore*, 50–52. DeGrow's name may also be a variation on the name "Moll Dyer," a well-known witch figure in the New Jersey/Maryland area.

70. Thomas, "The Relevance of Social Anthropology to the Historical Study of English Witchcraft," in Breslaw, *Witches of the Atlantic World*, 60–71.

71. Ibid., 66.

In the DeGrow tale, the witch may have taken delight in the misery of her neighbors, but every instance of her wreaking havoc follows upon some perceived injury—a slight which led to sour milk, an accusatory epithet which led to animal bewitchment. And her grudge against local families must have been severe if she unleashed death on their households. What exactly had they done to her? Of course, DeGrow may also be innocent of the last and most heinous of these acts, as she never admits guilt but merely "laughed and didn't deny it." Considering how often I've laughed in uncomfortable situations, I cannot help but wonder if maybe a little bit of shock and a lot of disbelief might not have been at play in that strange episode (that is, of course, all speculation on folklore, so please enjoy it with a hefty grain of salt). Whatever the case, we may believe that infanticide through magic is an overreaction, but it is a *reaction* nonetheless, and is rooted in a need for justice and communal responsibility.

With that point in mind, this chapter will be an overview of the types of folk magic commonly called "curses," "hexes," or "jinxes," although plenty of other folk names abound. There may be witches out there who find the idea of cursing distasteful, and plenty of non-witches who feel the same. That is, of course, okay. No one is ever obligated to perform curses, nor am I recommending them, as there are likely better ways of dealing with problems available to us now (but then, I write from a privileged place and not everyone has access to the same methods of problem-solving I do, so I also pass no judgement here). To pretend they don't exist, however—and to deny that there are powerful motivations behind them that may need to be addressed—ignores one of the central forms of magical practice found among New World Witches.

The Witch's Ire: The Wicked Deeds of Witches in North American Folklore

Tales of witches along the Eastern Seaboard generally present witches as somewhat sly and cunning, looking for opportunities to take advantage of any given situation. In some cases they sneak about at night wreaking havoc among the local townspeople in violent and forceful ways, and in other cases they operate more subtly, using magic to very slowly accomplish their purposes. Wherever the witch appears, however, she seems to be accused of casting curses. How does she do it? What is she trying to accomplish with her curse? I suggest that the witch targeted one of three areas when provoked into "hexation," so to speak.

Stolen Milk and Crooked Guns: Property Curses

A witch might focus her time and energy on a neighbor's property in some way. Often during pre-Industrial periods, the property was agricultural. A witch might put a curse on an enemy's livestock, causing it to waste away and die or to become useless, perhaps by failing to give milk. She might also curse the ground or a field, which would then no longer produce a harvest. In some cases the property she pursues is very specific: she might steal milk right from the cow using magic, or cause meat, eggs, or butter to go rotten, for example. Granny Lotz in Grayson County, Virginia, has a neighbor "get after" her about forgetting to close her gate, which allows his cattle to get loose. Because he ignores her age and persecutes her, she bewitches his cows to give bloody milk.[72] Tales of property damage often were the least severe and closely connected to the sense of injustice or need felt by the witches in question, at least in terms of long-term harm. While the loss of livestock or farm goods could certainly be devastating, in most cases the loss could be limited to a single event or an occasional inconvenience. A pair of stories from mountainous West Virginia entitled "How Witches Got Milk and Butter" and "The Milk Witch of Wood County" tell of witches who are portrayed as poor members of the community who keep their families fed and healthy by magically stealing milk from neighbors. In neither case do neighbors take any retaliatory action, however, recognizing that the theft is occasional and non-debilitating, and that the witches seem to need it more than the dairymen do.[73]

A person's money or home might also be cursed, although in both of those cases the hex is more abstract, manifesting in hauntings or general destitution. The witch could also curse a specific object, such as a wagon or a gun, preventing it from functioning properly. One tale tells of a rifle that gets bewitched by a "Yankee prisoner" during the Civil War so that it will no longer shoot straight for anyone who uses it.[74] In a few cases, the curse might be placed upon a specific object and carried for-

72. Davis, *Silver Bullet*, 35–36.

73. Gainer, *Witches, Ghosts, & Signs*, 167–68.

74. Davis, *Silver Bullet*, 49–50.

ward for many years, as happens with things like "witched guns," but most of the time a witch's curse on a neighbor's belongings would end with the destruction of the cursed item or creature. Unless, of course, she chose to escalate her vengeance, in which case the hex might become a more fate-oriented or bodily-oriented one.

Bad Catches and Forgotten Tubs: Curses Against Fate or Luck

Abstract curse targets include a person's "luck," generally leading to a bad run of it somehow. They might suddenly feel as though nothing is going right for them, or begin losing money hand over fist. Sometimes this could be tied to property loss or damage, as noted above, but it could also manifest in bad luck in gambling, love, marriage, or legal troubles. Spiritual curses put a sort of storm cloud over the victim, leaving them unable to shake off their woes until they meet some condition of the witch's making: leaving town, offering her something she wants, or even dying.

On the side of bad luck, a person who winds up the target of a witch's spell could be the victim of general misfortune or specific calamity. Ill magic might go after a person's livelihood, cause them confusion, or even be laid over an entire place or town in retaliation for poor treatment. We see this in the story of Moll DeGrow (or Dyer), who is eventually forced from her home by angry locals and left to die in the woods, but not before she leaves her handprints gouged into a rock and lays a curse upon the land around her house that it never be inhabited or farmable again (which, according to some accounts, is exactly what came to pass).[75] Some other examples of general "bad luck" witchery:

- A Maine witch named Emma Alley once went around asking for some contributions to help out an injured neighbor as he recovered, only to be rebuffed and insulted by a local fisherman named Charlie Mansfield. Charlie bragged about his prosperity in front of Emma, then denied her any help, and for that Emma cursed him not to get any more fish that year, which is just what happened.[76]
- In Maryland, a witch named Skidmore cursed a pair of watermen who mocked his "tub" (a type of simple cargo boat). His curse was fairly ingenious, as the men were forced to constantly remember the boat and want to share the joke

75. Carey, *Maryland Folklore*, 50–51.

76. Dorson, *Buying the Wind*, 60–61.

about it, but always forget it by the time they found someone to tell it to, thus making them look confused and foolish.[77]

- The Witch of Truro from Cape Cod Bay is reported to have cursed a ship's captain who purchased milk from her, causing storms to rise around his boat and making him act befuddled and confused while he tried to steer the ship toward shore. In this case the offense against the witch isn't recorded, although the story makes special note of the color of her shoes—red—and may be insinuating that she was a prostitute as well, which might have implications for her treatment at the hands of the captain (although that is obviously speculation).[78]
- In New Hampshire, one tale tells of a French Canadian witch who did not want to pay the price for room and board his landlady and her husband charged him, and so used a Pied Piper-like power to cause rats to come and infest the area. Only after acquiring a (slightly magical) cat who killed fifteen rats a day were they able to rid themselves of the curse.[79]

Spells targeting a person's general luck often reflect cultural standards against pridefulness or haughtiness. This can be seen in the way some of the spells deployed against individual fortunes are not simply pulled out of a momentary muttering of anger, but based on passages of biblical scripture! For example, one curse designed to "bring down one of high station" (e.g. a person who is acting haughty) involves carving a person's name into a piece of fruit out-of-doors (the spell is very specific about this), then reciting the passage Obadiah 1:3-4:

"The pride of thine heart hath deceived thee, thou that dwellest in the clefts of the rock, whose habitation is high; that saith in his heart, 'Who shall bring me down to the ground? Though thou exalt thyself as the eagle, and though thou set thy nest among the stars, thence I will bring thee down, saith the Lord."[80]

Of course, as the saying goes, pride goes before a fall, and a curse against a person's livelihood could very quickly turn into a curse against their life.

77. Carey, *Maryland Folklore*, 46.

78. Davis, *The Silver Bullet*, 46–47.

79. Botkin, *New England Folklore*, 230–31.

80. Mickaharic, *Magic Spells of the Minor Prophets*, 36.

FIG 6-1: A souring jar.

DIRT UNDER THE NAILS
A Souring Jar

While I do not advocate for cursing in this chapter, it can be incredibly useful to understand the mechanics of a curse, and perhaps one of the simplest and least lethal forms of cursing is the "souring jar" or vinegar jar found in several folk magical traditions. At one time, this may have involved using urine in place of the vinegar, as well, but most contemporary practitioners find the vinegar method effective. The spell requires:

- An image or token of the target (such as a photograph, a bit of their clothing or handwriting, or some of their hair)
- A jar full of vinegar (this can be the Four Thieves Vinegar found in chapter eleven, a simple white or cider vinegar, or even a jar full of left-over pickle juice—please note the person casting the spell won't be eating this after, however!)
- Any additional "hexing" herbs they might want to use: mustard seeds for simple hexing, red pepper to "heat up" a person's life, galangal root ("chewing John") for legal issues, or poppy seeds to cause confusion.

They can also just use the jar of liquid without any herbs if they so choose.

The witch will take the token of the target and mark it in some way to indicate her anger (crossing out the eyes to keep them from seeing things clearly, or the mouth to stop gossip spreading, for example). She will mutter words like "So long as you continue doing ______ (whatever it is the target is doing wrong), you will have no peace and your life shall worsen and sour like a pickle in a jar!" She then adds the image or item to the jar, along with the appropriate ingredients. She seals the jar, shakes it violently, and leaves it in a sunny windowsill to warm. Each day for nine days, the witch shakes the jar violently, then puts it back. If the target stops their bad behavior, the witch removes the image and disposes the ingredients appropriately, restoring the person's life and well-being. If they don't, the witch hides the jar in a dark place until the next month, then begins again (some might say this should be done during a waning moon, ending on the last night before the new moon—see more on magical timing in chapter eighteen). The curse goes on until the victim changes their behavior or the witch tires of the curse.

To that last point, I should note that I have used this method myself as a way of creating a mild inconvenience for someone who was causing me serious problems, but with whom I had no legal way of resolving my differences effectively. However, my heart was not in doing the hex, and so I failed to follow through on it for the allotted time, and nothing came to pass. Spell failures teach us as much as spell successes, though, and I learned there were better magical methods of coping with my situation (eventually turning to a spell that addressed a more specific part of the problem rather than the person themselves).

Live Things in You and a Hag-Riding: Bodily Curses

If a witch became very serious about her curse, she would enact a vengeance that specifically targeted a person's physical well-being (or the physical well-being of their family). They might experience sleep disturbances, illness and wasting away, violent injuries, or death at the hands of a properly pissed-off witch. These spells are often very much about revenge over a perceived wrong, something that put the witch in question in the path of potential harm herself, such as denying her food or slandering her name in public (which could lead to legal repercussions for her). In a few cases, the physical harm she did through cursing was part of a "price" she paid for her power, often to a devil or similar figure, but most tales seem to connect bodily curses to direct insult or injury.

When it comes to bodily curses, witches seldom play around. Frequently, the goal of a bodily curse is the slow, wasting death of the person targeted, although in some cases the witch may curb their attack if conditions are met before their victim passes. One witch named Old Deb from Rochester, Massachusetts, cursed the fourteen-year-old daughter of a man named Thankful Haskell during the late Colonial period. The girl insulted her by sweeping under Old Deb's feet (which may not seem like much, but could be a magical attempt to prevent Deb from marrying or a rude gesture to make the witch leave the house). Soon after, the girl began wasting away and getting sick, and only the intervention of a doctor and her father saved her.[81] In some cases, the witch may also be defeated doing a spell like this if a knowledgeable worker of countermagic is able to detect and reverse the curse in time (see chapter fifteen for more on this).

Happy endings are not the norm, however. There is also the tale of poor Mary Fisher of West Virginia, a seventeen-year-old girl who refused to let a local witch borrow anything from her house (which was a typical taboo about witches). The witch managed to snitch a bit of lettuce from the garden and curse the girl, who eventually died from the curse, according to the story.[82]

There are some bodily curses that do not lead to the eventual death of the victim, but merely cause them great physical suffering. One of the more vicious forms of bodily curses is the famed "live things in you" spell found in Hoodoo and some forms of Southern Conjure. In that spell, powdered materials from animals, such as snakes or spiders, are added to a person's food, which then become a horrible "crawling" sensation beneath the victim's skin, slowly driving them mad and making them sicker and sicker.

Even the Bible has its cursing applications. For example, one curse based in biblical lore involves reciting a variation of Psalm 137, saying "May your right arm wither and your tongue cleave to the roof of your mouth!" as a way of stopping slander or gossip

81. Botkin, *New England Folklore*, 229.

82. Gainer, *Witches, Ghosts, & Signs*, 151–52.

from an enemy. A spell based on Obadiah 1:9 uses a bowl of river water and an image of a person to weaken them as a way to cheat in athletic competitions (an idea that links back to Roman-era lead curse tablets often found near chariot racing tracks).[83]

One of the most delightful forms of bodily cursing involved "hag-riding" (although I'm sure it was not delightful for the victim). While this is discussed in much more depth in the chapter on witch flight (chapter nine), the basic practice involved a witch visiting a target in the night and "riding" him like a horse using an enchanted tool called a witch's bridle. The victim would awaken the next day bruised and sore, covered in grime or sweat, and only by making things right with the witch in question could he avoid repeated night rides.

Each of these three forms overlap, of course. The famed case of the Bell Witch haunting of Tennessee, while riddled with all sorts of variations and inaccuracies handed down through the years, generally revolves around a curse brought on by a potential land dispute (property-based) which led to extensive hauntings and bad luck in bringing marriage suitors around (the "spirit" or "luck" side of things), and also involved physical assaults by a poltergeist and the eventual death of John Bell (a bodily attack).[84]

FIG 6-2: Granny Tucker is often seen as a skilled but dangerous character.

83. Mickaharic, *Magic Spells of the Minor Prophets*, 38.; and Davies, *The Oxford Illustrated History*, 1–28.

84. Davis, *The Silver Bullet*, 92–96. See also Bell and Miller, *The Bell Witch of Tennessee*.

SINGING BONES
Granny Tucker

Granny Tucker is a folk character featured in a number of Southern stories along the Gulf of Mexico. She is usually characterized as a wicked witch or even a monster who lures children to her home and then devours them. When one young woman wanders into Granny's swamp home, she meets both the witch and her daughter, and lulls them to sleep with a fiddle tune. She swaps bedclothes with the daughter and sneaks out, and when Granny awakes she mistakenly murders her own daughter and then sets off after the girl in a fit of rage. When the girl is caught in a tree with Granny chopping away, she whistles for her dogs who arrive almost supernaturally fast and kill the witch. While this is the best-known version of the story, there are other Granny Tucker tales in which she offers magical assistance such as fertility remedies. She still has an edge to her, however, as one woman discovers after failing to pay the witch and having her child cursed to die by a horse's hoof (after a lifetime studiously avoiding horses, the child perishes by tripping in a hoofprint on a road and hitting her head on a rock). In many ways, Granny Tucker acts as a sort of Gulf Coastal counterpart to the Slavic witch Baba Yaga, neither good nor bad, but powerful, skilled, and sometimes very, very dangerous.[85]

Delivering the Curse: Methods of Hexing

Getting cursed by a witch may be a matter of balancing the scales of justice for some, but if you were the target of a curse wouldn't you want to know it? The tricky thing about curses, however, is that the way a witch might deliver such a spell varied widely. In some cases, she might be extremely open about her magic and leave no doubt that a particular person was the specific target of a curse. In other cases, the spell might be worked in secret and only after consulting a professional "witch doctor" or "power doctor" would the nature and origin of the spell be revealed.

While every curse seems to be unique in particulars, there are a few well-known methods for placing a curse upon an intended target in North American witch lore:

85. Hutcheson, "Old Granny Tucker," 735–36. See also Ancelet, *Cajun and Creole Folktales: The French Oral Tradition of South Louisiana*; Hurston, *Every Tongue Got to Confess*; and Schlosser, *Spooky Southwest.*

- **Witch balls**—These are little balls of wax and hair that are created by the witch for use in cursing. In some stories, she was given a specific number of witch balls by the Devil upon initiation and losing them meant undergoing some sort of punishment, so she had to choose her targets carefully and try to recover the balls if she could. The balls would be "shot" at the victim, either by throwing them, spitting them, or dropping them onto an intended target. They supposedly left a small bruise wherever they touched, and were frequently used for bodily curses involving illness.[86]

FIG 6-3: Dolls and poppets.

- **Poppets and dolls**—Crafting a poppet or a doll out of mud, clay, cloth, or other materials meant that a witch could easily work her curse from a distance (see figure 6-3). In a few cases, the cursed doll would also be delivered to the household of the target and left in a hidden spot, such as under the bed, to amplify the hex's effect. These are frequently used for bodily curses.
- **Speaking the curse**—Plenty of tales tell of a witch openly describing the curse or its outcome to the person or people involved. Tales of witches' curses on family lines or regional areas often involve the curse being spoken aloud. These

86. Davis, *The Silver Bullet,* 31–34; and Oberon, *Southern Cunning,* chapter five.

curses are fateful or property-oriented most of the time, although they can also be directed at a person's health as a bodily curse.

- **Spectral visits**—Much like the Bell Witch, some witches lodged their curses by visiting the victim in spectral or night-riding forms. This became a central point of contention in the New England witch trials, particularly the ones associated with Salem, where the idea of a spectral or astral tormentor was taken very seriously, much to the detriment of the law and justice.[87]
- **Foot paths**—Putting a curse into someone's path so that they must step on it appears in a number of African American magical systems. These can range from "dusting" someone's tracks so that they pick up a particular "poison" as they cross it to smashing a bottle of "war water" (a type of fetid, stagnant water full of unsavory items) on someone's porch so they have to cross over it. These would frequently be used to curse a person's body or fate.
- **Stolen or borrowed items**—A bit of hair or a feather taken from an animal is often enough for a witch to cast a powerful curse in a story, sometimes over all the livestock on a farm. Hair stolen from a person was similarly powerful. In a number of stories, a witch will also try to borrow something from a household, especially if she thinks they are working countermagic against her, because taking something from the target reaffirms her power over them.
- **Food and poison**—Curses could be delivered via food as well, as happens with the "live things in you" curse. Other hexes could be given in a similar manner, although the line between a "hex" and something more like outright poisoning is not a clearly defined one in some stories. There are also tales of slaves in the South who would grind up glass and include it in their masters' food, which was less of a hex and more of a plot on their lives (in many cases a justifiable one, given the horrors of slavery). As you can probably guess, most of these curses were bodily in nature.

87. While I do not cover a great deal of Salem history here, I do highly recommend the books *Salem Possessed: The Social Origins of Witchcraft*, by Paul Boyer and Stephen Nissenbaum, *The Devil in the Shape of a Woman* by Carol F. Karlsen, and *In the Devil's Snare* by Mary Beth Norton. These books provide a lot of careful, close examination of the Salem trials and their causes, proceedings, and outcomes. They also get heavily into the issues of spectral evidence (and the court of Oyer and Terminer established to try spectral witchcraft).

- **Bodily fluids**—Spit, urine, and phlegm all worked powerfully well to deliver a curse. Blood could also be deployed to leave a curse upon a place, as the blood would frequently become wet and fresh on the anniversary of the day it was spilled, creating a sort of fateful curse on a place. One type of bodily fluid curse involved taking a cheating man's semen and smearing it on a red cord, then knotting it to make it impossible for him to be sexually active with anyone but the person who cast the spell ever again, which made for a kind of bodily-fateful curse overlap.
- **Diabolical spirits**—In some stories, a witch's curse will be delivered by her fetch (a sort of shadow-self, so similar to spectral visitation) or by a familiar spirit of some kind. An imp or a bewitched animal might linger around a home, causing it to fall into disrepair (property-based cursing) or making the inhabitants grow sicker and sicker (bodily cursing).

These are hardly the only cursing methods found in all of North American folklore, of course. They do represent a wide swath of hexing techniques we see repeated in the stories of a number of folk groups, though.

Curses in stories are often undone by an experienced "witch master" or similar witch-fighting magical worker, so we only occasionally get to see tales featuring a witch successfully fulfilling whatever curse she's cast. Mostly, these narratives focus on the "justice" done in retaliation against the witches, although, as we've seen, plenty of the witches are seeking justice of their own. And in some cases, the curses they cast are not their fault at all.

Casting Curses by Accident: The Evil Eye

One final point I must address before we can close the chapter on curses is the infamous "evil eye." If you've ever been someplace and seen blue beads hanging all over, or seen a blue-and-white bead hanging from a person's neck, that may be an indication of evil eye deflection magic being used. The evil eye is essentially a curse cast by people with an innate power when they look at a particular victim. The eye is feared in numerous places, including Mexico, the American Southwest, Italian and Italian American neighborhoods, Turkish cultural zones, Greek areas, and dozens of other such spaces.

Importantly, many of the people who are believed to cast the evil eye are thought to do so without trying. They cannot help themselves, and they are even pitied for their condition of perpetual cursing of others. In some cases, they are located and treated with magical remedies for their evil eye, or taught methods to avoid casting it, such as trying to focus on the tip of their own nose. Usually, the evil eye comes out most strongly against people who might be the subject of envy by others: people with natural beauty or young children, for example. Parents in places where the evil eye is strong often dress beautiful children in ugly clothes to avoid the eye, and seldom will they speak of a child's beauty or talents to someone they do not know well. Any person with envy in their hearts might potentially cast the evil eye, so guarding against jealousy is thought to be one of the most important tools to prevent it.

What happens if you or someone you love is hit with the evil eye? Most often, a bodily curse takes form, with the target wasting away or becoming weaker over time. In some cases, the eye also stimulates a string of bad luck, creating a fateful sort of curse. The eye seldom extends to property curses (except in cases where property breaks as an extension of the fateful sort of curse).

The evil eye has been the subject of intense scholarly and non-scholarly research, and what I write here is the barest surface of the material available. For a scholarly take on the topic, I'd recommend picking up Alan Dundes' *The Evil Eye: A Casebook*, while a more accessible look at the phenomenon comes in Frederick T. Elworthy's *The Evil Eye: The Classic Account of an Ancient Superstition*.

The curses outlined here have not been provided as go-to examples with detailed "how-to" instructions, because cursing is a difficult subject. When used blindly or for revenge, curses often backfire or misfire in some way, and even when they are effectively deployed there's always the possibility of countermagic turning them back on the user. Still, understanding curse mechanics and how they get delivered to a victim can make them easier to detect, deflect, and destroy, so my hope is that if you gain nothing else in this chapter, you can recognize a curse a little better at the end of it.

THE WORK—Curses and Limits

I have often heard it said in Traditional Witchcraft circles that a witch must know how to curse in order to know how to cure. Another common saying is that "blessing and bane can grow on the same stalk," meaning that a poison and its cure are often part of the same plant. The metaphorical meaning, of course, is that we have to know how to apply our knowledge properly to get the right results—a poisonous plant like foxglove can work wonders for someone with heart disease, but a bit too much and that heart stops working.

The same is true for curses that don't rely on poison (and please do not poison anyone after reading this book, as the publishers get a bit tetchy about that). We have to know how we apply our knowledge, and just where the limits of our actions are. I highly recommend taking the time to think about what curses you would be willing to cast, and which ones you never would. Go back through this chapter and note down curses you think you could do, and ones you think you'd never be able to even try, marking them all "yes," "no," or "maybe." Then look at the ones you said "yes" or "maybe" to, and jot down the conditions under which you think you might do those particular curses. How far would someone have to push you? Would you need to take other actions first? Would you work them on behalf of someone else, someone who is in need of justice that they aren't likely to get otherwise? Would you work other spells that don't quite fit the "curse" mold and tackle the problem a different way?

Knowing just what your limits are, and the steps on the ladder required to reach your "curse level" of comfort, will help you define yourself and help you to understand just what the mindset behind cursing can be. Take the time to write those limits down for yourself and understand why you have them.

Recommended Reading

The Evil Eye: A Casebook, by Alan Dundes. The scholarship here on the evil eye (and to some extent other cursing traditions) follows the trajectory of this form of ill-wishing from ancient roots to contemporary sports like baseball. Dundes was a well-known folklore scholar and his casebook on the evil eye is a standout text on magical belief and its many forms, particularly focused on a widespread form of cursing.

Have You Been Hexed? Recognizing and Breaking Curses, by Alexandra Chauran. This book more properly belongs in the chapter on magical self-defense, but I place it here because it also has some excellent segments on *recognizing* a curse, which is very much in line with the goals of this chapter. Understanding what a curse looks like can be tricky, but Chauran examines both the curses and the casters in her book, offering some useful ways to spot curses in the "wild" of the reader's own life.

Southern Cunning: Folkloric Witchcraft in the American South, by Aaron Oberon. While I largely focused on the New England and Mid-Atlantic regions in this chapter, Oberon's book revisits some of the Virginia lore I discuss here from a Southern Conjure magical perspective. He is not afraid to bring up curses, and repeatedly points out that cursing is a way of dealing with problems that specifically belong to witches in these folktales.

FOURTH RITE: SECOND SIGHT

Or, Divination and the Discovery of the Unseen in Folk Witchcraft

"Old Veronica was old. No more joys came to her. By day she sat behind the closed shutters of her house and peeped out into the street, watching, watching eternally to see that none of her enemies 'dusted' her steps. As soon as night fell she would lift her gross body in bed and call to her nephew: 'Come, Pierre, give me my eyes.' Her 'eyes' were a deck of cards. She'd shuffle eagerly—riss, riss, riss! and cut them and spread them. 'See!' she'd cry. 'See that bitch! See 'em! Look at all my enemies working and plotting against me!' She'd keep this up till the early hours of the morning. (New Orleans, La.)"*

* Hurston, "Hoodoo in America," 406.

CHAPTER SEVEN

Wonders, Signs, and Tokens— Divination and Fortune-Telling

Fortune-telling in the New World does not begin with the Colonial era, but in that era we can see some of the best examples of the ambivalence and inner conflict that it raised. Increase Mather, a Puritan minister and writer, spoke against fortune-telling as a form of diabolical superstition in his work on "providences," many of which were essentially prophetic in nature. Mather's ire at fortune-telling was its lack of dependence upon God's revelation and the way it centered the power to know more about the created world than the supposed Creator of that world would naturally allow.[88]

That view of a world that remained solely understood by a distant God hardly comforted or guided people struggling to survive, often in new lands (or in the case of Native Americans, in new social relationships on old lands as Europeans invaded and settled near them). If you ask most people today just how much of a role they think things like fortune-telling and prophecy played in the development of North America, they are likely to say very little. What they may be missing, however, is just how central to so many pieces of American history and culture divination has been.

This chapter will explore the wonderfully diverse, often unique, and sometimes incredibly strange paths of divination, fortune-telling, and other forms of occult knowledge that have shaped us. I begin by looking at a handful of historical examples

88. See Mather, *An Essay for the Recording of Illustrious Providences*. See also Breslaw, *Witches of the Atlantic World*; and Hall, *Worlds of Wonder, Days of Judgment.*

to show the impact of a number of divination systems, key prophetic or divinatory figures, and movements built on divination. Then I spend some time looking at a few of the systems that have found a home here, or even been invented or expanded on North American soil.

My hope, of course, is the same as any diviner's—to see just what is hidden under the surface of the world we think we know. Let's see what the cards reveal.

A (Very Brief) History of Divination in the United States

Puritan pearl-clutching notwithstanding, fortune-telling has been a part of New World magical practices for centuries. Native groups, such as the Huron of the Great Lakes or the Quiyoughcohannock of the Algonquin Nation along the Mid-Atlantic coast, had very detailed and precise rituals for predicting and controlling natural phenomena such as weather. At times, invading Colonials joined with the Native groups, as happened with the indigenous Casqui people and Spanish conquistadores in 1541 when both worked together to perform rain divination and invitation rituals.[89] Far more often, however, Europeans in high-ranking positions of governance or church authority were incredibly suspicious of the divination practices of Native Americans and treated them as diabolical in nature, aligning their moral worldview more with Mather's.[90] That did not stop everyday European Colonists from engaging in fortune-telling and divination frequently. A "Mr. Lilley" of Connecticut possessed books of astrology and divination in the 1640s, a point discovered when another woman, Katherine Harrison, was accused of witchcraft and confessed that she told fortunes just as Mr. Lilley did. Accused Salem witch Dorcas Hoar owned fortune-telling books and read palms in the decade before the trials, and Rebecca Johnson told the Salem judges in 1692 that she asked her daughter to perform a divination rite with a sieve to determine if her son was dead or alive—hardly a diabolical question for a grieving mother.[91] Accounts of the Salem trials also note the use of a "Venus glass" by some of the young girls first afflicted, which may have been exactly

89. See White, "Shewing the Difference between Their Conjuration, and Our Invocation on the Name of God for Rayne."

90. See Breslaw, *Tituba, Reluctant Witch of Salem: Devilish Indians and Puritan Fantasies.*

91. Hall, *Worlds of Wonder,* 98–101.

the sort of device that Increase Mather referred to when he mentions putting an egg white into a water glass to determine a future husband's profession.

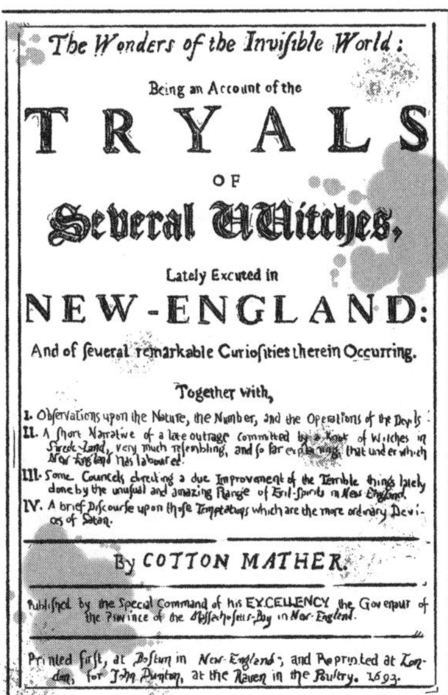

The Wonders of the Invifible World:

Being an Account of the

TRYALS

OF

Several Witches,

Lately Excuted in

NEW-ENGLAND:

And of feueral remarkable Curiofities therein Occurring.

Together with,

I. Obfervations upon the Nature, the Number, and the Operations of the Devils.

II. A fhort Narrative of a late outrage Committed by a Knot of Witches in Swede-Land, very much refembling, and fo far explaining, that under which New-England has laboured.

III. Some Councels directing a due Improvement of the Terrible things lately done by the unufual and amazing Range of Evil-Spirits in New-England.

IV. A brief Difcourfe upon thofe Temptations which are the more ordinary Devices of Satan.

By COTTON MATHER.

Publifhed by the Special Command of his EXCELLENCY the Governour of the Province of the Maffachufets-Bay in New-England.

Printed firft, at Bofton in New-England; and Reprinted at London, for John Dunton, at the Raven in the Poultry. 1693.

FIG 7-1: Cotton Mather's *The Wonders of the Invisible World,* a book about the Salem Witch Trials at which Dorcas Hoar was accused and convicted but escaped execution, became a primary source for understanding the role of spectral evidence and mass persecution in those trials.

SINGING BONES
Dorcas Hoar

Very little is really known about Dorcas Hoar, one of the women accused and convicted during the Salem Witch Trials. What we do know is that the witchcraft accusations of 1692 were not her first appearance in court, nor her first accusation of occult involvement. Court records from the decade or so leading up to the trial see her brought in on charges of theft, during which she was also noted to have books related to fortune-telling. These books—and her apparent reputation as a diviner—were enough to rouse frequent suspicions about her and earn her an accusation of witchery in 1692. She had just lost her husband the year before, a tragedy that saw her investigated for his murder (a point that infuriated Hoar to the point of stamping her feet and wringing her hands in court, demonstrating what court records called "a very greate pashtion" and calling her accusers "wi[c]ked wretches"). Now, brought up on witchcraft charges, Hoar's rage

> condemned her, as it was seen as evidence of a witch's temperament. In the end, she was tried and convicted, then sentenced to execution. Thankfully, she escaped the noose, as her sentence was not carried out before the trials were called into question by Massachusetts authorities. We know little about her life after Salem, but based upon probate records, she lived nearly two more decades before finally passing away.[92]

Over the centuries, divinatory techniques have waxed and waned like the moon or the seasons passing. As mentioned earlier, Native nations deployed a wide variety of techniques to gauge weather, hunting conditions, the outcome of wars, and migrations. These methods did not fade with the arrival of Europeans—plenty of Indigenous leaders sought answers regarding the relations between themselves and the white colonists from their diviners. Over time, Native groups would incorporate European models of divination into their own practices from time to time. In the twentieth and twenty-first century a significant number of non-Native people have turned to Indigenous methods of finding answers, even appropriating them outright at times in dangerous ways, as happened with in Arizona in 2009 when a New Age "leader" held a sweat lodge for high-paying clients, only to have several of them die, resulting in a conviction for negligent homicide for the leader. The sweat lodge was purported to be "Native American" in its nature, but the New Age version was a badly bastardized form of the more traditional—and much misunderstood—practices of groups like the Lakota or the Chumash.[93] Similar problems arise when non-Native practitioners pursue Native divination or ritual practices, such as the use of peyote or ayahuasca. Because the use of Native divinatory techniques is incredibly context-heavy and requires deep cultural understanding, getting those methods right remains very much a long-term and relationship-oriented process requiring years of community connection and participation.

The power of divinatory revelation may have made the early Puritan Separatists nervous, but over time spiritual forces erupted to reshape the North American landscape and divination found several gaps to fill. During the First Great Awakening—a period of Christian revivalism in the pre-Revolutionary period of North America—spiritual leaders sometimes began to take on the properties of prophets. One,

92. Karlsen, *The Devil in the Shape of a Woman*, 126–29; Hall, *Worlds of Wonder*, 99.

93. See Looking Horse, "Concerning the Deaths in Sedona"; Taliman, Valerie, "Selling the Sacred"; and "Native History: A Non-Traditional Sweat Leads to Three Deaths."

Jemima Wilkinson, underwent a near-death experience and one day awoke claiming she was a divine messenger, henceforth to be known as the Publick Universal Friend (PUF). The PUF—it's just too much fun not to use that term—was able to cross military camp lines between British and Rebel Colonial forces to deliver her prophecies and sermons, showing how wide her appeal was.[94] After the Revolution, a Second Great Awakening swept through the United States, ushering in a slew of prophets and seers including Joseph Smith, founder of the Church of Jesus Christ of Latter Day Saints. Smith believed that Jesus had come to North America and preached to the "lost tribes" of Israel, the Native Americans, after experiencing a powerful vision of Jesus and God—two separate beings in Mormon theology—and receiving golden plates that he translated using a special seer stone (or "peep stone" as it was sometimes called). Smith had experience as a diviner, and he and his father both engaged in magical treasure-hunting before Smith's revelation (see chapter eight for more on Smith's magical treasure-seeking activities). Other prophets, like William Miller, whose Millerite movement depended upon his prophecies of the world ending on various dates that always inevitably came to pass with little fanfare, were less successful than Smith.[95]

The big tent prophets, however, had nothing on the everyday, everyman access—and crucially every*woman* access—that came in the second half of the nineteenth century. In the late 1840s, sisters Margaret and Kate Fox of upstate New York began reporting mysterious spirit tapping in their home, drawing widespread attention. The Fox sisters were particularly important because they discovered they could *communicate* with the spirits around them by asking for knocks to indicate a "yes" or "no" answer based on the number of taps they heard. Eventually one of the sisters—on her deathbed, essentially—claimed that the whole thing had been an elaborate hoax perpetrated by popping toe joints under a table, but by that point the genie was out of the bottle and Spiritualism had taken off. Spiritualism's main draw was that any gifted medium could communicate with departed souls. In a post-Civil War era where many men had died—and in many cases, had left to join the war and never

94. Horowitz, *Occult America*, 17–22. Wilkinson is a fascinating figure, who also eschewed the use of gendered language after becoming the PUF, possibly making her a powerful, early nonbinary spiritual leader in some ways. She also preached against slavery and claimed that free will was a gift from God.

95. Albanese, *A Republic of Mind and Spirit*, 265–69; Horowitz, *Occult America*, 15–17.

been heard from again, leaving a number of unanswered questions behind them—women often became the lead figures in Spiritualist churches and séances.[96]

The power to retrieve answers from the dead was seen in a very positive light by many who believed it confirmed an afterlife and often let them feel their departed loved ones were at peace. Spiritualism made use of methods like tapping, automatic writing, mediumship, and even "talking boards" (more on those later) to communicate with the dead, and the sheer accessibility of the tools and methods for such communication made the movement incredibly popular. There are even newspaper accounts of séances in the White House during Lincoln's tenure, when Mary Todd Lincoln tried to communicate with her beloved dead son, Willie.[97]

Leading thinkers of the time were divided on Spiritualism's effectiveness. Some, like Transcendentalist Ralph Waldo Emerson, believed it all to be fraud, calling it "rat-revelation" based on scratches in the wall and "thumps in the table drawer."[98] Others, like the Shaker religious communities, embraced their own form of Spiritualism, believing themselves to be led by "Indian" spirit guides at times. One of the best-known Spiritualists was Andrew Jackson Davis, the "Poughkeepsie Seer" who became convinced by the Fox sisters of Spiritualism's power and developed his own seership abilities. Davis saw Spiritualism as something almost scientific, and believed that much of what happened was the result of a "magnetic" power between the spiritual and mundane worlds, something he built on the concepts of Franz Anton Mesmer (famous for "Mesmerism," which has some similarities to modern hypnotherapy). The "scientific" approach to divination and spiritual contact yielded other results, too. For example, in the mid-1800s a pair of German physicians—Franz Joseph Gall and Johann Spurzheim—began publishing about a concept that would mix science and divination in some radical ways: phrenology. Studying the shape of the head and its features, they believed, could tell us a great deal about a person's personality, even predicting their behavior. Phrenology, in turn, influenced other physio-psychological movements, including—nearly a century later—the rather

96. Albanese, *A Republic of Mind and Spirit*, 333–38.

97. Horowitz, *Occult America*, 57–62.

98. Albanese, *A Republic of Mind and Spirit*, 179.

horrifying eugenics movement (the one that gave rise to Hitler's "Aryan" supremacy idea).[99]

While the efforts to formalize and imbue authority into movements like Mormonism and phrenology gained ground, in truth the most widespread forms of divination were the ones people had been using all along, or the ones that anyone had access to. In places like Appalachia, the practice of dowsing for water or minerals—often called "water witching"—remained popular well into the twentieth century (and still retains adherents today). Similarly, astrological information regarding the movement of planets and stars through the different signs of the zodiac informed most of the early almanacs printed in the New World, and still remain a central part of rural farm almanacs. Predicting weather meant predicting crop growth, and in an agricultural society that sort of foreknowledge is incredibly valuable. Spiritualist churches emphasize informal structures, although some have attempted to become somewhat more organized, as has happened in Puerto Rican Espiritismo at various points.[100] Popular prophets from Christian churches like the Pentecostal and "Holy Roller" churches will frequently break into prophetic "tongues" during ecstatic worship, and found a wider audience during the early era of radio. Popular astrology ideas—mostly focused on the broadest interpretations of sun signs—became a staple of twentieth and twenty-first century newspapers. Divination has never really had to hide in North America, even as it has taken on different shapes and structures over the years. It has always had adherents and people interested in taking it to new places, discovering new methods of seeing the future or understanding the people around them.[101]

What we see over and over again in New World divination practices is a mixture of inherited traditions merged with improvisational methods and materials pulled from the immediate environment. Over time, the practice of divination became merged with both religious sensibilities and early forms of psychology, where divination became less about direct prophecy or prediction and far more about the

99. Albanese, *A Republic of Mind and* Spirit, 195–203; Davies, *America Bewitched*, 160.

100. Long, *Spiritual Merchants*, 29.

101. This is not to say divination has always been treated with welcoming and open arms. In a number of cases, it became the basis for legal action and persecution for people who were at the margins of society. For a very thorough look at the historical prosecution and persecution of North American fortune-tellers, see Davies' *America Bewitched*.

inner life and innate characteristics of a person. The art of divination comes down to knowledge, especially knowledge that comes from places most people either fear to look or do not know about.

The New World Witch knows, though. She always knows.

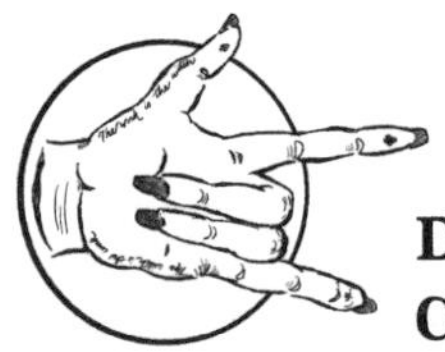

DIRT UNDER THE NAILS

Candle Wax Divination

This form of divination, known as ceromancy, resembles several systems brought over from Europe, and has been practiced in various forms since Colonial times. Typically, a bit of lead would have been heated and dropped into water to make the shapes divined by the participant. In Germany, this practice was known as *bleigießen* and was typically done on Christmas or New Year's Eve. Similar forms have been done in Britain and Continental Europe since at least Roman times. The candle adaptation gained popularity when lead's toxicity became apparent and fewer people had lead on hand in their homes (it was often used to repair cracked household items and simple machinery).

To perform this fortune-telling rite, you need:

- A sturdy container with fire-proof sides, such as a ceramic bowl
- Cold water (it doesn't have to be ice cold, but cool enough to harden the wax quickly)
- A candle large enough to pool wax around the wick (a large taper or small-to-medium pillar candle often works best)

The ritual works best when done around other people, as many people can ask questions that way and take turns. The basic rite simply requires that you turn out the lights in the room, light the candle, and ask a question about your future. Then, tip the wax around the candle wick carefully into the bowl of water from at least six to twelve inches above the water's surface. When the wax hits the water, it will harden into a shape. Based on the shape, you divine the answer to your question. For example, if you ask a question about your career, you may get a shape like a coin, signifying a coming raise. Or you may get a shape like an arrow, indicating a potential change in careers or travel coming in your future (a dream dictionary or tea-leaf reading symbol guide would be of great help to you if you're new to symbol reading).

The candle is then passed to the next questioner, and continues until everyone has had a chance to ask questions or until the candle burns out. This method of divination is popular even today, and has become—like séances or Ouija boards—a staple of slumber parties. It even managed to make it onto an episode of the popular animated television series, *The Simpsons* (season 3, episode 10, "Flaming Moe's").

The Medium's Methods, New and Old

Following European settlement in the New World, a number of divination methods spread based on Old World techniques. Practitioners of card-reading, palmistry, and various forms of lot-casting (sortilege, as it is known when it wears its fanciest of pants) all appeared early in areas settled by Western Europeans. A few forms of divination, such as dream interpretation, were held to be fairly innocuous, as were reading generalized signs and omens in everyday life. Others, such as reading palms or cards, could be seen as diverting amusements, serious tools of discernment, or outright frauds, depending on the situation. Often these more formal imported methods were associated with "undesirable" communities like "Gypsies" (in early American contexts, this population could be either the frequently-displaced and misunderstood Roma people of Eastern and Central Europe or nomadic subcultural groups such as the Irish "Tinker" communities).[102] Similarly, systems imported from Africa through the abominable slave trade sometimes managed—through the grit and perseverance of Africans and African Americans—to remain in use. Cowrie shell divination, for example, continued to be used in the Caribbean and the coastal, slave-holding communities of the southern United States through the nineteenth and twentieth centuries (and is still in use by many today). Mediumship by ritual possession continues to be a key part of systems like Vodoun as well.[103]

102. Davies, *America Bewitched*, 72; Bolton, "Fortune Telling in America To-Day," 299–307.

103. Raboteu, *Slave Religion*, 327–29; Deren, *Divine Horsemen*, 247–62. Chireau, *Black Magic*, 32.

The New World spirit of adaptation altered and adjusted many techniques for divination, and even spawned a few home-grown ones. Below is a list of methods that found favor at various points in North American history that became distinctly Americanized, for better or worse, and developed into systems still in use today.

Body Divination

This is a broad category, but the human body is thought to tell a great deal about the human psyche, and the potential of the individual. Palmistry is very much based on the principle that your life is written on your body, literally etched in the lines of your hands. Similarly, other markings and characteristics of the body reveal secrets to the discerning eye. A chapbook published in 1750 discussed the way different moles on a body showed potential fates of a person born with moles on the head and neck, saying that the person would be "witty, and to have good natural parts: but that he will die poor."[104] Inborn characteristics like a "broad face" could also be seen as indicators of a warm, friendly personality. Spots on fingernails have been interpreted as lies a person tells or as possible hints about the future, as indicated by an Ozark rhyme: "A gift, a ghost, a friend, a foe, a letter to come, a journey to go" (based on the number of spots, one through six, present on a person's nails).[105] One favorite and widespread proverb says "A dimple on the chin, a devil within," indicating a mischievous personality to match an adorable chin-dent. We also cannot ignore the power of body sensations. Itchy hands indicate money coming or going, depending on whether the receptive hand (money coming in) or the dominant hand (money going out) is the one itching. Your right foot itching means you are going on a trip, while the left one itching means you're going where you are not wanted. Burning ears mean someone is talking about you (hence, "My ears are burning!"), and an itchy nose means either a coming visitor or that someone wants to kiss you (possibly both in an ideal situation!).

Phrenology, while dubious as a science, holds that personality traits can be determined by head shape (as a divinatory practice this may have some untapped potential, but as a tool of "racial science" it led to some bad things). Mexican American folklore holds that people can have "hot" and "cold" natures (similar to

104. Anonymous, "Dreams & Moles, with Their Interpretation & Signification."

105. Randolph, *Ozark Magic*, 66.

Indian Ayurvedic medicine), and that those natures dictate personalities and bodily changes—a "hot" person might grow a great deal of hair, for example.[106] And, of course, there's the old dictum of "cold hands, warm heart," which many a devious person has claimed when sticking icy fingers onto an unsuspecting person's back (I may speak from experience here).

Water Divination

This category includes just about any sort of liquid-based divination method, including the use of the famed (and possibly dubious) "Venus glass" of Colonial-era witch trials.[107] While there are a few methods for conducting that rite, most essentially involve asking a question while holding an egg, then cracking the egg into a bowl, cup, or pan of water. Sometimes the water is heated before the egg is added, as well. Once the egg is in the water, the scryer (sign-reader) will look at the shapes made by the egg white or any markings on or around the yolk to determine answers to the questions. In some ways this very much resembles Old World rituals using melted wax or lead to divine future husbands or fortunes (see the inset in this chapter for a practical example). This method is still used in the *limpia* egg-cleansing rite of *curanderismo* from Mexican American traditions. Shapes like "curtains" might indicate spirits attached to a person, while blood on the yolk tells of witchcraft done against them.[108]

Other forms of water divination practiced in the New World involved using tea leaves—a method found in Old World forms as well, of course—and interpreting the dregs of the tea for symbols. Coffee is sometimes used in a similar manner. Some areas with large Russian and Eastern European populations have tea houses where readers may be on staff, or at least available to those interested in such readings. I recall having my tea leaves read at a shop in New Orleans once, a diverting but inaccurate session. I also had coffee grounds read by a Turkish friend while living in Central Europe, and her results were more accurate.

106. Neighbors, "Mexican-American Folk Diseases," 250.

107. Breslaw, *Tituba, Reluctant Witch of Salem*, 90; Breslaw, *Witches of the Atlantic World*, 134–35; Norton, *In the Devil's Snare*, 20–24.

108. See Curious Curandera, "The Basic Egg Limpia."

Bibliomancy

Quite simply, bibliomancy is book-based divination. One form involves simply opening a book—any book—to a random page and seeing what word or phrase you point to, then using that passage as an answer to whatever question you asked. While that version of bibliomancy is a part of New World divination, one that was much more common in the eighteenth and nineteenth century involved wedging an old-fashioned skeleton key into a Bible at a specific place—often Psalm 49, the Book of Ruth, the Gospel of John, or the Epistle of James—then binding the Bible up tightly. The questioner holds the book up using the key and her index fingers and inquires after whatever she wishes to know. The Bible will begin turning, possibly even jumping or sliding out of her hands, when the answer is "yes" to her question.[109] These practices have many Old World antecedents, but found particular popularity among religious groups in the New World as well, including some New England Congregationalists, spiritual seekers in the early nineteenth-century "Burned Over District" of upstate New York, and Pennsylvania Germans.

Playing Cards

Tarot cards are certainly popular among North American diviners. They have seen increasing sales in the early twenty-first century, even as physical book sales have been impacted by growing electronic markets for games and text.[110] The tarot is only one card system among many, however, and historically playing cards—the standard deck of fifty-two clubs, spades, diamonds, and hearts plus a couple of jokers thrown in for fun—have been just as likely to reveal the future as the more mysterious tarot (which, funnily enough, began as a game itself). In North American folklore we see multiple systems for reading playing cards, including the imported Lenormand system, ostensibly from France, and variations on Spanish systems in which the Queens are removed from the deck. The use of playing cards ranged over multiple classes and multiple ethnic groups, although it almost always met with resistance in particularly religious circles, with deeply religious critics claiming they lead to vice and ruin. In response to that criticism we find some folk accounts of soldiers—who often

109. Randolph, *Ozark Magic*, 184; arrowclaire, "Keys to the Hidden Door: Part 1"; Bilardi, *The Red Church*, 303.

110. See Kerr, "Tarot is Trending, and Dior Predicted this Months Ago."

kept cards to pass dull hours and win extra spending money—defending their card decks by claiming they functioned as "prayer books," with the threes reminding them of the Trinity or the Queens as four key women in the Bible. Cards are incredibly symbolic, and different systems appear in different places depending on context. For example, in one system from Kentucky, a Three of Diamonds meant "three pieces of good fortune together," while in another system from New York the same card meant good luck to men, but fickleness and shame to women. In the system I use, the Three of Diamonds means gifts or represents a fountain.[111]

Bones and Natural Objects

If you listen to much country music, you may remember bumping into a lesser-known-but-still-delightful Dolly Parton track at one point called "These Old Bones." In the song, a young woman visits the local mountain "witchy woman," who reads her future using a bag of bones, singing "These old bones will tell your story/ These old bones will never lie/ These old bones will tell you surely/ What you can't see with your eye."[112] Of course, she later claims she simply has a "gift" and the bones are "just for show," but the trope of telling fortunes with bones is effective in the song because using bones to discern past, present, and future appears in several key divination systems. The "bones" are not always animal bones, although they frequently can be. They may include other natural objects such as small nuts, roots, charms, dice, coins, keys, and seashells. The specific bones and objects are always highly dependent upon where the reader lives (although some readers may have a few objects collected from travels as well). For example, an Appalachian reader like the one in Parton's song would likely have things like a dog's tooth, a raccoon's penis bone (or *baculum*), a snake rib, a sheep's "knuckle" bone, and a possum's vertebrae, as well as perhaps a hickory nut, buckeye, a lucky penny, and a porcelain hand from a China doll.[113] A reader working with bones in Alaska might instead have salmon fin spines, a bear claw, a wolf's tooth, a carved whalebone fishhook, and perhaps a bit of ore or a gold coin. Many readers will work only with the bones of a single animal, as

111. See Hutcheson, *54 Devils: The Art and Folklore of Fortune-Telling with Playing Cards*, 5–8, 79–83, 97–99.

112. Parton, "These Old Bones."

113. Yronwode, *The Black Folder*, 71–73; Yronwode, *Throwing the Bones*, 5–8; Richards, *Backwoods Witchcraft*, 123–25.

well.[114] The bones are cast onto a mat made of animal skin or leather, although some will cast onto the ground into a symbol they have drawn there, and then "read" for significance related to the diviner's question. Many bone-reading systems are also *geomantic*, meaning they involve specific number combinations based on markings carved into or naturally occurring on "bones" or similar objects. For example, the Ifa divination system brought over from Africa with the slave trade uses a fixed number of objects—usually a type of nut or cowrie shells—and depending on how the objects land when thrown, each object is "open" or "closed" (for example, the cleft in a cowrie shell facing up is "open" and down is "closed"). That combination will provide a number that corresponds with a traditional saying, piece of literature, or other inherited knowledge to give an exact interpretation.[115] The Chinese *I Ching* divination system is another example of this kind of system, which often relies on yarrow stalks or coins to be the "bones" in the system.

Scrying

Essentially this method involves using a reflective surface to create a state of psychic receptiveness in the diviner, and images begin to appear that reveal hidden information. Perhaps the best-known version of scrying involves mirror divination, and mirrors are still sometimes used to foresee the future. Several contemporary "sleepover games" make use of a mirror and a spirit summoned into it to show the future (or frighten the summoner, as is the case in the "Bloody Mary" game). Often the scryer uses a mirror with a candle in front of it and focuses on the flame's reflection, although in some cases the diviner will hold a mirror in a way that allows her to look over her own shoulder until something appears behind her. The Laguna Pueblo people had diviners that would use obsidian polished to high reflectiveness for scrying the future or discerning why people were suffering from ailments or diseases.[116] One very famous scrying mirror is found in the British Museum: the scrying mirror of Elizabethan royal occultist Dr. John Dee, sometimes called his speculum. It, too, has a New World connection, as it is made from Aztec obsidian!

---

114. Richards, "When the Bones are Calling."

115. See "Ifa divination system," UNESCO Cultural Heritage.

116. Simmons, "Pueblo Witchcraft," in *Witches of the Atlantic Worlds*, 204–212.

Spirit Boards and Divination Games

When the Spiritualist boom of the nineteenth century began to ebb, it left behind a successful religious movement that—although diminished in adherents—remained very influential in other ways. The best-known contribution is the Ouija board, a game first produced for commercial markets by the Kennard Novelty Company in 1891 but based on any number of extant designs for "talking boards" associated with Spiritualist séance sessions from 1848 on. The board allows spirits to communicate by guiding the hands of "players" to different letters using a *planchette* (one version of a device used to aid spirit writing which included variations with room for a pen or pencil to do "automatic writing" on blank paper). The game remained popular throughout the twentieth century, but got a big boost when it was bought by Parker Brothers in 1967 and then had a dubious brush with fame when it featured as a medium for demonic possession in the 1973 film *The Exorcist.*[117] Ouija boards, of course, are not the only divinatory games out there, as anyone who has ever played with a childhood folded paper fortune-teller will attest. We may think of those sorts of divination devices as somehow less worthy or serious, but they have a sturdy pedigree. A 1684 book produced in London but sold in New World colonies provided a version of the game including a paper pinwheel that readers could use to decipher mysterious symbols from the text![118]

Signs and Omens

This is perhaps the most wide-spread and well-incorporated form of divination found throughout the New World. Virtually all people have their own culturally-specific "signs" that tell of events to come. For example, in Appalachian lore, dropping a dishrag means company is coming, while dreaming about gathering eggs indicates bad fortune to follow.[119] Dreams in general held numerous messages that could be decoded for the benefit of those who believed. In African American communities, "policy player" books offering to interpret dreams were designed to help those

117. Horowitz, *Occult America*, 66–79. See also McRobbie. "The Strange and Mysterious History of the Ouija Board"; The Talking Board Historical Society, https://tbhs.org/.

118. Hall, *Worlds of Wonder*, 112–13.

119. Gainer, *Witches, Ghosts, & Signs*, 124–28.

who had them win local lotteries (the "policies").[120] A bird flying into the house is a sign of a coming death, as is seeing a buzzard roosting on a roof. Having to turn back from a trip because you forgot something could very well mean disaster, and some people would delay a trip's beginning until the following day just to avoid the bad luck they thought they would encounter.

The well-known rhyme about red skies at morning or night predicting weather is a prime example of this sort of omen-based system: "Red skies at morning, sailors take warning. Red skies at night, sailors' delight" (also sometimes "shepherds" in place of sailors). Seeing all-white animals has a particular level of importance, as we see in stories about white deer from the Ozarks and New York state, or in the case of the Lakota Sioux sacred story of the White Buffalo Woman.[121] People would generally note that just about any form of slight variance from "normality" could be a sign or "token" as it was sometimes called. A bell that rang too loudly might mean a death for someone soon, but so could a barely-heard tinkling of bells, according to Ozark belief.[122] Signs and omens formed—and still form—a critical mental architecture for many people in the New World, demonstrating that the world is a place of mighty and terrible wonders.

Print Astrology

I specify "print" here because while astrology has had influence over any number of people in any number of places, the distinctive mass media print culture of the United States fomented a long-standing tradition of incorporating astrology into the everyday lives of ordinary people. Literacy rates in the New World tended to be uncommonly high compared to European rates during the Colonial period, and mass circulation of printed materials was absolutely crucial to the eventual independence of the Colonies from British rule. That also meant that many rural farmers took in newspapers and almanacs regularly, both of which frequently contained astrological information. While almanacs and astrology are more fully discussed in chapter nineteen, many farmers relied on almanacs for astrological information about when to plant which crops, and even those more removed from agriculture in the cities

120. Long, *Spiritual Merchants*, 122–26.

121. Jones & Molyneaux, *Mythology of American Nations*, 84; Erdoes & Ortiz, *American Indian Myths & Legends*, 47–52.

122. Randolph, *Ozark Magic*, 302–303.

sometimes followed stellar movements to understand things like weather.[123] Over time the regular appearance of astrological information became an expectation for most print media, and astrology often manages to remain in newspapers even in the digital age in the form of daily horoscopes.[124] The astrology we find in contemporary horoscopes is often only focused on the sun signs, which marks a remarkable transition from the much heavier emphasis on lunar signs in agricultural almanacs.

The selected list here is hardly a dent in the wide array of divination techniques found throughout the New World. In particular, it ignores some of the deeply culturally-specific methods found among particular immigrating groups, Native peoples, and contemporary methods in the digital age. However, I hope that the "quick-and-dirty" tour here shows just how deeply embedded divination remains in North American history and culture, even today. That point is particularly important, given just how frequently fortune-telling has been the center of prosecution in witchcraft history. Often that persecution comes down to an inability to hear the beliefs of others and regard them with the same weight we give our own beliefs. As folklorist Eric Eliason succinctly puts it, tongue firmly planted in cheek, "what *you* do is superstition, what *I* do is science or true religion."[125] Another way of thinking about New World fortune-telling, one which is perhaps more optimistic, is that virtually all people have looked at the people and places around them and decided that they live in a land of mysteries and wonders, one that seeks to interact with them somehow—whether through cards or dreams or the flight of birds simply depends on the tools we choose to use.

THE WORK—Signs and Omens

We all have personal omens that we follow, whether we like to admit it or not. Perhaps it's the black cat crossing your path that makes you nervous (kitties are delightful, and black ones like tiny panthers, so I adore them even if they do dash in front of me). Maybe it's the way the sun rises, or the flight of some birds. You might hear a song on the radio and instantly know it's going to be a good day (or a very, very bad one).

123. Hall, *Worlds of Wonder*, 21–70; Davies, *Grimoires*, 56.

124. Horowitz, *Occult America*, 253–54.

125. Eliason, "Seer Stones, Salamanders, and Early Mormon 'Folk Magic,'" 82.

Keep track of your omens. Write them down. Whenever you think of one that you subscribe to in any way, make a note of it. Even if you only half-believe it, or feel like it's silly, take the time to write it, because it means you're already paying attention to it. Then, test your observations. Which omens bear fruit for you in the wider world? Perhaps you notice black cats and then begin recording whether each day you see them is a good or a bad day (discovering in the process, of course, that they are delightful mini-panthers). You might feel an itch on your palm regularly, and discover that unexpected windfalls or expenses arise in conjunction with those scratchy feelings.

So many of the magic workers of yesterday and today spend time just listening and watching. That is how they discover the secrets of the world around them. Take the time to do the same, and systematically evaluate what you see and hear. You may find that you're speaking the secret language of the world (and the witches) better than you know.

Recommended Reading

54 Devils: The Art and Folklore of Fortune-Telling with Playing Cards, by Cory Thomas Hutcheson. This may seem like shameless self-promotion, but I wrote this little book several years ago to help guide readers through my personal system of divination. This is easily my most-used divination method, and I feel like it is the one I can offer the most insight on, so I include it here for anyone who has an interest in developing divination methods using everyday objects like the handy deck of Bicycle cards in your bedside stand. I also include an appendix of folklore related to other fortune-telling lore involving playing cards that may prove interesting to readers here, too.

Occult America: White House Seances, Ouija Circles, Masons, and the Secret Mystic History of Our Nation, by Mitch Horowitz. Horowitz's book is essential reading for anyone interested in the slightly off-center history of the United States, but to those who want to know more about prophets like Jemima Wilkinson, the history and cultural value of Ouija boards, or the importance of astrology in the twentieth century, it's a real can't-miss. It's written in a journalistic style and provides a lot of avenues for more exploration and discovery of U.S. occult history.

Worlds of Wonder, Days of Judgment: Popular Religious Belief in Early New England, by David D. Hall. While this text is an older one, it is absolutely marvelous (in every sense of that term). Hall's retrospective on early New England and its background of supernatural forces shaping and shifting against politics, domestic life, and even climate demonstrates just how well-integrated magic and omens could be. In many ways, what Hall describes resonates with many subsequent periods of history, including our own, and his thoroughness and thoughtfulness on this topic are delightful.

CHAPTER EIGHT

Bloody Sod and Silver Spade—Treasure-Hunting Magic

We all want to have a little extra in life, it seems. Most of us wouldn't consider ourselves greedy, but to live a life where our needs are met and we have a little bit left over for some luxuries? There are plenty who would say yes to that. Many contemporary spells are designed to bring an inchoate force known as "prosperity" into an individual's life. In some cases, Wiccan and Wiccan-influenced spellbooks contain workings that either target specific needs and cash amounts, or which seek to generally enhance the financial stability of the magician or his/her designated target (most Wiccan spellbooks also require that the magician have permission from the target even in beneficial magical workings like this).[126] Certainly, magical practices designed to bring a sense of bounty and abundance into one's life go back quite far—the cults of Fortuna and Tyche in the ancient world appeal to good luck, and the Roman cult of Pomona pursued the ideal of a fruitful life. Folk magic, however, has generally focused less on generalized prosperity and has drilled down to specific financial problems and advantages. The Wiccan spells that seek a specific sum of money to cope with a specific issue—a medical bill, a broken radiator, etc.—very

126. Please note this is not a knock at Wiccan prosperity magic or ritual. Participating in the Wiccan religion means adhering to its moral codes, and that discipline can certainly add to the magic and force behind a spell. If you don't feel comfortable doing spells on or for others without asking, that is perfectly fine and you should continue to follow your moral instincts on that count.

much mirror the sorts of spells done by people across multiple times and places as they tried to cope with uncertain finances and resources.

Some hoped for better luck, and some made their own. In many communities, popular lotteries and raffles offered bursts of material prosperity. Poker games and dice could turn a person's fortune overnight, for better or worse. Since risk and reward breed magic, gambling charms sprang up wherever these games of chance appeared. Additionally, the circulation of "Dream Books" in these communities offered ways for people to interpret their dreams in order to guess lucky lottery numbers. While gambling of the sort these charms and divinations were designed for has largely evolved, so too have the magical practices associated with them. That does not mean the use of such charms is much less common now. There are still plenty of people who will carry a lucky two dollar bill in their wallet or purse (perhaps even wrapped around a nutmeg for a little extra luck).

DIRT UNDER THE NAILS
Gambler's Charms

Somewhere between the world of the practical lump-sum spell and the highly ritualized world of treasure-hunting lay the commonplace and widespread "gambling charm." These were often small amulets or talismans crafted specifically to help the bearer win at games of chance. These charms were very common in poorer communities and among African Americans practicing variants of Hoodoo and Conjure work during the late nineteenth and early twentieth centuries (although by no means were such charms limited to those groups alone). One of the best-known charms (and one that I only include here as being of historical note, and *not* for practice in the modern day):

- Drilling out a core section of a nutmeg, filling it with quicksilver (liquid mercury—again, do not do this, as mercury is poisonous), and sealing it with some wax

Other charms that were far more innocuous and less likely to, well, drive you mad, included:

- Carrying a folded piece of paper money (often a two dollar bill or whatever the highest bill available was) and tuck it into the inner brim of a man's hat or inside of his belt. This would create a "money belt" effect that would ensure that the gambler never left the table with less than he started with.
- Sewing up a lodestone (magnetic stone) in a piece of flannel and dousing it with a special "feeding" ingredient, often either Hoyt's Cologne, Florida Water, or—in many cases—the urine of a woman, which was thought to be especially lucky
- Carrying a small pouch of tobacco with some collard seeds mixed in (this one is found in one of the famous "Brer Rabbit" stories recounted by Joel Chandler Harris)

Another brand of folk magic, however, did not work toward a specific sum, nor did it seek to bring a vaguely defined sense of wealth into someone's life. Instead, many spells targeted getting rich—quick! In some cases, the spell's target would be a gambler who worked to gain the advantage in games of chance, such as lucky hand talisman from the Hoodoo traditions of the American South. A few stories talk of acts of magical extortion, wherein a magician would either try to low-ball the purchase of land/livestock with the threat that failure to accept a paltry offer would result in the destruction of the commodity in question *or* a witch might place a curse on a neighbor and only remove the curse for a fee (you can find several examples of such stories in *The Silver Bullet, and Other American Witch Stories,* by Hubert J. Davis).[127]

If someone wanted to get rich *really* quickly, however, she would turn to magical treasure-hunting. Plenty of European grimoires had methods for finding lost treasures, usually with the help of spirits. Some grimoire texts that influenced American practices, such as *The Black Pullet,* spelled out in detail how to summon treasure-seeking daemons to work on one's behalf using a talisman and ring inscribed with the following sigils and markings (see figure 8-1):

127. See also Gainer, *Witches, Ghosts, & Signs: Folklore of the Southern Appalachians;* and Milnes, *Signs, Cures, & Witchery.* Appalachian tales frequently deal with hidden money detected by occult means, although just as often the money that has been hidden is ill-gotten through murder or robbery.

FIG 8-1: A recreation of talisman image no. 5 from *The Black Pullet*, thought to help those seeking treasure to be able to find it and raise it to the surface of the ground.

Once these tools were prepared, the old man guiding the treasure-hunting charm in *The Black Pullet* offers up the magic words "*Onaim, Perantes, Rasonastos,*" and seven spirits appear, one with a bird on its shoulder. The old man says the bird is the real driving force behind treasure-finding, as it can locate any treasure hidden on or in the earth.[128] Incantations like these and their accompanying symbols and objects were part of other magical practices, especially in places where the most common grimoire languages like German, Spanish, or French were spoken. Additionally, in the Old World, many times the same spells or books used for finding gold were also used for finding a companion for one's bed for the evening. Considering a great number of those who used these books were able to read because they were trained clergy, you can imagine the problem that presented to their superiors! The use of grimoires for treasure-hunting was never recommended, although the Church certainly welcomed new sources of wealth, but the strange combination of money and sex (not all that strange, really, to anyone who has ever watched television soap operas) frequently put grimoire-wielding priests into hot water. Penance usually involved the public burning of one's magic books with the hopes that the magical knowledge used to conjure bedfellows and bags of cash would go up in lit-

128. Anonymous, *The Black Pullet*, 37–8.

eral smoke.[129] Even finding a buried treasure by chance would have raised eyebrows because of its more common occult associations.

Of course, being able to find treasure only helps if treasure is already buried in the earth waiting to be found. In a largely unexplored land like North America (from a European perspective—Indigenous people knew the lands very well and had their own legends about hidden caches and vengeful protective spirits), the possibility of hidden wealth everywhere emerged in people's minds quickly and often. The stories of pirate treasures buried in the soil or wads of money buried during wartime and conflict flourished in an era where a well-sequestered pot was the closest thing to a bank that most people had. It was an easy recipe for treasure fever. In early New England (as well as the maritimes of other parts of the New World), a widespread belief in hidden golden caches secreted beneath the soil became the basis for a number of magical spells. A Maine man named Daniel Lambert, suddenly flush with money, faced suspicion from his neighbors who believed he had used occult means to find pirate treasure buried nearby. The supposition was that Lambert must have known evil spells because evil spirits were expected to guard every treasure.[130]

Magical Treasure-Hunting in the New World

Since the New World was vast and dangerous, people turned to magic to help find these copious buried (and frequently "cursed") treasures, and to remove any dangers that might arise during the expedition to unearth them. A number of "rules" for enchanted bounty-seeking developed, including:

- Treasure-hunting teams needed at least three members, as that number ensured magical success.
- Magical circles should be inscribed around the digging site to prevent any malevolent spirits from attacking the diggers.
- Implements of silver, such as silver spoons or spades, should be used to dig at least part of the earth to ensure luck in the hunt and to protect the diggers from harm.

129. Davies, *Grimoires*, 18–19.

130. Taylor, "The Early Republic's Supernatural Economy," 6–34; Dorson, *Buying the Wind*, 62–3; Hurley, "Buried Treasure Tales in America," 197–216.

- Blood offerings (animals usually) had to be made to quell the guardian spirits protecting the treasure—a belief related to the idea that a guardian spirit was usually a person who was killed and his blood spilled over the burial ground.

In addition to maritime treasures, the idea of "Indian" gold became very popular. Some European colonists and conquerors were sure that entire cities of gold were just waiting to be found in the dense, mysterious interiors of North and South America. Gonzalo Pizzaro and Sir Walter Raleigh both mounted expeditions to find such legendary places, frequently referred to as "El Dorado," or "the golden one." In almost every case, however, the site was protected by evil spirits, a curse, ghosts, or some other malevolent force.

In some situations, however, the spirit might actually *help* a seeker find his or her treasure. In several Ozark legends, ghosts guided wealth-seekers to a spot to find hidden riches, mostly because they wanted to reveal their secret and be at peace.[131] Additionally, these sorts of accounts usually seem to say that ghosts actually want their fortunes and personal effects to be enjoyed by others, which sounds like a mark of afterlife maturity. That's not to say that all spirits are so morally evolved, however. How one ensures that the ghost is not simply walking the magician into a trap is anyone's guess.

Pursuit of treasure through magical means represented something a bit deeper than simply a get-rich-quick scheme. America was—and often still is—seen as a land of "unlimited good," where anyone willing to put forth the proper effort could expect to be rewarded. This contrasted sharply with Old World expectations of class immobility. In peasant-based societies, people believed that wealth was only available in a limited quantity, and anyone who happened into wealth or treasure must therefore be diminishing the wealth of someone else. In the New World, however, treasure formed a concrete expression of the belief that the country was so ready to provide riches it literally required planting a spade in the earth and turning over a few shovelfuls to gain wealth untold.[132] Yet the treasure-seeker had to do *something* to gain that wealth, and could not simply expect it to rise to the surface of its own volition.

131. Randolph, *Ozark Magic*, 217–220.

132. Mullen, "The Folk Idea of Unlimited Good in American Buried Treasure Legends," 210. See also Alan Dundes, *The Meaning of Folklore: The Analytical Essays of Alan Dundes* (Denver: Universiy of Colorado Press, 2007).

The challenges presented by guardians, which might involve anything from natural phenomena such as wind or storms to the uncanny presence of dozens and dozens of lizards (as was recounted in one tale about Mark Island in Maine), to ghosts, wraiths, or even the Devil himself, all employed to guard pirate booty or a barrel full of silver. Even today, some of these guardian stories persist, as legends and rumors surrounding Oak Island, Nova Scotia can attest.

So far, we can identify a few key themes in these New World magical treasure expeditions:

- Treasure-seeking was seen as a dangerous undertaking, even if it could be lucrative.
- Finding treasure sometimes made one suspect of nefarious occult dealings.
- One often actually did need to have some occult dealings to find treasure, so point two is not wrong (even if "nefarious" is a bit of a strong word, since ghosts might not be particularly diabolical).
- A treasure hunter needed to know the landscape and the spirits they were dealing with before setting off on their quest.
- Crucially, they also needed to know how to either befriend or distract any local spirits or guardians set to protect a treasure. Having spirit allies of one's own helped, but offerings were a big part of the process.
- Having the right tools for the job could make the difference between success and failure, so once again, researching beforehand was crucial.

How often did people actually strike it rich with buried treasure, then? Well, while accounts of treasures found are remarkably thin compared to tales where things go wrong, there are situations where a person manages to pull up sacks of gold or an old box with valuables inside from time to time. The case of Daniel Lambert in Maine is one such example, as are some of the Ozark tales of finding buried money after someone's death. Perhaps the best-known case of finding treasure through occult means in nineteenth-century America led to something much different: a new religion.

Finding Spiritual Wealth in Burned-Over Places

Anyone who studies alchemy for very long knows that the fabled power to turn lead into gold was frequently understood as at least partly metaphorical. The pure "gold" derived from the transmutation of substances was an allegory for the evolution of the human soul into Divinity, or at least proximity to Divinity. The interwoven nature of spirit and material worlds was the underpinning for much of the world in the pre-Enlightenment era, but alchemy in many ways is one of the first experimental sciences, and its fascination with spiritual forces is not entirely incompatible with its fascination regarding chemical reactions. If we think of "treasure" metaphorically, then unlocking a better version of ourselves is very much like digging up and unlocking a hidden chest full of doubloons.

One of the best examples of magical treasure-hunting led to an entire religious movement in the New World. While the scope of this book does not permit me to explore the full magical heritage of the Latter-Day Saints, I would be remiss to omit at least a key part of their foundation story here. Joseph Smith, prophet and founder of the Mormon faith, used to hunt for treasure using methods derived from alchemy and hermetic science/magic. He reputedly followed the rules laid out above, offering animal sacrifices of white or black animals, such as sheep or dogs, within magical figures inscribed on the ground. This was largely the work he did prior to discovering his golden plates and having his angelic vision, which occurred during such a treasure hunt.[133] Smith's methods were not deviant or unusual. He used seer or "peep" stones to help find his hidden treasures, and his activity in the highly spiritually active area of New York known as the Burned-Over District was imitative of earlier seekers and followed by those who did the same. In fact, Smith was following very much in his own father's footsteps, as Joseph Smith, Sr. was an active treasure-seeker in Palmyra, New York. He once described his methods to a neighbor, saying "the best time for digging money was in the heat of the summer, when the heat of the sun caused the chests of money to rise to the top of the ground."[134] The tradition the Smiths followed required—like many grimoire traditions do—that the seeker be spiritually pure or else he would fail in his pursuits, a concept brought in from European hermetics and alchemy. The fervent spirituality and insistence on saintly

133. Taylor, "The Early Republic's Supernatural Economy," 12.

134. Brooke, *The Refiner's Fire*, 31.

behavior left a strong mark on the junior Smith, and helped him feel prepared for his prophetic role in revealing the Book of Mormon (which was originally inscribed on golden plates). For Joseph Smith, Jr., the "treasure guardian" tradition became transformed into a form of spiritual alchemy, with the golden plates representing the "gold" of spiritual truth, which could only be discovered by a prophet through the intercession of Divine beings—in Smith's case, the angel Moroni and later God the Father and Jesus Christ in physical form, as well.[135]

The story of Smith's discovery of the plates and his subsequent founding of his religious order could also be read through an alchemical treasure-hunting lens. He did, indeed, believe himself to be experiencing a physical perfection when visited by Jesus, and he saw the golden plates as valuable not for their substance but for what they promised in terms of human spiritual evolution. Eventually, though, he became the sacrificial lamb as he was killed by an angry mob outside a jail in Illinois (after escaping an angry mob in Missouri a few years earlier). There is always a price for this sort of magic, it seems.

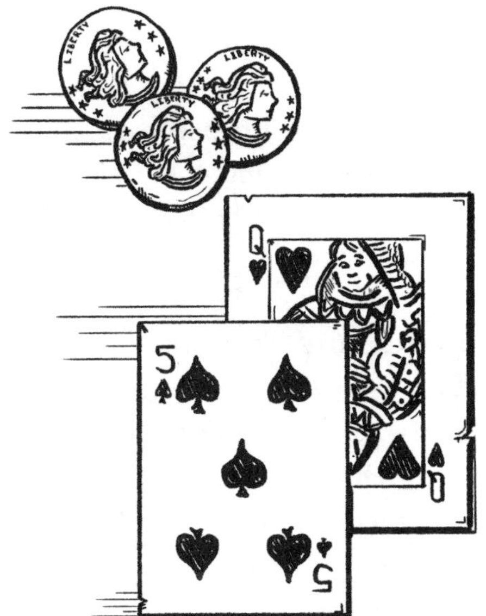

FIG 8-2: "Aunt" Caroline Dye was well-known around Newport, Arkansas, and elsewhere as a seer and conjure worker with a knack for knowing things and being able to find lost objects. She reportedly had thousands of dollars in cash secreted around her home when she died, a testament to how many people sought her services.

135. See Albanese, *A Republic of Mind & Spirit: A Cultural History of American Metaphysical Religion*. See also Horowitz, *Occult America: White House Seances, Ouija Circles, Masons, & the Secret Mystic History of Our Nation* and Bushman, *Mormonism: A Very Short Introduction*.

SINGING BONES
Aunt Caroline Dye

There are probably twice as many stories, songs, and legends about Aunt Caroline Dye (sometimes Dyer) of Newport, Arkansas as there are historical records. Still, her existence is well-documented, and she was consulted by people from hundreds and even thousands of miles away who would arrive in town on the train just to see her. While her birth date is uncertain, we are fairly sure based on her tombstone that she passed away in 1918 after a long life, putting her nascency in the early 1800s (although some accounts suggest a birth closer to the mid-1800s). She was a Black woman who grew up under slavery, lived to see Emancipation, and endured Jim Crow, all while operating a very successful business as a woman who could conjure and "find things" when they got lost or stolen. In this latter capacity, she frequently used playing cards as her tool of choice, although she could even find things like stolen livestock by a gift of "second sight" as well. Most stories say she gained her powers after a childhood illness or accident. When her gift showed itself, she began to bring in all sorts of clients, Black and white, and amassed a small fortune that enabled her to become a landowner and property manager in her community, all by dint of her spiritual and magical gifts. Her fame was so great that she was immortalized in folk songs, such as "Sundown Blues," by W.C. Handy.[136]

Doodlebugs and Witch Wigglers: Dowsing and Treasure Divination

In some cases, treasures of golden pieces and precious gems are not the target of the magic in the New World. Take, for example, the widespread phenomenon of dowsing, which allows a person to magically search for substances like water and oil beneath the earth (when searching for water they were often called "witch wigglers"). In some cases, the dowser might also search for veins of gold or silver or other valuable ores like iron. The method for making such a dowsing tool appears

136. Hutcheson, "Aunt Caroline Dye," 29–35. See also Parker, "The Hoo Doo Woman of Arkansas." Dillard, *Statesmen, Scoundrels, & Eccentrics: A Gallery of Amazing Arkansans*; Koch and Brantley, "Aunt Caroline Dye: 'The Worst Woman in the World?'"; and Wolf, "Aunt Caroline Dye: The Gypsy in the 'St. Louis Blues.'"

in John George Hohman's early nineteenth-century Pennsylvania German magical text, *The Long-Lost Friend*:

> TO MAKE A WAND FOR SEARCHING FOR IRON, ORE, OR WATER.
> *On the first night of Christmas, between 11 and 12 o'clock, break off from any tree a young twig of one year's growth, in the three highest names (Father, Son and Holy Ghost), at the same time facing toward sunrise. Whenever you apply this wand in searching for anything, apply it three times. The twig must be forked, and each end of the fork must be held in one hand, so that the third and thickest part of it stands up, but do not hold it too tight. Strike the ground with the thickest end, and that which you desire will appear immediately, if there is any in the ground where you strike. The words to be spoken when the wand is thus applied are as follows: Archangel Gabriel, I conjure thee in the name of God, the Almighty, to tell me, is there any water here or not? Do tell me!*
>
> \+ + +
>
> *If you are searching for iron or ore, you have to say the same, only mention the name of what you are searching for.*[137]

This version of magical dowsing incorporates high magical elements (such as the invocation of Gabriel) and strong folk magical ones (the clipping of the tree twig at sunrise and the straightforward dowsing methodology). On the simpler end of the spectrum, one could simply put a bit of whatever was being sought into the tip of the dowsing rod, as was the case in some Ozark lore, where the tradition of a "witch stick" (also known as a "doodlebug") involved attaching something like a gold or silver ring or coin to the end of the rod. Even "mixed ores" could be found by combining metals, such as wedging a silver dime and a copper penny together.[138]

Contemporary magical practitioners seeking to draw upon their forebears and the skills that have been used in North America for several centuries can still make use of treasure-hunting charms and methods (although I will not condone live animal sacrifice in these pursuits, as it is illegal in most places and you can usually acquire animal blood from a butcher to accomplish the same effect, if that's your preferred approach to treasure-hunting). Perhaps a modern practitioner would seek

137. Hohman, *The Long-Lost Friend*, 49–50.

138. Randolph, *Ozark Magic*, 188.

the unlimited good of spiritual gold, as Joseph Smith claimed he did upon finding the golden plates that became the foundation of a religion. Or a witch in New World society in the twenty-first century might use treasure-hunting as a way of finding objects or information of particular value (especially the latter, since we've shifted to a strongly information-based economy).

Times have changed, but the lessons of treasure hunters using magic more than a century ago can still be useful to us today. What are some of the big takeaways?

- Know what you're looking for. Are you pursuing something tangible, like real gold or money? Or are you after something less concrete? Or are you looking to protect your own stores using magic like a guardian spirit?
- Have the right tool for the job, be it a silver spade or something to distract hostile spirits.
- Bring offerings and learn how to make friends with new spirits (even if they aren't ones you regularly work with).
- Learn when a no is a "NO"—a good lesson in life generally, and when dealing with angry spirits, one you only need to learn once.
- Do your research! Local lore often gives you the best information about spirits of place, frequently in the guise of "ghost stories" or local legends.

The practice of hunting for buried wealth and riches spanned cultural and geographic boundaries throughout the New World. In many cases, very strict rules were followed, regarding purification and protection as well as actual seeking magic. Spirits would guide a magician to the site of a treasure, and in some cases might even be employed to raise it from the earth. In other cases, the spirits associated with the treasure were deeply malevolent and most of the magic employed was to placate or dispel any evil that might be lingering about the dig site. The payoff for an effective treasure hunter could be a sack of coins, a buried chest, or even a new branch of a religion, but the work required up front was heavy and intense. While gambling charms might take longer, the success rate was better overall. In the end, getting rich quick via magical means, it seems, has always been a labor-intensive and time-consuming effort, just like any other job.

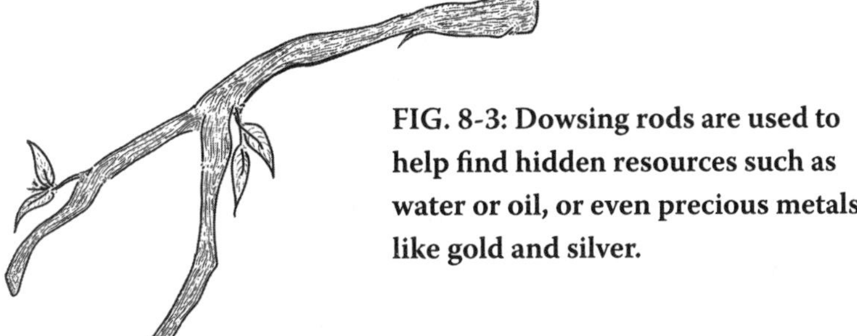

FIG. 8-3: Dowsing rods are used to help find hidden resources such as water or oil, or even precious metals like gold and silver.

DIRT UNDER THE NAILS
DIY Dowsing Rods

Dowsing may be one of the easiest folk magical practices to try your hand at, as many people have such a high opinion of it (or at least do not associate it with anything diabolical or evil). While getting practice dowsing using the traditional tree branch method is wonderful, you can also make a crude-but-effective set of dowsing rods from household materials. You will need:

- Two old pens (the kind with the plastic or cardboard casings)
- Two wire coat hangers
- A pair of wire cutters or pliers with wire cutters built-in

You begin by taking the pens apart. All you really need is the thin, tube-like outer casing of the pen. The rest you can recycle or use in other projects as you wish. Then, clip your two clothes hangers. You want to keep most of the long bottom wire and one of the "sides" of the hanger (but you can clip it before it gets to the twisted "neck" of the hanger). Gently bend the hanger side until you make a large wire "L" shape with it. Do the same with the other hanger. Put the shorter end of the wire "L" into the pen tube, and hold one tube in each hand. Try to start with your long wires parallel and pointing in front of you, and hold the rods at about chest level, maybe a foot or so away from you. Ask the rods to help you find whatever it is you're dowsing for, and slowly begin to walk back and forth over the area. When the wires drift closed into an "X," that's the spot your water/oil gusher/buried pirate gold is hiding. Or so the theory goes.

THE WORK—Guarding Your Treasures

The flip side to the idea of treasure-hunting is treasure protection. While the temptation to go out and dig up hidden gold is often strong, the first order of business is finding ways to hold on to what you've already got. So why not create your own protective spell around your most prized possessions and beloved treasures?

There are a number of traditions in which a magician creates a spirit form (such as a *tulpa* or an *egregore*) to assist in tasks or help find information for the creator. This hearkens back to Central European Jewish folklore, such as the story of Rabbi Loew and the Prague Golem.[139] In that tale, a learned and mystical Jewish teacher discovers that his congregation is under threat from the gentile population around them, so he takes a huge mass of clay and inscribes it with holy Hebrew letters. Then, he puts a scroll in the mouth of the creature and awakens it to protect his community. There is a restriction, however, as it must have the scroll removed periodically or else it will go berserk and begin attacking people (which it inevitably does, of course).

The magical helper creation practice also appears in some contemporary and historical Pennsylvania German Pow-wow or *braucherei* communities.[140] The creation of a "Butzemann," for example, as a protector of a farmstead during the planting and harvesting months, still has a home in some parts of the Keystone State. While those rituals are generally very tradition-specific, we know from sources like the famed Pow-wow manual *The Long-Lost Friend* that there were spells to compel the return of stolen goods relying on similar methods. For example, one spell involves going at sunrise to a juniper tree or bush and pinning a branch of it to the ground under "the skull of a malefactor" to compel a thief to return stolen goods. You might adapt this

139. See Schwartz's *Lilith's Cave: Jewish Tales of the Supernatural.*

140. See Schreiwer, *The First Book of Urglaawe Myths*; Phoenix, *The Pow-Wow Grimoire*; and Hohman, *The Long-Lost Friend.*

sort of spell by creating a small figure out of juniper twigs and giving it a carved clay skull (similar to the Golem), then giving it charge over all your most valuable treasures. Name each one so the spirit knows what it is protecting, and name the guardian as well.

Crucially, with all these spells, you should remember the limits involved. Like the Golem (and the Butzemann as well) these creations are employed only for a limited time, and must be given freedom or rest regularly. With your juniper guardian, you might give it employment for a year and a day, then set it free by taking it apart and burying it on your property with an offering. Retain one twig to incorporate into your new guardian, which you will make at the same time and name (perhaps even naming it something like "son of ___" or "daughter of ___" after the first one you created).

It's possible that you could even leave your helper (and the tradition of remaking and renaming it each year) to someone after you, and they might perhaps become the guardian of your treasures long after you're gone. Remember, though, that buried treasure is always *meant* to be found, and that someone will meet the conditions of your guardian at some point. Make sure your guardian knows and understands just who you would consider "worthy" of such precious objects and enchantments. In a way, this is a way to leave a very subtle, but very powerful, personal magical legacy. And who knows? Maybe some day people will tell the story of you and your strange clay-skulled juniper Golem and the shoebox full of treasures it guarded long after you were gone.

Recommended Reading

The Black Pullet, by Anonymous. This classic (and very digestible) grimoire contains several references to guardian spirits and various treasures. It has a number of talismans and designs that modern occult practitioners have found incredibly useful on their own, and is probably a good access point for a beginner trying to understand the more ceremonial aspects of magical ritual (including those rituals associated with buried treasures).

A Republic of Mind and Spirit: A Cultural History of American Metaphysical Religion, by Catherine L. Albanese. While I generally try to keep my recommendations aimed at a broad readership, I absolutely have to recommend Albanese's thorough history of American metaphysics here. Yes, it's academic in nature, but

Albanese weaves the stories of treasure-hunting occultists, Transcendental rebels, and New Age spiritual merchants together in such a rich and rewarding way. You begin to see North America as a place where the mystical has always thrived, even when it did so by conjoining itself to strange bedfellows like natural science or literature.

FIFTH RITE: FLIGHT

Or, Why Witches Take to the Skies for Reasons Magical and Malevolent

"This old witch used to tantalize people out in the country. They didn't know she was a witch; but every day there'd be something missing—diamonds, jewelry. She'd come in through a keyhole, or a crack in the door."*

* Gates and Tatar, *The Annotated African American Folktales*, 100.

CHAPTER NINE

Salting Her Skin—The Witch in Flight

Witches fly. Ask anyone. Virtually all lore regarding witches seems to make flight a recognizable characteristic of witch behavior. They soar along, mostly at night, to do whatever magical business they need to do—often nefarious business in folktales—and then return home by sunrise. When Halloween rolls around, you can be reasonably sure that in many places in North America, you will see witches. They will appear in windows as decorations, or as cookies, or as children timidly approaching your doorstep to ask for some candy. In any number of these incarnations, you are likely to see a witch toting a broom by her side or between her knees as she soars across the face of a bright yellow moon (or perhaps on to the next house to fill her plastic pumpkin).

Have you ever thought much about *why* witches fly, though? And why so many of the stories are so specific about the methods of flight and where they go? This chapter will be dedicated to answering those questions, as well as taking a look at a few of the "how do they do it?" methods of flight we find in North American folklore. Some of these examples will seem far-fetched or unbelievable, but then witches love that distant space at the margins of reality where those terms apply so well (and flight has something to do with that, as we shall see). The tales here are from a wide variety of traditions, as the belief in witch flight seems widespread.

A word of caution before we begin: while I will cover several methods of flight here, including ones that use specialized herbal formulas to achieve liftoff, I will not be providing any recipes for "flying ointments" or any similar concoctions. This is not because I do not believe they are effective—I very much do, and have seen them work in at least one form firsthand—but I am not an expert herbalist or equipped to provide detailed formulations of the recipes, which usually require some very persnickety ingredients. Those ingredients, dosed incorrectly, can have disastrous—even fatal—results, and so I advise you to read this chapter not as a "how-to" so much as a "why," and to seek out better, more detailed guidance for your preferred method of flight. That being said, I will provide a few details here and there that may enable you to experience witch flight without risking life and limb, so your level of participation is entirely up to you regarding what you read here.

Now, by yarrow and rue and our red caps, too, hie we to the skies!

The Witches' Excursion: Why Witches Fly

Witches take to their brooms (or a variety of other implements, as we shall see in the next section of this chapter) for a wide variety of reasons. The purpose of night flight will vary by witch, but we do see patterns of motivation develop. A folkloric witch flies because:

- **She must travel to a sabbat**—She is meeting with other witches, spirits, or devils and flight is her main method of getting where she needs to go.
- **She is stealing goods from her neighbors**—Several stories focus on witches traveling around and plundering the wealth of her neighbors in a semi-regular binge (as opposed to a more gradual attrition found in other stories involving stolen milk or butter that won't churn).
- **She is seeking justice (or vengeance)**—Often justice and vengeance are two sides of the same coin (see chapter five for more consideration of a witch's wicked deeds in light of the social obligations of her community). Many witches seem to go out at night to menace or harass others, usually those who have wronged or harmed them in some way, although in some cases they may be going after their community at large rather than particular individuals.

If we are to understand these flights better, and consequently understand witches themselves better, then we should consider more seriously the lore of each of these sorts of journeys and the goals of the witches involved. After all, it's all well and good to want to fly as a witch, but if we don't understand why we're really flying in the first place, what are we going to accomplish by hopping on a broomstick or slathering up with an ointment?

Sabbat Flights

Witches gathering together to perform strange and marvelous feats or share spells, ingredients, and enchantments is hardly a New World phenomenon. You need only think of the Weird Sisters of Shakespeare's *Macbeth* or the sensationalist accounts of late Medieval and early Renaissance clergymen—such as the infamous *Malleus maleficarum* or the lesser-known *Strigimagarum demonumque mirandis (On the Wonders of Witches and Demons),* published by Dominican priest Silvestro Mazzolini da Prierio in 1525[141]—to see vivid examples of how people imagined witch gatherings to go. Even writings about the late Roman period, such as the tenth-century *Canon Episcopi,* describe gatherings of women for magical and ritual purposes, usually associated with the goddess Diana.[142]

The association of sabbats (or sometimes "sabbaths," depending on the source) with flight, however, seems to have become more fully developed from the seventeenth century on, largely as a result of an increasing number of images and illustrations of these supposedly infernal get-togethers. Witchcraft historian Ronald Hutton notes that he thinks the eventual conflation of night-flying monsters from folklore and the idea of witches gathering in groups, especially as presented by Church authorities who wished to portray such convocations as satanic, largely became the basis for our image of the soaring, sky-skimming witch.[143] Witch flight as a sabbatical act, then, became a much more substantial part of the popular imagination in Europe at almost exactly the same time that Europeans were making major inroads

141. For a robust account of demonological texts and depictions of witches' sabbats in Medieval literature and art, see *The Oxford Illustrated History of Witchcraft and Magic* and Ronald Hutton's *The Witch: A History of Fear from Ancient Times to the Present.*

142. Davies, *The Oxford Illustrated History of Witchcraft and Magic,* 71; Cohn, "The Night-Witch in Popular Imagination," in *Witches of the Atlantic World,* 117–26.

143. Hutton, *The Witch,* 122–24.

into the conquest of North America. In an unknown and dangerous land, they saw devils everywhere.

The passage of the witch into Colonial lore meant that the sabbatical witch flying to her satanic meeting became an accepted image for European Americans in that period. At the same time, the emphasis on flight was often reserved for spectral attacks, with the soaring witch appearing more frequently as a literary figure than a literal one. Perhaps the best example of this is in Nathaniel Hawthorne's "Young Goodman Brown," a story about a New England Christian man who discovers his friends and neighbors are all witches. As he is walking along a path in the woods, seeking out the witch meeting to see it for himself, Brown encounters a man "in grave and decent attire," who turns out to be the Devil on the way to the same sabbat meeting. Eventually they bump into one of Brown's neighbors, who complains that another witch has stolen her broomstick, obliging her to walk to the sabbat. The Devil later loans Brown his staff, a serpentine cutting of maple wood, and when the mortal man grips it, he notes that "he seemed to fly along the forest-path, rather than to walk or run." Hawthorne seems to relate this to flying ointments, saying they are brewed from "fine wheat and the fat of a new-born babe," a pseudo-recipe he draws from sources such as Francis Bacon's *Sylva Sylvarum, or A Natural History in Ten Centuries*.[144]

If we see the sabbatic flight as an artistic and literary interpretation of things like witch gatherings and the use of flying ointments, then the purpose of flight seems to be breaking the bonds of physical limitation and—more potently—a chance to engage in risky, dangerous activity. The witch is not afraid to fly, or afraid of those dark, scary woods and strange nighttime sounds in the New World. She is, to paraphrase fantasy author Terry Pratchett, by far the scariest thing in the woods, the night, or the sky, and she knows it.

Theft Flights

Sometimes when a witch (or two, or even a whole coven) rides out above the darkened tree line, she is not seeking the formal revels of the sabbat, but more personal forms of enjoyment. A number of witch stories describe nocturnal ventures with

144. Cherry, "The Sources of Hawthorne's 'Young Goodman Brown,'" 342–48; Hawthorne, "Young Goodman Brown."

the specific aim of raiding a local cellar or storeroom, filling up on all the delights she can find—usually at least partly alcoholic—then returning home and leaving a mystery behind her about who has been stealing cheese, wine, bread, and ale in the neighborhood. Farmers use charms to hold witches fast during their night raids or to deter them from entering certain spaces like barns or storehouses. One widespread example is the use of a sieve or scattered grain by a door, which would force a witch to count holes or crumbs until dawn if she wanted to enter, so most would give up and try elsewhere.

A pair of stories from the Old and New Worlds essentially tell the same theft-flight tale in two different settings and offers us insight into the methods of flight and the cleverness of witches. The first is an Irish tale recorded in the late nineteenth or early twentieth century in a collection by William Butler Yeats and called "The Witches' Excursion." A man named Red James discovers a group of six witches in his kitchen, led by his housekeeper who had been slipping him a sleeping potion on previous nights but which he failed to drink on the night in question. He watches as they each put on a red cap, slather on a green goop from a jar, and grab a twig, then say, "By yarrow and rue, and my red cap too, Hie over to England!" James, of course, follows them, snatching his housekeeper's cap and twig. They fly from Ireland to an English castle, where they enter the cellar by a keyhole and drink until James passes out. He is found in the morning by the authorities and accused of plundering the cellar for a month, then sentenced to death. On his way to the gallows, a witch calls out to him in Irish to remember his red hat, which he asks to be placed upon his head. When given the opportunity for last words, James recites the rhyme, and shoots "through the air in the style of a sky-rocket" and back home.[145]

The second tale is from the Appalachians, where a good many Irish and Scots-Irish settlers made homes. In the New World version, the witches' cabin is located on Roan Mountain, and the interloper is a traveler named Riley who is invited to stay the night with the Dobbs sisters. Roan Mountain is a real mountain on the Tennessee/North Carolina border, but the "roan" referred to could be tied into the "red" of the red cap being used to induce magical flight in the Yeats tale, with "roan" derived from Old French from "red" or "ruddy." Or, "roan" could be a variant on "rowan," which is a mountain ash tree (which derives its name from its red berries, and thus

145. Booss, *A Treasury of Irish Myth*, 168–70.

could still have the "red" connection). The rowan tree is loaded with magical significance—some of the most potent anti-witchcraft charms are crosses made from rowan twigs bound with red thread. However, it could also be used to make magical tools as well, such as wands or staves, or perhaps twigs for flight. The witches put their guest to sleep using a drugged squirrel stew, but he wakes and sees them slathering themselves with grease and flying away. Once again, he follows, using their flying ointment and their phase: "Willie Waddie, I have spoke. Willie Waddie, remove this yoke, and let me rise like chimney smoke." Once again, they raid a local storehouse, and their victim is left behind. In this case, he only escapes having his ears cut off by agreeing to marry one of the sisters, who then whisk him away, leaving only a greasy footprint behind.[146]

FIG 9-1: Some evidence suggests that witch flight was achieved through the aid of *entheogens*, or hallucinogenic substances, such as the fungus *Amanita muscaria*, commonly called the "red cap."

The unguent used in both stories seems to be, basically, a flying ointment. In the version from Yeats, this could be a mixture that incorporates fly agaric fungus (*Amanita muscaria)*, but I base that almost entirely on the fact that the "red cap" is a key feature of the tale and that particular fungus has a long history of connections to witches and fairies. In both stories, the mixture is activated by the recitation of a short, rhyming phrase, which seems to be a common enough way to trigger witch flight in many stories. In some tales, the non-witch makes a mistake and it causes some sort of comic misfortune, like being lifted up and dropped to the floor unexpectedly. An interesting difference between the two tales comes during the heavy drinking portion of the tale (don't all interesting things come during the heavy drinking portion of the tale?). In the Old World version, James knows his witch lore and remains silent while in flight, but in the "Greasy Witches" variant, Riley has to say

146. Russell and Barnett, *The Granny Curse*, 3–12.

additional magical words while in flight to follow the Dobbs sisters. I've had a gifted witch tell me that when making a profound crossing like this, silence is better, and I trust that idea.

Tales like these seem to make magical theft a sort of game or challenge, a way of testing one's abilities for other forms of witch flight. The thefts are usually targeted at the wealthy, or at least those who "have" rather than those who "have not," and in the Appalachian tale whatever the sisters are plundering, they are using it to welcome travelers lost on their mountain. In a way, they rebalance the resources around them. It's nice to know witches are good for something other than breaking-and-entering, right?

Justice Flights

The last purpose of witch flight to consider is something I am calling "justice," although it may seem much more like vengeance to many. While I get into the specifics of community justice and witchcraft much more fully in chapter six, it may be worth recapping here a central point about why witches do things like curses (or even, to some extent, steal things using magic). The witch often has little or no legal recourse in her favor—she is either outside the law somehow, or the law is not likely to ever be on her side due to her reputation, circumstances (e.g. poverty or an unorthodox lifestyle), or the influence of her enemies. Added to that, she seldom curses in folklore without some sort of provocation first. Her reaction may be overzealous—for example she might blight all the livestock on a farm if the farmer refuses to sell her a pig she particularly likes—but it is rooted in a sense of social obligations that have been overturned or upended by other people first.

To that end, much of the lore of spectral night rides into neighboring homes or farmsteads in the witch lore of pre-modern North America takes for granted that the witch is using her ride as a way to claim some sort of revenge (i.e., justice). One story I relate in more detail in the "Singing Bones" section of this chapter is an account from early New England of witch Betty Booker, who rides a skinflint skipper like a horse all night in retaliation for his lack of generosity and rude behavior.). In a similar story from Maryland in the late nineteenth or early twentieth century, a witch curses a fisherman who refuses her some of his catch, then as he walks home that night she overtakes him and turns him into a personal horse. That may not sound like flight, exactly, but in most cases these spectral horses are ridden great distances in a single night. That implies flying, and indeed this tale says that she rode him "some hundred miles through marsh and brambles and brush" as a punishment for his inhospitable nature.[147]

FIG 9-2: Betty Booker's ride across the New England countryside seems like a little bit of wicked fun at first, but also served to punish the old skipper who had been so ungenerous with his halibut.

SINGING BONES
Old Betty Booker

I cannot help but share one of my favorite tales of hag-riding here, which features all the different curse forms at different times. It involves a nineteenth-century witch in Maine known as "Old Betty Booker" and a local captain named Skipper Perkins. The skipper is greedy and often treats locals poorly and has little charity. In response to a request for "a bit of halibut," Perkins refuses her, which makes her shake her head at him, enacting a curse. He fails to catch any more fish and his ship is damaged in a storm (the curse on property and luck); then when he finally drags himself home to bed that night, he is visited by Old Betty and her coven, who use a magical tool called a witch bridle to mount him and ride him like a horse all over the landscape. He suffers scratches and pricks, bruises and exhaustion, before Betty finally returns him home with the warning not to treat poor old ladies so badly again.[148]

Booker's story is largely the stuff of folklore and fantasy, but Booker herself may have had a connection to a real-world woman named Betsy Booker

147. Carey, *Maryland Folklore*, 53–4.

148. Hutcheson, "Old Betty Booker," 734–35.

who lived near Kittery, Maine in a place known as "Brimstone Hill."[149] Betty's night ride may seem a severe response to someone acting uncharitably, but in this case she is acting not just on her own behalf, but on the behalf of the community. Skipper Perkins is not acting in a way that supports community values of charity and compassion, and for that, he is treated like a brute animal and asked to learn a very specific lesson. Curses and justice, it seems, go hand in hand.

African Americans similarly have night-flying witch stories, one of the most well-known of which is the "boo hag." This witch slips off her skin and then rides out at night to punish errant husbands, young men who play with "bad girls" (likely construed as sexually promiscuous women or prostitutes), or the children of slaves. The boo hag is usually defeated by filling her stripped skin with pepper and salt, which makes it impossible for her to put back on before sunrise, destroying her.[150] These "skin-changing" sorts of night flights have parallels in stories of *lechuzas* (owl witches) and other animal-transformation witch forms from the American Southwest and Mexico.[151]

Justice flights could also take the form of purely spectral attacks, in which a witch's ghost, spirit, or "fetch" form would be sent out of the witch's body to attack someone. In some cases, these attacks were designed solely to psychologically torment the victim or their family, while in other cases there are reports of pinches, pokes, slaps, and blows delivered by the spectral witch. This spirit-form became a central crux of the Salem witch trials, which created the Court of Oyer and Terminer ("to hear and to determine") specifically to handle spectral attacks in those cases. Famed Virginia witch Grace Sherwood, the "Witch of Pungo," was accused

149. I base my assertion that Booker may have been real on historical accounts found in historian George Alexander Emery's *The Ancient City of Georgiana and the Modern Town of York (Maine) from Its Earliest Settlement to the Present Time* and *Maine Pioneer Settlements: Old York*, although these accounts mix Booker's story with several other reputed witches in the York area.

150. One variant of the story tells of a charm against a boo hag that involves counting out thirty-three needles or pins, and putting them into a bottle with a cork when a boo hag visits, which will send her away and keep her from doing any harm to that household again so long as the bottle remains sealed. For a wonderful collection of boo hag stories, see Henry Louis Gates, Jr.'s and Maria Tatar's *The Annotated African American Folktales*.

151. Bowles, *Border Lore*, loc. 1072–1118; García, Nasario, *Brujerias*, 76–79.

of making these attacks on her neighbors (most of whom had accused her of various wrongdoings and most of whom she would then countersue in response to their accusations).[152]

The divisions here are not hard and fast, of course. A witch raiding a neighbor's pantry on a theft flight may also be administering a form of justice or vengeance by reclaiming goods that are being unfairly hoarded. Some witches soared out to the sabbat bearing stolen goods—or people, especially children and infants, if you believe some of the most sensational accounts—as a way of placating their infernal helpers and masters. Is a child stolen from the home a theft or revenge? Is a sabbatical ride on a rude neighbor, mounted like a horse, also justice? As with so many things in witchcraft, the borders between things bleed and seep into one another, leaving a lot of gray spaces for us to see (and perhaps a few greasy footprints).

Pitchforks, Skunk Grease, and Red Caps: Methods of Flight

The "why" of flight in folklore shapes the experience of witchcraft for the witch and those around her. Her purposes are her own, and we are obliged to make room in the sky for her. The "how" of flight is another critical detail, and on this point the methods are varied. Partly this is because there are no singular, "one-true" ways of witch flight. Cultural, regional, and individual differences play a part in how witches move about, and even within a particular time or place multiple forms of flight may be considered typical of a witch. We do, however, see a number of methods repeated often enough to draw some general conclusions about them, which is just what I will do in this section.

Staves and Brooms

This is the method we often think of first, with a witch climbing onto a broomstick and physically soaring into the sky. Broomsticks are a bit of a latecomer to the game, and many tales point to other farm implements like rakes or pitchforks as the likely steeds for witch flight. Domestic tools like cooking spoons and spindles are also used, building on the witch's associations with the hearth and her subversion of conventional "women's" roles. Slavic witch Baba Yaga soars in a mortar and pestle, for example. In some older versions of tales, the witch will usually mount the broom

152. Howe, *Penguin Book of Witches*, 184–85, 214–19.

"backwards," with the bristle end up, like a hobby horse. There has been a good bit of back-and-forth argument over the use of these poles as applicators of flying ointments, which is not something I will rehash here. Instead, I will say that witches mounting these objects are sometimes presented as nude, sometimes not, sometimes flying physically, sometimes not, and it does not seem to change the outcome of the witch's flight all that much; she still visits those who have wronged her or soars off to a sabbat just the same.

I will also share that I really enjoy this method of flight as a form of ritual. During May Day, Midsummer, and Hallows bonfires[153], I have often taken a broom (one that I made by hand) and practiced the old custom of fire-leaping. I wait until the fire is a manageable size, but still big enough to be a slight challenge, and then I stand astride the broom, charge, and leap over the flames to the other side. I am not recommending this method, but as a ritual this has given me a unique "flight" experience and I often seem to feel very much "out-of-body" when I do it.

Flying Ointments/"Witches' Grease"

To those who study witchcraft, the lore of flying ointments—an oily salve that gave witches the reputed power of flight, although the nature of just what "flight" is varies—can be an in-depth line of study all by itself.[154] "Young Goodman Brown" author Nathaniel Hawthorne is thought to have penned a short article (published anonymously in a periodical written almost entirely by Hawthorne and his sister) on witch ointments for *The American Magazine* in 1836 in which he repeated an older recipe that required "the fat of children, digged [sic.] out of their graves, and the juices of smallage, cinquefoil, and wolfsbane, mingled with the fine meal of wheat."[155] The inclusion of wolfsbane, or aconite, in the recipe reflects the common belief that these mixtures required the use of toxic herbs (aconite is quite deadly, and similar herbs like belladonna or mandrake root appear in other recipes). These would be brewed

153. For a good discussion of bonfires and holidays like these, see Ronald Hutton's *The Stations of the Sun: A History of the Ritual Year in Britain* (New York: Oxford Univ. Press, 1996).

154. If you are a serious student of entheogens—substances used in religious or spiritual ceremonies to achieve altered states of consciousness—I would highly recommend Dale Pendell's three-volume *Pharmako* series, which goes into incredible detail on the history and practice of using these formulae to achieve various kinds of "flight."

155. Cherry, "Sources of Hawthorne's 'Young Goodman Brown,'" 343.

into a fat-soluble (the "fat of children") concoction that blended with an oily base. While the use of children's fat may have an eerily evil impact in the stories, the use of animal fat to render salves and ointments is incredibly common. In addition to readily available lard, we also see the frequent use of wild animal fats, especially "bear" or "skunk" grease as a delivery method for topical treatments.[156]

Ointments made today are sometimes done with vegan substitutes or with reclaimed animal fats (although it is crucial you find a trustworthy source to avoid poisoning and death, which put a real damper on flight).[157] To activate the power of the grease, the witch needed to know magical words or phrases, like the "Willie Waddie" rhyme in the Appalachian tale. The "flight" of the grease is usually represented as a real one, with the witch suddenly sliding up a chimney or through a keyhole as in the "Greasy Witches" story from Appalachia, but a number of tales also seem to indicate that once greased, the witch seemed to fall down in a stupor or as if dead while her spirit made the flight.

Transformation

In the American Southwest, a number of stories from tribes like the Pueblo people or the modern-day Diné (Navajo) people mention transformations into creatures like coyotes or "skinwalker" beasts. I deal a bit more fully with shape-shifting in chapter thirteen, but I mention it here because several stories discuss witches transforming into night-flying creatures. Romans used the word *strix* to mean "owl," and that may have eventually given rise to a similar word for "witch," even to the point that the contemporary Italian word for witch is *strega*.[158] The *lechuza* owl-witch from the U.S.-Mexican borderlands is a transformed enchantress, and some accounts of the boo hag from African American lore also describe her as being very birdlike in her flight. Animals like bats or crows could sometimes be thought of as witches in disguise, as well.

---

156. Milnes, *Signs, Cures, & Witchery*, 98.

157. My personal recommendation is the Bane Folk plant medicine shop, run by Sarah Anne Lawless. She has a depth of experience with these formulae that goes into her handmade products, and she is very, *very* careful about how she blends them. You can find more at her website: https://banefolk.com.

158. Hutton, *The Witch*, 69–71.

- **Animals**—Even if a witch didn't transform herself into an animal, she might well ride one into the sky on her way to a sabbat. Multiple engravings and printed depictions of witch flight show her astride a goat, calf, or pig—usually mounted backwards—as she soars over houses to the tops of mountain peaks for her holiday gathering. Virtually any animal could be used this way, but farm animals are some of the most frequently represented. Horses were sometimes thought to have been ridden by witches in the night if they were tired and damp with sweat in the morning.

FIG 9–3: Witch bridles allowed a witch to ride a human like a horse.

- **Witch Bridles**—Of course, why ride a horse when a man will do just as well? Plenty of stories tell of a human being who has earned the ire of a witch only to find that he is now going to be used as her "steed" as she travels around, as we see in the case of both Betty Booker and the witch who rode the fisherman in the story from Maryland a few pages back. To accomplish this flight, the rider made use of a special "witch bridle," a magical object that rendered the wearer completely under the witch's power. One folklore collector claimed that this instrument was made from horsehair, tow (a rough-twisted fiber like jute or twine), and yellow birch.[159] The bridle could be turned against the witch,

159. Botkin, *Treasury of New England Folklore*, 226–28; Cox, "The Witch Bridle," 203–209.

however, if the one being ridden managed to pull it off somehow. The power of the horsehair in the bridle would likely be transformative, while the tow uses knot magic to "bind" the power and will of the target. The birch would have rendered the victim pliant to the witch's will, and forced him to obey her commands.

- **Fire**—This is essentially another form of transformation, but instead of becoming an animal the witch will simply transfigure herself into a floating flame or a ball of fire. A belief in this type of night-flying witch can be found in the Caribbean, where she is known as the *soucouyant*, and behaves a bit like a mixture of a witch and a vampire. Certain versions of this witch are also called a "loogaroo," which shows a connection to the French term for werewolf, the *loup-garou*. The Algonquin wendigo, while not strictly made from fire, occasionally seems to leave a pile of ash after it takes a victim, which may indicate some connection to this transformation (although the wendigo is *not* a witch, but a cannibalistic spirit).
- **Spectral Forms**—Witches who send their spirit—sometimes referred to as their "haint," "fetch," or "double"—seem to be able to do so with or without the aid of these other tools and techniques. Several stories show witches whose physical bodies lie at home in their beds while their spirits roam about to torment neighbors. Sometimes these spirit forms take over animals, like cats or rabbits, and the physical harm done to the critter will show up as harm on the witch's body once her spirit returns. These spirit-form flights may simply be a type of lucid dreaming or even astral projection, in modern parlance. There is also the phenomenon of the "Old Hag," or "mara," a creature who would visit a person in the night, sit on their chest, and drain away their life. This literal "night-mare" riding experience has been linked to the medical phenomenon of sleep paralysis, in which a person consciously wakens during the night, but their body—which is paralyzed by the brain during REM sleep to prevent injury—will not respond.[160] The Old Hag may be medically explainable, but that doesn't mean that folkloric ways of understanding her are entirely wrong, either. If a person has anxiety about their social environment, including the way their neighbors are being

160. See Hufford, *The Terror that Comes in the Night: An Experience-Centered Study of Supernatural Assault Traditions.*

treated, waking to an Old Hag sitting on their chest might very well be a sort of consciousness projection of some kind. Or, it could just be a bad dream. Only the witch in the next house over knows for sure.

DIRT UNDER THE NAILS
Dream Flight

One form of witch flight that most people can at least attempt is using your dreams as a launchpad to spectral soaring. The goal here is not exactly lucid dreaming—which implies that you control what happens in the dream-space—but rather a more broadly guided "setting" to your dream that allows you to experience the flight in a relaxed, visceral way.

To do this, you will simply need a comfortable place to sleep and a journal or some paper. If you like, you can drink a bit of dream- or sleep-stimulating tea, such as mugwort with a bit of honey (if you are medically able; be careful of allergies and other reactions). Before you climb into bed and go to sleep, take several deep breaths. Tell yourself where you will be going on your night flight. Picture it as clearly as you can in your mind. Draw a map of it in your journal if you need to, and write down details about it. Do all you can to prepare your mind to go to this space, and then relax. Let yourself drift off and dream.

Whatever you dream about, write it down as soon as you wake up. Jot down notes, scribbles, doodles of whatever you can. Just get it down on paper. Then go back later in the day and reread what you wrote. Try to write it out again, as clearly as you can remember it, adding any details you can recall that you may have missed when you first woke up. Reread the journal entry again before bed, then repeat the process of breathing, telling yourself where to go, writing it down, and falling asleep.

It may take a few tries to get this to work consistently and effectively, but when it does you will be surprised how clear this kind of night flight can be (I once had a remarkable dream flight where I visited my childhood home and managed to see changes and additions that the new owners had made, which turned out to be fairly accurate when I followed up on them later).

Rise Like Smoke: Listening to the Night-Flying Witch

We may be horrified by what we see witches do in folktales like the boo hag, where she preys upon the children of slaves. We may be scandalized by the idea of witches coaxing lost travelers into marrying them by leaving them for dead and drunk in a storehouse only to rescue them at the last moment. We could be disgusted by stereotypical images of witches kneeling before the sabbat Devil and giving him a profane kiss on his hindquarters, or mixing up salves and ointments from the fat of dead infants. What if we were as fearless as the witch, though? What if we did not turn away right at the moment of shock and horror, and instead steadied our gaze and looked closer to see why she is really flying out at night?

In the fall of 2017, then-outgoing American Folklore Society (AFS) President Kay Turner shared her paper "The Witch in Flight" at the Society's annual meeting. Turner, a feminist lesbian queer woman and scholar, took a closer look at a boo hag tale "The Witch Wife" from Americo Paredes' *Folktales of Mexico* and the artistic interpretations of witch flight by artists like Hans Baldung Grien and Francisco Goya. She sees witches as a transgressive and contrary example of womanhood, reveling in their "unnaturalness" and "abnormality," rejecting a dualistic worldview of good and evil, male and female, right and wrong. As Turner puts it, "witches bitch the binary."[161] Not only that, but the night-flying witch unsettles the troubling reduction of women to angelic figures of motherhood and childbearing or satanic figures of lust and seduction. She is a creature who takes back the power from male-dominated culture around her. Turner points out that the witch-wife flies out from her home, and that her husband wants to "punish her" by chopping up her skin and salting it. Of course, when she returns and cannot put her skin back on, she is distraught, and flies away into the air, becoming an omen of death to all who hear her. The witch-wife, though, escapes from an abusive husband and strict domestic and social control through this story, which seems to be exactly why she was slipping her skin and flying out at night in the first place. She needs a time and place of her own—she will be a wife by day, so long as she can also be a witch by night. The husband's brutal control of his wife's literal flesh—a strong metaphor for hyper-masculine marital roles—is undone when she becomes flying bones. In losing her skin, she gains power, and the husband loses all control of her. What Turner sees in this story is a

161. Turner, "The Witch in Flight: AFS Presidential Address."

tale of patriarchal abuse and feminist rejection, or as she puts it, "the witch-wife flies in the face of men and gods who cannot conceive of women as their equal."[162]

The flying witches we have seen in this chapter all fly in the face of their own abuses, whether individual or social. Why do boo hags murder slave children in African American tales? For one, these witches are frequently portrayed as the master's wives or daughters, and slave children are frequently the master's children as well, given the brutal rape-based slavery system of reproduction (or, as it is sometimes portrayed in nineteenth-century slaver literature, "breeding"). A witch terrifying neighbors who are ungenerous also seems an obvious quest for justice, but what if we also see that the witch may be howling through the night because her neighbors refuse to see or hear her during the day, especially if she is suffering from things like abuse at home? What if we look at the sabbat flights from the lens of a woman who has been taught that her local church and religious community is charged with caring for the poor, but she has felt none of that generosity herself? How would we see her diabolic revels, then, at a ceremony where she is literally feasting, dancing, and surrounded by others like herself who teach her spells and give her power?

The witch in flight tells us not to be afraid, and not to accept the proposition of "either/or." She is a "both/and" sort of woman. She tells us that we can do more than we are told we can, and that sometimes we have to become frightening to free ourselves from fear. We fly towards our fears with open arms, and we bitch the binary on our broomsticks.

THE WORK—Flying Things

Witches are not the only things that fly. Many of the stories we read about tell of witches transforming into already winged creatures like birds or bats or even insects. Since folk magic and folkloric witchcraft are heavily invested in seeing and understanding the world around us through enchanted eyes, what happens if you spend time watching the creatures that already inhabit the air and sky? What happens if you look for their magic?

Spend time with flying things. Take a few minutes each day, an hour or two a week perhaps, and watch the birds. Study the bees and the buzzards. Observe the swoop of a petrel or a gull if you're near the seashore. Spot owls and hawks if you live

162. Ibid.

closer to forests, and see how they hunt and soar. Look to bats emerging from their haunts at dusk to gather their meal of insects, and study the buzzing fly or mosquito even as it drives you mad. What is driving the flight of these creatures? Can you move your mind into theirs, understand their motions and the mechanics of their bodies with your own somehow? What if you imitate them? Mimic their soaring and flapping? What do you learn about them, and about yourself?

What sort of flight could you manage?

More importantly, what sort of fear will you conquer in your flight?

Recommended Reading

Pharmako/Poeia: Plant Powers, Poisons, and Herbcraft, by Dale Pendell. This is the first in Pendell's series of *Pharmako* books, which provide some of the most detailed information on the "poison path" of entheogen use. If you have any interest in flying ointments or the use of herbs to provide various forms of non-corporeal witch flight, this book is the place to start.

The Witch's Broom: Craft, Lore, & Magick of Broomsticks, by Deborah Blake. This is part of the "Witch's Tools" series from Llewellyn, and Blake is well-known for her accessible, personable writing. Here she turns her warm tone to the topic of brooms and broomsticks, and provides some interesting lore about flight and riding in addition to other broom-based magical work.

Video: "The Witch in Flight," a presidential address from Kay Turner, outgoing president of the American Folklore Society. From the AFS YouTube channel: https://www.youtube.com/watch?v=ALw2Zw_4hyI. Turner's astoundingly insightful reading into the role that night plays in creating a safe space for magical transformation is one of my absolute favorite things, and I highly recommend watching this video (I think I may even be in there somewhere cheering and applauding).

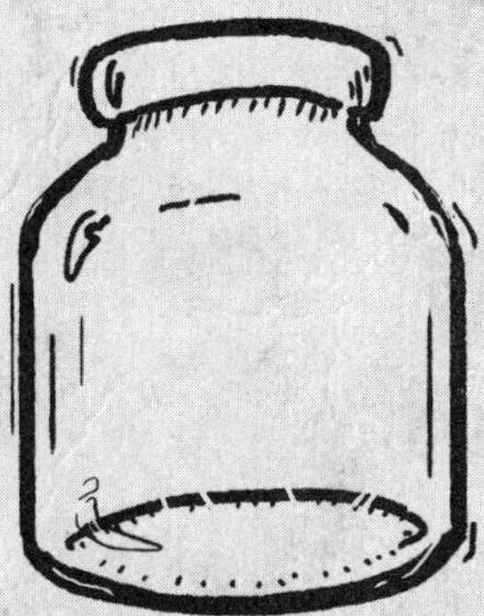

SIXTH RITE: CHEWING THE ROOT

Or, the Material Miscellany of Folk Witchcraft from Gathering Ingredients to Crafting Enchanted Objects

"Originally I would tell people, when they asked for my thoughts about some arcane system of magic in which I had no interest, 'I'm just a rocks and string kind of guy.' This usually stopped these lines of inquiry, and it was actually true. In time I started to call it dirt sorcery, and rocks and string remain important parts of my practice!"*

* Wachter, *Six Ways: Approaches & Entries for Practical*, 155.

CHAPTER TEN

Hidden in Plain Sight—Everyday Magical Ingredients

If we imagine ourselves as witches, we think of ourselves in a little cottage secluded in the woods, bundles of herbs drying from the rafters, arcane ingredients stored in strange old bottles. I'm not knocking the aesthetic appeal of that image, and I know some people who make this a reality (good on them!). However, we also need to account for the fact that most folk magic doesn't come from strange and obscure herbs imported from exotic locales, and that while growing our own supplies of anything is a definite goal, we shouldn't be afraid to turn to what we have and use it.

This chapter will be a little different than many of the others, in that it will be "tour" of an imagined home, a home that could be just about anyone's. We will wander through rooms, picking up and putting down objects to see what magical purposes we might find for them in folklore historically, and how we might imagine using them now, too. We will begin by looking in those familiar places like bedrooms, bathrooms, and kitchens to see the potential magic they house in their wares and furnishings, as well as how specific rooms can become spaces of magical action as when, for example, a child's bedroom becomes a necromantic portal during a sleepover Ouija board session. This is not a chapter about the quirkier magical ingredients such as bones, which will be covered more in the next chapter. Nor will this chapter explore the crafting of magical tools and talismans from the mundane objects listed here, as that is better suited to chapter twelve. Instead, this is a chapter looking at the very ordinary and everyday sort of magic that is likely already around you in the places and things within your reach.

FIG 10-1: One common method for preventing witches and other supernatural forces from entering a home includes filling jars with beans, rice, sand, or rocks and placing them near the door.

Magic Under Your Sink and Enchantment in Your Cupboard

Every room in your home has the potential for magic in it if you know where to look, but the best place to start might be before you even enter your home.

Doorways

In folklore, the concept of the "liminal space" is very important, because it often represents a location that is not fully of one world or another, but a gray zone between two places. If you've read myths and legends, you've likely encountered stories of heroes who could only accomplish a task or be killed while they were in some paradoxical situation, such as "neither walking nor riding on a horse," in which case the hero would likely be riding a goat with their feet dragging the ground to meet the criteria of a prophecy.

We cross through these liminal spaces all the time, if you think about it. When you stand in your doorway, are you outside or inside? The door is open, so it's basically outside, right? But at the same time, your door and the threshold are still part of your house, so it's kind of inside, too. The wonderful thing about these spaces is that they are so useful in folk magic. Doorways are often the best place to put up charms or wards to protect your home because they are charged with this "in-between" magic. You might lay down a line of salt or red brick dust—common in Hoodoo and Southern Conjure magic—in order to create a barrier against anything harmful coming inside. You might anoint your door with holy water or olive oil to provide a barrier and a blessing simultaneously. Many who practice the Chinese house alignment system of feng shui will place mirrors near the front threshold as a way of deflecting harm, a practice mirrored in other parts of the world as well. A spell derived from Mexican folk magic recommends putting obsidian stone chips into the frame of your doorway to cut any evil spirit that tries to cross over[163], and a number of European traditions state that leaving a jar near your door and filling it with small objects—rice, sand, pebbles, or something similar—will deter wicked witches or things like vampires from entering because they'd be forced to count everything in the jar before doing so.

You can also use the passage through the front door as a ritual space. Bri Saussy, in her 2019 book *Making Magic*, discusses setting up a small altar space or even just a little oasis of calm by your front door so that when you enter after a day of work, you can leave your "business" life out in the world, and feel welcomed and comforted by your home every day.[164]

The Cleaning Closet

One of the deepest wells of domestic magic, other than cooking, is cleaning. The use of cleaning agents and methods as a form of enchantment goes back centuries in North America, and a clean home often indicated a place that was protected from evil influences. If you think about what's in your cleaning closet, you might find a few of the following:

- **Pine-Sol**—This commercial floor cleaner basically evolved out of Hoodoo floor washes in Mississippi when chemist Henry A. Cole used local pine forests to extract oil to use in a household floor wash. Pine already had a reputation in African American cleaning solutions for being extremely effective as well as nice-smelling, and folk beliefs about pine's potency for purifying and stripping away spiritual dirt as well as physical dirt made the Pine-Sol brand extremely popular.[165] Beyond the traditional pine scent, floor cleaners often use lemons as a fragrance agent and chemical enhancement. Lemons have a cut-and-clear

163. Anonymous, *Magical Powers of the Holy Death*, 23.

164. Saussy, *Making Magic*, 35–46.

165. Yronwode, *Hoodoo Herb & Root Magic*, 155.

effect on a space, and have long been associated with destroying curses and breaking hexes.

- **Ammonia**—This is a somewhat harsh chemical, but one used since ancient times. Author and folk magician Draja Mickaharic recommends a simple floor wash of ammonia and salt added to mop water, and it really makes a wonderful cleansing and protecting wash water.[166] It can really neutralize almost anything thrown at you, magically speaking, and it disinfects beautifully. Mickaharic also recommends a little ammonia down every drain when you finish cleaning (just a teaspoon or so), to finish off your magical housecleaning.
- **Vinegar**—The medieval formula called Four Thieves Vinegar is popular as a counter-curse wash, and as a protective mix-in for a mop water (see chapter eleven for a recipe). But really, any vinegar will help get rid of unwanted energies and protect the home from invaders and malicious forces. If the scent is strong enough, it may protect you from visitors altogether.
- **Urine**—This one is very traditional in Hoodoo, though much frowned upon in modern use.[167] It has, however, been long used as a cleaning agent, and a little urine diluted in some mop water can be very powerful for "marking your territory" and protecting the home. It can also instill a sense of good luck in the place, and ensure fidelity in your mate and passion from your lover—if they don't catch you doing it, of course.

There are lots of other cleaning agents out there that you can use, of course. Almost anything scented probably has at least some tenuous connection to a magical formula, so a little homework can help you transform that bottle of Mop-N-Glo into a powerful apothecary's potion.

---

166. Mickaharic, *Spiritual Cleansing*, 94–5.

167. I currently have quite a reputation because I let it be known once that I sometimes take a *tiny* bit of urine and mix it with a soapy solution to wash my front door and create a magical boundary line. This practice is extremely common in Southern folk magic, but tends to make a few people squeamish. Just wait until they hear about what you can do with menstrual blood…

FIG 10-2: Many specialty shops and even drugstores in places where Hoodoo and Southern Conjure are found carry premade jars of magical "condition" oils and formulas designed to help with specific situations.

DIRT UNDER THE NAILS
Floor Washes

Magical floor washes do more than just wipe away dirt. In traditional Hoodoo, they can be used to enhance magical effects in a space, providing protection, business boosts, or even romantic potency where they are used. Consider trying some of these formulae—usually available for purchase in magical supply shops or online, but especially try to find them made by African American creators to support the community whence this magic comes—and seeing if they add any extra magical "oomph" to your cleaning routine. One of the best-known examples is the hex-breaking Chinese Wash, which reputedly derives from a mixture sold in Chinatown (which Chinatown is never particularly clear) and contains things like lemongrass, vetiver, and broom straws. Other formulas include mixtures such as Van Van (for luck and purification), Fast Money (a spicy sweet mix used to draw rapid prosperity), Wall of Flame/Fiery Wall (a protective formula), or Chuparosa (which means "hummingbird" in Spanish and is thought to bring love and attraction with its sweet scent). If you want to try to make a simple version of a cleansing/purifying floor wash yourself, brew a strong "tea" of the following:

- Nine lemons, cut into pieces
- A handful of pine needles
- A handful of salt
- Nine crushed eggshells

Strain and add this liquid to your mop bucket, topping with hot water. In some systems, such as Hoodoo, tradition dictates that you would mop from the back of your home to the front, and dispose of the mop water by tossing it out your front door or in the direction of the rising sun.

One important magical tool we find in the cleaning closet is the infamous "witch's broom." Many traditionalist witches insist that a broom used for mundane cleaning should not be used for magical work, and others claim that a broom can be used for both. Historically, of course, a broom—sometimes called a "besom" in British sources—would have been a domestic tool *and* a magical one. Leaving aside the broom as an instrument of flight (which is better discussed in chapter nine), we still encounter a lot of folklore about brooms as magical objects. Ancient Roman rites involving brooms offered protection to laboring mothers and newborn children, for example.[168] Laying a broom across a doorway prevents a witch from entering, as well (assuming you should want such a thing).[169] Want to get rid of a guest overstaying their welcome? Put a broom with the bushy part turned up in the corner behind the door, and they'll soon leave.[170]

Brooms not only protected, but predicted, as a number of superstitions relate to brooms falling, breaking, or sweeping in ways that tell the future of a member of the household. Sweeping under someone's feet was almost always a bad sign. In most cases, it meant the person who had been "swept" would not marry.[171] If you break a broom handle you will soon break someone's heart, too.[172] Sweeping the house after dark was also thought to bring sorrow in love and romance. In some cases, though,

168. Burriss, *Taboo, Magic, Spirits,* 28–9.

169. Puckett, *Folk Beliefs,* 156–57; Thomas, *Kentucky Superstitions,* 282; Randolph, *Ozark Magic,* 281–84.

170. Puckett, *Folk Beliefs,* 317–18.

171. Hyatt, *Folklore from Adams County,* 227–28; Puckett, *Folk Beliefs,* 397–98; Randolph, *Ozark Magic,* 182.

172. Hyatt, *Folklore from Adams County,* 228.

if you did find yourself sweeping at night, you could expect a "gentleman caller."[173] Young unmarried women could wet the bristles of a broom and sprinkle the water around their houses to invite love into their lives.[174] If an engaged girl dropped a broom, she could divine her romantic future by the way it fell: if the handle pointed north, she or her fiancé would break their engagement. A south-pointing broom meant she would marry him and live a happy life.[175]

The connection between marriage and brooms goes beyond the bride seeing one, as well. In the antebellum United States, when African American slaves had few or no rights, marriage was often not a legally binding union for them. Instead, cultural and social marriages would be sealed by "jumping the broom" together.[176]

One of the most interesting themes in broom lore has to do with relocating a household. If one is moving, for example, one should not take the old broom along. Likewise, when you are moving, you should break your old broom and burn it before leaving the house. The superstitious believe that a new broom should be one of the first things you bring into a new home.[177]

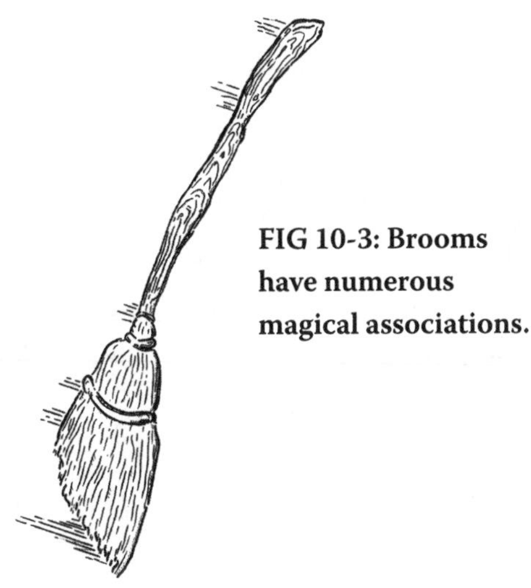

FIG 10-3: Brooms have numerous magical associations.

173. Thomas, *Kentucky Superstitions*, 136–37; Puckett, *Folk Beliefs*, 395–96.

174. Hyatt, *Folklore from Adams County*, 228.

175. Hyatt, *Folklore from Adams County*, 227.

176. Chireau, *Black Magic*, 87–88; Raboteau, *Slave Religion*, 228–30.

177. Thomas, *Kentucky Superstitions*, 134; Puckett, *Folk Beliefs*, 397–98.

Bathrooms

Taking a shower or a bath as a child can feel like a blessing (when bubbles and toys are involved) or a chore (almost any other time). As we get older, time in the bathroom somehow becomes a luxury. It is time to ourselves, and bathrooms offer us a sanctum where we can occasionally escape from the demands and needs of others—although, as many parents will attest, those demands are not completely barricaded by a bathroom door. Perhaps because of the bathroom's combined utility and privacy, people have developed a number of important rituals around bathroom use, some of them very magical. Looking around the washroom proper we can see plenty of potential magic waiting to happen.

A long soak in a bathtub can be intensely relaxing, but there are also a number of traditions that employ bathing as a way of aligning ourselves spiritually or magically. After all, as some witchy folk have pointed out, a bathtub is essentially a large cauldron.[178] In traditions derived from Africans kidnapped from their homelands such as Hoodoo, Vodoun, or Lukumi/Santeria, bathing can be used to cleanse a person of hurtful spirits or draw specific spirits and benefits to the bather. Some simple but popular additions to a bath include:

- **Lemons**—useful for cutting and clearing away any spiritual attachments (often both good and bad, so be careful how you use this idea).
- **Hyssop**—a ritual purification herb that is easy to grow. It is specifically mentioned in Psalm 51, and thus has a potent ability to remove "sin"—broadly conceived—or any undesirable trait.
- **Rose petals**—as you would probably guess, these are great for drawing love to you, or for helping you love yourself (and the body you're in).
- **Black walnuts**—washed and often boiled before being added to the bath, they make a dark infusion that can stain (they are also an excellent fabric dye), so be careful. Magically, they remove curses and obstacles from your path.
- **Salt**—both sea salt and Epsom salts can be used here, and they are good for warding off evil spirits or harm.
- **Cider vinegar**—a bath that reportedly strips away harmful energy and also makes the skin softer and better-looking.

178. Zakroff, *The Witch's Cauldron*, 203–208.

- **Coffee**—adding strong, already brewed coffee to a bath adds vitality, and is supposed to be good for boosting energy or helping your body heal after an injury (obviously consult with a physician on this point).
- **Milk**—milk baths are thought to enhance beauty, especially for women or people who wish to present as feminine. Goat's milk is considered particularly good for beauty in some places.
- **Water**—this may seem a bit silly, but various kinds of water added to a bath are thought to boost the magical effects of bathing for the user. Sea water is thought to be purifying in many Mediterranean bathing spells, while holy water is frequently used in Irish and Mexican folk cures. Water infused with moonlight (left in the light of a full moon) can also be a powerful ingredient in magical baths.[179]

In many traditions, the bathing ritual itself requires certain actions, such as washing from the head down to remove something (like an evil spirit or a bad habit, for example), while washing from the feet up adds power to the bather (such as bringing love or prosperity).

If you shower more than you bathe—and many people only have access to a shower—you can still get many of the benefits of a spiritual bath by infusing your chosen ingredients in a jar, straining off the solids, and using the liquid during your body washing (but be aware, the magical formula water will be much colder than the water coming from your showerhead!).

A toilet may seem like a strange place to work magic, but toilets have a long provenance in spellwork. In folk magical traditions from the Appalachians and other parts of the South, the historical outhouse was the place where a vengeful person might drop a poppet or other magical representation of a target in order to really ruin their life. Similarly, several candle-based curses call for candles to be extinguished by dunking the flame in toilet water in order to really seal the doom of the intended victim.

Toilets can also be a place to collect an ingredient used in folk magic that often causes people to scrunch up their noses: urine. In Hoodoo, for example, the "strongest" urine, magically speaking, is the first release of the morning, and so collecting

179. Illes, *The Encyclopedia of 5,000 Spells*, 207–215; Mickaharic, *Spiritual Cleansing*, 39–60.

a bit of urine in the toilet before a morning shower can be useful (not least because you can shower off right afterwards).

The bathroom mirror also has some magical potential. I know several people who are terrified of mirrors, especially mirrors in a dark bathroom. This may all stem from playing sleepover games as children, but it also speaks to the power of the bathroom mirror as a portal to strange and uncanny places. When we do summoning rituals like "Bloody Mary" using a mirror, we expect to see our world reflected back at us, but with a twist—a person approaching behind us, for example. Bathroom mirrors, which are often the largest mirrors in the home, thus provide a very powerful gateway for working with the Otherworld. Holding a séance or a scrying session in a bathroom can be potent because the mirror seems like a door waiting to open.

Bedrooms

We may feel vulnerable in the bathroom (as anyone who has ever sped through washing their face after watching *Psycho* can attest), but we have some of our highest vulnerability in the bedroom. Where else are you going to lie unconscious for six to twelve hours a day, protected by a few layers of cloth? Because of that vulnerability, we do see a few spells regarding safety during sleeping hours pop up. For example, stories from the British Isles and the Appalachian Mountains both tell of leaving a sieve over the bedroom door handle as a way to deter malevolent spirits, witches, and vampires (they must count the holes as they would the grains of sand in the jars by the threshold described earlier).[180]

Spellwork in the bedroom, however, often focuses on other areas of vulnerability. Sleep and dreaming are seen in many cultures as times when we are susceptible to spiritual attack. The well-documented phenomenon of "hag-riding" or the "nightmare" who sits on a person's chest while they sleep has been linked to the medical condition of sleep paralysis, and some research has indicated that folk responses to this affliction are as effective as medical ones.[181] The ubiquitous "dream catcher" derives from very specific lore in the Ojibwe Nation about preventing these sorts of attacks during sleep. The spiderweb-like design is supposed to entangle harmful entities much in the same way the sieve stops them at the door. Some people leave

180. Davis, *The Silver Bullet*, 132–33.

181. See Hufford, *The Terror that Comes in the Night.*

a glass of water by their bedside both in the event of nighttime thirst and so that their soul will not wander far in search of water, and thus be able to find its way back before morning. Pieces of iron, such as railroad spikes or iron frying pans, are sometimes placed under the bed to fend off invading spirits, as well, as iron is thought to weaken or upset them.

Another area in which we are often deeply vulnerable is our intimacy with another person, and that gets reflected in bedroom lore as well. Plenty of charms focus on heightening the allure of the bedroom. Even the trope of rose petals scattered on the bed is an extension of love magic, with the red roses and their soft petals acting as an invitation to sensuality. Spritzes of fragrances such as vanilla, jasmine, or carnation are reputed to inspire passion and desire for those who tangle themselves in the sheets. Lavender is used for men to entice other men, a fragrance secret often used by male sex workers in the nineteenth and twentieth centuries. Other charms include stashing a lodestone—sometimes anointed with a formula like "Look Me Over" or "Fast Love"—between the mattress and box spring or under the bed, with the thought that the magnet will draw a lover to bed.

Beyond seduction, however, an enormous number of charms focus on fidelity and keeping a bedmate faithful. Several Hoodoo-based spells involve a woman using a red thread or yarn to measure her partner's sex, then wetting it with their combined sexual fluids and knotting it to ensure they will be unable to perform with anyone else.[182] One simple charm involves taking two items of clothing—one from each partner, such as underwear or socks—and tying them together in a knot. This is then left latched half-in, half-out of a trunk or between the mattress and box spring to hold a lover. A Mexican folk charm involves tying two large *chiles pasillas* in a cross with a red ribbon and hiding it under the bed or pillow to ensure fidelity.[183]

The combinations of knots and the intimate space of the bedroom seems to be the fundamental connection between many of these spells, and doing things like "tying" a lover often seem like an imposition on a person's free will to us now. However, it is worth remembering that in many situations, a vulnerable partner—often a woman—would lose things like financial security or a parent to help with childrearing if the philandering partner decided to bolt permanently. With little legal

182. Hurston, "Hoodoo in America," 366; Hyatt, *Hoodoo-Conjuration-Witchcraft-Rootwork*, 917.

183. Madsen, *A Guide to Mexican Witchcraft*, 81.

recourse and intense social stigmas around divorce and separation, acts of love-binding were sometimes acts of stabilization and addressing injustice (which can still be true today).

Finally, the bedroom as a ritual space can often be transformed into a gateway to the Otherworld in much the same way a bathroom could be. The presence of mirrors, low lighting, privacy, and comfort allows a bedroom to host necromantic rites like slumber party Ouija board sessions or small ancestral altars readily (for example, with Mexican *retablos*).[184] And, of course, we can't forget about the early magic of a child's favorite blanket or stuffed animal acting as a protector against invading monsters from the liminal spaces of inside the closet or under the bed!

DIRT UNDER THE NAILS
Spirit Water

One bedroom ritual that I regularly practice is to leave a glass of water near the bed, but not to drink. Instead, place the water in a glass or bowl in the room where you sleep and leave it there overnight as a combination offering/trap for spirits. Spirits who come in search of sustenance will choose the water over draining the sleeper in most cases, and what's more, the reflective surface of the water can act as a transfixing mirror for many harmful spirits.

Kitchens

Of all the rooms in the house to inspire magical work, the kitchen easily takes the cake, if you'll pardon the expression. In contemporary magical practice, there is even a whole branch of witchcraft called "kitchen witchery," which involves using cooking, cleaning, herbs, spices, and appliances for magical purposes. While I will be digging into the potential ingredients in a witch's spice rack when I tackle supermarket sorcery in the next chapter, tools and techniques of kitchen witchcraft go well beyond

184. See *Home Altars of Mexico*, by Ramón Gutiérrez, S. Scalora, D. Salvo, and W.H. Beezley. I have also encountered bedroom ancestral, saint, or spirit altars in versions of Filipino Catholicism and Santería. See more about the latter in Kristine Junker's *Afro-Cuban Religious Arts: Popular Expressions of Cultural Inheritance in Espiritismo and Santería.*

the bottle of bay leaves or cellar of salt on the counter. Here are a few of the tools that can do some serious magic in the hands of a kitchen-oriented witch:

Pots and Pans

Cooking magic often happens at the hearth or stove, and we cannot help but be drawn in by the idea of a witch standing over a bubbling iron cauldron. Stories of magical pots derive from many cultures, from versions of the "Raven Steals the Sun" stories in Pacific Northwest Salish traditions to the charming Italian story of the never-ending pasta pot that has been immortalized by children's author Tomie de Paola in his book *Strega Nona*. Using a pot as a tool for combining ingredients is common enough, but it can also be a tool for casting spells or seeing the future. Scrying into a pot of bubbling water or simmering sauce can sometimes provide valuable insight to the chef-witch doing the cooking.

Utensils

Both knives and spoons are useful tools in the kitchen, and a talented magical worker can do a lot with either. Spoons stir pots, of course, but they can also be used to bang them as a way of scaring away evil spirits. The way a witch stirs her pot can also add influences to the food or formula she's preparing, with clockwise stirs thought to add positive effects, and counterclockwise stirs thought to create banishing or negative outcomes. Decorative spoon-carving or painting can also incorporate folk magical attributes, such as using a particular wood like oak for a protective effect. Dropping a spoon or fork means the arrival of a visitor, spoons meaning a woman and forks meaning a man.[185] Knives also inspire a great deal of magical lore, mostly around the giving and receiving of them. Knives in general must be paid for, even with a sum as small as a penny, or else they will inevitably turn on their new owner and accidents will follow. A dropped knife is much like a fallen broom, indicating the arrival of company—sometimes ominous company like a bill collector or the police, but just as often a visit from a relative or friend. Mountain folklore often describes the handing over of knives to be a tricky business, because if the knife doesn't draw blood before being put away it will nick someone as it is being transferred to satisfy its "thirst."[186]

185. Gainer, *Witches, Ghosts, & Signs*, 123.

186. Ibid, 124.

Knives also cut herbs and flowers, and bread and cheese, and meat and potatoes, so they can be used to cut other things, as well. One spell involves taking a knife outside before a major storm and driving its blade into the ground with the edge pointing into the oncoming winds. This will magically "cut" the storm and prevent it from doing serious harm to the person or home where the knife is planted.[187]

FIG 10-4: Butter churn.

Appliances

You may already be wondering what spells you can work with your toaster, but using kitchen appliances and larger tools for or with magic has a long pedigree. Butter churns often needed a bit of enchantment to get them going. One such charm went: "Come, butter, come!/ Peter stands at the gate./ Waiting for a butter cake./ Come, butter, come!"[188] If the churn failed to produce butter, that could be a sign of witchcraft, and a silver coin—sometimes heated—might be dropped into the churn

187. Randolph, *Ozark Magic*, 33. A version of this appears in Scott Cunningham's *Earth Power* involving an ax (127). One correspondent has told me that she believes this spell helped her evade one of the most damaging tornadoes she had ever seen, although I should also caution that modern weather prediction and safety precautions are far more effective than the knife method.

188. This rhyme has appeared in numerous collections and forms, including even some Mother Goose books. The Library of Congress has a recording of such a charm-rhyme done by folklorists John and Ruby Lomax, sung by Irene Williams of Mississippi in 1940: https://www.loc.gov/item/afc9999005.11770.

to break the hex (see figure 10-4).[189] In contemporary times, we have a number of spells that rely on appliances to work. The "freezer" spell has become very popular for dealing with aggravating coworkers or neighbors, and simply involves writing the person's name on a piece of paper (or if you can get a bit of their hair or clothing that works even better), then putting it into a container of water and freezing it. The person performing the low-level hex "chills" the target and the goal is to prevent or reduce potential conflict between people. Witches are not the only people who know how to use a little kitchen magic, too. Realtors famously know that baking bread or cookies in the oven before showing a house leads to more offers and a better impression of the home because of the inviting aromas. You can harness that magic, too, by simmering water on your stovetop with mixtures like cinnamon, sugar, and clove (to stimulate pleasant conversation and create warmth between people) or lemons and limes (to cut through any negativity lingering in the air, not unlike the lemon Pine-Sol mentioned earlier).[190]

Towels and Rags

The "soft goods" of a kitchen can also be extremely useful for magic. They have remarkable divinatory power in folklore. Like knives and brooms, a dropped dish towel means company is coming, and should it be dropped twice you can bet they will come with an appetite. Dropping a dirty dishrag sometimes meant that news was coming your way (likely from that hungry visitor), often about an upcoming birth. Two people using the same dish towel indicates a quarrel about to start.[191] Letting animals chew dirty dish rags was once thought to keep them from running away and help to break sickness when they were ill (although I would not recommend this method at all today).[192] Wiping blemishes with dish towels and rags and then placing them in a coffin with a corpse was sometimes thought to take away the offending marks. You could also simply rub the mark with a towel and toss it over your shoulder someplace you wouldn't find it again to get rid of things like moles, warts, and corns. A contemporary witch might adopt a practice like this, and might adapt it to contemporary needs, too. For example, if you were trying to quit smoking you might

189. Randolph, *Ozark Magic*, 294–95.

190. Mickaharic, *Spiritual Cleansing*, 85.

191. Randolph, *Ozark Magic*, 53–54. Hyatt, *Folklore from Adams County*, 285.

192. Hyatt, *Folklore from Adams County*, 47.

use a dirty towel to rub a cigarette, then discard it and walk away to break the addiction (from experience I can say any extra boost to help with this process is welcome).

DIRT UNDER THE NAILS

Stone Soup Incense

A Russian story (with variations found throughout the world) tells of a soldier who could find no charity in a village and found himself on the brink of starvation. He cleverly pulled out a pot and put it on the fire, filling it with snow that became bubbling water. He then began looking around on the ground, attracting the attention of the locals, who wondered what he was doing. "Looking for the right stone for my stone soup," he replied. They scoffed at him but continued to watch with interest. When he finally found a nice, big stone, he cleaned it off and dropped it into the pot, then inhaled and let out a satisfied sigh. Locals began to gather, wondering what he smelled, for they could smell nothing. "It's the most delicious soup in the world, stone soup. But what would make it even better would be some carrots." Immediately, one villager chimed in saying he had a few carrots, and ran to retrieve them. He returned and the soldier added them to the pot. Then he said the soup only wanted an onion, and another villager obliged. So it went until everyone in the village had contributed, and a truly delicious soup had been concocted, with enough for everyone to enjoy a bowl together.

This story may not seem inherently magical, but sometimes magic is in the thinking. The soldier's cleverness ensured everyone—himself included—had something to eat, and that everyone contributed. This is a marvelous way to hold a potluck among magical practitioners, too. You could easily have everyone bring a bread, dessert, or drink, plus a single ingredient to add to the soup, and create a mutual love feast to share together.

One tradition I have enjoyed with a magical group was to adapt this principle to other forms, as well. We had great success creating a "group incense" with everyone adding an ingredient that they felt represented themselves. It would be burned at any group ritual as a way of getting people on the same magical page, and some of it was given to every member of the group to work with on their own, so that they could draw upon the power of the group even in their solitary working. If you have magical friends (or even friends or family members without particular magical leanings), try a method like this and see what sorts of lovely combinations you generate together!

Around the House

In this section we have considered a few of the "key" areas in which magic gets highly propagated, but this is not the whole story. What of the shared living spaces where we might keep a bowl of pennies and a lodestone to draw in financial security every time someone passes by and drops in a coin? What of yards and porches where we bury witch bottles or throw curses at enemies (see chapters eleven and five, respectively, for more on those topics)? We have backyards that become the sites of lunar rituals, gardens that grow the herbs and roots we use to work spells, and laundry rooms packed with traditional magical ingredients like bluing or needles and thread.

Clearly there are so many ways that a home can be seen through magical eyes. The rooms and spells covered here are far from comprehensive and, considering how much of our lives we spend in our homes, that makes a great deal of sense. Our homes are representations of ourselves, and if we are magical, we want that magic to be expressed through our domestic spaces. If we also consider how many types of "home" there are—from apartments with fire escapes and shared hallways to motor homes with composting toilets and fold-out beds—we have a nearly endless supply of magic available to each person, and that magic will be as unique as the individual wielding it in their own personal space.

THE WORK—Waking Your Home

Hopefully this chapter has offered you several tools in and around your own home that could potentially be serving you magically. One of the main problems we run into with magic in the twenty-first century is believing that it must be arcane and eldritch in some way or it isn't valid. It is all well and good to have your more exotic ingredients and spells drawn from far-off lands and the distant past, but the folk magicians who have always been here generally use what's around them. They understood the world as a living, vibrant place with spiritual power everywhere. Even your own house can exude a life force or power of its own, one that you can connect with.

The work I mention here and that I highly recommend is something I heard from contemporary magical practitioner, artist, and poet Lisa Marie Basile, author of *Light*

Magic for Dark Times. She described a friend of hers who made sure to say "good morning" and "good night" to her home every day, and spent some time thanking it for sheltering her and offering her peace and comfort. Not everyone's home does that, but if yours does, consider adopting a ritual like this to begin developing your own long-term relationship with your space. Even if it is just your bedroom or your bed or a favorite hiding spot, making that connection can open up immense possibilities for magic because you come to see your home and space as something not of stone and plaster, but living and breathing. That is a truly enchanted worldview.

Recommended Reading

Spiritual Cleansing: A Handbook of Psychic Self-Protection, by Draja Mickaharic. This is an essential and very easy-to-read sourcebook on keeping your home (and yourself) spiritually clean. It offers many simple, thoughtful ways of dealing with protecting your spaces and making them magically useful to you. Mickaharic incorporates magic from a number of sources, but does so with simplicity and style, and the author's charm and directness make this a pleasure to read, as well.

The Magical Household: Spells and Rituals for the Home, by Scott Cunningham and David Harrington. This is perhaps one of the classics of home and domestic magic. The authors tackle many of the subjects in this chapter, including a section on "By Broom and Rag," and their suggestions are incorporated into a framework of natural magic. They also cover important issues like what happens when you move from one place to another and need to carry some of your household magic with you.

Light Magic for Dark Times: More than 100 Spells, Rituals, and Practices for Coping in a Crisis, by Lisa Marie Basile. Basile's thoughtful book is largely focused on concepts of self-care and personal magic, but that also means there is a tremendous amount of domestic magic in its pages. She incorporates bathing rituals and the use of household objects like bowls and beds in ways that feel comfortable and even occasionally challenging, but in a good way.

CHAPTER ELEVEN

Roots, Stones, and Bones—Gathering Magical Supplies

A woman's friend has been having bad dreams at night, horrible dreams that leave her unable to go back to sleep and which are causing her to have real problems in her daily life. She struggles to stay focused, feels depressed all the time, and even gets a bit paranoid now and then wondering if her dreams are somehow going to come true in her waking hours. The woman sits her friend down in a chair and tells her to close her eyes. She has picked up some simple tricks from an aunt of hers who was reputed to be a *curandera,* a folk healer in the Mexican tradition. The woman wraps a rosary around her waist and slips a stone she considers lucky into her pocket for protection. She then pulls out a few saint candles she picked up at the local grocery and lights them, reading the prayers aloud on each one. She gets a bowl of water and whispers a prayer over it, sprinkling in some salt from her pantry. She takes a cutting of rue from her garden and sprinkles the blessed water all around and over her friend. Finally, the woman takes an egg and begins rubbing it gently over her friend's body, from head to feet, murmuring prayers. She cracks the egg into a glass of water and sees some bubbles, as well as a "shroud" in the floating white, indicating that a nasty nightmare spirit may have attached itself to her friend. The woman flushes the egg and water down the toilet, sprinkling blessed water after it and everywhere it had been, and doing the same to her friend again. They embrace and the friend leaves, assured that her nightmares should not bother her again. Both sleep soundly that night.[193]

Magic in North America often happens this way. The ritual above would be recognizable in Oaxaca, Los Angeles, El Paso, and New York to many residents, although each place would likely have its own slight variations—the water might need to be official holy water from a Catholic church in some places, for example, or a bundle of sage or stick of palo santo wood might be burned in place of the rue and water used here. Magical work depends very much on where you are and what you have around you, and for a number of people that also means limited access to the more esoteric ingredients or artisanal occult supplies. The internet has collapsed some of these distances, of course, and made virtually any ingredient—even human bones in some cases—available to those who will pay for shipping right to their doorstep. Still, the world of grocery-store candles and lucky stones found on a beach remains a rich source of magical components for many spiritual workers. In the pages to come we will look at both spell ingredients and where magical practitioners find them, as well as discussing how we can use them and source them carefully, wisely, and well.

Supermarket Sorcery

This chapter will begin with a tour of the local grocery store aisles, where you can often find a number of valuable magical ingredients waiting for you, and not just in the spice aisle (witches do love herbs, but those aren't the whole story, magically). We will see the value of understanding how to work with what you have and what you can get quickly and cheaply without raising an eyebrow in the checkout lane. I will also discuss gathering magical supplies from the world around you—sometimes from unexpected places—and spend some time looking at the more esoteric or imported supplies we find in North American folk magic. The examples here are largely drawn from traditions such as the Mexican American *curandera* practice or variations of Southern Rootwork, Conjure, or Hoodoo, because all of those systems

193. This account is a slight fictionalization of the rites outlined in several texts on *curanderismo*, including "The Basic Egg Limpia," by Curious Curandera; Torres, "Cheo," *Curandero: A Life in Mexican Folk Healing*; Avila, *Woman Who Glows in the Dark: A Curandera Reveals Traditional Aztec Secrets of Physical and Spiritual Health*; and Buenaflor, *Cleansing Rites of Curanderismo.*

are inherently deeply practical about their ingredients. That being said, most folk magic is built upon practicality, so other systems will be recognizable here, too.

The goal here is not a comprehensive list of every possible ingredient you could find, nor an exhaustive table of folkloric correspondences for each item listed. This is all simply a way to look at the everyday world a little differently and turn a walk in the woods or a trip to the market into a doorway for magic. Your grocery list can double as an inventory of magical potential, and many people working with magical traditions in the past and present have done their best spellcraft using a few things picked up at the store or pulled from the pantry.

The grocery store is not the end-all be-all of magical supply houses. I prefer by far to grow or wildcraft my own botanicals (a point I will address near the end of the chapter), use hand-crafted incenses from a local occult shop, and carry talismans picked up at the nearby Catholic bookstore in a lot of cases. Supporting community commerce and doing work oneself fits in as well or better with most magical practices than grabbing a mass-produced box of incense from a five-and-dime shelf, but there are always going to be cases where magic must be done on short notice or with supplies not readily purchased at the witchy store. In some of the cases below, it should also be noted that the grocery stores where one can find these ingredients are not the big chains, but rather local *bodegas* or international markets. You are far more likely to find chewing john (galangal root) in an Asian market than in a big chain one, for example. I'll talk a bit about navigating the tricky road of imported magical supplies later on, but for now let's get back to those automatic sliding doors and the rickety rattle of a grocery cart on our way to casting spells.

Aisle One: Herbs and Spices

The common image of a witch huddled over a cauldron working spells generally also involves her casting handfuls of herbs—among other things—into the bubbling pot. There are a number of excellent books on herbal magic and medicine out there, so I will not cover every single potential herb from anise to za'atar blend here, but instead hit a few you'd be likely to pick up for various cooking and baking needs. Folk magicians in the New World are a practical bunch, so herbs that couldn't be used for a combination of cooking, cleaning, medicine, and magic would have had to be remarkably potent if they only served a single purpose.

- **Allspice**—This is a good success spice, but also good for stimulating conversation. I like to vacuum with cinnamon and allspice sprinkled on the carpets before guests come over to encourage a warm, friendly atmosphere.[194]
- **Bay Leaves**—These stiff little leaves of the bay laurel tree are useful for a lot of magical work involving success or achievement. This association may come from the use of laurel leaves to crown victors in Roman sporting events, but it seems to be fairly widespread. They are also good for marking with magic words or sigils, then hiding in places like shoes or under pillows (just be aware they can be a bit pointy at times).
- **Cinnamon**—Creates a sense of prosperity and joviality. Some use it for business success, but I find it creates more of a personal confidence and comfortability than anything purely financial. It's also useful for working on "warming" feelings between people, and thus sometimes gets included in love spells.
- **Cloves**—Yummy in gingerbread, but useful in magic that inspires love or lust, as well. Cloves are sometimes burned to ward off evil spirits, and are supposed to be particularly effective when burned to stop others from gossiping about you.
- **Dill**—Not just for pickles anymore! Dill essentially makes people like you, so it can be used to create spells that influence others' opinions. Dill is added to court case spells to help convince the judge or jury to side with the spellcaster, for example.[195] Washing in a dill-infused bath can draw love or luck, and carrying dill seeds in your wallet can help attract money your way. Some also use dill to break love spells, too, and an Ozark cure cites dill as a cure for hiccups.[196]
- **Ginger**—Ginger is a very multi-faceted herb that can do a lot, magically. It is used to "heat up" any spell you need to get working in a hurry. It inspires love, luck, and lust in equal measure, but can also bolster courage when added to infusions, incenses, or packet spells like mojo bags. It's also reputed to be good for digestive health (but consult with a doctor before using it for medical purposes).
- **Mustard Seeds**—These come in "black" or "white" (actually closer to yellow in color) varieties. Each variety can have its own uses, with black ones more often

194. Mickaharic, *Spiritual Cleansing*, 85; See also Curious Curandera, "Herbs Used in Spellwork."

195. Yronwode, *Hoodoo Herb & Root Magic*, 85.

196. Randolph, *Ozark Magic*, 100.

used in hexing work, but in both cases they can be used to break up harmful effects as well. Yellow mustard is particularly thought to be protective when scattered in corners or at thresholds, and can also be used to stimulate love or fertility in some beliefs.

- **Oregano**—Keeps meddlesome influences from interfering in your life. Makes a nice "law-keep-away" substitute, and discourages nosy neighbors. Some authors note that it helps dispel sadness and depression as well (but see a doctor or therapist rather than relying solely on a spice cabinet for your mental health, please).
- **Pepper**—Black pepper or red pepper (or even pink pepper or green pepper)—these little desiccated berries add a punch of flavor and a little flame of heat to the foods they touch. Similarly, in magic, they add heat and potency to spells. They are often used in hexing charms or banishing spells. A palmful of salt combined with pepper can be tossed after an unwelcome visitor to ensure they don't return, for example.
- **Poppy Seeds**—Poppies are used to control others or cause confusion. They can be added to things like mustard seeds to create discord and disagreement, especially in things like legal spells where a hung jury might be the best outcome. They also can be used to target an enemy and make them feel weak or befuddled.
- **Rosemary**—Good for domestic bliss, as well as helping those who smell it focus and think clearly. This is one of my favorite fumigatory (smoke ritual) herbs, and always has a very maternal feel to me. Added to bathwater it is also thought to help the bather retain a youthful look, and left under a pillow it can bring good dreams.
- **Sage**—This is not the white sage *(Salvia apiana)* used by Indigenous peoples of the Americas, which has its own benefits but also comes with a lot of complicated cultural concerns about appropriation and overharvesting. Instead, this sage is your typical cooking herb, but it provides magical benefits such as a boost to wisdom or insight, an increase in longevity, and a spiritually cleansing effect.
- **Salt**—Great for stopping any hexes put upon you and removing unwanted spiritual energies from your home. I use a salt-and-baking-soda mixture sprinkled on carpets before vacuuming to both absorb odors and remove pesky curses.

One author on Hoodoo records a method of preventing unwanted guests from returning that simply involves sweeping salt after them when they leave.[197] Salt is famed for being a good "barrier" sprinkle, used to line doorways and windows to prevent anything harmful from entering (as any fan of the television show *Supernatural* will know). It can also be added to water to help imbue it with magical properties, something that often happens during Wiccan ceremonies.

- **Sesame Seeds**—Like mustard, this comes in white or black varieties, but the distinctions between the two shades aren't as severe from a spellwork perspective. In traditional Chinese medicine they are thought to have a "draining" effect and clear out buildups of negative *qi*.[198] Additionally, they can be used to attract money (similar to dill) or reveal hidden secrets (think of the famous "Open Sesame!" line from the tale "Ali Baba and the Forty Thieves").
- **Sugar**—A little sprinkle of this will add a sweetness to your home, though make sure you get it all and don't use too much—a little sweetness may be great, but a lot of ants aren't. If you are airing your house out, a little honey, brown sugar, molasses, or even table sugar might be a good thing to burn or warm on the stove, as it will provide a sublimely "sweet" feeling to the area. You can also store the names of people you want to like you in your sugar jar as a way to lend a little sweetness to those relationships.

How you deploy the magic of these spices depends on the system you're using, or on your personal needs at the time. You might use these as an incense or heat them on the stove to infuse them into the atmosphere (or simply cook a recipe with them). Some of them are also good as "strewing" herbs, lightly tossed over the floor and then vacuumed up after. The basic method is to sprinkle everything, let it sit for a bit (if you can stand letting it sit for twenty-four hours, that is lovely, but probably a little excessive—thirty minutes is often plenty of time, and even a five-minute wait will give you a quick dose of magic).

197. Haskins, *Voodoo & Hoodoo*, 136.

198. "Black Sesame Seeds/Hei Zi Ma," Me & Qi.

Aisle Two: Produce

What would a Colonial-era folk magician or yesteryear *curandera* make of the vast variety of produce available in a modern supermarket? Plums imported from Chile, cherimoya from Mexico, bananas from Costa Rica? For one thing, they would likely be able to expand their magical repertoire with so many variant ingredients available to them. They would also likely be a bit overwhelmed by some of the selections, since a number of the items used in folk magic don't translate easily from one culture to another (and there are some serious consequences to all this global traffic to consider, both magical and mundane). Still, if we look at the produce aisle through the eyes of a witch or folk healer, we can see myriad spells ready to toss into our carts and head to the cash register. Below I share a few selections that could be found in a typical grocery (or in some cases a grocery serving a particular community, which are fairly common in most North American cities now). This, like the herbs and spices list on the previous pages, is hardly comprehensive, but should give you an idea just how much potential you have for magic in every grocery trip.

- **Coconuts**—A coconut can be rolled and kicked throughout a home while speaking spells of banishment to remove evil spirits or harmful spells. The "milk" inside is often incorporated into a Vodoun ritual of head-washing because of the way the liquid both strips away evil influences and leaves behind sweetness. That sweetness can also make the coconut a good home for sweetening spells (after you finish draining the milk and getting all the good stuff out of the inside, of course).
- **Corn Husks**—The papery, stiff-but-pliant corn husk is absolutely essential for making really good tamales. Usually these come in huge packs (because if you're going to go to the trouble of making tamales, you may as well make a lot of them), and they're often dirt cheap. So what sorts of magical mischief can you get up to with all those husks? If you're not making ensorcelled tamales, you might consider saving a few husks and turning them into doll babies for working various kinds of poppet magic. In some cases, the husks would be bound to the cob, along with various herbs and things like hair or clothing from the intended target to work a spell on them.[199]

199. Casas, *Working the Root*, 245–54; Wigginton, *Foxfire 3*, 453–60; Dr. E, "Making Doll Babies for Spiritual Use," 36–38.

- **Galangal Root**—Often found in Asian grocery stories, but frequently making its way onto chain supermarket shelves, too, the spicy galangal root adds heat and sweetness much the same way ginger does. However, one of its most effective uses is from the Hoodoo tradition of "chewing the root." Galangal is known as "Chewing John," one of the three key "John" roots of the tradition, and it was frequently used in court case spells to make the judge favor the chewer's side. The most famous example of this is South Carolina rootworker Dr. Buzzard, who would sit in court and "chew the root" on behalf of his clients to ensure they won their case.[200]
- **Garlic**—Garlic cloves are famous for repelling evil, but in some cases they repel, well, everyone. The crumbled dried skins of garlic bulbs will leave a distinctive odor in the air when burned. Burning a few of them or adding them in powdered form to a vacuum powder can keep away the nastiest of spirits, but may keep away friendly faces, too. Garlic is also sometimes added to the famous blend "Four Thieves Vinegar," which is reputed to be very protective (and yummy when made well!).
- **Hot Peppers**—There are so many varieties of chili peppers it can be hard to choose, and most groceries now have both fresh and dried peppers in staggering assortments. Using the peppers in hot-footing charms to remove unwanted people from a person's life is typical of Hoodoo charms, as is a charm involving slitting open a habanero pepper and stuffing it with someone's name to apply some serious pressure to them. In an account of Haitian Vodoun rites, alcohol, such as rum, is stuffed with hot peppers until it is nigh-undrinkable, then used during ecstatic trance-possessions to offer visiting *lwa* (spirits) like the Ghede (the dead).[201]
- **Lemons (Citrus)**—Lemons, oranges, and limes really fit here, because citrus fruit has long been associated with magic and spellcraft. An Italian spell recorded in the nineteenth century involves sticking pins into a lemon to break the effect of the evil eye.[202] Sticking things like cloves into an orange and dusting it with orris root (powdered iris roots) turns it into a pomander, a charm

200. Pinckney, *Blue Roots*, 48; Montgomery, *American Shamans*, 30–34.
201. Deren, *Divine Horsemen*, 104; and Hurston, *Tell My Horse*, 158–64.
202. Leland, *Aradia*, chapter V.

often hung up at the holidays to spread its lovely scent through the home (and to confer a blessing of bounty and abundance to all within). Citrus was also frequently given as a gift during the holiday season because of its connections to prosperity and abundance.

- **Potatoes**—The humble potato is a lovely addition to magic in the New World because it comes from South and Central America, but has made itself absolutely essential to other cultural cuisines. It's also a cheap, plentiful food that offers a lot of nutrition (make sure to eat the skins, though). That low cost and high availability has also made the potato useful in magic. Wart charmers in the Appalachian and Ozark regions would slice a potato in half, rub the warts with part of the potato, and bury the rest. As the potato rotted away, the wart would disappear, too. Potatoes can also make effective "dolls" for spellwork (think Mr. Potato Head, which originally was just doll parts and facial features you stuck in a real potato). British folklore says that carrying a small potato in your pocket relieves rheumatism as well, although that power is more often ascribed to buckeyes or nutmegs in the New World.[203] The potato acts as a proxy for you, absorbing all hurtful conditions (which sometimes extends to things like colds or gout).
- **Rose Petals**—I'm sneaking these in here because many grocery stores have a fresh floral section near the produce aisles, and rose petals have plenty of magical uses. They encourage love and passion when crumbled around the home and left for a bit before sweeping/vacuuming, or infused into bathwater as a love-building wash (and the love being built can be for yourself, too). Sleeping with rosebuds or petals under your pillow is thought to bring clairvoyant dreams, as well. Depending on the color of the rose petals you can use them for other forms of magic, too—white petals can be used to settle an untranquil home in some traditions, for example. Roses are just one possibility, of course, and many floral sections have a variety of flowers you might be able to use magically.

203. Opie & Tatem, *Dictionary of Superstitions*, 314.

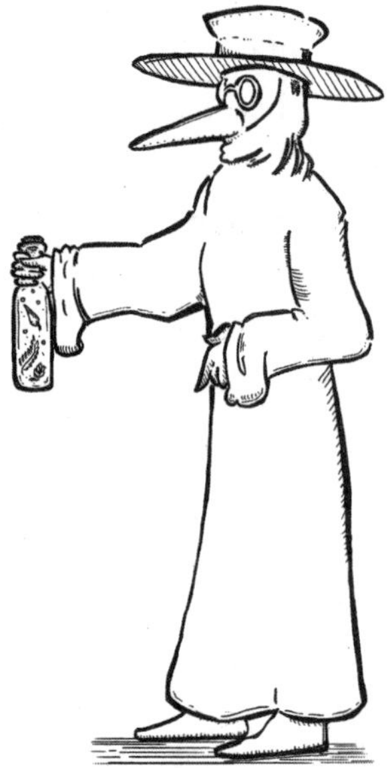

FIG 11-1: The recipe for the famed "Four Thieves Vinegar" allegedly stems from the Black Plague.

DIRT UNDER THE NAILS
Four Thieves Vinegar

The fabled origins of the formula known as "Four Thieves Vinegar" are murky at best. The first reference to the formula in English doesn't appear until 1825, although versions in other languages like French or Italian date back a bit farther. Supposedly the legend is that sometime during the plague years of the sixteenth and seventeenth centuries, a story went about that four spice merchants had discovered a secret formula that made them immune to the plague and which they'd rub on their bodies before robbing corpses ravaged by the disease. That formula was eventually revealed to be a strong red wine vinegar with a number of different spices—reputedly one for each thief—most notably a lot of garlic. Vinegar and garlic have some strong antiseptic properties, so it's not hard to imagine that in a time before Leeuwenhoek's discovery of microorganisms in 1675, any application of anti-microbial formula would help prevent a communicable disease. The formula was still in use even in the 1790s in North America, where it apparently played a role in managing a yellow fever outbreak in Philadelphia.[204]

Whatever the origins, Four Thieves Vinegar is still a popular magical formula, with benefits that range from keeping away illness to breaking hexes and even being used to lay a curse now and then. Here is a version of the recipe based on one I learned, with a few minor modifications of my own:

Ingredients:

- One pint mason jar, filled to just about ¾ full with good cider vinegar
- One head of garlic, peeled of skins (around 8–12 cloves)
- One large handful of red chili flakes
- One large handful of black mustard seeds (if you can't find black mustard, yellow will be fine, though you might want to toast them to release their oils and blacken them a bit)
- One handful of salt—kosher or sea salt are best
- Optional ingredients include: a sprig of rue (I usually include this), black peppercorns (just a small handful of these), rosemary, other types of chilies such as habanero or jalapeno, guinea pepper grains, galangal root, ginger root, etc. You only need a little bit of any of these to boost the overall strength of the mix.

Put your ingredients into your mason jar, making sure it doesn't overflow. Cap and seal, then shake vigorously for thirty to sixty seconds. Put it in a cool, dark place or a refrigerator. Shake daily for two weeks, then keep stored in a dark pantry or a fridge.

The way I was taught to make this follows the rule that the recipe should be not only strong, but edible. It should, in fact, make quite a tasty addition to an oil-and-vinegar salad dressing, with the added bonus of keeping you free from any hexes, curses, or bad luck!

This list is obviously incredibly small considering how many options you have in a produce section. Exploring what's available is more important than following any

204. See Stough, "The Yellow Fever in Philadelphia 1793," 6–13.

list, so look at what you see regularly for sale in your local grocery and build upon that foundation. Research the plants, fungi, and flowers that you can get readily and easily. Farmer's markets are also great for this because you begin to see what is seasonally available in your area, so your magical produce is connected to the land and sky and waterways around you, too.

Aisle Three: Everything Else

Grocery stores are not just about what fresh fruits and veggies you can buy, nor about the aisle packed with spices you can shake into your bubbling brews and cauldron creations. Folk magicians use what's around them, and in the case of a grocery store, there are so many possibilities. The list below is just a simple flyby of things you might find in a typical supermarket with a suggestion or two of how they are used by working folk magicians today. Again, this is not comprehensive, but just a way of thinking about how much magic is readily waiting for you and your wobbly-wheeled shopping buggy every time you go to the store.

- **Bread**—Blessing bread and giving it to an ill person or animal is said to speed their recovery. A Scandinavian belief says that stealing the last piece of someone's bread steals their luck, and dripping hot lead or wax into a bowl of water through a hole in a loaf of bread can help predict the future.[205] I have often given bread, salt, and a coin as a house blessing to anyone I know who moves into a new home, a tradition I inherited from my Slavic ancestors and have found in other cultures as well, such as Jewish lore.
- **Butter**—Butter sometimes gets incorporated into folk magic and folk healing. Carving figures out of butter is common in places like Wisconsin and Pennsylvania, and butter can burn like oil in a lamp to do fire-based magical rites. I had a student whose Mexican American mother used butter as a topical treatment for burns and cuts, as well (although this is not a medical recommendation at all).
- **Candles**—Most groceries have at least a few candles available. Taper candles or jar candles provide long-burning options for spellwork, while birthday candles can be good for "quickie" spells. Often you can find incense near the can-

205. Gardbäck, "Nordic Bread Spells," 57–62.

dles as well, although your selection may be very limited (and not particularly "natural"-smelling).

- **Coffee**—Coffee has its own potency and everyday magic, at least for me. It also has a place in folk magic, as well, and can be added to magical baths to give a boost of energy and stamina. Coffee grounds can also be used to scrub off negative influences (and even help make your magical garden grow).

FIG 11-2: The use of eggs as magical cleansing agents is seen clearly in the *curanderismo* ritual of the *limpia*, which removes negative influences from someone and allows the *curandera* to "read" the egg in a glass of water to find out what's wrong.

- **Eggs**—The ritual I described at the beginning of the chapter involved using an egg to cleanse someone of harmful spiritual influences. That ritual is better known as a *limpia*, or "cleaning," and usually involves a freshly-laid egg. However, in contemporary times, many practitioners simply use a standard grocery store egg (left out to get to room temperature, of course).
- **Jars**—The typical grocery will have a small selection of canning supplies, including trays of glass jars with lids. These are wonderfully useful for anything from making oil-based candles with floating wicks and lots of magical ingredients to crafting witch bottles to protect a home (see chapter twelve for more on that).
- **Meat**—Lots of spells use meat or butchery products (although if you're vegetarian or vegan you probably want to skip these). Raw chicken was once used to "draw" infections from a wound (not recommended medically!), and people still sometimes use raw beef to soothe bruises and black eyes. Boiling meat can predict poverty or wealth, depending on if it shrinks (poverty) or grows (wealth). Some cuts of meat, such as a cow's tongue or chicken's feet, are used for specific spells. The tongue is used to "shut up" someone gossiping, and the

chicken's feet can be used to remove harmful spirits or energy from a person, both spells found in Hoodoo traditions.[206]

- **Paper and Markers**—There's often a "school supplies" section for harried parents needing to pick up some poster board for a last-minute class project a child has conveniently remembered only the night before it is due. That also means there are tons of paper products, envelopes, sticky notes, pens, pencils, and markers you can use for doing written charms or inscribed sigil magic and petition-making.
- **Peas and Beans**—As mentioned in the previous chapter, a jar of grains by the door deterred evil spirits and witches from entering, and peas and beans can also be used to fill those sorts of apotropaic (anti-bad-stuff) wards. Additionally, there are strong luck associations with eating things like black-eyed peas on New Year's Day in the South. A single bean or pea can also be added to the Mardi Gras King Cake to act as a divinatory aid, with the person finding it inheriting luck for the coming year (and possibly chipping a tooth).
- **Rice**—Rice has associations with luck and money, largely because of its abundant nature. Tossing rice into the air can invite rain, while tossing rice at a newlywed couple is often thought to bring fertility (although birdseed is now more common as it is better for wildlife, and also likely available in the pet section of your grocery). Carrying some rice dyed green with food coloring in a little sack or envelope is thought to bring you good luck.
- **Sewing Needles and Thread**—Often you can find little sewing kits with needles and thread, or even just a tin of pins and needles, near the laundry aisle. These are extremely useful when doing carved image/doll/poppet magic, of course, and are also a key ingredient in the powerful witch bottle. Thread or string can be used in binding rituals, or to help create a "witch's ladder" (see chapter twelve).
- **Tea**—Some of the herbs you might need for magical work are not readily available as bottled spices, but you can find them in a number of pre-made teas. For example, star anise is found in a lot of cinnamon-orange tea blends, and chamomile (great for calming ritual baths) is easy to find in "sleepy time" blends. You

206. Haskins, *Voodoo & Hoodoo*, 182.

can get a good deal of mint for magical formulae this way. Black and green teas are also good magical cleansing agents themselves, and of course, don't forget about divination using tea leaves!

- **Vinegars and Oils**—I've already mentioned the famous Four Thieves Vinegar, but the uses of vinegars and oils in magic is widespread. You can easily make a "vinegar jar" to sour someone's life. Olive oil can be blessed and used to mark windows and doors with protective signs like crosses or circles. Pouring olive oil into water slowly is also sometimes used as a cure for the evil eye.

This short collection of potential finds in your store barely scratches the surface. I'm sure that your local grocery has more than three aisles, and it may seem a bit unfair to bundle up all the "miscellaneous" items here, but really the point here is less about using the specific ingredients listed and much more about looking at the options you have around you from a magical perspective. A slight shift in the way you see a bag of rice, peas, or beans can open up all sorts of spellwork possibilities that you might not have considered before.

Exotic Ingredients: Shopping International and Import Markets

If you live in any mid-to-large-sized city in the United States (or for that matter anywhere in North America), you are living in a cosmopolitan world made up of people from a rich variety of backgrounds. If you have a particular ethnic background or cultural connection, chances are you also have a market somewhere nearby that can supply additional culturally-specific ingredients for magical work that speaks directly to you. Plenty of cities have international markets specializing in ingredients that big-name chains don't bother with. Markets specifically catering to a non-white ethnic clientele are likely to have even more particular ingredients available. There's an entire pharmacopeia in a well-stocked *bodega* (which primarily serves a Latinx clientele), with everything from aloe vera (the gel and the live plants) to *nopales* (prickly pear cactus, sometimes used in *curanderismo* for treating diabetes) to chicken feet and cattle tongues (both edible, but also both used in various Hoodoo spells as well and mentioned in the "Aisle Three: Everything Else" section). In these markets you can often find a number of saint candles as well. I've found everything from the standard Virgen de Guadalupe to Santa Muerte, Seven African Powers, Just Judge/Justo Juez, and even a Lucky Lotto Numbers candle just by browsing a little.

Similarly, Asian markets often have a staggering amount of ingredients available, including herbs from traditional Chinese medicine or even lucky talismans or specially designed amulets for warding off evil, as well as incenses from India, Japan, or Singapore. Middle Eastern and Mediterranean markets may have rose water (useful in love work) and blue glass beads for deflecting the evil eye, among other options. West African markets may have things like "black soap," which is useful for removing curses (and has a unique and pleasant scent, in my opinion).

Some of these items may not even require you to go to a different store. Plenty of major markets have international grocery sections where things like candles, body products, and other ingredients are available alongside your Cocoa Puffs and bananas. For example, if your grocery has a Jewish section with kosher options, they may sell Shabbat candles. They frequently come in boxes at a very reasonable price, and are specifically designed to be used for spiritual purposes (albeit non-magical ones in most cases). These burn longer than birthday candles but much more quickly than novenas, and so might be good for mid-range spell work.

This last point about international sections of major chains brings up something worth considering, however. Importing ingredients is not unusual in magical practices, and has happened frequently since even before European colonization, when Native civilizations such as the Mississippian city of Cahokia near modern day St. Louis, Missouri traded with groups located in the Rocky Mountains and the Great Lakes (not to mention other major Mesoamerican civilizations like the Aztecs).[207] Trade, exchange, and movement are not inherently bad, but it may be worth considering if magical ingredients you source from distant lands are procured ethically and responsibly. Additionally, if you are buying imported magical ingredients in a chain store, you are likely not sending much financial support to the cultures of origin for those ingredients, because conglomerates and corporations eat most of the profits. Buying from a neighborhood *bodega* or Middle Eastern market may be slightly less convenient or slightly more expensive, and it won't always resolve every ethical issue (especially if you're not a member of those communities in some way), but at least you're putting money back into the community that sourced the magical supply you're using.

207. See Mann, *1491: New Revelations of the Americas before Columbus.*

Growing Your Own Ingredients and Wildcrafting

Treating magical ingredients as commodities to be bought and sold is not a particularly new phenomenon, but it can feel really uncomfortable for some practitioners. The good news is that no matter where you live in North America, chances are very high that you'd be able to gather your own ingredients for folkloric witchcraft from the landscape around you (or maybe even from parts of your daily life you're not thinking of as "magical," such as the dinner table, but we'll get to that in a moment). You can also opt to grow your own plant-based magical ingredients in some cases, a time-honored tradition among numerous herbal healers of the past and present.

The trick to both wildcrafting (a term for gathering ingredients from the land around you) and growing your own ingredients is that you have to be responsible about it. You may want to plant some mint for use in hex-breaking spells and protective charms, but as anyone who has ever grown mint will tell you, you should grow it in a pot and *not* in a garden plot bordering your neighbor's yard. Why? Because mint has a tendency to "get away" and spread quickly. Similarly, you need to think about cultural responsibility. If you're growing a particular herb like white sage for your personal use in smoke-cleansing rituals, are you being careful not to appropriate terminology (like "smudging") or specific rituals from the Diné (Navajo) or other Native peoples? Are you sourcing your seeds from Native growers to ensure that at least some money goes into the communities responsible for most of that herb's propagation and restoration in its native habitat?

This is not to say you need the thought police overseeing your every move, or that you cannot grow what you want. In the end, only you can make the decision about what is ethical and responsible for the magic you use. In terms of aligning with folk magic more generally, it's worth remembering that plenty of cultural exchange has happened and continues to happen, so as long as you're being respectful about the traditions of others, you can learn and grow with new magical ideas you encounter.

When you're harvesting from the wild, another major concern is overharvesting of native plants, minerals, and animals, and ownership of the land and all that lives on it. You may very much want to nab a bloodroot plant to help boost your relationships at home (as it is thought to be good for both domestic bliss and sexual intimacy), but if you're on federal or private lands you have to consider the laws you'd be breaking. Additionally, you may be stealing a plant that is only tenuously establishing itself in an area, or one that has become endangered through aggressive harvesting (something that has happened a lot with Appalachian ginseng hunting). Similarly, gathering stones or animal parts in the wild can be tricky because those may be protected in some way. For example, migratory bird feathers are not supposed to be picked up or harvested due to concerns about poaching, even though feathers are a crucial ingredient in a witch's ladder.

If you live in a city or somewhat more urban area, some of these concerns may seem like they don't apply to you, but often there are very specific rules or laws about what is okay to "take" from public spaces, especially in terms of plants. The real trick is to familiarize yourself with the rules and make your decisions about harvesting based on your ethical code in relation to those rules. In some cases, you may find rules that are bendable—even if wild harvesting of plants is generally restricted, most places are not going to mind you pulling up a few dandelion roots, which make a good tea for clairvoyance (just make sure that any plants you intend to ingest or use on your body are gathered from pesticide-free zones and away from busy areas of traffic and pollution!). You may even be doing people a favor by nabbing invasive species like kudzu (the bane of the South, but a vine plant that can be used to make baskets and binding hexes).

Below I've listed a few examples of plants or other magical ingredients that are likely easy for most people to gather on their own, along with a little bit of the folk magic associated with each.[208] Again, it is up to the practitioner to learn about and decide how to follow rules for ethically gathering these, but these examples usually have few restrictions and their commonplace occurrence means you'll likely not raise many eyebrows collecting them.

- **Antler Sheds**—Deer often shed their antlers in the late winter or early spring, so you may find them on nature walks. If you're a hunter you may have access to antlers as a by-product of a day out in the field. Antlers can be used in bone-casting divination or in spells for personal power.
- **Bindweed**—A common and invasive morning glory species. Good for, of course, binding enemies from doing harm. The root can be dug up to be used

208. See Cavendar, *Folk Medicine in Southern Appalachia*; Cunningham, *Cunningham's Encyclopedia of Magical Herbs*; Curious Curandera, "Herbs Used in Spellwork"; Randolph, *Ozark Magic & Folklore*; Yronwode, *Hoodoo Herb & Root Magic*; Yronwode, *The Black Folder.*

in spells of mastery and personal empowerment (especially "masculine" power, as you interpret that term).

- **Chicory**—A common roadside herb with a bitter, sturdy root. Used in spells to gain favors or weaken enemies.
- **Clover**—A four-leaf clover is commonly known to be good luck, but carried in your shoe or wallet it protects from harm and loss.
- **Coins**—See a penny, pick it up... a common luck charm with meanings that can change based on the image. Be careful about picking them up at crossroads, where they may have been left to "pass on" a cursing spell.
- **Dandelions**—Yummy leaves and a seed head good for making wishes, but the roots can also be brewed into a tea to aid in psychic endeavors.
- **Feathers**—From domestic species only (chicken feathers or farm-raised goose feathers, although you can sometimes get ostrich feathers as well if you're feeling ostentatious). Good for use in a witch's ladder and spells for sending messages to others far away.
- **Fleabane**—A stringy little daisy-like plant, it has been used as a natural bug repellent (hence its name) and it can also be employed to dispel evil spirits.
- **Glass Bottles**—If you find glass bottles abandoned, why not clean them up and use them for bottle or jar spells? Bonus: recycling!
- **Holey Stones (Hagstones)**—Often found near bodies of water, these are stones with natural holes worn in them. They allow you to see fairy or spirit activity if you peer through them, and bring luck and protection when worn as an amulet.
- **Mullein Stalks**—Tall gangly plants with thick tops. They were once dipped in wax and used as candles, and thought to keep demons and witches away. Also good for warding off nightmares when a bit of the plant is kept under the bed or pillow.
- **Nails and Railroad Spikes**—If you live near an active rail line, you can sometimes find iron spikes that rattle free from the rails or get discarded there during maintenance. These are great for securing your home and protecting it. Found nails, especially iron ones, are also good for this. Be extremely careful when gathering these and avoid accidents!

- **Nettles**—Stinging nettles are used to make spring tonics to purify the blood, and also get used in jinx-breaking herb blends.
- **Nuts**—Each nut has its own symbolism and magic. Acorns are powerful charms against lightning strikes and harm, while walnuts are thought to boost brain power. These are often easily found on the ground during autumn so learn what nuts grow in your area and what they can do.
- **Pine needles**—Good for uncrossing and refreshing a home. They can also protect against evil entering the home.
- **Plantain**—An invasive plant sometimes called "white man's foot," it has been used as a poultice on bruises, cuts, stings, and other minor injuries in many rural magico-medical practices.
- **Pokeweed**—Sometimes called "poke salat" and the young leaves are eaten as a spring tonic. The berries can be poisonous. The root is good for sending away enemies.
- **Queen Anne's Lace**—Once used as an abortifacient in Appalachia, it has also been used to treat boils or skin eruptions. Careful of the poisonous look-alike water hemlock!
- **Seashells**—Be careful about collecting from protected areas, but good in divination spells or in spells designed to draw beauty or wealth (try including them in a bath for this purpose).
- **Sea glass**—Beautiful and often easily found, sea glass can be used in charms to deflect evil spirits from a home, especially hung in windows or kept near entrances.
- **Snake sheds**—Shed snake skins are fairly common (watch out for snakes and treat them well, please, as they are valuable members of our ecosystem). The skins are used frequently in cursing spells.
- **Wishbones**—Having chicken or turkey? Keep the wishbone and use it for luck, or as they do in the Ozarks, to attract a mate (usually used by women trying to attract men, see figure 11-3).

What you find around you will inevitably vary by your region and your circumstances, so the best thing you can do to improve your wildcrafting and harvesting is get out and look around. See what grows wild, find out what is native versus invasive, observe what people leave on the ground or what washes up in waterways and shorelines, and get to know the animals that live around you. Folk magic depends upon an observant mindset and patience—those who grow their own learn to watch everything from other plants and animals to the movements of the moon to discover new magical secrets.

The twenty-first century gives us a lot of choice. Previous generations of folk magicians might well be jealous of the easy availability with which we find and gather our ingredients, but in the end folk magic is based on what you have, what is around you, and what you know how to use. In that way, an egg from the local supermarket or a dandelion pulled from your back yard can be just as deeply magical as any talisman inscribed upon a plate of pure silver.

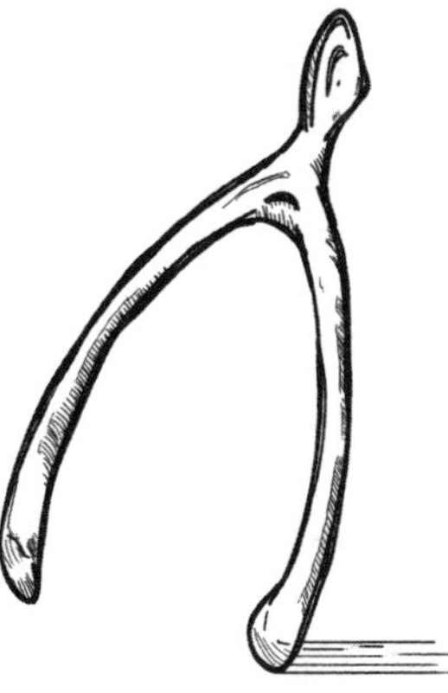

FIG 11-3: In places like the Ozarks, wishbones would be nailed or placed above doorframes as a way to draw in potential suitors for young women.

THE WORK—Folk Magic in the Spice Rack

Working with what's at hand sits at the root of most North American folk magical practices. Often, though, we forget just how much truly is at hand for us, and what we already have available to us for magical use.

At the end of chapter ten, I recommended taking stock of your magical household based on your rooms and the activities you do in them. Here I suggest doing something very similar, but in a more focused way. Specifically, spend some time with your kitchen cupboard, your spice rack, or your pantry. What ingredients do you already have there? Which ones do you use most often? Make a list of the herbs and spices you are already using on a daily basis (even if that's just pepper and salt). Take the time to really pay attention to what you're keeping on hand.

Now think about what food you cook on a regular basis. It doesn't matter if "cook" to you means making a frittata from scratch or if you're microwaving a frozen burrito. Specifically, think about the foods you prepare, and then make a list of the major ingredients. Also note any spices you can on your list. Now find a book that breaks down the ingredients and components of your meal (I have several good suggestions on the next page) and see just what kind of magic is already associated with each aspect of your dish. What if you treated that dish like a spell? What would you be casting with your lunch selection? Do you have something featuring beans and rice with spices like cayenne pepper? That might be a "fast money" sort of working, since beans and rice are both prosperity-oriented and the pepper is supposed to "heat" the spell to work more quickly. Maybe you make a chicken salad with fruits and nuts mixed in that might bring prosperity (or perhaps you like a savory chicken salad featuring herbs like sage, poppy seeds, and lemon, which might provide clear thinking and insight on a particular problem).

Keep working on this list, honing in on the sorts of ingredients you keep on hand, and what effects you might potentially create with your daily menu planning. In time, you may start to see a deeper relationship between your kitchen, your plate, and your magic.

Recommended Reading

Cunningham's Encyclopedia of Magical Herbs, by Scott Cunningham. This has long been seen as a fairly essential book of magical herbalism. Cunningham was an enthusiastic collector of folk magic, and while you certainly should not take this book as gospel on every magical plant listed, it proves incredibly useful for fielding simple spell correspondences and ideas.

Folk Medicine in Southern Appalachia, by Anthony Cavender. This is a fairly academic book, but does an excellent job looking at both the folk cures (herbal and magical) *and* the folk ailments found in parts of the mid-to-lower Appalachian region. Cavender acts more as a documentarian here, but the information gets at the underlying structure of how the beliefs and the cures work together in the Appalachian region.

Hoodoo Herb & Root Magic: A Materia Magica of African American Conjure, by cat yronwode. Yronwode's compilation of Hoodoo-based herbal ingredients, curios, and objects stands out as a solid reference for that particular branch of magic. It covers a lot of ground, and is very no-nonsense. Like Cunningham's work, it shouldn't be taken as gospel (even for Hoodoo practitioners), but it is useful and valuable in terms of the sheer volume of its entries and information.

A Modern Herbal: The Medicinal, Culinary, Cosmetic and Economic Properties, Cultivation, and Folk-lore of Herbs, Grasses, Fungi, Shrubs & Trees with Their Modern Scientific Uses (2 Vols.), by Margaret Grieve. This two-volume collection is hardly "modern" in the sense of being twenty-first century and up-to-date, but that doesn't really matter. Ms. Grieve's *Herbal* is a quintessential collection of plant lore that covers an immense amount of practical information and interesting folklore. Like so many of these books, it is not a hard-and-fast gospel of herbalism, but certainly well-researched and incredibly informative.

CHAPTER TWELVE

Ladders, Dolls, and Bottles—Crafting Magical Objects

If you walked the streets of Memphis, Tennessee, in the early- to-mid-twentieth century, you might have occasionally heard a little bell-like sound coming from a woman as she passed you. She might have given you a sweet smile or passed right by you, but if you were a man with a bit of money or lust to offer, that sound might have caught your attention. It told you that a woman had her "nation sack" on, a small bundle of cloth she wore discreetly out of sight. The jangling sound came from one of the only ingredients we are reasonably sure it included—a silver dime—since the nation sack was considered a woman's secret charm and very few women ever talked about it. It could be worn to attract customers for sex workers or to entice men to treat a lady well for the evening, although in most cases its primary use was to keep an unfaithful man from sneaking around on his woman.[209]

Nation sacks are a type of "mojo," or bundled spell made from cloth, herbs, minerals, animal parts, and various other ingredients. Their magic was built by hand from scratch for each woman who carried one, just as most mojo bags are built—very few practitioners of Hoodoo prior to the late twentieth century had "pre-made" mojo bags, although plenty of them might have some of the pieces ready to go on short notice and only need a few ingredients to personalize one. These bags had a life of their own, a personality of sorts, and could demand things of the person carrying

209. Kail, *A Secret History of Memphis Hoodoo*, 47–49; Hazzard-Donald, *Mojo Workin'*, 141–42.

them, like offerings of whiskey or rum or coffee to "feed" them. The effort put into a magical charm like a mojo bag means that it has a lot of significance. It represents time and thought and learning and sustained relational work with something handmade and magical.

What follows dives into the material creation of folk magic in North America. Witchcraft is and long has been a very physical practice, no matter how many spells are muttered under the breath. There is always something a person practicing magic *does* to make the magic happen, and often that involves something the person *creates* as part of the spellcasting process. The handmade and magical is what this chapter is all about. It will be a more hands-on chapter with several more spells and methods for the reader to try on their own. Additionally, I do my best to connect each version of magical handicraft I discuss to its cultural origins or environment, because understanding that these crafts have roots in particular places and peoples is vital to understanding how their magic works. After all, if you found yourself in a car with a steering wheel on the "wrong" side of the car, you might not understand how to drive it unless you'd spent some time in England or Japan.

I have divided my discussion—somewhat arbitrarily—into brief overviews of container spells, packet spells, cord and knot spells, and dolls, but as I will note near the end there are still many types of craft I am not covering here. The selection below, though, should at least whet your appetite to turn witchcraft into work, physical and messy real work that says "magic was here."

Container Spells

At their core, container spells are about "bottling up" the magic to be done, creating a working space for enchantment that holds the ingredients, spoken words, emotional investment, all of it. Everything is together and pushing against everything else, sugar against paper or roots against bones. Container spells are often also done at home, or at least in places where they won't be disturbed, and usually are not carried around. This is slow, active magic. If you've ever made homemade pickles or dealt with a potted plant, this kind of work will be familiar, as it takes time to really begin to manifest. Once it does, however, the results are often remarkable and strong.

Sweetening Jars

Common in contemporary Southern Conjure and Hoodoo, a sweetening jar is filled with something like sugar, honey, syrup, or molasses. A person might use their household sugar bowl to do this. Usually a target's name is written on a slip of paper and pushed into the sweetener, then the spell worker tastes the sweetness on their fingers and tells the jar that it will make the target "sweeter" or give them a sweeter life. Some workers also burn candles on top of these jars for a series of nights, repeating the spell's verbal part, to increase its power, and some workers will include things like hair or scraps of the target's clothing to help it focus more. Some conjurors place more than one target in the same sweetening jar, and some feel there should be separate jars for each target. Workers can also make "souring jars" to do the opposite and make the target's life *worse* (see chapter six for an example). To stop the spell, the target's name is removed from the jar.

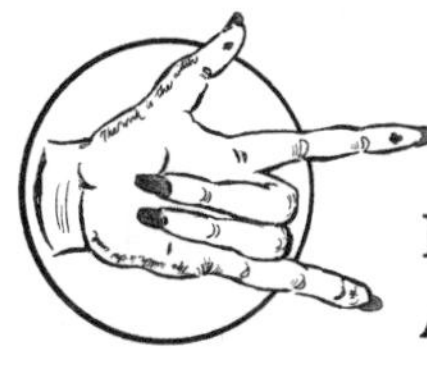

DIRT UNDER THE NAILS
A Sweetening Jar

In chapter six, I included a spell for a "souring jar" to trouble someone's life, and this is essentially a spell with the opposite effect. The goal of this working is to make someone "sweet" toward you, and that can have various shades of meaning. In general, most people doing this today are trying to alter the bad attitudes of a person in their life who bothers them or causes them anxiety and frustration. However, by mixing things into the sweetening agent like rose petals (love) or shredded currency or bayberries (money), you might sweeten a person's disposition and make them a future lover or a generous bank loan officer. The following version is designed to sweeten someone in friendship towards you.

Ingredients:

- A jar of sugar, honey, molasses, or syrup (use something locally produced if possible, but even table sugar is fine)
- A jar (like a mason jar) with a lid
- A pinch of cinnamon
- A pinch of allspice
- A pinch of cloves
- A piece of paper with the person's signature on it (or alternatively, their business card or a paper with their name on it if you don't have anything else)

To begin, fill your jar with the sweetening agent. Leave a little room at the top, and add your pinches of the spices. Close up the jar and shake it, mixing the botanicals with the sweetener as best you can (if using a syrupy sweetener you can stir with a spoon, but leave the spoon in the jar until you're done with the spell). Hold the name paper in your hands and tell it firmly what kind of friendship you want. Describe the feelings you want the person to feel when they see you, the way they'll glow when you walk into a room. Tell the paper you want to be able to share your thoughts, too, and feel the same sweetness towards them. Breathe on the paper three times, then push it into the jar of sweetener as far as you can. When you pull your fingers out, lick them clean, tasting how sweet the spell is and imagining that as the sweetness of your relationship with the other person now. Stir it with the spoon if you need to in order to really get it covered up, and pull the spoon out, licking it clean as well. Seal the jar and put it away someplace private but accessible. Each day for the following month, take it out and shake or stir it (always tasting it if you open it up). Watch as the bonds between you grow stronger and you find things to talk about. Once you are friends you can ritually dispose of it by offering it to a tree or plant, or mix it with some water and toss the water into the east while the sun rises.

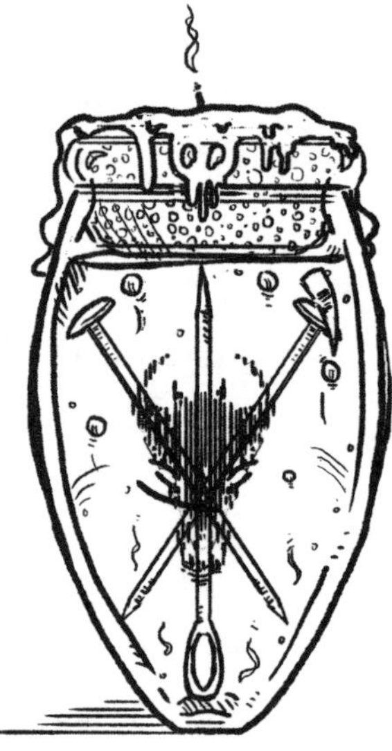

FIG 12-1: The witch bottle is a container of sharp objects along with the urine of the intended person.

Witch Bottles

Witch bottles are often used in practices of Hoodoo, Mountain Magic, New England Cunning Folk, Southern Conjure, and multiple other systems. The use of bottles as magical containers is centuries-old, and archaeological excavations of British and European historical sites have turned up many examples of these. In England, a variety of bottle spell called a "bellarmine" used a pottery jar with a face imprinted or sculpted on it. In most places, however, a simple jar or bottle would work for these sorts of spells. These either deliver a curse or offer protection to those who dwell where a witch bottle is placed. They are filled with sharp objects such as pins and needles—sometimes bent to mark them for witch work—and then the urine of the witch, her family, or her target would be added (see figure 12-1). In some cases, additional objects like hair or nail clippings might go in, or a symbol like a leather heart if a love spell was intended. These jars are often buried on the property of the person they are intended to work on. In the case of a magical defense mechanism, they are designed to draw the attention or attack of any evil spirit so that they will get "trapped" in the bottle when they come searching for its creator. One variation on this from Contemporary Feminist Witchcraft that I love is the "personal underworld" spell found in Lisa Marie Basile's *Light Magic for Dark Times*, which involves using stones in a jar to make a private "underworld" to hold the darker parts of ourselves and offer us an underworld space for shadow work. Another variation found in Hoodoo and some Appalachian lore includes the "walking boy" bottle, in which a witch (or anti-witchcraft "power doctor") would keep a small insect like a beetle. The bug bottle would be used by the magician as a divinatory tool to help find any harmful spells or negative conditions lingering in a household.[210]

Box Spells

Often found in Hoodoo and Southern Conjure practices, box spells work similarly to the sweetening jars above, except that they can be used to create a variety of conditions for a target. Many people inadvertently seem to create these sorts of spells by storing up keepsakes in shoeboxes, hatboxes, or cigar boxes, but the intentional creation of a box spell is more involved. Usually items representing a target—such as a dolly (see below), hair or nail clippings, or a bit of the person's worn clothing—are placed in the box with other ingredients. For example, if a person were being a gossip, they

210. Chireau, *Black Magic*, 101–102.

might be placed in the box with alum or lemons to constrict their ability to blather. The mirror box is another good example of this kind of spell. Bits of mirror or even tin foil are placed around the interior of the box, with the representation of the target sealed inside it. Any harm they try to do will then be reflected back at them. A variation on the mirror box involves placing the mirrored surfaces on the outside of the box to deflect any harm directed at the target.

Bowl Spells

Bowl spells are common in Hoodoo, Mountain Magic, and Southern Conjure. The use of bowls in spellwork is hardly limited to North America, but there are a few interesting versions of bowl-based spells found here. For example, a bowl of holy water may be placed near a door to prevent any wicked or harmful spirits from coming in (and offer people entering a chance to bless themselves to cleanse any ill intentions or troublesome spirits away). Money bowls are fairly common, as well, with bowls of coins acting as an innocuous magnet for good fortune. Bowls seem to either draw in a good influence or hold good power for later use, as we see in some Buddhist practices where a bowl of water will be placed near a bodhisattva or divine image statue to bring peace and tranquility.[211] A North Carolina counter-curse involves keeping a hexed doll in a bowl of blessed water to negate the spell.[212] The water can also be sprinkled around to offer blessings or prosperity to those who occupy the dwelling.

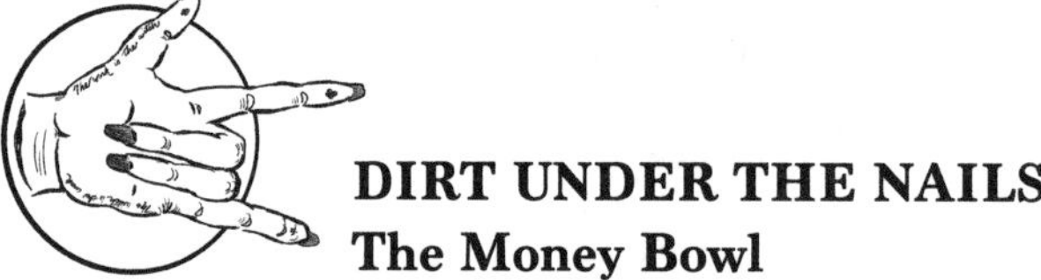

DIRT UNDER THE NAILS
The Money Bowl

This is a relatively simple spell with a lot of adaptations that you can make. At its core it requires only:

- A bowl
- Some loose change

211. See Lee and Nadeau, *Encyclopedia of Asian American Folklore and Folklife.*

212. Hand, *The Frank C. Brown Collection of North Carolina Folklore*, 103.

- A lodestone (or other magnet)
- Some iron filings (available from educational supply companies or you can buy those "draw a mustache with a magnet" toys at the dollar store, break them open, and use those)

If you wish, you can also use an attraction oil or money-drawing condition oil and rub it into the magnet/lodestone before you begin. Otherwise, simply add the stone to the bowl and tell it to bring money into your home so long as it is fed. You may wish to pray a psalm over it (psalms are traditional in Conjure and Hoodoo spells). I recommend Psalm 65, emphasizing the section that says "He has crowned the year with success, and his paths drip fatness," but you may also use Psalm 85, emphasizing "The Lord shall give that which is good, and the land shall yield her increase." Then, add the change to the bowl and a pinch of the iron filings. Make sure the change touches the magnet. Each day, add a bit more change (even dollar bills and other currency as you go along, if you like). Once a week, add a pinch of iron filings, too, and repeat the spell or psalm you used to charge it. You can also take change from the bowl and carry it with you, so long as you replace it with more change that same day. Over time you may start to add larger denominations as your finances increase to reflect the way you are being "fed," and feed the bowl accordingly.

Face Jugs

The use of jars or bottles with faces on them—usually carved or sculpted although they can be made in other ways—appears in a few different traditions that have wide-ranging applications for them, such as Candomble, Mountain Magic, New England Cunning Folk, Regla de Ocha/Lukumi, Southern Conjure, and Quimbanda. I mentioned above the use of face jars called bellarmines in English folk magic, a tradition that carried across the Atlantic a bit into some New England areas. Face jugs—a specific type of pottery derived from African traditions and made extensively in the Southern mountain regions—often housed "off-limits" items, such as moonshine liquor, but could also be used to house ashes of deceased relatives as happens in some African and African Caribbean practices. In some cases, jugs would be pasted and decorated with mementos of a loved one to create a "mourning jug."[213] Similarly, a "memory jug" can be used to memorialize the dead, often by affixing glass beads, seashells, and other objects to the outside and leaving them at gravesites. These can also be devotional items, as seen in the concrete-and-cowrie shell Elegua heads used in Quimbanda, Candomble, and Lukumi practices, where they serve as a locus for spiritual forces and a guardian at the doorway of a home.

Packet Spells

Container spells are slow magic, but packet spells are the magic of the witch or conjurer on the go. These are usually small bundles (there are exceptions to this) that hold in a spell or spiritual force that benefits the person who carries them (or on rare occasions can be used to cause harm to someone else). These are assembled with thought and care and empowered through ritual workings, then usually given ritual boosts (or "fed") every once in a while, for as long as they are around. I suppose there are a lot of ways to think about these packets, but the way I often feel makes the most sense is that they are like little spirit houses that you carry with you. You invite a beneficial spirit into them through enchantment and adding ingredients that the spirit likes, and then maintain the home as best you can to keep the spirit happy there. That long-term relationship is often mutually beneficial and you gain the benefits of always having a spirit helper close at hand.

Mojos

As a part of Hoodoo, Rootwork, and Southern Conjure practices, these bundle spells, sometimes also called "hands," "gris-gris," "jacks," "wangas," "trick bags," or "tobies," are some of the best-known examples of packet charms. They frequently involve creating a little bundle of spell ingredients (always in an odd number) wrapped in a piece of red flannel (often cut from the user or target's clothing, especially underwear). The mojo (sometimes called a "jomo" in a few locations) is then "fed" regularly with offerings of strong drink, tobacco smoke, bodily fluids, or something similar. A bit of the offering gets dabbed on the outside of the bag, sometimes while muttering a prayer or spell to "recharge" it, and sometimes with a breath from the user to reinvigorate it. These charms are seen as alive, a sort of living spirit house that bestows particular effects based on the ingredients enclosed and the spell used to create it. Often these are worn close to the body—some older methods men-

213. See Richards, "Grave Traditions: the Southern Mourning Jug."

tion tying them under the armpit or around the waist under one's clothes with a red thread. The nation sack mentioned at the beginning of the chapter is one type of mojo worn by women used to control men, either to attract them or keep them faithful, and its components largely remain a mystery today.[214]

FIG 12-2: Charms made into bags and packets are usually constructed of specific combinations of ingredients designed to invoke particular powers or conditions.

DIRT UNDER THE NAILS
A Success Bundle Spell

This mojo is one of the ones I've personally had the greatest relationship with, because it saw me through two advanced degrees and still boosts my classroom and research work when I need it. I call it an "academic success mojo," but you can adjust it to help with other areas of your life as well. It's based on the "Crown of Success" formulations found in Hoodoo and Southern Conjure.

Ingredients:

- High John/John the Conqueror root (a whole one, but you could use chips if that's all you've got)
- Gravel root

214. See Kail, *A Secret History of Memphis Hoodoo*, 47–49; Hurston, "Hoodoo in America," 328–29; Chireau, *Black Magic*, 47; Hazzard-Donald, *Mojo Workin'*, 140–143.

- Rosemary (dried)
- Sage (dried)
- Frankincense tears
- Small psalm scroll*
- Red flannel square
- Twine
- Crown of Success oil

Take the red flannel square and lay it out on your working space. Begin adding each of the ingredients one at a time in a little pile in the center. You can speak the spell or psalm you've chosen while you do this, or just silently focus on the results you want.[215] After all the ingredients *except* the oil, flannel square, and twine are in a pile, fold up the corners of the square and twist them to make a little round "ball" with the corners of the square pointing up. Wrap the "neck" of the ball tightly with twine (tight enough to keep it from spilling open and high enough on the neck to hold all the ingredients inside—the intention is not to open this again unless you're destroying it). Bind off the twine and tie three knots in it, then breathe three breaths on the ball. Dab your finger in the Crown of Success oil (or a similar blessing oil) and touch the mojo with it, asking it to wake up and help you with your academic endeavors. Keep it fed regularly with the oil (or as a reasonable substitute I've found strong black coffee works wonderfully!).

Medicine Bags

Native peoples from the Plains (such as the Lakota) to the Eastern Woodlands (such as members of the Iroquois Confederation) often create medicine bags as a part of their practice. These are also called "medicine bundles," and they are not intended as medical supplies in the Western European-influenced sense of that term.[216] Instead, they are essentially proxies for the person who carries them, filled with plant, animal, and mineral representations of a person's life. Frequently these bags or bundles

215. I usually use Psalm 65 for success work, with the passage "You crown the year with success, your paths drip fatness" as the part I write down for inclusion here, but Psalm 119 works here, emphasizing, "I have declared myself and you heard me; teach me your statutes, make me to understand your ways so I may tell of your wondrous works."

216. Jones & Molyneaux, *Mythology of American Nations*, 53.

are large, highly decorated, and get buried with their maker or keeper upon their death, but sometimes bundles are passed through friendship or family connections as a memorial to the departed. These are religious objects more than spells, although healing work (or, if a person is unlucky, cursing work) can be done using the medicine bag of a particular person.

Paper Packets

Found in Hoodoo, Mountain Magic, New England Cunning Folk, and Southern Conjure practices, in some ways these packet spells are similar to the mojos mentioned above. They are essentially spells based on the ingredients included—bay leaves and marigold petals used for luck, for example, or mustard seeds, pepper, and black salt for cursing—all wrapped into a paper envelope of some kind. One worker I know uses a dollar bill to wrap things like Solomon's seal, clove, and pyrite pieces in order to attract money to her.[217] Others will take written portions of biblical scripture (or even torn pages from desecrated Bibles—ones badly damaged and thus bound for the garbage bin) to wrap their spell and add an extra charge to it. Similarly, sometimes a handkerchief is used to wrap something like some asafetida or sulphur along with "sweet" herbs like angelica or clover in order to dispel hurtful spirits when worn around the neck (it may, in fact, dispel anyone, given the odor of the main ingredients). Usually these are "fixed" by being wrapped in a red thread, and they may need regular "feeding" like the mojos, depending on the tradition and formula. They are often worn around the neck or carried in the pocket.

Knits and Knots

Plenty of people do knot magic and don't even know it. Think only of how many young children weave friendship bracelets and wrap them onto each other's wrists with a final binding knot to cement their connection. At its heart, that is knot magic. The spells involving cords, thread, or yarn all involve forms of binding or releasing, whether that's binding up harmful spirits to keep them away from sleeping children in an Ojibwe dreamcatcher, releasing the winds using a knotted cord on a seashore, or even tying off a headache using a knotted amulet worn on the wrist. Spells like these are quicker than the container spells and packet spells above, but they are no less successful for those who use them, and something about their simplicity seems to add to their power.

217. Casas, *Working the Root*, 188–89.

Measures

Often practiced in British Traditional Wicca, Hoodoo, Southern Conjure, and Traditional Witchcraft, cord charms are a widespread phenomenon, and can be found in virtually any culture producing both textiles and magic. In direct connection to witchcraft, we have the witch's ladder (see figure 12-3), but also the idea of a "measure" or a "cord of sovereignty," signifying initiation into witch work.[218] This involves taking a cord longer than a person's body and using it to measure and knot various lengths associated with that person, such as the height from their feet to the crown of their head or between the fingertips of outspread arms. In Wicca, that cord is called a *cingulum* and is used as both an initiatory item and a potential link to a coven (in some covens, witches who break oaths of secrecy have their cords destroyed as a way of punishing betrayal, although that seems to be less common now). This practice has connections to Masonic initiation rites, and often other measures are incorporated, such as feet to groin or head to heart, and the cord becomes the symbolic proxy of the initiate. Cords used to measure other body parts can have other uses, too. In Hoodoo, for example, a cord used to measure a partner's sexual organs, wetted with the sexual fluids from copulation, and knotted will prevent a partner from ever straying.[219] Measures also work on objects: a simple book-binding charm involves wrapping the book in a cord and knotting the book's height, width, and depth, then keeping the cord in a safe place to ensure the book's return when it is lent out (which makes me wonder if there are secret rooms in libraries full of knotted strings).[220]

Knot Charms

Even broader than measures, we have knot charms used for healing or controlling various phenomena, often used in Maritimes Witchcraft, Mountain Magic, and New England Cunning Folk practices. In Cunning Folk practices and several healing traditions, we find charms for relieving headaches by creating a knotted halter from a hanged man's rope.[221] Similarly, some cures involve wrapping an aching or

218. Orapello & Maguire, *Besom, Stang, & Sword*, 34; Illes, *Encyclopedia of Witchcraft*, 691–92.

219. Hurston, "Hoodoo in America," 361–62.

220. Cunningham, *Earth, Air, Fire, & Water*, 50–51.

221. Baker, *The Cunning Man's Handbook*, 254.

injured body part in red thread, then knotting it seven or nine times (depending on the tradition) to stop the pain, a treatment also used for warts.[222] Undoing knots also has power. During a birth in the Appalachian Mountains, women were advised to unknot their hair and all knots in the birthing room were untied to ease the labor. A maritime charm for raising winds at the seashore or on a becalmed ship involves taking out a cord with seven knots in it and untying them one at a time. Usually only one or two knots needed to be undone, as seven would release hurricane-force gales!

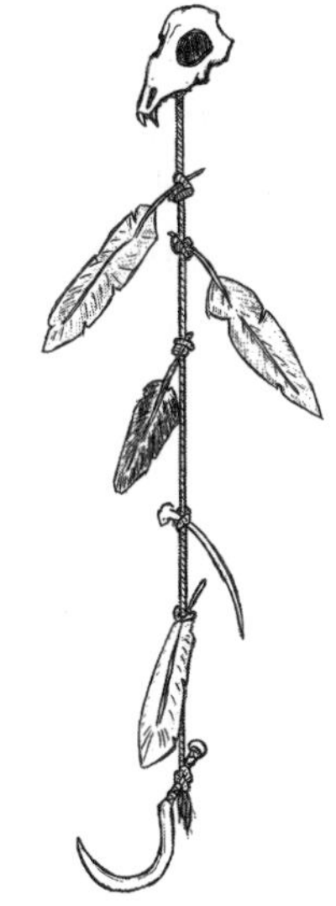

FIG 12-3: The witch's ladder.

Witch's Ladder

While much of what I've mentioned thus far has been positive or neutral magic, the witch's ladder comes out of cursing magic. Often found in New England Cunning Folk and Traditional Witchcraft practices, it involves braiding three cords together and knotting them nine times, placing an object into each knot (usually a feather from a hen or a goose, connecting it to mythological and folkloric figures like Frau Holle), and cursing the target with each knot tied. These ladders are hung in secret places—the target's home if possible, but the witch's home if not—and the person under the spell begins to suffer and eventually die unless the knots are unbound, or

222. Hand, *The Frank C. Brown Collection of North Carolina Folklore*, xxix, 147–48.

the ladder is destroyed somehow. Late twentieth-century Wiccan author Scott Cunningham revised the witch's ladder a bit for more positive purposes, turning it into the "wishing ladder," which uses similar magical structures to create charms that get a witch what she wants out of life.[223]

Fabric and Cloth Knots

In addition to taking a partner's "measure," Southern folk magic practices, such as Hoodoo and Southern Conjure, also include spells that involve taking two pieces of clothing, one from each lover, and tying them into a knot together, then placing that knotted charm under the bed or in a trunk, half in and half out of it (so dangling from the lip of the trunk, essentially). That would keep a couple together and prevent infidelity. Similar clothing-knotting charms appear in other places as well, such as knotting the corners of a woman's shawl to give her protection, or alternatively, bind her to a partner or home.[224] The use of fabric pieces touched to a wound or sore, then nailed into a tree (sometimes called "plugging"), also has some precedence in Mountain folk magic.[225]

God's Eyes and Dreamcatchers

God's eyes and dreamcatchers are common in native Huichol, Lakota, and Ojibwe peoples' practices, as well as folk magic worldwide. The best-known version of the *ojo de dios* or god's eye talisman comes from the Huichol tribe in south-central Mexico where it was called the *sikuli*, but versions of it appear all over the world.[226] The Huichols wrap a cross of sticks with yarn in color patterns to make a diamond-like "eye" that hangs from ceremonial arrows and acts as both a shield against harm and an "eye" ensuring that evil deeds meet with justice. The origins of this talisman are obscure, but may date to Peruvian civilization around 500 C.E. in the Americas. Similar crafts include the Brigid's cross of Ireland, the rowan cross of Britain, Scotland, and Scandinavia, the thread crosses in Nigeria and Angola, and an *unruh* charm made in Bavaria, Denmark, and Sweden. In most places, these talismans ward

223. Cunningham, *Earth Power*, 97.

224. Hurston, "Hoodoo in America," 348, 378.

225. Randolph, *Ozark Magic*, 289.

226. See Potts, *The World's Eye*.

off evil, especially the evil eye, and the *unruh* is even said to stop moving in the presence of a witch (it's normally hung in a window or from an overhead beam, where it will spin or rock gently). A somewhat similar but unrelated craft is the dreamcatcher of the Ojibwe and Lakota people around the Great Lakes and northern plains. This device, when made by Native practitioners, is designed to be a spiderweb-like creation (the origin story for the craft is about a spider character, usually Iktome or Spider Grandmother)[227] that traps bad dreams or spirits and keeps them away from sleeping people—usually children. Sadly, most dreamcatchers sold today are mass-produced and do not support the tribes from which they originate.

Sewn and Knitted Charms

There has been a strong trend in the last part of the twentieth century and the first part of the twenty-first, especially in Contemporary Feminist Witchcraft practices, to return to handicrafts, and many people are picking up knitting, crocheting, and embroidery work as a hobby. One of the innovative and delightful ways I've seen this manifest magically is in feminist witchcraft circles, where some witches are needle-pointing charms to hang on their walls based on old spells (such as the famed SATOR square) or creating counter-patriarchal and empowering embroidered pillows with phrases like "Hex the Patriarchy!" on them.[228] Some witches are spinning their own yarn and incorporating fibrous magical herbs or even the hair of certain animals to create spellcrafting skeins. I include mentions of these here because this is very much what folk magic is about: meeting contemporary needs with traditional methods and being able to modify them appropriately to work your own particular spell.

Dear Dolly—Poppet Spells

Dolls, doll babies, dollies, poppets—whatever you call them, figural toys seem to have the power to evoke fear in people and act as powerful proxies for magical and supernatural work. We have eerie examples such as Robert the Doll in Key West, Florida (who was once reputed to have appeared on an owner's bed, brandishing a kitchen knife) or the famed Annabelle "Raggedy-Ann"-style doll kept by paranormal

227. Erdoes & Ortiz, *American Indian Myths & Legends*, 381–82; Jones & Molyneaux, *Mythology of American Nations*, 74.

228. See Henderson, *Sew Witchy: Tools, Techniques, & Practices of Sewing Magic.*

investigators Ed and Lorraine Warren (and subject of several films). Most tales of dolls and magic in the New World are not as spectacular as these. That doesn't mean there aren't some very interesting uses for dolls in American folk magic. There most definitely are, and we can start in Salem, during the famous witchcraft trials of the early 1690s.

A slave from Barbados named Candy was the focus of one early investigation (although her fate was not, as far as we know, the gallows). Candy confessed her use of folk magic, including the use of a handkerchief that she transformed into a doll.[229] Candy's use of the knotted handkerchief gets at some of the main reasons that doll magic seems to be popular and widespread. Firstly, it involves easily found or acquired resources—in this case cloth from the intended target, making the materials doubly enticing. Secondly, doll magic is sympathetic magic, and the connection is easy to see. If I make a piece of someone's long johns look like a person, particularly the person whose backside the doll so recently covered, it seems likely that those two things will share a connection.

This point, that something that *looks* human but isn't has uncanny powers, gets echoed in a lot of folklore as well, some of which connects to the folk magical systems of early Americans. Imported stories, such as tales about Anansi, refer to the use of dolls as agents of trickery. One account of Anansi tells how he tricked Tiger, and Tiger avenged himself on Anansi by putting a gumdoll in a field. Anansi gets angry when the doll won't respond to him, and strikes it, becoming stuck to it.[230] This tale is likely best known by American audiences as the tale of Brer Rabbit and the Tar Baby, of course, which replaces Anansi with the wily trickster rabbit and uses tar in place of tree gum. An Apache tale recasts the narrative as Coyote fighting with a lump of pitch, placed in a field by a "white man" to catch the sneaky food thief.[231] The story keeps reappearing across different cultural backdrops, with new characters but the same basic structure. In all cases, the doll in question does nothing—that is one of the reasons Brer Rabbit and his compatriots dislike the thing—but still manages to get the best of its target.

229. McMillan, "Black Magic," 99–117.

230. Gates, Jr. & Tatar, *African American Folktales*, 162–63.

231. Erdoes & Ortiz, *American Indian Myths & Legends*, 359–61.

Dolls, much like the Tar Baby or gumdoll, don't necessarily have to do anything to be effective in folk magic, either. Jason Miller recounts a story in his book *Protection & Reversal Magic* in which a doll's effect is clearly psychological, but nonetheless potent:

> A santera I know was having problems with her neighbor being loud and obnoxious at all hours of the night and leaving garbage on her lawn. She asked her madrina (her teacher) what she should do. The madrina told her to make a doll that looked like the neighbor, blindfold it, tie its arms and legs, and nail it to the tree in her yard facing her neighbor's front door. My friend was a bit shocked and said, "Good Lord! I don't want to hurt him! What will happen?"
>
> "Nothing," replied her madrina, "but it will scare the living crap out of him!"[232]

Miller's account of the santera's doll experience resembles other accounts in American folk history, such as those referenced by Newbell Niles Puckett in his *Folk Beliefs of the Southern Negro*. Puckett describes cases in which dolls in black caskets are left in front of a person's door to warn them of a curse or ill intent. The dolls may or may not actually have a magical effect, or they might simply convey the sender's sentiments about how they wish to see the recipient suffer.

Dolls that do nothing, however, are not as much fun as dolls that do *something*. Dolls can have powerful magical agency, according to folklore. Paper dolls are used in Japanese and Chinese American folk magic, often to curse a target, but sometimes to bestow a blessing upon them.[233] Corn husk dolls appear in rural cultures and in Latinx communities, and can be effective dolls for burning rituals. Dolls are often crafted with local flora (and occasionally fauna) for a combination of practical and symbolic reasons. Spanish moss is frequently used to stuff or wrap doll babies in Delta-area conjure practices, both because it grows ubiquitously on trees in the region and because as a plant it acts semi-parasitically (it doesn't actually feed off of the oak trees it grows upon directly, but it can limit their growth), thereby sharing life with a host as a doll is supposed to. Even more potent than Spanish moss, however, are doll components that come directly from the intended target, such as pieces

232. Miller, *Protection & Reversal Magick*, 30.

233. Cummins, *Dark Side of Japan*, 66–68.

of their clothing, as noted above in the example with long johns.[234] In contemporary times, we see ubiquity and necessity fueling new ways of doing doll magic. Dorothy Morrison, in her book *Utterly Wicked: Curses, Hexes, & Other Unsavory Notions,* discusses using dollar store plastic dolls and stuffing their little torsos and heads with baneful herbs as a way of creating a cursing poppet.

Dolls today have a lot of the same stigmas attached to them: they are objects of fear and superstition as well as simple objects of play. Magically, they can be used for a number of purposes that resemble and also modify the traditional folk uses I've outlined here. One informant shared a story with me about a sloth doll she uses to overcome issues with chronic lethargy, letting the doll absorb any feelings of laziness from her, for example.

All of which is to say, dolls are a big part of magical lore and practice, and don't seem to be going anywhere soon. And they watch you while you sleep. So sweet dreams and all.

Works in Progress

The crafted objects of magic I've listed here—witch bottles and mirror boxes, poppets and witches' ladders—represent only a small fragment of what folklorists like to call the "material culture" of witchcraft. Virtually every spell has its physical components, and there's a reason that witchcraft is called, well, witch*craft*. Things get made so that other things get done, and the magic is both in the making and in the having made. Sometimes it's even in the unmaking, as we see in cord magic or some doll spells.

I would be a little remiss if I didn't acknowledge that there are a number of traditional crafted objects, and some created in more recent iterations of folk magic, that I've had to skip here. Take, for example, witch balls, which can be one of two different crafts. In British-derived traditions and Cunning Folk practices, these are glass balls used to fascinate witches and break their spells or to ward off evil spirits much the same way witch bottles do. In many Mountain Magic practices, however, witch balls are little wads of hair and wax provided to a witch by the Devil for her to use in cursing.[235] Both objects are important, and both are unique, and fitting them into a chapter like this (beyond a mention here) could spill over into pages and pages

234. Hyatt, *Folklore of Adams County*, 456.

235. Oberon, *Southern Cunning*, chapter 5; Davis, *The Silver Bullet*, 31–34.

of material. That's not even getting into brooms, which I cover briefly in chapter ten but which have their own magical lore associated with their fabrication. I could also mention things like the Devil's club that Southern folk magician Aaron Oberon describes in his book *Southern Cunning*, a tool based on traditional models but also something he created on his own, too.

Witches and folk magicians are a crafty lot and trying to cover everything that they can and do make could be its own dedicated volume (and who knows, it may be some day!). My hope, though, is that this chapter unscrews the lid from the jar a bit, or opens up the box a crack, and lets out a few of the craftier imps that linger in North American folk witchcraft's cupboard. There is so much to explore, and I hope that readers will seek out crafts of their own for study or use, and find magic in the making as well.

THE WORK—Handicraft to Witchcraft

Virtually everyone I know has the power to make *something*. That something could be as intricate as a cable-knit sweater or as simple as a gum wrapper chain or a cut-out paper doll. Wherever you are in your life, you likely have made things before, and very likely still make things. Perhaps you even make things with magical intent behind them already—herbal blends or soaps, poppets, candles, and so forth.

What I offer as a challenge to you, then, is to look at a handicraft you do (or pick one up, if you are so inclined) that you have not previously associated with magic. Maybe you make your own herbal soaps with witchy ingredient blends, but you don't really consider sewing a button on a shirt with any magical regard. Perhaps you love brewing magical oils for spellwork, but when you fold origami out of Post-It notes you are doing so without a second thought to magic.

This is my invitation to you to change that. Take a handicraft, something you can make, and spin it magically. Maybe you home-preserve jams and jellies. Is it something you could turn into a container spell? How would you do that? Perhaps you like making collages or coloring with your children. How might you be able to turn that into some kind of poppet magic? Do you sew up tears in a favorite pair of slacks or add a button back onto a shirt when it pops off? What might happen if you slipped a little knot magic into that process, creating a "wish ladder" or a protection spell of some kind?

Challenge yourself to make your everyday crafts into magical ones. Draw upon your crafting skill set to build up new kinds of magic in your repertoire, and you may be surprised at just how many spells you already have at your disposal.

Recommended Reading

Working the Root: The Conjure Workbook, Volume One, by Starr Casas. Starr's book is not only a good overview of Southern Conjure practices, it is intensely hands-on and guides the reader through the creation of bottle spells, packet spells, dollies, and more. She gets into a bit of the lore behind each, but focuses largely on the practical effects of using these spells and how they fit into the everyday practice of a Southern Conjure worker.

Earth Power: Techniques of Natural Magic, by Scott Cunningham. This was one of the first books full of folk spells I remember encountering, and it still stands as a wonderful resource today. Though Cunningham "Wiccan-ized" a number of the spells he recorded, the roots for each enchantment are there and he does point the way to other ways of working with his ideas. Additionally, virtually all the spells here are very practical and down-to-earth, pulling from the folk magical tradition of using what you have and what's around you to get the job done.

Magic When You Need It: 150 Spells You Can't Live Without, by Judika Illes. I'm always a fan of Illes and her practical, down-to-earth, and folklorically-rooted magic. This book is not just about the physical objects of magic work, but there are a good number of them in here. Additionally, she pulls from folk traditions to address timeless needs, such winning a court case or protecting your home, while also using magic to deal with modern problems like getting a green card or collecting child support.

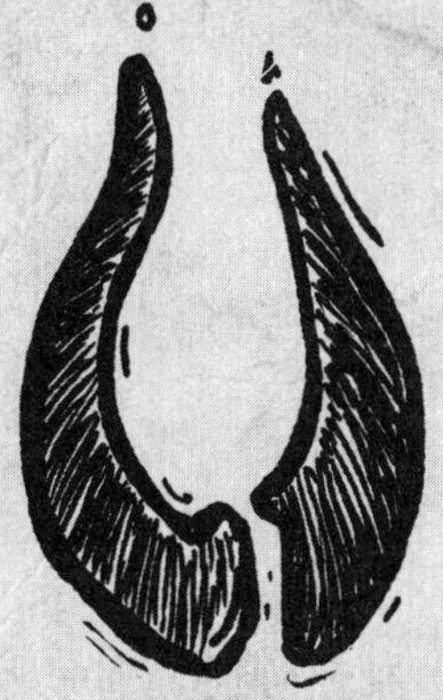

SEVENTH RITE: THE FAMILIAR

Or, a Witch's Relationship with Creatures Seen and Unseen

"Nobody could shoot a rifle better than John … But it got so that for some reason he could not shoot straight at all. In the evenings he would go out, and every time he went he would see a large doe. Try as he would, he could never hit it. There was an old woman who lived not far from his place and lots of folks said they thought she was a witch … He made a silver bullet and the next time he saw the doe, he shot at it and hit it in the leg. It ran, but he followed it by the trail of blood, and it led him right to the door of the old woman … He knocked at the door, and one of the girls came to the door and told him that grandma had hurt her leg very bad and couldn't see anyone. He knew that this witch had turned herself into a doe, and when he shot the doe, he was really shooting the old woman. After that he had no trouble with his rifle."*

* Gainer, *Witches, Ghosts, & Signs*, 157.

CHAPTER THIRTEEN

The Witch's Companion—Creatures and Witchcraft

In the areas around the Mexican-U.S. border, the sound of an owl hooting or screeching can put an icy feeling in the pit of a person's stomach. While plenty of people can get spooked by sudden sounds in the night, an owl is particularly unsettling in that area because owls are believed to be transformed *lechuzas*, a night-flying witch that often brings destruction or bad luck to those who see it. In some stories, lechuzas come to the windows of children, pressing their heavy bulk against the glass or poking their heads into darkened bedrooms with enormous glowing yellow eyes. There are local stories of these owl-witches chasing down cars and pursuing adults, too. They may come and visit the home of a person who is about to die.[236]

Owls, of course, are hardly the only animal associated with witchcraft in North America. Cats, rabbits, deer, coyotes, and more feature in tales of witchery and magic. Sometimes these animals are not simply the bodies of transfigured witches, but companions who live with or work for a particular witch. Sometimes witches draw upon the animal kingdom for spell ingredients. People who might not consider themselves particularly witchy might even engage with strange magical rituals involving animals, such as putting black hens in the yard to scratch up bad luck or hanging a dead snake from a tree to call for rain during a drought.

236. Bowles, *Border Lore*, loc. 1072–1118.

FIG 13-1: In the Southwest, witches called *lechuzas* transform into owls.

The deep connection between magic, humans, and other animals will be the focus of this chapter. We will look at some of the folklore surrounding different animals, including how they fit into a magical pharmacopeia, how transformation into animal forms can be useful (and dangerous) for a witch, and how rituals and magic in the New World frequently draw upon creatures great and small to maintain the enchantment of the world around us. While the examples here are not exhaustive (and how could they be, given how many different animals get associated with witchcraft?), hopefully you will see how the deep relationship with the animal kingdom shapes New World Witchery in a number of important, powerful ways.

Telling the Bees: Connecting with the (Magical) Animal Kingdom

Relationships between animals and humans in the New World, as in so many places, require give-and-take. Humans must learn to listen to the animals in the world around them and follow their lead. That sort of "reading" of the landscape is useful not only for a seventeenth-century fur trapper in the wilds of Ohio or Michigan who needs to know where the beaver are going and how to avoid the bears, but also for the twentieth-century farmer who watches cattle or sheep lying in a pasture and knows a storm is coming in. That last bit of lore is not scientifically founded, yet many people living in partnership with animals in some way will pay attention to them because of years of close observation, even if their observations go against more empirical science.

Just as there is a practical relationship between the animals around us and ourselves, there is also a long tradition of magical relationships between animals and people. For example, in many rural areas, beekeepers still practice the custom of "telling the bees" whenever there has been a major shift in the household—usually a death, but sometimes also a birth or marriage. This is done so that the hive will not grow upset at the changes and abandon the hive eventually.

In other forms of North American magical lore, we also have a plethora of animals with significance for magical practitioners. Some of them work as omens, some as bringers of magic, some as sources of spell ingredients (see chapter eleven on the use of bone curios in magic). Below are some examples of the magical menagerie of North American creatures, along with a bit of the lore associated with them.

Cats

Cats are one of the animals most strongly associated with witches, particularly black cats. They may act as companions or familiars—animal helpers that are sometimes thought to also act as vessels for the witch's imp or devil—and some may be the witch herself in a transformed state. One particularly gruesome connection with cats and folk magic is the procurement of a "black cat bone" in several forms of Conjure and Hoodoo.[237] That bone, which empowers its carrier with magical gifts such as invisibility or control over others, is acquired by boiling a cat alive in a cauldron at a crossroads at midnight—a brutal and heartless way to gain magic from an animal so willing to lend its fur, whiskers, and purrs to spells when adopted and well-cared for.

Dogs, Wolves, and Coyotes

Canids (dog-like animals) also have strong associations with folk magic and witchcraft. Wolves frequently seem to be either the companions of witches or at least present in their spaces, such as dark woods. They also have strong mythological forms, such as Coyote the Trickster in Aztec lore, where he is known as Huehuecoyotl.[238] Helpful or tutelary spirits may take the form of a black dog, a common motif in English folklore (think Sherlock Holmes and *The Hound of the Baskervilles*) and one repeated in tales about meeting the Man in Black at the crossroads in Southern folk stories.[239] Dog hair and teeth are frequently used in folk magic, often to cause a change in another person. Dog hair and cat hair may be combined to break up a couple, for example.

237. Hurston, "Hoodoo in America," 387.

238. Bowles, *Feathered Serpent, Dark Heart of Sky*, 68–9.

239. Hyatt, *Hoodoo-Conjuration-Witchcraft-Rootwork*, 103–105.

Raccoons and Possums

Both of these creatures have folkloric associations, and sometimes get used as stock characters in folktales. For instance, folklore derived from African American storytelling traditions often include mentions of Brer ("Brother") Possum, a character who is generally unassuming and nice enough, if a bit dim. Raccoons, on the other hand, are frequently tricksters like Coyote, as in the Abenaki tales of Azeban. Raccoon bones have value in Hoodoo, where the baculum, or penis bone, of a raccoon is used as a gambling or protective charm.[240]

Rabbits

In Western European lore, rabbits and hares are frequently associated with witches. Isobel Gowdie, a self-confessed Scottish witch, famously used a charm to turn herself into a hare as a means of attending sabbat rites and doing witchery. In North America, the magical lore of rabbits also marks them as witch animals, although mostly in locations where European influences established that trope. Rabbits are also trickster figures, as anyone who has read stories of Brer Rabbit from African American lore will know. Additionally, rabbits provide one of the best-known magical charms: the lucky rabbit's foot, which is usually collected from a rabbit in a graveyard to maximize its power.[241]

Bears

Several different bears inhabit the North American continent, and wherever they go they carry stories of magic with them. The Nariticong people of New England used bears as representations of chiefs or respected warriors, and in folklore from Michigan's Upper Peninsula, several stories tell of shape-shifters who are half-man, half-bear, known as "bearwalkers."[242] Once again, stories from African American lore offer up Brer Bear as a somewhat slow-witted animal who is nevertheless not to be trifled with. In magical practices, wearing bearskins or using bear "grease" (the rendered fat of a bear) works as a shape-shifting method for some witchy folk.

240. Yronwode, *Hoodoo Herb & Root Magic*, 161.

241. Hyatt, *Hoodoo-Conjuration-Witchcraft-Rootwork Volume 2*, 1486–87.

242. See Dorson, *Bloodstoppers & Bearwalkers*, 1972.

Deer and Buffalo

While deer may seem docile and timid, they can also be fiercely protective of their herds or their young, and they have an uncanny way of dissolving into the forest almost silently (and here I speak from experience, having watched a young buck do exactly that). Witch stories that identify deer as magical often describe the deer as special in some way, such as being all-white. That is exactly the case in the New York state-based legend of local witch "Auntie Greenleaf," who could turn herself into a white deer. Antlers are also used in bone divinations and have occasionally been used as a form of virility tonic as well.[243] Buffalo similarly appear in North American myths and legends, often as bearers of wisdom or knowledge, as in the Lakota tale of the White Buffalo Woman, who established important traditional ceremonies.

Snakes

Wily serpents have plenty of magic all their own, with their ability to shed their skins in self-transformation or slip into the chthonic (Underworld) spaces with a slinky slither. Additionally, snake parts are frequently represented as having magical qualities, with the skins getting used in cursing works and the bones being used in bone-casting divinations. Rattles from rattlesnakes are considered lucky, and some blues musicians even kept a rattle in their guitars to bring success (I did a variation on just this charm as a gift to a couple of musician friends of mine, and they've done all right for themselves, so who knows?). Haitian Vodoun and New Orleans Voodoo traditions both have sacred associations with serpents, including Marie Laveau's famous snake, Zombi, whom she wore draped around her neck during some rituals. The Vodun *lwa* (sacred persona) Damballah is often represented as a snake, as well. Some farmers in the rural Midwest and Appalachia also hang dead snakes in trees to bring rain.

243. Schlosser, *Spooky New York*, 171–77.

FIG 13-2: The custom of "telling the bees" required that any major news be reported to the bees kept on a property.

Spiders and Insects

I have already mentioned the custom of "telling the bees" at the start of this chapter, and honey is used magically for spells such as "sweetening" work. Spiders have a magical significance of their own, too. Several traditions maintain it is bad luck to kill a spider in your home. Spiders appear as tricksters (most famously Anansi) in African stories and thus sometimes show up in African American and African Caribbean lore.[244] The legendary Iktomi is a well-known and cunning spider-human spirit in Lakota mythology, while Diné (Navajo) stories tell of a Spider Grandmother named *Na'ashjé'ii Asdzáá* who acts as both a helper to her people and their equivalent of the boogeyman.[245] Spider and insect eggs are used in hexing spells in the Hoodoo and Conjure traditions, especially to perform the dreaded "Live Things Inside You" curse. Spiders can also be used to help find lost things in Appalachian folk magic, if one says the following charm to a spider in her home: "Spitter, spitter spider, tell me where the [lost object] is and I'll give you a drink of cider."[246] Some

244. Gates, Jr. and Tatar, *African American Folktales*, 9–12.

245. Jones & Molyneaux, *Mythology of the American Nations*, 74.

246. Gainer, *Witches, Ghosts, & Signs*, 125.

witches keep insects as pets or familiars as well, as in the story of Rindy Sue Gose of Virginia, who kept a beetle in a bottle and fed it nightly from her shoulder.[247]

Birds

There are entire books written about the lore and folk magic of birds, and individual birds can have specific magical meanings. Magpies, for example, can be counted to predict coming events, as in the nursery rhyme, "One for sorrow, two for joy, three for a girl, four for a boy, five for silver, six for gold, seven a secret never to be told, eight for a wish, nine for a kiss, ten for a time of joyous bliss."[248] Some other examples of species-specific bird lore:

- Loons portend bad weather because they are the souls of dead sailors.
- Whip-poor-wills calling indicates death or bad luck soon to follow, although some believe it may just be a sort of "closing time" whistle at the end of a hard day's work.
- Killing barn swallows will cause your cows to give bloody milk.
- To cure a backache, wait until you hear a whip-poor-will call, then roll on the ground three times.
- It is bad luck for a hen to crow.[249]
- There are also more general magical beliefs about birds, too. If a bird gets hold of your hair (for example, by you brushing it outside) and weaves it into her nest, it is said to cause madness or headaches. If a bird builds a nest in or out of your clothes—say an old hat or boot—it is a token of death coming within the year.

Of course, trying to list every possible North American animal and its magical associations would generate multiple volumes of lore, so the list above is necessarily limited and incomplete. Other animals have strong magical significance for very specific groups or locations. For example, the groundhog is vitally important to Pennsylvania Dutch folklore and has some magical associations such as weather and initiatory lodges. In the Pacific Northwest, salmon have additional meanings and

247. Davis, *The Silver Bullet*, 16–19.

248. Opie & Tatum, *Dictionary of Superstitions*, 235–36.

249. McAtee, "Odds and Ends of North American Folklore on Birds," 169–83.

also help keep track of the rhythms of nature. Most witches in North American lore seem to be well-versed in the comings and goings of their animal neighbors and to have special relationships with a few in particular.

Sop Paws, Witch Hares, and Skinwalkers: Shape-Shifters and Folklore

Beyond the symbolic associations of animals and their roles as providers of magical insight and ingredients, many witch stories also feature tales of shape-shifting and transformation into animal forms. In most cases, a witch adopts an animal form to travel from one place to another, and we frequently see the concept of witch flight linked to such transfigurations (see chapter nine for more on flying witches). Sometimes that travel means meeting other witches, as in the tale of the Sop-Paw from Appalachia. In that story, a traveling man seeks shelter in an old barn, and as he sits around a small fire, a huge black cat slinks from the shadow. The man tries to ignore it and continues cooking his food, but the cat puts its paw into the frying pan and stirs, saying in a distorted-but-human voice, "Soooooopppp Paaaaaaawwww!" Soon, another cat shows up, and the first cat stirs again, repeating its strange incantation. Slowly more and more cats arrive, and when the man has had enough, he takes out a knife and whacks off the big cat's paw, sending the whole group scattering. He later finds out that the cat was a witch in disguise and that they were gathering to meet the Devil, with plans to kill the man when he arrived. A local woman (typically the wife of the farmer who owns the barn) is usually identified as the witch, and she'll often have a severely injured hand or be missing one altogether, which is how she is caught.[250]

Similarly, rural stories from all over North America talk of "witch hares," wild rabbits who seem to be unafraid of human hunters and who somehow evade capture or killing. Hunters will frequently describe trying to sight just such a strange looking animal—often wild-eyed or oversized—only to find their gun will no longer fire straight or even at all. Traditions like Pow-wow and Conjure frequently have spells for taking a hex off of a "witched gun" after an encounter with a shape-shifted rabbit-witch. Using a silver bullet will sometimes break the spell, too, and if a hunter hits the rabbit-witch with a silver bullet, it can kill or injure her even in her human form,

250. Gainer, *Witches, Ghosts, & Signs*, 146–49; Chase, *The Jack Tales*, 76–82.

much as we hear in twentieth-century lore about werewolves (in some cases, the link between werewolves and witches is very strong, especially in Europe).

The *lechuzas* mentioned at the beginning of the chapter are not the only shape-shifters from the Southwest, either. A number of stories from the Diné tribe talk of creatures called "skinwalkers," who transform themselves into large animal-like creatures by putting on the pelts of beasts such as bear or coyotes. These transformed forms have superhuman powers of speed and strength, and are thought to prey upon the families and communities of the shape-shifted witches (who are seen as unquestionably evil in that tradition). Similarly, Hopi stories tell of witches who shape-shift by using enchanted hoops to turn into things like coyotes or birds.[251]

Transformation seems to be largely a feature of escape—most of the witches in these stories are members of families or households where the use of witchcraft is strictly taboo. It also seems to provide unique powers and abilities to some of the witches, as in the case of skinwalkers who gain speed and strength, *lechuzas* who gain flight, and rabbit-witches who are able to magically confound hunters. The act of self-transformation and the adoption of an animal nature seems to be an empowering act for most witches, then, even while it is often viewed as a violation of her social roles. But then, howling at the moon is a lot of fun, and damn what anyone else thinks about such things, right?

DIRT UNDER THE NAILS
Go into a Hare (Mask-Making)

One of my favorite magical people, Peter Paddon, used to teach workshops on leatherworking that involved creating animal masks for sacred and magical practices. While leather work can be a very involved skill and take a great deal of time to learn, it produces absolutely gorgeous final products that really have a feeling of power in them.

251. See Malotki and Gary, *Hopi Stories of Witchcraft, Shamanism, and Magic*; Games, *Witchcraft in Early North America*; García, *Brujerias: Stories of Witchcraft and the Supernatural in the American Southwest and Beyond*; Simmons , *Witchcraft in the Southwest.*

Even if you can't tool leather, though, you can tap into the power of mask-making for magical transformation. I have done rituals on my own and with groups involving the use of animal masks, and the results are always surprising because a piece of me seems to melt away and something else—something a bit wild and a bit messy, but incredibly powerful—seems to take its place for a while.

To make a magical mask, you can buy a pre-made blank mask at a craft store (but know that many of those are plastic and if that will interfere with the magic for you, find an alternative). You could also put a very thin layer of petroleum jelly or a similar product on your face and have a friend lay strips of papier-mâché over you until you have a good covering, about three to five millimeters thick (about an eighth to a quarter of an inch). Let that dry enough to hold its form, then remove and let dry completely. Cut into a final shape and make space for your eyeholes and holes to use ribbon, yarn, or cord to attach the mask to you on the sides.

Decorate your mask with the animal that you want to invite into your transformation. If possible, consider ethically sourcing some of that animal's parts to make the mask: legally acquired feathers for bird transformation, for example, or snake bones from a company like the Bone Room to have a serpentine shape-shifting experience. If you do not have access to these supplies, of course, just do your best with what you've got and use paper, cloth, cardboard, or whatever you have on hand to create your mask. So long as *you* recognize what it is you're becoming, it will be fine.

When your mask is decorated and complete, make the time to take it out someplace wild where you won't be disturbed. Draw a circle on the ground (or in the air around you with your finger) and sit in the middle. Focus on the mask and remember the stories of the creature you're "putting on." Try to think of what it looks like, smells like, sounds like. Think of the myths and legends you know, and the way you have interacted with the creature in your own life. Say its name, and repeat your intention to transform, saying for example, "Rabbit I am you; now I am rabbit." Raise the mask to your face and put it on. Feel the creature you've slipped into filling your body and wrapping itself around you like a second skin. Let it guide you, and follow its lead: jumping, running, howling, rolling on the ground.

When you are ready, return to your circle and remove the mask. Give yourself some time to readjust and reorient yourself, and just rest on the ground for a few moments. Thank the animal for being with you, for becoming you, for letting you become her for a bit. Store the mask carefully in a cloth or some other protective covering, and use it only for magical transformation (and feel free to combine other transformative methods with this, as well, such as safely-sourced flying ointments or drumming).

It Had No Tail: Fearsome Critters of the New World

The animal kingdom has a magic all its own, but still we humans love to see mythical or quasi-mythical beasties around us as well. Medieval European unicorns, the guardian dragons of China, the fearsome Nandi bear of Kenya, the reluctant Yeti of Nepal, and other strange creatures dot our global landscape and have become deeply entwined with local legends and cultures in many cases. In the late twentieth and early twenty-first centuries, we began referring to some of these creatures as "cryptids," a diminutive nickname derived from the concept of "cryptozoology," or the study of mysterious and unknown (frequently unverifiable) animals. Not all of these creatures are mythical or fabulous. Take, for example, the okapi, which is a creature that seems like a mash-up between a zebra and a deer, although it is actually more closely related to the giraffe. When it was first reported by local central African tribes to Europeans in the nineteenth century, most colonial naturalists wrote it off as legend. Then, in the very early twentieth century, Europeans found the creature alive and well, although in small numbers, and they moved from mythic beast to zoological curiosity (and it should be noted that the African people from the surrounding areas never thought of these as mythical at all; they knew okapi were real right from the get-go). Similar tales could be told of the coelacanth, a fish that was generally thought to be extinct until a South African fisherman brought one to shore in the 1930s.

FIG 13-3: Author's rendering of the infamous Jersey Devil.

Cryptids may be interesting folklore, but what do they have to do with magic? In folk magical practices, we often see that witches and other spellcasters become involved with local spirits and animals. That is also true of several cryptids in North America, and in some cases these beasts can act almost as local deities, providing a link to magical lore or omens portending doom to those who know how to read them. Two excellent examples are the Jersey Devil of the Pine Barrens in New Jersey and the Mothman of Point Pleasant, West Virginia. The Jersey Devil has been talked about in local legends for more than two centuries, and was even the subject of a story attributed to Napoleon Bonaparte's brother when he hunted in the area. While the story of the Jersey Devil varies in the telling, many accounts trace its origin back to a woman named Mother Leeds. She is frequently described as a witch, and the Jersey Devil is her thirteenth child, cursed by her from birth with a monstrous shape resembling something like a bat-goat-kangaroo hybrid (some believe that this creature is simply a blue heron, indigenous to the region but which can look a lot like the Jersey Devil's descriptions when molting, see figure 13-3). Some practicing witches in the area have taken the Leeds Devil—another nickname for the beast—as an icon with which to work.[252] Even the New Jersey National Hockey League team is called, of course, the Devils.

252. Orapello and Maguire, *Besom, Stang, & Sword*, 171–74.

Similar stories surround the Mothman, who began appearing in West Virginia in the 1960s. It is often described as a large, dark figure with enormous wings and glowing red eyes who will follow drivers in their cars or swoop out of the sky near unsuspecting people. Its home was thought to be an abandoned munitions dump, although it was seen in numerous places around Point Pleasant over a one-year period. Then, in December of 1967, the Silver Bridge collapsed into the Ohio River, killing nearly fifty people, and the Mothman sightings slowed and then ceased altogether. Many linked the two, thinking that perhaps Mothman was a harbinger of destruction. Mothman was also linked to UFO activity at times, and alien encounters are sometimes a good proxy for the sorts of abductions and Otherworldly experiences reported in European fairy lore.[253]

That is not to say that every cryptid or alien is magical in nature or to be considered a local land spirit. Certainly, there are also plenty of hoaxes out there (such as the infamous Hodag of Wisconsin, created essentially as a publicity stunt), and many creatures may simply be a known species seen by those who do not quite understand what they are seeing, as with theories of the Jersey Devil as a confused vision of the indigenous blue heron. Still, there are plenty of strange creatures in our folklore, and some of them may well be incarnations of local entities that those interested in magic can work with.

An excellent example of localized lore reflecting magical experiences of Otherworldly creatures comes in the form of lake monsters and water serpents. We have lore about krakens and sea serpents dating back centuries, millennia really. In North America, a number of lakes and rivers have localized water serpents associated with them, such as Chessie (in the Chesapeake Bay), Champ (in Lake Champlain between New York and Vermont), the Beast of 'Busco (in Churabusco, Indiana, which is actually an oversized snapping turtle), Ogopogo (in Okanagan Lake in British Columbia), Manipogo (in Lake Manitoba), Slimy Slim (in Lake Payette, Idaho), and the White River Monster (in Newport, Arkansas). I have even spoken with someone living near Niagara Falls who told me of a legend of a "dragon" living in the cave nearby.[254] Many of these resemble stories of horned serpents found throughout Native American lore, as well, and may be local manifestations of just such a beast.

253. Ellis, *Aliens, Ghosts, & Cults,* 142–60.

254. *New World Witchery,* "Episode 126—Magic and the Great Lakes," 2018.

Similar tales can be told about creatures like the Wampus Cat of the American Southeast and paralleled with stories of jaguar-like beasts in the Southwest and Mexico. Mexican *duendes* often resemble gnomes or goblins from European lore, although they are also distinct in many ways. Multiple locations have lore about sasquatches and ape-men, with localized incarnations attached to different legends. In the Mormon cultural region around Salt Lake City, for example, the "bigfoot" legends get attributed to encounters with a dark, hairy wanderer who turns out to be the biblical Cain, still walking the Earth under an eternal curse—immortal but unable to rest (combining the sasquatch legend, the story of the "mark of Cain," and European legends about a figure known as the "Wandering Jew").[255] Many places have legends of phantom hitchhikers or ghostly "gray ladies" or "ladies in white," who seem to act as both memorials to past tragedies and guardians of a particular place. The wailing La Llorona in Mexico and parts of the United States fills a similar role, while also being a boogeyman to terrorize errant children. In the Ozarks and Appalachians, that boogeyman is known as Raw Head and Bloody Bones, a sort of phantom wild boar under the command of a local witch. In the Baltimore area, some African American communities have a similar story about the ghost of a headless hog who wanders through the streets at night.

Looking into local lore for animals both concrete and wondrous opens up all sorts of possibilities for magic. What may seem like a silly legend could turn out to be the gateway to an entire vein of localized spiritual forces that are untapped or misunderstood. Or, they could get you haunted, hunted, and killed. Those seem to be the risks with magic in so many cases, though.

THE WORK–The Wildlife

Get to know your local wildlife—your local domestic life, too, while you are at it. Spend time discovering what animals in your part of the world do, and how they behave. Count the birds, carry treats for neighborhood dogs and cats, put earthworms back on the soil after rainstorms to keep them from being crushed underfoot. Watch how birds migrate—or don't—when the seasons change, and pay attention to when the first fireflies of summer appear (or the last mosquitos disappear). When do the owls come out at night, and can you identify them by their calls? Can you

255. See MormonThink, "Bigfoot."

make friends with the local crows, or spend some time putting out water dishes with pebbles in them for the bees and other local insects during hot summer days? Find the connection to the creatures around you, and you will find they begin to mean more to you, reveal things to you. Stories about snakes mean something very different once you've discovered how helpful and friendly a garter snake or rat snake can be. You may see animals you love pop up in divinations or even unexpectedly in art or music or conversations around you. Pay attention then, too, because that network of relationship is very much at the heart of North American witchery.

In my own life, animals have long held an important place. I am not always sentimental about them—as someone who lived and worked on a small sheep farm for much of my youth, I understand very well the cycle of life and death that weaves us all together. I have, however, loved a number of animals and felt their love in return, and seen some truly magical moments with them. I still remember one night in particular when my mother, who had been recently diagnosed with the cancer that would steal her from us in a little more than a year, left the house in an emotional cloud of rage and sadness. She dropped to her knees in the sheep pasture, sobbing and wailing, and I had no idea how to comfort her. Within moments, however, our sheep—led by our ram Patrick—had come over to her and began nuzzling their woolly faces against her. Slowly, she calmed down and began stroking their fleecy necks, and the sobs subsided. Sometimes, magic happens in ways we don't expect, and comes from creatures we would never imagine had such power all along.

Recommended Reading

Border Lore: Folktales and Legends of South Texas, by David Bowles. While I could probably recommend a number of books on shape-shifting witches (and please do see the recommendations in chapter nine on witch flight), Bowles has written an excellent guide to the lore of the Mexican-U.S. border which covers shapes-shifters like skinwalkers and *lechuzas* with wonderful narrative verve. I highly recommend this book as a jumping-off point for shape-shifter lore of the Southwest in particular.

Chasing American Monsters, by Jason Offutt. Sadly, one of my favorite books on cryptozoological creatures (Daniel Cohen's *The Encyclopedia of Monsters*) is now out of print. Thankfully, Jason Offutt, a paranormal researcher and journalism professor, has done a marvelous job of collecting many of the best stories of

American mythical and legendary creatures in his book. He breaks down the catalog by state, making them very easy to find (but missing Canada, Mexico, and Central America, unfortunately). The stories range from the whimsical to the dark, but often provide good insights into local customs and traditions surrounding the creatures he describes.

What the Robin Knows: How Birds Reveal the Secrets of the Natural World, by Jon Young. Young's book is about learning to listen, to birds in particular but also to the natural world around you. In a vein similar to Tristan Gooley's excellent guides to observing nature, this book unlocks some of the ways even a casual birding enthusiast can learn to hear the twitters and tweets around them with new ears. This makes a good first step to learning how to pay attention to animals in general, and offers a great approach to opening yourself up to the highly active realm of nature and animals surrounding you.

CHAPTER FOURTEEN

The Dark Man in the Woods—Diabolical Rumors and Rites

Almost everyone who grows up in the United States hears something about the Salem Witch Trials at some point. Mostly it seems to be treated as an episode in mass hysteria, with people loving to blame silly superstition, or strange fungi in the crops, or (rather insidiously) the volatile whims of mean-spirited adolescent girls for the eventual legal entrapment of more than a hundred people and the final, tragic death of nineteen of them. While there have been some wonderful scholarly excavations of the hidden motivations for the "witch hysteria" in New England,[256] something that often gets overlooked is the very real worldview held by so many at the time: witches were (and are) real. And if witches were real, that meant accepting the even more frightening truth that the Devil was real, and actively stomping a cloven foot around when no one was looking. If witchcraft was happening at your neighbor's farm and you heard stories of strange yellow birds or fierce black dogs roaming the area, the next pair of eyes you spied in the dark might very well be a sign of infernal forces creeping up to your back step (even if those eyes belonged to your own dog, or sheep, or your friendly pet goat Black Phillip).

One of the longest-standing charges against witchcraft in the New World (as well as the Old) is its inherent alliance with diabolic forces. A person simply could not be

256. See Breslaw, *Witches of the Atlantic World*; and Boyer and Nissenbaum, *Salem Possessed: The Social Origins of Witchcraft.*

a witch without being bound in some way to the Devil or one of his minions, according to popular conceptions, which remain strong even today. If you have seen the 2015 Robert Eggers film, *The Witch*, then you know that Colonial-era conceptions of the Devil made him look like an attractive alternative to starvation in the wilderness, especially if one liked the taste of butter or wished to "live deliciously." The notion of witchcraft as a Satanic practice is, of course, inaccurate—many Satanists have nothing to do with witchcraft, and many witches have nothing to do with Satan (that name here being used for the adversary of the Judeo-Christian God). There are certainly Satanic witches, just as there are Jewish witches or Neopagan witches.

I prefer to draw a distinction, though, between Satan and the Devil (or devils in general, the capital "D" being used when referring to a singular entity). In most cases, Satan appears in biblical lore as a being concerned with the overall cosmology of Heaven and Earth, leading wars against God, and presenting deep philosophical and theological complications into the story of Creation. Devils, on the other hand, are creatures interested in particular individuals, usually offering them power or temporal gifts in exchange for a soul, a service, or as a reward for exemplary cleverness. They stem from myriad sources, including the Teutonic Teufel, the trickster spirits of African and Native American mythology, mischievous European deities or spirits like the Norse Loki, and British devil-figures like "Old Nick." In North America, the Devil gets distilled into a creature that can certainly be malevolent, but who also has a number of facets to his personality.[257] Two in particular that bear wicked but useful fruit are the Devil's roles as both an initiator figure and a trickster figure.

Some Devils

Depending on the situation, the Devil's power to initiate someone may be a lifelong commitment or a period of temporary instruction. The legend of blues musician Robert Johnson (more accurately attributed to backwoods bluesman Tommy Johnson) meeting the Devil at the crossroads and selling his soul for musical power and fame is a variation from most crossroads lore. Usually, a person seeking to be a better musician, gambler, or pursuing other paths associated with vice would meet the Devil at the crossroads in a series of midnight rituals. The Devil would then either

257. A brief note: I use male-coded terminology because the Devil as represented in North American lore almost always takes on a male form, even appearing as male animals like roosters.

trim the person's nails, play their instrument or use their cards or other tools, show them how to play a song or something similar, or some combination of those elements. After, the Devil would leave and the person would have fame and success and demonstrable talent for their trade. In most cases the notion of "selling one's soul" is not an explicit contract in these transactions, although folk belief often seems to lean into saying there's a price paid for taking such shortcuts, such as a briefer lifespan or a violent end. Crucially, not every tradition explicitly names this initiator the Devil, but often he is called a "Man in Black" or a "Dark Man" at the crossroads. This Dark Man may also meet those seeking him in the woods.[258]

In other lore, however, the trade is more explicitly a diabolical compact. The Dark Man or Devil offers something to the one seeking him: power (usually magical or political), fame, money, or gifts, such as an imp or familiar. In some Appalachian traditions, the Devil provides "witch balls" made of hair and wax to be used in spellwork, and the cost of losing these is a severe beating by the Devil at an annual sabbat meeting.[259] In exchange for what the Devil offers, there is almost always a price. Vance Randolph noted that when the Devil initiated witches in the Ozark Mountains, it was akin to a baptism in its power but came with a heavy cost—the loss of a loved one as a sort of natural or unintentional sacrifice.[260]

Other things a witch might stand to lose include her family (who would shun her once she was a witch), a part of her body (often a withered finger or a bit of blood), or—of course—her soul, contractually signed away in the Devil's famous "book" (see chapter nineteen).

What the Devil offers is so tempting, however, because the power gained is tremendous. A witch will be able to provide food for herself and anyone she wishes to feed, usually by means of magical theft, using dishrags to siphon off milk magically, or flying at night to raid the larders and cellars of her neighbors (see chapter nine). The gifts gained by becoming a witch through compact with the Devil often must be exercised regularly in order to remain potent. Lapsing in witchcraft seems to lead to torment on the witch's part if the Devil finds that she's not been keeping up her end

258. Hyatt, *Hoodoo-Conjuration-Witchcraft-Rootwork*, 100–107; Puckett, *Folk Beliefs*, 553; Hurston, "Hoodoo in America," 392.

259. Milnes, *Signs, Cures, & Witchery*, 167–8; Davis, *The Silver Bullet*, 31–4; Oberon, *Southern Cunning*, chapter 5.

260. Randolph, *Ozark Magic*, 268.

of the bargain by using her powers. I would posit that while the folklore here superficially portrays the Devil as a cruel master, he may instead be a necessary goad. After all, what great musician or momentous artist ever became who they are without practice? Again, the Devil may be a stern teacher at times, but one that provides the necessary impetus for improvement in one's craft.

In all of these particular aspects—tutor/schoolmaster, mentor/sponsor, bookkeeper/librarian, and gift-giver—the Devil rather reminds me of a faculty member at a university, taking a student under his wing, and helping the young witch succeed in her field of calling, which is perhaps why in much European lore the Devil winds up in league with students or junior academic types, such as the famous Faust. Imagining the Devil as some doddering old professor is foolhardy at best, though, and no small amount of projection on my part. He is, of course, wilier than I give him credit for, particularly in the New World.

The lore about trickster Devils is not a New World phenomenon, of course. There are several tales from Europe and Africa which feature a Devil or a diabolical trickster figure of some kind, such as the Grimms' tale "The Devil's Sooty Brother" or the Ashanti tales about Anansi the Spider.

Just as often as he tricks someone, though, the Devil also gets tricked or outwitted in some way, as in tales of Clever Jack, who outwits the Devil time and again until he is finally rejected from both Heaven and Hell for his trickery.[261] This flip-side to his role provides a number of amusing tales, but I tend to think there's a subtle willingness to play the fool on the Devil's part, making the whole scenario one big trick in the end. But I'm getting ahead of myself. Sometimes the Devil's trickster competitions are with angels, saints, or even God. In these cases, the Devil almost always loses, but often whatever occurs in the story has some lasting impact on the world. The catfish, according to one Southern folktale, gets its distinct and ugly appearance from a brush with the Devil. God created the fish, then took the evening off to go up to the "Big House" with his archangels and eat supper. When he came back down to the river, the Devil was sitting there descaling the fish. God demanded he put the catfish back and the Devil agreed. The catfish rolled in the mud to make up for its lack of scales but never grew them back again.[262]

261. Schlosser, *Spooky Maryland*, chapter 22.

262. Leeming and Page, *Myths, Legends, & Folktales of America*, 59–60.

Another tale, immortalized in folk song, claims that the Devil is responsible for certain nigh-uninhabitable parts of the country. In these tales, the Devil hides on Christmas morning and waits for God to walk by before popping out and shouting, "Christmas gift!" (an old folk custom that required the one surprised by the phrase to offer something for it, a bit like "Trick or treat!" at Halloween; this custom was widespread especially among African American slaves in the southern United States, who could manage to get a few extra provisions for themselves from otherwise stingy masters and neighbors this way). When God hands out his "gift," it is a parcel of land inhabited by dangerous creatures like scorpions or alligators, and often a place hot or otherwise uncomfortable such as the desert areas of Texas or the swampy Florida Everglades.[263]

Sometimes, of course, people get the better of the Devil. In a piece of Maryland folklore which parallels the Ashanti story of Anansi and Anene, a woman named Molly Horn (who is never quite identified as a witch, peculiarly enough) enters into a contract with the Devil and outwits him at every turn, getting him to accept inedible parts of crops as payment and leading to an argument. Molly eventually "struck the devil a terrific crack and skidded him across the marsh to the edge of the bay. When he stood up and shook the mud off himself, it formed Devil's Island, then he dove overboard and made Devil's Hole."[264]

Sometimes, though, people don't quite get the best of the trickster Devil, and pay a gruesome price. Zora Neale Hurston records the tale of High Walker in her book, *Mules and Men*, in which the titular Mr. Walker gains necromantic powers from the Devil only to eventually be tricked into losing his head, literally, in a graveyard.[265]

As a final point about the Devil as a trickster, I'd like to look at the Devil's music. As most probably know, the Devil loves music, especially fiddle music, and can be lured into a fiddle contest on a moment's notice. If you've ever heard the Charlie Daniels Band perform "The Devil Went Down to Georgia," you know this story (a mariachi band once sang this to my wife and me at a large Mexican wedding, which was a pretty phenomenal experience). While it is an entertaining song even on its own, it has precedents in folklore, too. Appalachian folklore associates fiddles with

263. Schlosser, *Spooky South*, 166–70.

264. Carey, *Maryland Folklore*, 49.

265. Hurston, *Mules and Men*, 173–75.

the Devil, nicknaming it things like the "Devil's box" or the "Devil's riding horse."[266] There's even a serpentine association, as many players (of both fiddle and guitar) keep rattlesnake rattles in their instruments to ensure good luck when playing.

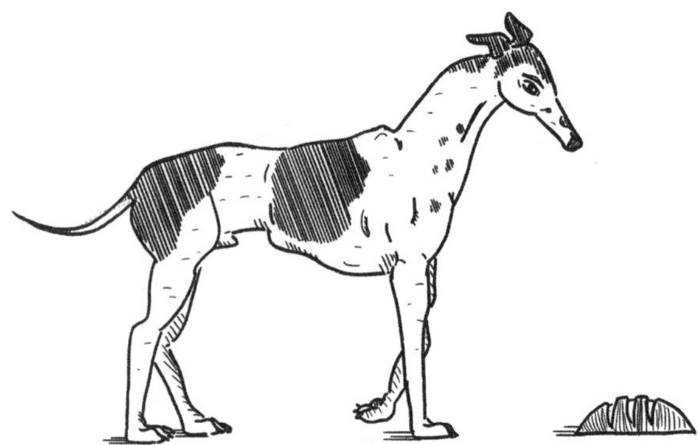

FIG 14-1: A witch cake, containing a victim's urine, was fed to a dog in order to break a witch's power.

SINGING BONES
Tituba, Candy, and Mary Black

For a figure at the center of one of the most-researched and discussed periods of North American history, we know surprisingly little about Tituba from the Salem Witch Trials. To begin with, her origins are murky—historians believe she may have been a member of the South American Arawak tribe or more specifically the Taino people, but even those points are uncertain. She is often referred to as Samuel Parris's "Indian Woman," which gives us very little to go on. Tituba is frequently depicted in fiction such as Arthur Miller's *The Crucible* or Maryse Condé's *I, Tituba* as at least partly African in origin. We do know she was Parris's slave when he left his failing fortunes in Barbados during the 1680s and took up his post in Salem. Tituba cared for her master's daughters (and their cousin), and some accounts have her teaching them fortune-telling games or sharing her own childhood stories with them, points which later counted against her during the trials. When she was interrogated in the public meeting house, Tituba shared a range of sensational and diabolic images likely drawn from European witch-lore learned from the English around her. While much of the Salem Witch Tri-

266. Milnes, *Signs, Cures, & Witchery*, 153.

als hinged on what was known as "spectral evidence," or the visions of the alleged victims, some accounts do indicate folk magical practices among the villagers. The use of a witch cake containing a victim's urine and fed to a dog (see figure 14-1) in order to break a witch's power is reported in one account, in which Mary Sibley ordered the Parris's slave Tituba to make one.

Even less is known about Barbados slave Candy, who worked for high-ranking gentlewoman Margaret Hawkes and who was questioned about potential involvement with witchcraft and demonstrated methods of poppet magic she knew for the interrogators. Mary Black was a slave stolen from Africa and in the subjection of Nathaniel Putnam (the Putnams were one of the rival family factions in the trials). While undergoing interrogation, she was asked to pin her neck cloth, which caused the afflicted girls to go into fits as if they were being prodded with pins.

Crucially, all three women of color were not executed. Mary Black continued in Putnam's employ, and while Candy turned her accusations on her mistress, she was also released. Tituba languished in jail for some time, but all indications are that she was released by whomever paid her jail fees and never mentioned again in historical records.[267]

Summoning Devils

In my time working with folkloric materials about witchcraft and folk magic, I've written a few different times about the Devil of North American folklore. Almost invariably when I do, one of the questions I receive in response is, "but how do I meet him?" Is the Devil an entity anyone can just summon up? Do you have to be careful to call the "right" devil so as not to wind up with more on your plate than you can handle? And if you do meet the Devil, how do you come away with your soul intact (assuming you want to)?

Broadly speaking, there seem to be two distinct flavors of diabolical summoning: the ceremonial invocation found in medieval grimoire traditions, and a folk-inflected series of methods that vary a bit depending on location, circumstances, and need. If

267. See Howe, *The Penguin Book of Witches*; Karlsen, *The Devil in the Shape of a Woman*; Norton, *In the Devil's Snare: The Salem Witchcraft Crisis of 1692*.

you've ever read Christopher Marlowe's *Dr. Faustus*, you know how the ceremonial invocations go: theatrical props such as lampstands and staves or wands, markings on the floor pulled from medieval tomes, and a contract (usually signed in blood) presented by a demonic creature contained within a "magic circle" or "triangle of arte" of some kind. Grimoires used in these rites include *The Greater Key of Solomon the King* (or just *The Key of Solomon*), the *Goetia* (or *Lesser Key of Solomon*), or more recent ones such as *The Grimoire Verum* and *The Sixth & Seventh Books of Moses*. These are all well and good for those who enjoy the ceremonial side of sorcery, but I unfortunately cannot write about those methods with very much authority.[268]

Then we have the folk summonings. Some of these methods call a figure that may or may not be the Devil, but which certainly shares traits with him (a trickster nature, Otherworldly knowledge, the granting of gifts, etc.). A word of warning, however, permeates virtually all devil-conjuring lore: Do *not* attempt any spiritual summoning work or diabolical contact without the proper precautions—while these sorts of spirits can be powerful allies, they also can have a dangerous side and should be treated with respect and caution.

So, how do you meet your devil?

The Crossroads Meeting

In many stories, the Devil can be found at a crossroads of some kind, frequently in a rural environment, although there are exceptions (many modern stories of meeting the Devil involve transportation or big cities with things like streets or train tracks taking the place of crossroads, e.g. Robert Bloch's *Hell-Bound Train*, Ray Bradbury's *Something Wicked this Way Comes*, and the cult film *Rosemary's Baby*). Probably the most famous ritual involves visiting a crossroads over a series of nights, usually seven, nine, or thirteen, and being met by increasingly frightening black creatures (a rooster, a dog, a bear, etc.). The last figure to show will be the Dark Man/Man in Black, with whom you make your deal for fame, fortune, or magic.

268. In addition to the grimoires I've already mentioned, I will also recommend reading both *Dr. Faustus* by Christopher Marlowe and *Henry VI, Part II* by William Shakespeare. Both of these texts contain summoning rituals designed to be performed on the Elizabethan stage, but rooted in grimoire magic, so they may offer you a way to visualize not only the ritual but how people acted and reacted during it. And, after all, literature is often a good way to take existing material and dress it well for everyday use, so why not turn to Shakespeare and Marlowe for inspiration?

The Forest Meeting

Meeting the Devil in a dark forest at night is also a popular option, second perhaps only to the crossroads in North American lore. The forest or wild place meeting is a common folkloric theme across many cultures. There are, of course, the Teutonic tales of meeting various wild spirits or devils in the forest, as in the Grimms' tales of the Devil (see "The Devil's Sooty Brother," or "The Devil's Grandmother"). There are biblical precedents for these sorts of meetings as well—Moses encounters the burning bush in the desert (an analog for wilderness in biblical terms), which is at least terrifying if not outright diabolic. Three of the gospels also recount the story of Jesus being tempted in the desert. American folklore picks up this thread, and stories of meeting the Devil in wilderness are quite common. "Young Goodman Brown," by Nathaniel Hawthorne, features such a meeting, and at least one scholar has brought the idea into the twentieth century by suggesting that "Men in Black" sightings associated with UFOs in rural areas may be connected to Devil lore.[269]

The Graveyard Meeting

The other alternative to the forest meeting is the graveyard meeting. Usually in this version of the story, the person meeting the Devil must also do battle with him. It can be a battle of wits, but just as often it is a physical wrestling match which parallels the interior struggle of the person confronting his or her fears by meeting the Devil in a graveyard in the first place. A folktale from Florida has famed conjure-man John the Conqueror stealing the Devil's daughter from him through "West Hell," a euphemism for an unconsecrated burial ground.[270]

The astute reader will probably already see that in each of these cases, the folk ritual attempts to meet the Devil where he is, requiring the magician to undertake a journey into a liminal space in order to gain the magical outcome desired. This runs counter to the ceremonial approach, which attempts to force the Devil (or other infernal spirit) to come to the enchanter and be bound by them. Both methods have their adherents and seem to have a history of success for those who use them, so the decision on how to approach a meeting like this lies entirely in your hands.

269. Ellis, *Aliens, Ghosts, & Cults*, 207.

270. Schlosser, *Spooky South*, 182–85.

DIRT UNDER THE NAILS

The Forest at Midnight (Meeting the Devil)

If you really want to meet the Devil (the North American folkloric Devil, that is, without any particular satanic connotations), you can pledge yourself to him in a dark forest and he may just show up!

Ideally you will want to find a clearing in the forest big enough that you can make a ring of stones and build a small campfire (make sure you are far enough away from trees to avoid sparks catching in them, and be cautious of any dry season or fire hazard conditions in your area). In a perfect scenario, you'll find a clearing with two trees nearby that have grown together, creating a natural archway (brambles grown this way with a tunnel under them can be used the same way, and both are thought to have the power to "strip away" things attached to you).

With the fire lit, go just beyond the fire's light (or just beyond the tree arch), and call out, saying you've come to meet with the Devil. Bring along an offering of some kind: candy, apples, pawpaws, tobacco, or black animals like chickens or mice are all fairly common (only do this if you are comfortable with animal sacrifice and understand its implications—do not do this lightly, as there are perfectly reasonable substitutions available). Put one offering at the edge of the fire's light/tree arch, then enter the space. Begin circling the fire slowly, walking counterclockwise, until you start feeling heavy. Your feet will begin to drag, and things will seem to slow down around you. When that happens, present the second offering by the fire. Then, put one hand on the sole of your left foot and the other on top of your head.

Say, "All that lies between these two hands I pledge to the Devil!"

You will, if all goes according to plan, receive some sign of his presence. It might be the appearance of an animal, sudden changes in the wind or the movement of the fire, or strange sounds around you. You can then ask for a boon if you like. Then, smother the fire completely and depart.

The trick is that you will want to leave back through the arch, thus clearing you of the obligation you just made (if you don't want to remain pledged to the Devil, that is). If you don't have the arch, make sure you leave by a different way than you came, and perform a ritual cleansing bath when you get home.

FIG 14-2: Wouldst thou like to live deliciously?

The Devil's Trick: Does the Devil Belong in Witchcraft?

So what is the point of getting tangled up with the Devil in the first place? After all, a number of witches practicing under the fold of Neopagan practices have actively spent decades trying to combat the perception of their religion as anything diabolical.[271] Why bring him into anything at all? Isn't that just courting disaster?

Yes, and no. The Devil is part of witchcraft lore, just as spells and moonlit dances and broomsticks are. But witches don't always have to have broomsticks, or dance in the moonlight. Some people call themselves witches and stay far away from spells, preferring the label to be a religious one. There are a lot of ways to be a witch, and doing work with any sort of Devil is just one potential option among many. Devils are tricksy creatures, and they do offer some wonderful gifts to a practicing witch, including spirit aids (the imps and familiars found in lore) or even guidance on spell creation or ingredients. They also can add a tremendous amount of power to other workings, and sabbat rites can become truly Otherworldly when a devilish figure joins in (I say this having experienced it several times both with others and on my own).

More crucially, when we fear the Devil we let him become our master. If you pay attention to the stories, the Devil is really a threat to those who do not know

271. Adler, *Drawing Down the Moon*, 476–81.

how to manage him, those who rely on the intervention of other spiritual forces like angels or God to stave off his wiles. Those who *do* know how to deal with him—the Molly Horns and John the Conquerors and Clever Jacks of the world—often gain his instruction, his gifts, and even occasionally his favor by outwitting him. Cunning is an essential part of witchcraft. It requires thinking flexibly on the fly, crafting solutions that others cannot think of, a sort of lateral problem-solving skill that sees the unseen mechanics of an enchanted world and uses them wisely and well. That is the Devil witches meet, the one they can outsmart because that is essentially why he's there.

In a number of Christian traditions, people believe that the Devil was the snake in the garden of Eden, offering Eve the fruit of the tree of knowledge of good and evil. One of the important points that frequently gets missed in that tale is that the snake never lies. He tells the truth and asks why God forbids Adam and Eve from eating everything in the garden (they cannot eat everything, because the tree is forbidden). He points out that if the humans eat the fruit, they will be "like God" and know good from evil, and still be essentially immortal (God punishes their disobedience by removing the tree that gives the fruit of immortality, which was *not* previously forbidden). All of this is true. If the snake and the Devil are one (and I tend to think that they weren't in the original, but I like the folkloric revisions made over the centuries), then the Devil wanted us to be wise, and cunning, and smart.

Meeting the Devil gives us a chance to demonstrate those things. It's a sort of riddle, a puzzle, a challenge we can rise to. Charles Baudelaire once noted that the greatest trick the Devil could play was convincing us he didn't exist.[272] I rather like Baudelaire, but I tend to think the Devil's greatest trick is to make us think for ourselves and prove our worth. Witches do that well, because magical thinking requires a kind of cunning even greater than the Devil's. Witches meet him not as a master, the way so many fearful Christians might, but as an equal, and we play the game before us wisely, well, and occasionally, wickedly.

THE WORK—Revisiting the Contract

What would you give for witchcraft? For magic? What would you do to meet the needs in your life, or the life of those around you? In short, what would your magi-

272. See Baudelaire, "The Generous Gambler," in *Paris Spleen*, 61.

cal contract look like? If you've never thought about this question, it's one worth addressing. If you don't know what your boundaries and limits look like, you don't know how far you can go (or what sort of challenges you can face as you reach those limits). Being a witch sometimes means being able to make sacrifices, accept changes that seem overwhelming, or looking for the place where you can twist Fate just a little bit through your own cleverness.

Petitions have a long and valued history in magical work. Many traditions use written papers as a way to focus a spell's intention on a particular target or to achieve a specific desired effect. Drawing up your own "diabolical contract" is one way to do that, too. I mentioned this in chapter four's "The Work" section, but here I want to offer you an expansion beyond initiation, something that moves and changes and grows with you. Design the terms of your life and figure out what you are willing to give up to achieve your goals and dreams, and what dreams and goals you will be willing to give up to hold on to what you have. Explore what magic means to you, and how dearly you hold it. Point to the pieces of your own magic that have grown strong, and what pieces you still need to collect. Use this as a road map for magical exploration and development, and as a biography of the enchantments you've already wrought.

Write your own contract, or update the one I challenged you to start earlier. Know it well enough to let it become a part of your daily guidance, leading you to be open to the things that fulfill its terms. Build in loopholes (remember the value of cunning) so that you will always be able to bend with new changes, rather than break under them. Make this a living contract (perhaps that's why these so often get sealed with blood, because they are more animate than a property-based will or contract). Animate it and use it to guide you. You needn't sign yourself away to the Devil, although you can if that's your inclination and you wish to make him a partner in your magical life. You are really, at a fundamental level, using this contract as a way to sign yourself away ... to *yourself*.

Set your own terms, and decide the gifts you want in return. Offer what you can, give what you will, and be the mistress of your own Fate.

Recommended Reading

The Demonology of King James I, edited by Donald Tyson. This is a highly influential work that certainly gives a sense of what it was like to live in an age surrounded by demons, witches, and everything in between. While much of this book is a problem because of the hysteria it helped to fuel, it's an excellent insight into the side of the magical worldview from the perspective of those who *didn't* know how to handle diabolical forces. This edition done by Donald Tyson annotates the text with helpful historical information and includes additional materials related to witch trials in Scotland.

Dr. Faustus, by Christopher Marlowe. Sure, this is fiction, and yes, I know there are other versions of the Faust story that play down the drama and play up the existential angst. But Marlowe's version is just so much fun, and even if it is telling the story of someone not quite smart enough to outwit his devils, it gives a good insight into the rituals, actions, and reactions that a good diabolical summoning might entail. It's a delight to read, even if it is a bit out-of-fashion.

The History of the Devil, by Paul Carus. While this is not quite as spectacular as the sadly out-of-print *The Devil in Legend & Literature,* by Maximillian Josef Rudwin, it comes close in its scope of tracking the progress of the Devil as a cultural and literary figure over human history. While some of its assertions are a little overly broad (and it leaves folkloric devils largely out of the discussion), it does cover a cross-cultural comparison that can be useful for seeing diabolical figures not as a singular massive entity, but as more of an archetype that has proven useful to people throughout the ages.

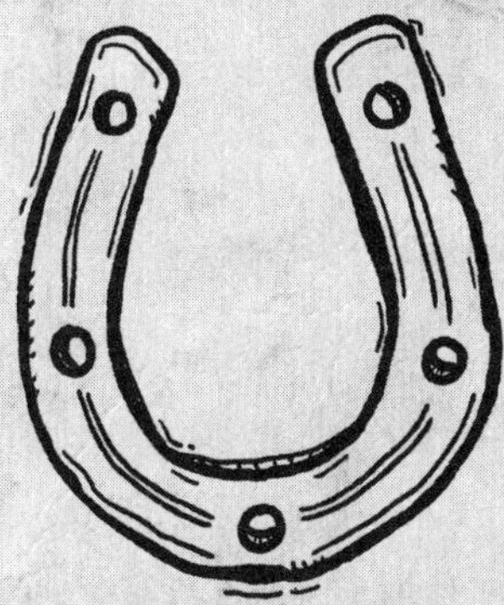

EIGHTH RITE: HALLOWING THE GROUND

Or, the Spaces and Places of Witchery Both Domestic and Abroad

"A sliver of moon haunted the sky, and the stars seemed very bright. A night wind stirred the graveyard shrubbery; crickets chirped, and bats flew down after the moths drawn to the lantern. It was a perfect time and place for magic."*

* Gandee, *Strange Experience*, 332.

CHAPTER FIFTEEN

A Scratch Above Her Eye—Defending Home and Hearth from Witchery

Let's say your cow has stopped giving milk. Or worse, let us say that your cow has started giving bloody milk. Or your butter won't churn properly. Perhaps the cow (or cows) all seem to be afflicted with some illness, and are growing weaker by the day. As you think back through what the potential causes might be—was there white snakeroot somewhere in the pastures, or have there been wild dogs spotted nearby that might be stressing the animals?—an image of a neighbor pops into your head. You recall this older woman stopped by and admired your cows while they were grazing, and somehow you got uncomfortable standing and talking to her. She made a joke about how much butter and cream they produced, and how you should give some to a poor old lady now and again. At least, you thought it was a joke.

When you tell your friends in town about it, one of them nods solemnly, saying the same thing happened to an aunt's farm several years ago, and in the end, they had to consult a local witch doctor about what to do. They were told to take the clabber—the soured milk from the afflicted cow—and toss it onto the fire, then beat it with thorny canes clipped from a blackberry bush while it burned and sizzled. After that, all would be well again.

What harm could it do, right? After all, if you lose this cow, you have to pay to replace it, and you lose the income or the household sustenance her milk provided.

The cure may seem odd, but it involves very little risk on your part, so you try it. As you're beating the thick stinking slime of milk on the hot coals, you feel a bit silly, until you hear a faint shrieking sound. It's almost like a scream. Soon after you hear a knock on your door and it's the neighbor who eyed the cows the other day. She looks sick, bent over and hunched in pain, a cold sweat on her face. She begs you for a cup of milk she can take to ease her stomach, but your friend warned you about this. You tell her to go and never darken your doorstep again. It feels harsh, but then, witchcraft is a harsh thing, and you are locked in a battle with a witch. As you return to the fire and continue beating the milk, you do not feel silly anymore, but strong, powerful. You think you can hear sobs coming from the milk as it boils away, and a flicker of a smile turns up your lips. In the war of witchcraft, you have won the day. Your cow will heal, your neighbor will remember not to cross you. If this is magic, witchcraft... well, maybe she used it for harm, but not you. You are using magic for good. To take back control. And you like it.

Witches were viewed as a very real phenomenon during the Colonial period right through until the nineteenth century, and even well beyond in certain areas. In New England, the belief in witches was prevalent enough that "witchfinding" was a legitimate pre-Revolutionary career, just as it was in England. It was not limited to the Europeans alone. In 1806, a group of Delaware tribe youths attempting to eliminate all traces of witchcraft began an organized persecution of both their tribal elders and the local Moravian missionary community in the White River settlement area of Indiana. A regional "expert" named Tenskwatawa was summoned to help identify other potential witches in the area, leading to a brutal raid which saw the young men attack their old chief, Tedpaschsit, with a hatchet and throw him, still alive, into a fire.[273] Other colonies, such as Virginia and Pennsylvania, took a more publicly liberal stance toward witchcraft, and regarded it as "bad behavior" rather than any indication of diabolic allegiance. William Penn once ordered a woman accused of witchcraft to simply "practice good behavior" and insisted to her accuser that there was no law against "riding a broom."[274] By the nineteenth century, the Calvinist influence on the upper Appalachian colonies made them more willing to regard witchcraft as superstition, a thing ascribed to Catholics, at least publicly. However,

273. Games, *Witchcraft in Early North America*, sec. 29.

274. Milnes, *Signs, Cures, & Witchery*, 37–8.

the prevalence of anti-witchcraft charms, talismans, and amulets in all the colonies demonstrates that in private, many folks believed much as the Puritans did—witches existed, and they were dangerous.

Elsewhere in this book you will find curses and hexes deployed by malevolent (or sometimes maligned) witches and conjurers. Yet a great bulk of magic practiced in North America aimed to break those curses, reverse the hexes, and disarm the witches sowing discord and harm. To that end, protection magic needs to be addressed, and in the following pages we will see how many people used magical solutions to solve their magical problems.

Disarming the Witch

To combat curses, a victim has a few distinct options. They might simply try to appease the witch in question, giving her what she wants if the cost is not too dear. This sometimes works and sometimes doesn't, because it does not break the witch's power over her victim, only alleviates the symptoms. To actively undo witchery, a target has choices ranging from the fairly simple to the outright aggressive.

Reversal Spells

The butter churn that failed to make butter or the cow giving bloody milk both had simple treatments for their enchantment: simply reverse the curse. The silver coin under the churn or milk tossed onto a burning log breaks the basic spell cast by the witch and sends her hex back on her. She might suffer some physical harm—often witches are reported to have scratches, marks, burns, or bruises after these sorts of magical operations—but seldom would a simple reversal kill her. In Hoodoo and Southern Conjure practices, reversal magic sometimes involves things like a bicolored candle (often red and black) burned to send a witch's spell back at her. Older versions of that spell involve physically cutting and remelting a candle so it burns from the "wrong end."

Denying a Witch's Request

If a witch's curse is reversed, many folktales see her coming back and asking for something—anything—from the victim or their home in order to reactivate the curse. A cup of sugar, or even simply a dipper of water, might be enough to give the witch power again. Denying the witch, however, seems to not only break the curse but also offers some magical insulation. In mountain folktales, the witch frequently cannot curse a target anymore after being denied her second (or sometimes third, in that great fairy tale numerical tradition) request. However, if a person were to provide the witch so much as a matchstick or a bite of bread, the curse could return with a vengeance and be nearly unbreakable without outside interference. Could a witch *steal* something and make this work, too? That depends very much on the witch and the place—most stories seem to indicate the target must freely give something to the witch, although occasionally a tale pops up where a witch can twist a leaf off of a plant on her way out of the garden gate and manage a bit more mischief, although it never seems to be as powerful.

Getting Professional Help

If a person couldn't halt the progress of a curse directly, the next step on the ladder involved seeking out the guidance of a "professional." Frequently these professionals were known as some form of a "doctor": witch doctor, fairy doctor, power doctor, yarb [herb] doctor, conjure doctor, or two-headed doctor are some of the terms that get used when writing about these curers. In the Pennsylvania Dutch communities, these workers might be known as *hexenmeisters*, while in Cajun regions like Louisiana they might be called *traiteurs*. Most of these professionals could offer magical or herbal cures to various ailments, but many also specialized in breaking or reversing curses. A German Appalachian curer named Dovie Lambert, for example, would prepare a "ticket"—a paper with the target's name and a Bible verse on it—to be burned to reverse the curse.[275] These professionals are not limited to the distant past, either. Chicagoan Nestor Gomez recalls that when his mother was struck with a mysterious illness, his family summoned in *la bruja*, a witch, to come and remove it.[276] Ozark power doctors sometimes made images of the witch and shot or burned them to deactivate a curse. These professionals frequently also helped to identify the witch doing the cursing, and even occasionally might be in league with or locked in magical combat with them as happened between Sheriff McTeer and Doc Buzzard in the sea islands of South Carolina, for example. They might also be working both sides of a curse on their own, as in the case of Nestor Gomez's bruja encounter, or

275. Milnes, *Signs, Cures, & Witchery*, 76–79.

276. Washington, "The Curse."

witch/witch doctor couples like Mont and Duck Moore from Appalachia (see chapter two).[277]

Destroying a Cursed Object

Frequently the main recourse a professional had in dealing with a witch was to find whatever the witch had used to cast the curse and destroy it. Sometimes the victim could do this work themselves, discovering a doll somewhere in the house and tossing it into the fire or some running water. Most victims, however, did not perform those sorts of operations, either because they did not know how to do so, they couldn't find the object, or they feared to touch something cursed and thus exacerbate their conditions. The power doctors dealing with a hair-and-wax witch ball or a broken bottle of war water, however, would usually know how to gather up all the ingredients involved without touching them directly, then be able to "deactivate" them and dispose of them carefully so as to avoid any "reinfection" through contact with the curse. Sometimes this method proved excruciating for the witch doing the cursing, and she might hurry to try and find out if her doll baby or packet spell had been discovered, only to be turned back by the conjure doctor at the door. The hex breaker might also prescribe proactive preventative remedies like the use of certain psalms (Psalm 52 is considered very powerful for this purpose) or the placement of iron, a sieve, or a pair of shears around the house to stop future attacks.

Attack the Witch

Finally, if nothing else worked, a direct attack on the witch could undo her work. Generally this involved killing her, although in some cases the attack might be much less gruesome. One long-standing tradition inherited from Europe said that a witch would lose her power—and thus all her curses would be undone—if she could be scratched until she bled above her eyes. A quick cut on her forehead, then, might be enough to clear away any remaining curses, although of course most accused witches were not eager to undergo this solution. Shooting her with a silver bullet—even an image of her—could sometimes cause her powers to fade, as could attacking her when she was in a shape-shifted form (such as the cat in the "Sop Paw" tale in

277. See Pinckney, *Blue Roots: African-American Folk Magic of the Gullah People*; and Davis, *The Silver Bullet, and Other American Witch Stories.*

chapter thirteen). Religious attacks using prayer, Bibles, or other holy objects could also sometimes make her weaker or kill her, although much of that lore seems to be shared between both witches and vampires in places like New England.

Often the stories told about witches involved more than one of these remedies, and in many of them the response to witchcraft involves a quick escalation from a mild reversal to an outright witch hunt. Plenty of witches get away relatively unscathed, however, or the curse disappears without any particular witch being singled out as the cause. All occupations, even magical ones, have their hazards, it seems.

FIG 15-1: Galangal root, or "Little John to Chew," a favorite root of Dr. Buzzard.

SINGING BONES
Dr. Buzzard and Sheriff McTeer

Few rivalries are as bitter—or as interesting—as the one between South Carolina's Dr. Buzzard and Sheriff J. E. McTeer. Buzzard, whose real name was Stephaney Robinson, maintained a bustling Rootwork practice in the area around Beaufort, South Carolina, frequently providing magical and pseudo-medical cures for diseases (and, crucially, draft-dodging during World War II). He was also famed for his court case work, and would show up in court wearing dark sunglasses and chewing galangal (or "court case") root (see figure 15-1) to intimidate witnesses and judges alike. When junior lawman J. E. McTeer took over for his father, the local sheriff, after the elder's death in 1926, he inherited Dr. Buzzard as a problem. McTeer took an "if you can't beat 'em, join 'em" approach and began to learn about—and *use*—Rootwork and folk magic against Dr. Buzzard. Both men seemed to be quite good at what they did, and the war between them resulted in mounting arrests and then suddenly incapacitated witnesses during subsequent trials. Things finally reached a head when Dr. Buzzard's son was killed in a car crash and the old root doctor offered a peace between the two sides. He died soon after in 1947, and McTeer lived on until 1976, carrying both a respect for his deceased enemy and the renown of being a powerful root-worker himself.[278]

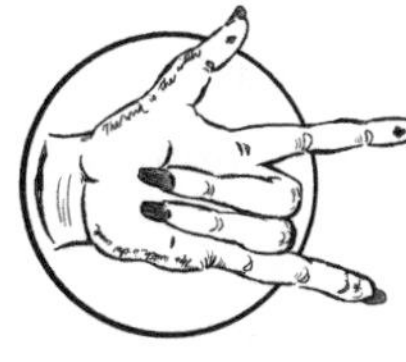

DIRT UNDER THE NAILS
Reverse the Curse!

When dealing with a curse where no physical object is present to destroy, what can you do? In both Hoodoo and Southern Conjure, the development of candle magic in the nineteenth and twentieth centuries offered a solution: reversal candles. Frequently these are now made by (non-Black-owned) manufacturers like the Lucky Mojo Curio Co. or Indio Products, although some shops still make their own or dress pre-made candles to customize them for clients. You can create your own, however, with relative ease and in a way that has some magic in the ritual as well.

You need:

- A red candle
- A black candle (both candles should be the same type and size, such as tapers or pillars)
- A sharp knife
- A lighter or matches

Reversal herbs or oils (optional, but helpful—suggestions include using Devil's shoestring, knotweed, ginger, black or red pepper, and salt).

To make this spell work, all you must do is cut both candles in half, then cut the "tops" (where the wick protrudes and you'd normally light the candle) off of them as well. The idea here is that you're making a new candle out of the "wrong ends" of two other candles. Carve the new "bottom" of the

278. Pinckney, *Blue Roots*, 91–109; and Montgomery, *American Shamans*, 39–50.

black candle (where you cut it in half) into a point until the wick emerges and clean the wick off enough that you will be able to light it. Using the lighter, a match, or a bit of tin foil in a skillet on a warm stove, heat the flat areas where you trimmed the "tops" away from both candles, then stick them together. Try to make sure the wicks line up between them as best you can. Let them cool a bit, and you should now have a two-color candle with the black on top and the red on the bottom. Roll your candle gently in any herbs or oils you want to use, and carve the name of the one who made the curse down the side of the candle, if you know it. Light the candle and speak your desire to break the curse on you and send it back to its creator (use Psalm 52 if you cannot think of words of your own). Let the candle burn until it has burned all the way through the red portion and the black is ignited. Then you can either continue to let the black candle burn until it's gone or you can snuff it and relight it a little each night over nine nights to really make the reversal stick.

FIG 15-2: A protective charm imported from Europe involves taking rowan twigs and binding them into an equal-armed cross with red thread, then hanging the talisman over the doors or windows of the home.

Guarding Against Witchcraft

In addition to performing effective countercurses, any number of magical practitioners (even casual ones without any pretensions to witchcraft) deploy protective magic to shield themselves from harm. These can be elaborate—some people like to use carefully made seals taken from medieval grimoires, for example—or very simplistic, such as a jar of sand or salt left near a doorway. The latter forces a witch to count every grain before entering, and thus deters her. Below are some common, fairly easy-to-find magical methods of building up a layer of enchanted personal protection.

Salt

Most people who get involved with magic know this one. Salt nullifies magical effects, particularly harmful ones. Laying a line of salt along a threshold or windowsill can usually halt magical attacks on a home. Leaving a jar of salt near the door will force a witch to count the grains before entering, and that can be an effective deterrent. Even sprinkling a little salt in the corners of a room can dissipate any hurtful spells in the area, while a saltwater bath can sometimes ease or break a curse.

Silver

Silver is often associated with purity, and even has some slight purifying effects on things like water. Thus, silver jewelry is often used to deflect any curses or harmful energy, and a silver weapon is frequently used to harm or kill a witch (or a werewolf, vampire, or other supernatural fiend in stories). One of the best-known North American charms involves taking a silver "Mercury" dime and tying it on a red thread around one's ankle for magical protection.

Blades

Cutting through witchcraft seems to be an effective protection method, too. Leaving a knife or an axe under the bed is thought to deflect harmful magic, as is placing a pair of shears or open scissors near a doorway or window. In one Mexican tradition, shards of black obsidian—a volcanic glass so sharp it has been used in surgical instruments—are wedged into doorframes in a home as a way to "cut" any witchcraft that comes through into ribbons.[279]

279. Anonymous, *Magical Powers of Holy Death*, 23.

FIG 15-3: The "INRI" Cross is a written charm that uses Latin shorthand for the name of Jesus as a powerful anti-evil spell.

Written Charms

The use of written charms is widespread (see chapter nineteen), but certain ones are thought to be particularly effective at keeping out hurtful magic. The famed SATOR square is a well-known protective charm, as is the INRI cross (see figure 15-3). Writing down Psalm 52 or Psalm 140 can also be effective. These papers are then slipped into the doorframes or window jambs to finalize the protection (they can also be put into places like light fixtures—away from the bulbs—or even inside things like couch cushions or throw pillows).

Markings

Carved images such as the six-pointed star or rosette have been found on homes and barns dating back centuries. The Pennsylvania Dutch have long had a tradition of making barn signs with ornate marked designs on them, although many specifically say these are simply decorative and not magical (it remains a point of intense debate).[280] Crosses, flowers, birds, and magic words—the SATOR Square again is quite popular—all show up in painted, carved, or otherwise marked form as protective aids.

280. Donmoyer, *Hex Signs*, 9–11.

Guardian Spirits

Invoking an angel of protection or another similar spirit can offer a degree of insulation from witchcraft. Many Protestants will simply ask the protection of Jesus (or, in a very occult turn of phrase, "pray the blood of Jesus upon" whatever is being harmed or cursed). In a few cases, guardian spirits are created, either by burying an animal somewhere nearby (if you have a beloved pet that has passed away this works well if you continue to honor and make offerings for it) or by creating a doll-like object (such as the *deitsch* Butzemann, see chapter seventeen).

Smoke

Sacred smoke is a great way to clear away harmful spells, and has been used by Catholics for centuries in church and private ceremonies. Many Southwestern Native groups and those coming from Mexican Indigenous roots like the Mexica or Nahuatl will burn bundles of white sage as a way of creating magical barriers to witchcraft. This practice has been widely co-opted by non-Natives, which has created problems with appropriation and access to white sage supplies for Indigenous communities (a similar fate has befallen palo santo wood when it is harvested irresponsibly). Using sacred smoke is not limited to any one culture, but choosing ones rooted in your own traditions, ones you grow yourself, or ones from your own region would be just as effective without causing problems for Native peoples.

Red Brick Dust

This derives from Hoodoo practices, and as such is best suited to those from within that cultural framework. It involves sprinkling ground-up red bricks—often taken from places like cemetery walls or old churches, although almost any good red brick will do—at key points of entry like doorways or thresholds. A similar protective charm that is more broadly accessible would be salt (see page 277), or one could use sand as well. There are some who speculate that the red dust is based on an idea of red representing blood, so sprinkling a bit of lamb's blood (from the butcher shop) or menstrual blood can be incorporated for protective effects.

Holy Water

Most Catholic churches and many Episcopal ones have fonts on the premises where you can fill a small bottle with holy water. You can also make your own by passing a bowl of it through a sacred smoke, mixing some salt into it, leaving it in the light of the sun or moon, or even dropping a piece of silver in it for a little while. The water is then used to sprinkle (or asperse) the area you want to protect, creating a magical shell around it.

Mirrors

Mirrors were once made with silver, and thus they have many of the same associations. Mirrors deflect magic back at the sender, and create additional light in the space where they are found, so they can be powerful agents of protection.

Hematite

This is a newer protective charm, one that seems to have emerged with a New Age fascination with gemstones and rocks as magical charms (stones and rocks have long had magical associations, but the current glut of them on the market is a new phenomenon and one with some potentially negative environmental and human rights impacts). Hematite, which is an iron oxide-based mineral, is thought to deflect negative energy due to the iron and its often shiny surface when polished. Bonus, hematite's name comes from the Greek word for "blood," as it leaves a reddish streak when scraped on porcelain, thus linking it to blood-based protections.

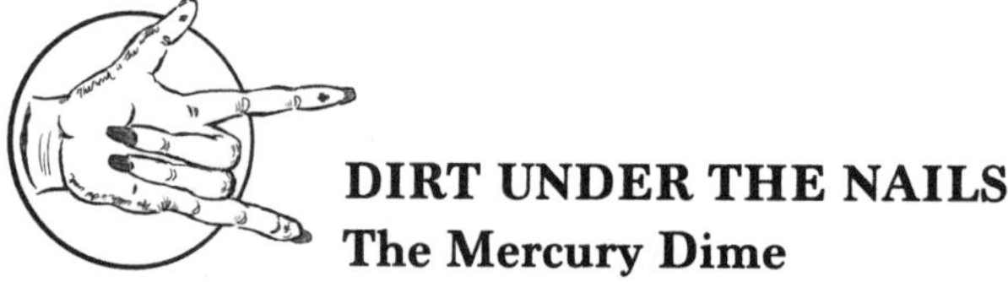

DIRT UNDER THE NAILS
The Mercury Dime

The silver "Mercury" dime is actually a piece of U.S. currency made from around 1915 to about 1945 and containing a fair amount of silver for its size. It doesn't depict the Roman god Mercury, however, but a figure called "Winged Liberty." Still, the resemblance to Mercury, as well as his associations with silver, stuck, and the coin has had magical value almost since it first appeared.

In several traditions, most notably Hoodoo and Southern Conjure, a Mercury dime is a powerful protection spell, mostly due to its silver content. A hole was drilled in the top of the coin's face (right around Mercury…er, Winged Liberty's cap). The coin was then tied on a piece of red thread or string and worn around the ankle. It would continue to repel witchcraft so long as it stayed shiny, but the more curses it deflected the darker it would turn. Once the entire surface was black, it would be replaced.

While finding a Mercury dime can be difficult, you can use the principle easily. Simply get a silver charm—one with magical meaning in the symbol would be very effective—and make an anklet out of it. The idea is that your feet are likely to walk over any curses laid out for you, so the charm will stop them before they can get "into" you. You can also slip a silver coin or charm into your shoe for that purpose.

Silver Bullets: Witches, Werewolves, and Vampires

You may have picked up on the point that any number of these protective charms resemble ones found in lore about other mythic creatures, such as vampires and werewolves. This is a point at which the witch as a fairy-tale figure and the witch as a real-world person jostle against one another. Beliefs about witches often made them out to be essentially supernatural beings in folklore and fairy tales. Indeed, some witches seem to be derived from fairies or Otherworldly entities in British and European lore. At the same time, the belief in people who could perform magic—especially malefic magic—also required the use of the word "witch," and so the conflation of those ideas became common as well. In general, a person telling a story about a witch knew just what kind she meant, as did her listeners, but we sometimes stumble over those distinctions in ways that storytellers didn't.

Add to that the problem of the werewolf, a creature whose lore is frequently conflated with witches. In France, werewolf lore included things like intentional shapeshifting rituals and satanic pacts, and witches are often seen as essentially women doing evil magic while men doing the same might be werewolves.[281] Hunts for witches, including legal or semi-legal ones, parallel the same sorts of hunts for werewolves in some parts of Europe during the late Medieval or early Modern period. Silver is deployed to kill them both, with a silver bullet or a silver sword being used to strike down a transformed witch or wolf, only to have their human form later appear wounded or dead of the same blow.

In North America, the lingering associations with werewolves were less prevalent, except in the form of silver bullets that might be fired at a witch hare or an image of a witch nailed to a tree. Those methods broke a witch's power and very often led to her

281. Hutton, *The Witch,* 195; and Davies, *Oxford Illustrated History of Witchcraft,* 144.

physical injury. Werewolves on the whole are not as commonly reported in the New World (shape-shifting, however, is frequently found in folklore here). On the other hand, vampires were a real threat in some places, even leading to a period known as the "New England Vampire Panic" in the nineteenth century. Families struck by diseases like tuberculosis often suspected evil magic, and witches or vampires became the ones to blame. The graves of suspected vampires were often dug up to examine the bodies, which would then be reburied with the heads severed, the hearts pierced or removed, or large stones in the mouths of the dead to prevent them from rising from the grave. Funnily enough, many of these methods are also found in stories about killing and burying witches to prevent *their* vengeance from the grave.

Disentangling the folklore of all these creatures is not easy, and there always seems to be some overlap in terms of powers and protections. Perhaps one day we will see movies about a brooding vampire having to choose between the werewolf and the witch he loves?

The Witch Must Die?

Witches in general get the short end of the stick when it comes to tales told about them. That's true in fairy tales (the written-down, literary ones not told as "true," necessarily) and folk legends (the ones where the listener is expected to believe what's being shared at some level, even if not all of it). Witches who do anything bad—curse a victim, steal a child, or threaten a community—almost always wind up dead or severely injured. Why is that? Because, as fairy tale scholar Sheldon Cashdan puts it, the witch represents our own darker selves, and we kill her because "only by destroying the evil in the story can justice be served and undesirable tendencies in the reader mastered."[282] For most people, the witch is something to be feared, something as untamed as a werewolf, something with powers beyond control.

Yet not all witches die. Many survive, or even thrive. Baba Yaga in a number of Slavic tales is not destroyed, and in variations on the Russian story "Finist the Bright Falcon" she acts as a guide for the heroine, offering her magical aids to help her on her way.[283] The New England tale of Betty Booker sees her riding the ungenerous skipper all over the countryside and then going on her way, having taught him

282. Cashdan, *The Witch Must Die!*, 83.

283. Forester, *Baba Yaga*, 19–27.

a valuable lesson about kindness to his neighbors (see chapter nine). Even tales of Mont and Duck Moore, a pair of magical racketeers, ends with them dying peacefully within a few days of one another (see chapter two), and the locals discovering a cache of goods they'd saved from all their years of magical service to the community ("service" here being a loosely construed term).

For those who are not afraid of a little darkness, it seems, witches have a place. They belong in the world, and chasing them out with silver bullets and witch hunts is unnecessary. It may even be harmful. After all, facing the darkness is part of life, and witches do that pretty well.

Still, it's good to keep a cellar of salt on hand, and maybe a bit of silver. Just in case.

THE WORK—Warding in Daily Practice

So often in the folktales of wicked witches witching wickedly, what we see is a balance between the forces of proactive and reactive magic. The witch is usually proactive, using magic to pursue her goals tenaciously, sometimes at the expense of her neighbors, but in other tales we find that her activity is done on behalf of one of those neighbors as well. Someone will hire her to place a curse or cast a spell, and then she's perpetually caught in the middle as reactive magic sends a curse back on her, while her client/neighbor gets little of the blowback.

On the other hand, proactive magic is often the right first step to avoiding those entanglements with magic. A magical "first alert" system in the form of a silver dime on the ankle or a witch bottle by the front door slices through potential harm. Spells of this type are so often about dedication and maintenance: keeping a witch bottle buried and intact, wearing a charm daily, feeding a mojo bag regularly, replacing door ward SATOR square slips every year.

What systems do you have in place right now? What are your proactive magics? Do you have ancestors watching over you that you feed on a regular basis, or spirit guardians, perhaps? Do you keep your front steps clean, or store a broom behind your door in case of unwanted company? Do you pick out certain jewelry or even clothing and deploy it as a magical guard against trouble and harm? Do you consult your divination tools often, or grow things in pots or garden beds that need regular care? Are you paying attention to your neighbors, making sure their needs are met if you can, and asking for help when you need it (magically or otherwise)?

Turning magic into your daily practice does not have to be about adding in new things—a silver dime on the ankle or an INRI cross in the window jamb. It can be putting the folk magical touch on the things you already do, running a charm bracelet through sacred smoke once a week or whispering to your front doors when you lock them at night, asking that they protect you for another day. Folk magic is practical, and proactive folk magic is seldom a disruption to your daily rhythm. Instead, it fits in like a new line of harmony under the melody you were already playing. Find your rhythm and touch it with magic that keeps you safe, makes you strong, and builds your relationships (even with inanimate objects).

Recommended Reading

A Century of Spells, by Draja Mickaharic. Mickaharic is a master of the straightforward, contemporary spellbook. While this may sound like old magic based on the title, the "century" the author refers to is the group of over one hundred spells in this slim but potent volume. This book goes well beyond protection, but that makes up a significant portion of the work and the spells can almost all be integrated easily into daily life.

Protection and Reversal Magick, by Jason Miller. Miller's book is often thought of as a quintessential and fundamental guide to psychic protection and self-defense. He draws upon both ceremonial magic and folk magic to craft a book that is accessible, but which also has plenty to offer the practical magician looking to keep out the nasty bits.

The Tao of Craft: Fu Talismans and Casting Sigils in the Eastern Esoteric Tradition, by Benebell Wen. This chapter largely focused on the protection methods found in a small handful of traditions, but there are so many more out there! Wen's book is marvelous in that it brings Chinese sigil craft accessibly to the reader and offers ways to think about using Fu sigils to create peace and balance in a home, offer protection both personal and domestic, and develop magical systems that can respond to negative energy or magical attack. Wonderfully thorough and thoughtful, anyone with an interest in Chinese and Chinese American folk magic would benefit from this book.

CHAPTER SIXTEEN

The Devil's Tramping Grounds—Magical Spaces and Places in the New World

Near York, Pennsylvania, high school–aged people grow up hearing about a place where the world of homework and math problems fades away, and something much darker and eerier opens its doors. They share the legend of the "Seven Gates of Hell," a series of gates set into trees, fields, rocks, and woods that opens upon the Underworld itself. An intrepid explorer need only find the first gate and pass it, then travel to the next—usually a good distance away from the first but close enough to be discernable from the previous gate—and so on until they reach the last gate. The gates may all be different: some made of metal and bearing latches, others rougher affairs made of wood (possibly even mostly rotted away). The gates may test each traveler, presenting terrifying sights or sounds after each passage. The reward is dubious: the opportunity to look upon Hell itself, and possibly never return.

Folklorists know that excursions like these, commonly known as "legend trips," are not really about getting to the seventh and final gate (since virtually no one ever does). They are about the experience of doing the challenge and sharing it with friends. They act as an initiation of sorts, but also bind groups together as they make the journey and the attempt together. Do people believe these gates really allow nefarious passage to the lands of the damned? It depends on who you ask, but most will say they don't *really* believe it. Yet the places where the gates are reputed to begin frequently become the target of police patrols and have dozens of "No Trespassing" signs posted because of how often these trips occur, lending an air of credibility to the stories.

Variations on the Seven Gates of Hell legend can be found in Illinois, Virginia, and Massachusetts. There are likely more versions of the story circulating in some form in other states, too, places believed to be entrances to the Underworld or special "tests" for encountering dangerous occult beings. There are hills and mountains where witches are believed to gather, or statues in cemeteries that supposedly come to life at night and walk among the graves. In several cemeteries there are "witch's chairs," stone benches or seats that will supposedly hold fast anyone who sits on them. Many states have "gravity hills" where a car parked on a slope will mysteriously begin going backward up the hill when left in park or neutral. Some believe the Skinwalker Ranch in Utah to be a site of regular alien visitation, and the ranch itself derives its name from legends about evil witches who use transformation to torment neighbors and enemies.

The places we associate with magic matter. Sometimes those places are a nexus of supernatural activity in stories dating back hundreds of years or more, and sometimes they are places with relatively new spirits to haunt them. Often the spiritual forces found in a location have occult connections—witches, as already mentioned, or special occult challenges designed to test those who would meet or summon uncanny forces, as we see in the story of the Seven Gates of Hell. Frequently, these places are "wild," spots that have little-to-no human contact or context, although they may have once been inhabited by people in some accounts. Abandoned buildings, like hospitals or jails, can become just as wild as a patch of land in the woods where nothing ever grows, or a circle of mushrooms on a moonlit hill. They can be places abandoned only at a particular time, as we see in legends about deals made at crossroads in the night, places where traffic during daylight hours might be frequent.

In witchcraft, the spirits of place matter, and we can often learn a great deal from folklore about those spirits and those places. A folklorically-inclined witch, then, should be able to find and use places of power, the wild places, to amplify her magic in remarkable—if potentially unnerving—ways. This chapter will look at those places and those spirits in folklore and examine how any landscape is likely hiding a few pockets of spirits that have a thing or two to tell us about magic.

Visiting the Midnight Crossroads, or Wild Places of Folkloric Witchcraft

Places have power. If you've ever been in a graveyard after dark, you've likely felt the eerie power of fear, rational or irrational, that creeps over you. Similarly, most of us have places that feel like "home" in some way—places where we are on familiar ground or where we can relax and be comfortable (this doesn't have to be a family home, of course, as those can sometimes be deeply *un*comfortable, but perhaps a favorite restaurant where friends gather or a gym where we go to play basketball with people we like). Cities have a certain "feel" to them, as do quiet country lanes. Barns feel one way, and train stations another. A witch is able to tap into those powers and use them for her benefit, and in North America those practicing witchery seem to favor certain spaces over others.

Traditional Witchcraft (capital letters here) often places emphasis on *genius loci*, or the spirit of places (plural: *genii locorum*). Plenty of traditions around the world have such a concept, and often you will find small shrines, roadside offerings, sacred trees, or standing stones in locations thought to be particularly sacred to a localized spirit. Animism—the belief in a spiritual life that inhabits all things—seems to be the oldest "religion" in the world (although it is more of a worldview than a formal religion in many places). Seeing places as spiritually alive, then, is not strange or aberrant, but fairly typical, and only in recent centuries do we seem to have tried to siphon off active life from our immediate surroundings.

I begin with the "wild" spaces, or those that are not immediately associated with city landscapes. Additionally, I am not discussing "home" spaces and their spirits, as I cover a lot of information about the home in chapter ten instead (but rest assured that most homes seem to have spirits of their own, too).[284] We'll begin in the deepest, darkest wilderness.

Forests

The forest at night is a frightening place for some, and a comforting place for others. Of course, even during the day the forest can be a tricky beast to manage, and plenty of people get lost in the woods every year. In folklore, history, and legend, we

284. For more on spirits of the house, I highly recommend Lecocteaux's *The Tradition of Household Spirits: Ancestral Lore and Practices.*

see forests often associated with spirits and witch meetings. During the Salem trials, several accused witches claimed they went into the woods around the village to meet with devils (or sometimes Indians, who were perceived by some Colonists as diabolical anyway).[285] While those confessions should be taken with a grain of salt, they also point to an inherited body of lore that painted the woods as a place of witchcraft and sorcery. Hawthorne's "Young Goodman Brown" features Puritan witches meeting in the heart of the woods for their satanic rites, as well, and a forest of "dwarf pines" surrounds the sorcerous meeting place in his "Hollow of the Three Hills" as well.[286] Woodland clearings are considered a place of witch meetings and diabolical activity.

In North Carolina, a place called "The Devil's Tramping Grounds" is reputed to have occult powers, with those who try to camp there being chased by strange creatures or sounds at night, or waking up to find their campsite has been moved away from the clearing in the dark, presumably because the space was needed for witch dances.[287] The woods are where witches gather ingredients, too, collecting herbs or curios at night. Travelers in the Appalachians may see strange lights among the trees, known as "foxfire" and thought to be enchanted witch light or the spirits of the dead (in reality it is a bioluminescent fungus). Those who chased the foxfire into the dark could be lost and never heard from again.

Creatures and cryptids—which are essentially local spirits and thus a form of *genii locorum*—are thought to live in particular woods, such as the dense forests of the Pacific Northwest (in the case of Bigfoot) or the New Jersey Pine Barrens (in the case of the Jersey Devil). Some witches are associated with regional forests. For example, Aunty Greenleaf was a witch thought to live in the woods near Brookhaven, New York, and accused/exiled witch Moll Dyer left a cursed stone in the woods near Leonardtown, Maryland (although the stone has since been moved into town, apparently carrying the curse with it!).[288] The woods do not need to be vast expanses of forest, either. My own magical partner and I long used a narrow strip of woods near my suburban home as a meeting place for our witchery, and it was sufficiently "wild" for our purposes. An Alabama witch that I know related to me that he learned

285. Howe, *Penguin Book of Witches,* 126, 136–39, 212–13.

286. See Hawthorne, *Twice-told Tales*; and *Mosses from an Old Manse.*

287. Bledsoe, *Carolina Curiosities*, 94–5; Harden, *The Devil's Tramping Ground,* 45–51.

288. See Schlosser, S. E. *Spooky New York*; and Carey, *Maryland Folklore.*

much of his spellcraft from the woods near his home, including particular rituals or even sigils imparted to him by the forest and land.[289]

Crossroads

If you've ever heard the story about a famous blues singer meeting the Devil at the crossroads at midnight to sell his soul in exchange for musical fame, then you know that crossroads have a deeply magical reputation (see chapter fourteen). In a number of traditions, crossroads—the places where two or more roads intersect—are home to all sorts of occult lore and forces. European witch lore positions them as the locus of the famed mandrake root used in spellcraft, born from the semen of the criminals hanged from crossroads gallows.

FIG 16-1: Papa Legba, the crossroads guardian between the worlds.

In the New World, the slightly sinister reputation these spots enjoy holds the promise of magical aid, just as in the blues story above. African American lore (and lore from the broader rural South) says that if you want to master any skill—particularly skills like music, conjuration, or gambling—all you needed to do was go to a crossroads under cover of night, where you would meet a helpful spirit.[290] Skills might be musical, focus on gambling abilities, or the power to do magic or be invisible. Similarly, in Vodoun traditions, illustrations called *vevés* are used to represent

289. B. F., personal communication, June 5, 2019.

290. Hyatt, *Hoodoo-Conjuration-Witchcraft-Rootwork*, 99–100. See also chapter fourteen of this book.

various spirits, known as the *lwa*. One of the best-known *vevés* is that of Papa Legba, thought to be the crossroads guardian spirit who will appear as either an old man with a cane (often dark-skinned or wearing black clothing) or as a young Black boy. His *vevé*, or spiritual marking, is specifically designed to look like a crossroads (see figure 16-1). He likes offerings of sweets, and welcomes toys and cigars as well.[291]

In Maine folklore, legendary lumberjack George Knox was reputed to have sold his soul to the Devil at a crossroads to gain great strength and the ability to play mischievous tricks on his fellow foresters.[292] In Guatemala (and some other areas with a strong Mayan and folk Catholic presence), a figure called Maximón—syncretized to San Simón/St. Simon—is often seen seated at a crossroads in his imagery. He's a bit of a tricky figure, but gets called upon to help protect people from witchcraft, provide sexual gratification, defend Indigenous peoples, and unblock the paths of devotees (including removing legal obstacles). He's frequently depicted wearing a black suit and hat and holding a rifle, and often found in wooden effigy form. Offerings include rum, sugar, tobacco (his effigy frequently smokes cigars or cigarettes), and money.[293]

Graveyards

The local cemetery is probably full of spiritual activity, and it can be one of the places ripest for magical work, too. Sometimes you can find specific graves or monuments with powerful stories associated with them, as in the case of the Black Aggie grave in Maryland, the Weeping Lady monument in Utah, or the graves of Mary Black and the Witch's Chair in Pennsylvania cemeteries.[294] In some cases people will work with these spirits, summoning them in Halloween séances or by making legend trips to these locations.

In Hoodoo and Conjure lore, graveyards provide valuable working spaces and tools, as well. Many workers will use dirt gathered from the graves of specific individuals—often based on their occupation in life—to use in spells later. In these cases,

291. Illes, *Encyclopedia of Spirits*, 626.

292. Bisset, Carina, "Lumberjack Tales," in Fee & Webb, *American Myths, Legends, & Tall Tales*, 630–31.

293. See Pieper, *Guatemala's Folk Saints*.

294. Carey, *Maryland Folklore*, 93–98; Hardy, "Shhh ... Do you Hear Someone Weeping?"; and White, *Witches of Pennsylvania*, 88.

the workers do not just take the dirt, but "buy" it by leaving offerings of things like whiskey or rum, favorite objects of the person they are buying dirt from, or silver coins (see chapter twenty). Additionally, they may bury work in a graveyard to give it a boost in power. A mirrored box with a target's doll or effigy inside might be buried in a graveyard to keep the individual from doing harm to anyone and make them pay for their wrongs, for example.

Cemeteries don't have to be spooky places, either, as many people use them for communion with their own beloved dead. The rural South has a long-standing tradition of Decoration Day when people will visit the graves of family members to clean and decorate them, a tradition that has strong parallels with the Mexican Día de Muertos celebration (see chapter seventeen). Ancestral work can be done by simply maintaining the graves of the departed with respect and reverence (I frequently like to volunteer for local cemetery clean-up days for this reason). However, it's also worth noting that there are likely to be a number of legal restrictions on anything you do in a graveyard. None of the lore listed here is intended to be a recommendation, especially if it goes against your local laws.

Bodies of Water

If you've been to the ocean, you've probably felt just how big and powerful it is. Water has a deeply spiritual power in a number of magical traditions, holding either pieces of human and divine memory for all eternity or acting as a cleansing and purifying force. Moving bodies of water like rivers or seashores are considered immensely potent. Bathing in seawater is a good way to remove any curses or spiritual suffering a person has. Witches at the seaside are reputed to summon up storms and winds by whipping strands of seaweed around their heads, and seashells can be useful divination tools. Rivers are used in Appalachian witch initiation rites (see chapter four) and to find the infamous "black cat bone" of Hoodoo and Conjure.[295] Rivers may house sacred entities or creatures as well. The Columbia River is sacred to the Secwepemc, Yakama, and Colville First Nations tribes (among many others), and the Ojibwe have a number of legends about the waterways around the Great Lakes and Niagara Falls, including stories of a dragon-like creature that lives there.

295. Hurston, "Hoodoo in America," 387; Hyatt, *Hoodoo-Conjuration-Witchcraft-Rootwork*, 74–97.

Lakes in general can house creatures like dragons and serpents, such as the famed "Champ" in Lake Champlain, Vermont or the beloved Ogopogo in Okanagan Lake, British Columbia (see figure 16-2).[296] More stagnant water sites can also be sources of powerful magic and lore. The bayous and swamps of Louisiana and Florida have plenty of folktales about strange creatures and magic. Marie Laveau conducted St. John's Eve rituals (around Midsummer) at Bayou St. John, immersing herself in the water wrapped in her snake, Zombi, then reemerging renewed and refreshed (and reputedly much younger).[297] The Florida Skunk Ape (a variety of sasquatch) is thought to roam near the swamps in that state. Swamp water is often used for harmful work in Southern Conjure and Hoodoo, including acting as the base for "war water"—a jar of swamp muck with rusty nails and other noxious ingredients inside, left to steep, then broken on an enemy's doorstep to curse them. Even ditches can have their magic. In the Mexican town of Tlayacapan, for example, the border ditches around the town are thought to be inhabited by spirits capable of offering magical power, or potentially great harm—a pattern we can also see in border lore about the famed La Llorona (Weeping Woman) in places like Austin or San Antonio, Texas.[298]

FIG 16-2: The Okanagan, British Columbia, serpent known as Ogopogo.

296. There are so many lake serpents or monsters that trying to capture even a sliver of them here would be a fool's errand, but I highly encourage anyone to locate a large body of water near themselves and look into the local legends about it. There's almost always some sort of creature there, and usually that means a local spirit of some kind.

297. Tallant, *Voodoo in New Orleans*, 65–66.

298. Ingham, *Mary, Michael, & Lucifer*, 103–105.

Hedges and Borders

You may have encountered the term "hedgewitch" if you're reading this book, and there's a reason that hedges are sometimes associated with witchcraft and magic. In British folklore the hedge was a truly wild place, dense and thickly grown over many years and designed to act as a natural barrier between properties. It frequently housed foxes, owls, and other wildlife and provided thorns, wild herbs, or wood for use in folk spells. In North America, hedgerows seldom take on the significance they do in England. However, there are places where fences or gates can become sites of magical ritual. Stone walls sometimes have lore about meeting supernatural creatures, such as the Devil or Death, if a person walks their entire length without falling. The "turnstile" found in some walls, which requires stepping up, turning the body, and stepping down, is sometimes a place of magic where strange creatures may appear. The Seven Gates of Hell story that began this chapter shows how a sequence of walls or gates can become a pathway to Otherworldly encounters.[299] Similar to hedgerows, sometimes overgrown or wild areas may exist at the edge of a garden or forest. Probably the best-known example of this is the story of Brer (short for "Brother") Rabbit and the briar patch from African American lore. In that tale, Brer Rabbit avoids being killed by his enemies—Brer Fox and Brer Bear—by tricking them into tossing him into the briars, his natural home where they can't chase him.[300] There's more than a hint of magic in the tale of a trickster passing through a seemingly impossible barrier like that, I think.

Caves and Mountains

Considering we have cave paintings going back to the dawn of humanity depicting rituals and ceremonies with magical components, it's little wonder that caves in the New World often have connections to magic as well. Sometimes caverns and underground passages have been used as sacred places for centuries, as in the Actun Tunichil Muknal cave in Belize, which was a holy site for the Maya (and a locus of their sacrifices, where you can still see the famed Crystal Maiden, the skeleton of a woman—possibly sacrificed—whose body has been covered in calcium crystals). More recent lore has given rise to the legendary Bell Witch Cave in Tennessee,

299. Meley, "Adolescent Legend Trips," 5–24.

300. Gates, Jr. and Tatar, *African American Folktales*, 133–66.

thought to be home to the spectral entity responsible for hounding the Bell family. Mountains are also held to be sacred in many places in North America. Pele, the Hawaiian goddess responsible for much of the islands' volcanic activity, has a sacred home in the crater of Kilauea. She's also thought to be very protective of her mountain, as many people who have taken even small pebbles from Kilauea have found themselves facing terrible streaks of bad luck until they return the rocks to the National Park Service (which maintains an archive of the stones and the letters of apology people send with them).[301] In North Carolina, Brown Mountain and Roan Mountain have local legends about witches and witch lights appearing on their peaks. A bit of a cross between caves and mountains are mines, which often have lore associated with them about hidden treasures or guardian spirits. Perhaps the most famous of these is the Lost Dutchman Mine in the Superstition Mountains (appropriately enough) of Arizona.[302] Even those who go searching for the mine often end up dead or lost in the mountains, and the legend says a vengeful and protective spirit guards the mine's location closely.

DIRT UNDER THE NAILS
Meeting the Man in Black (or Other Local Spirits)

The tradition of meeting a *tutelary spirit* (spirit teacher) crosses a number of traditions. The infamous "Man in Black" at the crossroads is probably one of the best-known of these spirits, and one that can be met with a simple ritual. You need to have a strong sense of purpose when you are doing this rite, as meeting this entity is supposed to grant you a boon or power, and summoning a spirit without a good reason may just end up backfiring on you (especially given the tricky natures of crossroads guardians).

Identify a crossroads that you can visit repeatedly. Some people will say this is an X-style crossroads where two roads intersect, while others say it should be where three roads meet and form something more like an asterisk. Either way, bring an offering of something (sugary treats or rum is often

301. Hammond, "The Tourist Folklore of Pele: Encounters with the Other," 159–79.

302. Probert, *Lost Mines and Buried Treasures*, 25–38.

recommended, although tobacco makes a good offering, too). Wait at the crossroads at midnight for nine nights (these can be consecutive nights or nine of the same nights, like Sundays, over nine weeks).

There are a number of potential "skills" you can gain by this contact. Zora Neale Hurston mentions a ritual like this that will give you a "slick hand with people" and allow you to control others.[303] Musical mastery is a well-known option. You can let the Man in Black hold a talisman or charm you've made to improve magical skills, or a deck of cards to improve divination or gambling abilities.

You may see or hear strange things, and things that frighten you, as you get closer to the ninth night. Make sure to stay at least through midnight each night and leave your offering at the crossroads. Go home by a different route than the one you came (to make sure nothing malicious follows you). On the ninth night, you will likely run into a person there, dressed in dark colors or with a dark appearance. Offer them something to eat, drink, or smoke. If you've brought something like a guitar, you may want to let them hold it for a bit. Try to be calm and collected and respectful.

Oh, and avoid traffic and cars. It is a crossroads, after all.

City Witches, or the Urban Landscape and Folk Magic

It always surprises people when I bring up cities and urban environments in connection with folklore and folk magic. I think that this is partly because we have been told that "folk" has something to do with old, rural populations that have their "ways" threatened by anything "city-fied" or modern. We often see people lamenting that some aspect of folklife is being "lost" or "forgotten," although considering that argument has been going on since the nineteenth century, it sure seems to be taking a while to lose and forget things. Much early folklore research focused on things like "occupational folklore" (a fancy way of saying "the traditions associated with working people in groups"). While some of those occupations were rural, like lumberjacks or farmers, there were also plenty of studies being done on railroad workers, police officers, and medical professionals because those jobs seemed to breed folklore at a fast

303. Hurston, "Hoodoo in America," 392.

pace (one of the "rules" of folklore is that it often springs up in places with higher risks of some kind, so any life-or-death sort of job would be likely to have folklore).

I say all of this because the city can have just as much active folklife—and folk *magic*—as any rural crossroads or hidden mountain cave. Cities are concentrations of people, often people from diverse backgrounds that all have their own folk magical traditions. When people are wedged together, those folkways conflict, adapt, adopt, and transform one another, and new forms of magic appear alongside the old ones. Some of the most vibrant magical communities in North America happen to be in cities: the Vodoun communities of Brooklyn or Philadelphia, for example, or the "witch market" of Mexico City. Baltimore has a long tradition of Hoodoo candle shops, and Hoodoo itself has distinct forms that appear in places like Memphis (home of the nation sack), Chicago, and San Francisco/Oakland (to say nothing of the incredibly cosmopolitan New Orleans). Portland, Oregon has a vibrant culture of mixed magical practices that draw upon Native Chinook and immigrant Russian, Spanish, Chinese, and Japanese traditions, among others. A high concentration of contemporary Neopagan magical practitioners has settled in the Minneapolis-St. Paul area, lending it the nickname "Paganistan."

City magic has its own distinct flavors, of course, but that does not make it less useful to those who live there. The connections between Jewish merchants in New York and Chicago and the development of Hoodoo in the early twentieth century vitally changed the practice, but also offered new forms of magic, new sources of magical instruction, and new ingredients for magical formulae which have all become standards in the time since.[304] The places in a city can also reinterpret magic in new and wonderful ways. Consider the following list of urban spots and the potential magical uses I suggest. What would you add to this list?

- **Abandoned places**—If you think caves are magical, imagine an underground tunnel or an old warehouse hollowed out of its former industrial life. The graffiti on the wall might include a number of magical sigils (or you might add your own sigil to the cinderblock canvas). Empty buildings can be good as liminal spaces, spots to contact spirits, or places to leave completed spells and offerings.
- **Train stations**—I often imagine the afterlife will involve something like a train station and a ride somewhere (I may have watched a few too many of

304. See Long, *Spiritual Merchants: Religion, Magic, & Commerce.*

Hiyao Miyazaki's films). Trains and transit stations are places of movement and change, good for meeting trickster spirits, for death work, hot footing an enemy out of town, or getting guidance from a tutelary spirit. And, of course, any travel-related magic you care to do.

- **Hospitals**—Hoodoo often recommends collecting dirt from places like hospitals, especially if you need to ask for healing for someone. Adding the dirt to a dolly of a person might help with their recovery, or you might roll a St. Jude candle in the dirt to direct healing at a specific person and place. Since hospitals are also where you go when sick, you might be able to creatively swing a curse, too.
- **Courthouses**—The famous rootworker Dr. Buzzard of South Carolina was known to hang out at courthouses on behalf of his clients, "chewing the root" (usually galangal root) and spitting the juice on the courthouse floor to make sure the trial went in his clients' favor. Gathering courthouse dirt can also be a way to do legal protection work.
- **Dance clubs and bars**—If you've ever wandered into a club when the music, dancing, and intoxication is at just the right mix, you've felt that strange mixture of threat and allure that likely comes from any number of Otherworldly spaces. Using the energy of the club is a good way to get a boost in love or lust magic, or just experience ecstatic release and trance. Even a low-key club might be able to provide a magical experience, as a bit of alcohol and music creates a surreal, Otherworld liminal zone where anything could be a sign or omen waiting to happen.[305]
- **Malls**—Admittedly more suburban than urban, a mall can be a space that reeks of consumerism and commercialism, or it might be a strange zone where that energy has ebbed away and left something empty and hollow given the state of many American malls. In either case, these spaces can be a place to meet spirits—marketplace ones in some cases, or the ones that are more ready to "buy" away your problems and enemies, for a price.
- **Schools**—In particular, schools in urban environments have a powerful folk culture of their own, with students creating fortune-telling games or inventing

305. For an excellent discussion on the trance-space magic of the club, see Orapello and Maguire's *Besom, Stang, & Sword.*

mythical stories about spooky teachers all the time. Picking up a bit of dirt from the school grounds could make for a good "brain-boosting" spell.

DIRT UNDER THE NAILS
Magical Mixology

When it comes to urban magic, what could more resemble a witches' sabbat quite so much as a strobe-lit, high-energy, musically frenzied, alcohol-fueled night club? As a college teacher, I hear more than a few students discuss their drinking lives, and I know plenty of them like to "pre-game" their evening at a club or party. While I do not advocate that they drink (or that anyone does, for that matter), I always like to approach things from a magical perspective. So what if your night out involved drinking with *intentionality* and a magical focus? What if you made a few cocktails with friends into a liminal space for magic as well? Some drink examples and their potential magical effects:

- **Bloody Mary**—Contains spicy peppers, so good for protection magic or keeping away undesirable influences. Also has tomatoes, and spicy food can warm the blood, so this works as a lust potion as well. To up the protective factor you could add olives (for the salt and evil-eye appearance), while a phallic stalk of celery might boost the aphrodisiac qualities. *Alcoholic alternatives:* Michelada (protection) or Sex on the Beach (sex, obviously). *Non-alcoholic alternatives:* Virgin Mary or ginger ale.
- **Margarita**—With the heavy emphasis on limes and citrus flavors, plus the soothing burn of the aloe-like (but unrelated) agave tequila, the margarita is a good "cut-and-clear" drink for removing blockages. That could be good for forgetting an ex or opening the roads to better things ahead (it's a pretty solid break-up drink). *Alcoholic alternatives:* Whiskey sour. *Non-Alcoholic alternatives:* Lemonade or limeade.
- **Irish Coffee**—The coffee will act as a stimulant, and the whiskey as a depressant, but between the two of them these drinks are known for

making people *talk*. If you're looking for a drink that motivates conversation (and goes well with an aphrodisiac dessert), this is a good one. *Alcoholic alternatives:* Vodka and Redbull or a Black Russian. *Non-alcoholic alternatives:* Good coffee.

- **Sazerac**—This is a smooth drink invented in New Orleans. The hint of absinthe in the glass and the dark amber surface of the drink make it a good visionary cocktail. Useful for opening the gates to the liminal and turning a night at the club into an Otherworldly journey. *Alcoholic alternatives:* Absinthe cocktail. *Non-alcoholic alternatives:* Mugwort or green tea with honey.
- **Piña Colada**—This is a drippingly-sweet cocktail built on the back of thick, creamy coconut milk and sugar-distilled rum. The bite of pineapple only makes the sweetness sharper. If you're trying to sweeten up your personality (or someone else's), this might be a good (if cloying) option. The coconut might also act as a cleansing, purifying element here. *Alcoholic alternatives:* Gin fizz, Tom Collins, or a Daquiri. *Non-alcoholic alternatives:* A cane sugar-based cola.

When you make your first selection of the night, you might take a moment and whisper your intent or desires over it, or even trace a sigil into it with your cocktail stick. You can use supporting drinks throughout the night for a bit of a boost to the original intent (for example, following your Bloody Mary with a bit of ginger ale later, or having a cup of coffee with your brand-new group of friends at 3 a.m. in the diner down the street after you've drawn them all in with your sparkling Irish Coffee-fueled conversational skills).

Of course, balance is important in magic as well as cocktails. Make sure you are consistently fueling your body with one of its most vital potions, water, to keep yourself and your magic healthy.

THE WORK—Mapping Magic Around You

Getting to know your personal magical landscape is absolutely essential to witchcraft. Journeys to midnight crossroads and grabbing a bit of dirt from the local hospital work well at a broad level for magic, and fit in with the traditions of witchcraft and folk magic generally. At the same time, the particulars are often what really shape the magic of a place, and the magic a particular witch performs in that place.

What are your local places of power? What places and spaces already have lore associated with them? Do you have local buildings or wild spots with a reputation for being "haunted"? Do you know of local legends about strange or uncanny things in the woods, on a particular road, or in the local graveyard? These do not have to be places with national fame like the Bunnyman Bridge or the Skinwalker Ranch. The more local your lore is, the more likely that you're going to connect with it since you share the land and air and water with whatever exists near you.

Make a map of the spaces you can get to easily. If mobility isn't a major issue for you, try to make these all places you could walk to or reach in half an hour or less by transit. Take the time to really get to know all the spaces around you. If you have mobility challenges, can someone bring you something from a nearby place of power? Look for bodies of water, strange trees, roads. Think about the names of rivers and creeks in your area, or why certain streets have certain names attached to them. Make up some stories about them if you need to as you get started. Then begin looking in local newspapers, books by local authors, or in conversations with people from the area for hints about the stories behind what you've mapped out. Mark your map with the locations of anything uncanny. Note where the best places to leave offerings might be. Circle the spaces that might be good for rituals or spells. Make a point to study your map, get to know it, and visit the places you marked.

And don't forget to bring offerings when you go.

Recommended Reading

The *Spooky* series, by S.E. Schlosser. Schlosser's books are all collections of regional folktales in North America (generally just in the United States, unfortunately). In most cases she not only includes really lovely retellings of local folktales, but each book will have a map of where those tales connect with a particular town or region. This is a useful tool for finding lots of local spirits and creatures.

The Encyclopedia of Spirits: The Ultimate Guide to the Magic of Saints, Angels, Fairies, Demons, & Ghosts, by Judika Illes. While it covers the globe in terms of its scope, Illes' book has more than enough lore on North American spirits and just where they can be found to justify adding it here. You can discover all sorts of interesting information on the various spiritual entities around you, plus learn about their holidays, preferred offerings, and the risks and rewards they provide.

Magical Destinations of the Northeast: Sacred Sites, Occult Oddities, & Magical Monuments, by Natalie Zaman. While this only covers the Northeastern United States (roughly New England, although it ventures a little beyond those borders), it is an incredibly thorough and informative guide to the potential magical hot spots in that area of the country. My hope is that there will be even more of these done for the rest of North America at some point, and that this is just the first of them.

NINTH RITE: CALLING THE MOON

Or, the Times of Enchantment by the Clock and Around the Year

"Di büne blanzt mer im iberschtëede ... "
("Plant beans when the horns of the moon point upward")*

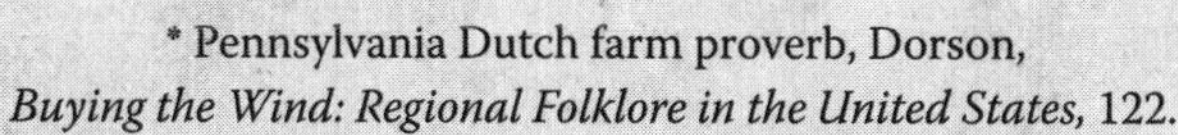
* Pennsylvania Dutch farm proverb, Dorson, *Buying the Wind: Regional Folklore in the United States,* 122.

CHAPTER SEVENTEEN

Topsy-Turvy Days—A Calendar of Bewitched Days

I love Christmas. Not just the day of it, the whole "season" of it, starting from late November when the end of Thanksgiving in the United States marks the official "beginning" of the winter holidays, until around January 6th when my decorations come down and get packed away for another year. The entire celebration feels so much bigger than one day, and indeed, for me it encompasses a complex mix of traditions I've both inherited and absorbed over time. Those include baking gingerbread houses with little bear figures to run around in the thick royal icing "snow" to the more recent "Christmas pickle" ornament buried in the tree and picked up from the Pennsylvania-German neighbors around us where our family lives now.

Not everyone feels this way about the winter holidays, of course, and that is perfectly reasonable. For many, these holidays are bittersweet, or simply bitter, because of family complications and trauma. For others, the hegemony of American "Christianity" over the winter holidays is frustrating and oppressive, stifling other traditions under the weight of a strange combination of nativity scenes and holly, jolly Santas that seem inescapable even in completely secular spaces. Still others may chafe under the weight of obligations that gift-giving creates, putting people into debt for what can be a crassly commercial and capitalistic holiday. These criticisms are all perfectly valid, as are other critiques I've not covered here.

And yet, even with all the complicated tangles of tinsel and the gritty, dark underbelly of a red fur suit to contend with, I love this holiday, and many others do as well. The critiques point to one of the reasons why: it is not just one holiday to one group of people, but can be many things to many people, all collected under a massive banner of winter celebration (even as that banner can seem more like a blanket covering over other traditions).

For several years, I also participated in a winter holiday procession in Philadelphia, the Philadelphia Parade of Spirits. The point of this parade is not the ho-ho-ho sort of Christmas spirit, but the embrace of the darkness of the holiday, especially through the horned, devilish figure of Krampus imported from Austria and Germany. Krampus, and other similar figures like Gryla of Scandinavia or Père Fouettard of France, Perchta, or Baba Yaga, as well as figures from North American lore like the Belsnickel, does not give gifts but threaten naughty children with switches and growls and even being stolen away or eaten. He is the dark side of the holiday, the "scary ghost stories" part of the Christmas tune (see figure 17-1).

FIG 17-1: A design for a mask worn by the author during Philadelphia's Parade of Spirits.

When I celebrate Christmas, I am celebrating both the gingerbread and the Krampus. I am experiencing the holidays as what anthropologist Alessandro Falassi called "time out of time," a way of breaking away from the everyday and piercing the uncanny space of ritual, mystery, and magic.[306] I do that with cookies and with costumes, with presents to my family and offerings to spirits that might destroy

306. Falassi, *Time Out of Time*, 4.

my home or steal my children otherwise. The holidays are, for me, a "traveling liminal space" (a phrase borrowed from witchy friend and author Chris Orapello), and because of that I feel particularly tapped into magic during the winter season.

This chapter builds on that "traveling liminal space" and looks to the way that holidays and festivals punctuate the calendar and create key places and times that elevate magic. This is not a typical "wheel of the year" scenario, however, and I hope to emphasize that the folkways of many people use different holidays in different ways, and that those traditions are all valid and valuable for those using them. Just because you don't celebrate the Christmas holidays the way I do—or perhaps at all—doesn't take anything away from your own calendar. You have the power to build the connections and the cycle that means the most to you, just by tapping into the folkways of your own community, your own traditions, and your own environment.

A Handful of North American Holidays

While I may have gushed rather heavily about Christmas on the previous pages, it is one of many holidays we see taking root in North American folk traditions. Some are more regionally celebrated than others, and some are culturally specific and require a certain amount of insider knowledge to participate fully. Below I outline a few—well, more than a few but not nearly so many as I could—holidays and the magical traditions associated with them. Some of them are very much rooted in particular religious traditions that you may not like or which may not be your own, but often those holidays have secular avenues that let community members from outside the religion participate in some ways. This is not a carte-blanche invitation to pick up any of these holidays or a demand you adhere to some sort of "magic schedule," but instead an effort to see the calendar as a place already inhabited by magic that may be accessible to you based on your local customs.

I will also point out that this is not, strictly speaking, an agricultural calendar. Agricultural moments punctuate it, true, as we see during the Thanksgiving/Harvest Home season for example, but there are many festivals that mean plenty to those who celebrate them without the addition of farming cycles. Most holidays are rooted at least partly in the seasonal shifts, but the relationship between those shifts and crop-planting or reaping are highly variable. I personally find the Wiccan Wheel of the Year beautiful, but even it faces issues when exported beyond Britain and northwestern Europe because seasonal cycles in other places differ so greatly (as Australian and New Zealand Wiccans can likely tell you). Add to that the problems instigated by climate change and even the deeply agricultural Wheel of the Year is untethered from specific farm activities and moved into the realm of symbolism. That doesn't rob it of value at all, however, so if that model fits your worldview best, the holidays below may just be a lovely way to add to or expand what you already do. Similarly, if you follow other liturgical calendars, such as the Muslim or Jewish holidays rooted in a lunar calendar or the Catholic calendar tied to saints' feast days and cycles connected to the story of Jesus, these holidays may simply expand or augment your existing celebrations.

New Year's Day

Virtually every culture has its own New Year's celebration. In much of North America, that comes at the beginning of January, and the holiday is loaded with significance and magical possibilities. Lore from the Ozarks and Appalachians says that whatever a person is doing on New Year's Day they will do for the rest of the year, so starting a new project can be beneficial, while those attempting to recover from alcoholism may refrain from drinking.[307] The first twelve days of the year symbolize the twelve months to come, so some people note the weather of each day as an indicator of the weather for the following year. Many cultures have food-based traditions for New Year's Day. Mexican lore says that eating twelve grapes gives you twelve months of good luck to follow. Pennsylvania Germans cook sauerkraut and pork for luck,[308] while Southerners often eat collard greens and black-eyed peas to provide a lucky year. The "green" of the collards or cabbage is sometimes equated folklorically to the green of money, and indeed some people cook a dime into their vegetables for such luck, but the provenance of that belief is a bit spotty in the historical record. Many people "shoot in" the new year by firing rifles or shotguns into the air (powder charges only, please, as firing live ammunition up means it comes down somewhere and may give someone a very unlucky new year when it does so). The "shooting in" has become the use of fireworks to welcome the new year and dispel any harmful spirits lingering around. Asian American New Year's festivities, which come later

307. Randolph, *Ozark Magic*, 78–81.

308. See Yoder, *Discovering American Folklife*, 283–86. See also Bronner and Brown, *Pennsylvania Germans: An Interpretive Encyclopedia*.

after a lunar-based calendrical cycle, sometime around early February, also deploy fireworks and large costumes like dragons to frighten away wicked spirits. Gifts are given in red envelopes as well, a way of offering luck and good fortune along with the gift itself.

FIG 17-2: The groundhog, or *grundsau* in Deitsch, is seen as an Underworld messenger in traditions like Urglaawe.

Groundhog Day

While many people know about this holiday, few take it very seriously. In Pennsylvania, however, it is a much-feted and celebrated day, particularly in places like Punxsutawney, where the local celebrity groundhog (also known as a woodchuck) Punxsutawney Phil emerges with great fanfare from his official "den." He then determines if people should expect a longer winter (if he sees his shadow) or a shorter one (on a shadowless day). The groundhog is the basis for a series of lodges (much like the famed Elk or Moose Lodges) in Pennsylvania, and lodges often have some slightly esoteric and magical practices associated with them. The Pennsylvania German Heathen community known as the Urglaawe also build their protective Butzemann spirits during this holiday period.[309] The tradition of Groundhog's Day is rooted in the holiday of Candlemas—associated with Imbolc on the Wiccan calendar—which involves blessing candles for the remaining winter, so many of the traditions associated with this day involve looking for light to return after the long, cold, dark nights.

309. Schreiwer, *The First Book of Urglaawe Myths*, 15–27; See also Schreiwer, "Requirements for Butzemann Construction."

In Europe a Candlemas Bear or Badger filled a similar function to the groundhog here, and weather lore has long been associated with the day, as evidenced by lines from an old English nursery rhyme: "If Candlemas Day be fair and bright/ Winter will have another flight./ But if it be dark with clouds and rain,/ Winter is gone, and will not come again." Candlemas is also associated with love divinations, tying it to a more commercial February holiday, Valentine's Day.

Mardi Gras, Lent, and April Fool's Day

Lent, the forty days before Easter, is typically a period of abstinence beginning on the mournful "Ash Wednesday" sometime in mid-to-late February. That also means that the final Tuesday before Lent—often called "Fat" or "Shrove" Tuesday in many places—is a day of heavy indulgence. In areas with Pennsylvania Dutch populations, people make *fasnachts*, a type of very rich doughnut intended to use up all the sugar and butter or lard in the pantry on the pre-Lenten "fasting night." A similar tradition from England and Western European origins involves making pancakes for the same reason. In New Orleans and other areas where French-speaking Cajun populations abound, the celebration of Mardi Gras (literally "Fat Tuesday" in French) would be incomplete without the famous "king cake." This cake is usually a rich dough baked in a ring shape covered in festive icing and sprinkled with decorative sugar—frequently in the green, gold, or purple hues of Mardi Gras. A bit of magic is added through the inclusion of various charms in the cake. Frequently a coin or a small figure of the infant Jesus will be baked into the batter, and the lucky person who finds these tokens is seen as the "king" for the day or otherwise believed to inherit good fortune (if they do not break their tooth on the charm, that is). Huge parades are held for the pre-Lenten rites in many parts of the Gulf Coastal South, the most famous of which are in New Orleans. Costumes and disguises are everywhere, and a tradition of trading lucky glass (now often plastic) beads for applause, alcohol, or—in some cases—nudity turns the streets into a massive party. Following the revels, many people give up indulgences for the forty days until the Easter celebration (or at least attempt to), in ways similar to New Year's resolutions. This short period of self-discipline may be more attainable than the full year, however, and even a number of people from non-Christian traditions will use the Lent season as a period of quiet self-reflection. All that self-reflection can get tedious, however, and the arrival of a topsy-turvy day of mayhem in the midst of it all can be a delightful reprieve. The tradition of naming an April Fool goes back to Roman times when Saturnalian feasts involved a day when servants became masters and masters became servants for a day. The reversal of social order allowed a sort of "purge" of pent-up hostility (or so the theory goes), although anything done by the servants would likely be remembered the next day when order was restored. Over time this day has come to be associated with other ways of bringing out gleeful, controlled chaos, and that makes this an especially good day for those who love tricks and tricksters to strut a bit.

FIG 17-3: In many Ukranian-influenced areas, the tradition of elaborately decorating eggs is called *pysanky*, and is a sort of artistic representation of grace and prayer associated with the Easter holiday.

Eastertide

At the end of Lent comes Easter, the Christian celebration of death and resurrection. It's easy to see the rebirth of spring in this holiday, and even the symbols linked with "Easter" are often very much about the natural world's renewal. Traditions of egg-dying and hiding speak to newly hatching spring chicks, and many people create incredibly elaborate egg decorations such as the detailed beeswax-and-dye patterned *pysanky* derived from Ukrainian traditions (see figure 17-3). The weather on Good Friday—the Friday before Easter Sunday—is believed to foretell the prevailing weather for the next forty days (similar to the groundhog traditions above). It is thought to be an ideal day for planting or setting eggs for new chickens. Being born on Good Friday enables a person to see spirits, or gives them extraordinary luck. Elaborate meals break the Lenten fast and people frequently consume ham or lamb on Easter, but in some places with German or Czech populations the animal may be represented by a loaf of sweet bread or a large hunk of butter molded into the shape of a lamb. Hot cross buns are a sort of Eastertide *Fasnacht*, with rich dough full of fruit covered in icing (in a protective equal-armed cross shape on top). The return of spring also means that many people in Appalachia are consuming spring tonics, herbal infusions designed to "build up the blood" and prevent sickness as the weather grows warmer. One such tonic is a strong infusion of sassafras tea, which can taste a bit like a weak root beer and is thought to purify any illness from the body.[310]

May Day

The rush of blood and warmth as the days grow longer can lead to the planting of more than flowers. For many people, the celebrations of May Day are connected to sex and fertility. Dancing around the maypole, a tall pillar festooned with flowers and ribbons that get woven together by young dancers growing ever closer with each passing turn, even raised the ire of local Puritans in Nathaniel Hawthorne's story, "The Maypole of Merrymount." On May Day, young women wash their face or eyes with the morning dew at dawn before speaking in order to preserve their youthful beauty. Children gather baskets of flowers to hang on neighbors' doors in the sweetest possible version of "ding-dong-ditch" (making this holiday tradition, which lies calendrically opposite of Halloween, a sort of counterpoint to trick-or-treating). The night before May Day also has plenty of significance, especially to witches. It is known as "Walpurgisnacht" (the night dedicated to St. Walpurga, known in Germany as a protector against witches). Walpurgisnacht rites involve witch-meetings on mountaintops and leaping over flaming bonfires, sometimes on broomsticks, which makes this night an ideal one for crafting your own broomstick.[311] These revels often involve spirits, imps, or devils as well, and if you've ever seen the "Night on Bald Mountain" segment of Disney's *Fantasia*, then you probably have a sense of what people imagine on that night.

Midsummer and St. John's Day

The summer solstice has a fair number of customs associated with it, although far fewer in North America than the winter solstice season does. The Lakota Sioux

310. Milnes, *Signs, Cures, & Witchery*, 92–94.

311. Raedisch, *Night of the Witches*, 75–86.

often hold their famed sun dances around the time of the summer solstice (although it is not necessarily directly tied to that date). While we often associate the "dumb supper" with Halloween, there are multiple accounts of the ritual being done on Midsummer's Eve (the night of June 22nd, usually). Performing the dumb supper required all who participated to remain silent as they prepared the food and set the table (usually backwards), although the meal could be as simple as some bread and cheese.[312] If done properly, an image of a future spouse would appear. In places with Catholic traditions, such as Louisiana, St. John's Eve (June 23rd) was the focus of celebration. Several stories place famed "Voodoo Queen" Marie Laveau at Bayou St. John for this holiday, noting that she would submerge herself into the water and come out looking youthful and renewed (even leading to some speculation that she swapped places with her daughter during one such ritual).[313]

Independence Days

With nearly two dozen countries in North and Central America, the dates of independence celebrations are all over the calendar. However, early July is the date for both Canada (July 1st) and the United States (July 4th), so I situate my discussion of these dates here. Of course fireworks are frequently involved, which means gunpowder—a magical ingredient used in a number of spells focused on purification and banishment. Some women used gunpowder to magically induce abortions, and in Hoodoo practices mixing gunpowder with an enemy's footprint cursed them. The celebration of Juneteenth (on June 19th, which honors the final emancipation of slaves following the Civil War) is usually marked by the consumption of foods like hot sausages and red strawberry soda. Some participants will prepare altars of food for their ancestors, much as we see during the Día de Muertos rites of Mexican Americans.[314] Haiti's Independence Day is January 1st, but they certainly have some magical history to celebrate, as some accounts say that the Vodoun *lwa* (spirits) were invoked to aid the fight for independence there.

312. Hyatt, *Folklore from Adams County,* 225; and Randolph, *Ozark Magic,* 178–81.

313. Hurston, *Mules & Men,* 193–95; and Tallant, *Voodoo in New Orleans,* 62–66.

314. See Taylor, "Hot Links and Red Drinks: The Rich Food Traditions of Juneteenth."

FIG 17-4: At Michaelmas, many Christians celebrate the victory of the Archangel Michael over Satan, sometimes called Lucifer (although they are also distinct and different entities in many traditions).

"Back to School" and Michaelmas

Sending children off to (or back to) school can be either emotionally taxing or a big breath of relief for parents—sometimes both. While these aren't officially "holidays," when the children are back to school we see some folk magical rituals spring up after them. For example, some parents will take a handful of dirt from the front yard and toss it lightly after the departing children, making sure they don't see, in order to protect them and bring them back home safely. If children pick things up on the way to or from school, a wise parent will burn them in case they were left by witches to curse the child.[315] School's start is often near the seasonal rite of Michaelmas (September 29th), which features lore about the Devil and St. Michael the archangel (see figure 17-4). Blackberries shouldn't be eaten after this date or they will be cursed by the Devil, and snakes can be signs of luck when seen on this day. A love divination on Michaelmas involves carving the initials of all potential suitors into apples or crab apples on Michaelmas Day, then seeing which one rots last. The initials that last longest are the ones belonging to the true love of the love-seeking diviner. Kids develop their own spells, too, as anyone who has played with a folded paper fortune-teller

315. See Hyatt, *Adams County*, 466.

will know. A more contemporary version of the crab apple spell involves flexing the tab of a soda can back and forth while reciting the alphabet. When the tab breaks, the last letter spoken is the first initial of the person's next significant other.

Harvest Holidays & Thanksgivings

I often explain to my students when teaching American Studies courses that the reason we have Thanksgiving in November is because the early Puritan colonists were bad farmers. That's a bit of an exaggeration on a lot of fronts (including calling them "Puritans," which isn't quite technically correct, and I use that statement to explain that history is, well, complicated), but it does boggle the mind a bit that we in the United States celebrate our harvest festival so late in the season. Canada is a bit more realistic, setting the date in early October. There are lots of folk magical moments in the harvest season. The well-known turkey wishbone charm offers a free wish to whichever person gets the larger half when two people pull on the prongs of the bone. Turkey bones are also used in the Ozarks by young women who want to attract suitors (see chapter eleven).[316] They nail the wishbones above their doors to summon in the parade of gentlemen (or possibly gentlewomen) callers. Thanksgiving is not the only harvest festival, though, and many places observe a "harvest home" celebration. Large county fairs are held in rural locations, which sometimes feature fortune-telling tents or other acts of divination (even electronic "love tester" devices have a touch of the strangely magical when surrounded by hay bales and the smell of corn dogs, I think). Harvest Home was a bit contentious in Pennsylvania Dutch areas, where it conflicted with "English" or "Yankee" Thanksgiving.[317] Often during harvests, farmers leave a little bit of their fields unmown and free-standing. I had a contact in Maryland that sent me photographs of these "verges," and there are several potential meanings; they could be left in case anyone poor and hungry needed to come and glean them (which matches biblical practices), or they could be offerings to the "spirits" of the land and harvest ensuring another good planting and harvesting season the next year. Animal slaughter also has a number of rituals associated with it, including specific religious restrictions in kosher Jewish or halal Islamic communities, and the blood can sometimes be saved for sprinkling over the

316. Randolph, *Ozark Magic*, 167.

317. Yoder, *Discovering American Folklife*, 227–46.

farm land to protect it. The whole Thanksgiving meal, in its way, is what the television show *Buffy the Vampire Slayer* once called "a ritual sacrifice ... with pie!"

Halloween

Dressing up in spooky costumes and begging for treats sounds like a good time, doesn't it? Even more so when you add in all the eerie ambiance of haunted houses, ghost stories, and late-night graveyard séances. Halloween night is associated with a number of magical traditions, including the sharing and begging of "soul cakes," which are sort of the dryer, scone-like antithesis of the Easter hot cross bun. Halloween is said to be an excellent time for divination, and is even known as "Nutcrack Night" in places with a strong rural British influence because of a nut divination ritual. Two sweethearts would toss nuts—usually walnuts or chestnuts—into a fire. If both burst, they were truly in love, but if only one did or they both fizzled, the romance was not to last. Apple bobbing sometimes worked as a love divination game. Young people carved their initials into the apples and set them to float in the water, then took turns bobbing for them. If you got someone's initials on the apple you caught with your teeth, they were to be your sweetheart (although in many cases this worked more like a very soggy "spin the bottle" and you were simply obligated to give them a kiss). Dumb suppers sometime get performed on Halloween, while visiting graveyards on Halloween adds power to rituals there, including rituals to summon up ghosts or spirits and ask them questions. Those same rituals can be performed at home, too, although they seem somehow even more dangerous in that situation, as with the case of contemporary spirit summoning rites like "Three Kings" or "Midnight Man" (see chapter twenty-two for the "Three Kings" ritual). Guising and using costumes means that you can also play pranks in the "merry misrule" traditions while also protecting yourself from any wandering or roving spirits that might be hunting that night. Leaving lit jack-o-lanterns out protects one's home from harmful haunts and provides a pathway for the dead to find their way back to their homes to visit loved ones in the night.

FIG 17-5: During the celebration of *Día de Muertos*, images of the skeletal maven of the festival known as *La Catrina* are frequently created and shared.

Day of the Dead

While it can be tempting to overlap Halloween with its frequent skulls and ghosts with the traditional Day of the Dead on November 2nd (although in many places the celebration runs from October 31st to that date), these are not equivalent holidays.[318] In North America, the best-known version of this celebration comes out of Mexican traditions, where it is known as *Día de (los) Muertos*[319] and involves visiting the cemeteries and decorating the graves of beloved ancestors and friends. Often these decorations include offerings of favorite foods on altars called *ofrendas*, where photos and curios belonging to the deceased are kept as well. Marigolds are a preferred flower for decoration, and many people light candles or lanterns for the dead as well. Skulls are everywhere: from the *papel picado* (literally "cut-up paper") decorations to the sugar skulls marked with the names and initials of the dead left on

318. For a good discussion of why these holidays are important to separate, and why Mexican identity is often very closely associated with *Día de Muertos*, see Brandes, "The Day of the Dead, Halloween, and the Quest for Mexican National Identity."

319. While I speak and read Spanish, I have been told on many occasions that the preferred term is *Día de Muertos* without the article "*los*." However, I have also seen native Spanish-speakers use the *los* as well, so I include both versions here.

the *ofrendas.* Beautiful skull masks and makeup are worn by some revelers. And we can't forget about the beautiful *La Catrina*, the gorgeous skeletal woman who acts as a semi-official "face" to the holiday (see figure 17-5). Much of this holiday is about celebrating life by remembering that death is a great equalizer, but it also helps celebrants to see that they have a form of eternal life in the memories and hearts of their descendants. While the Mexican variations are the best-known in North America, other communities with strong folk Catholic heritages—such as Italians, Irish, and Polish groups—often have versions of the holiday, too.

The Christmas Season

A massive number of holidays fall under this broad and snowy blanket, although not all of them are strictly "Christmas"-related. Generally things kick off around December 6th, with St. Nicholas' Day. The holiday is found throughout Europe, although the Dutch tradition has children leave their shoes out by the door, as well as carrots or oats, in the hopes that St. Nicholas and his horse (or reindeer in some versions) will stop by and fill the shoes with treats and small toys. This is also the potential date of a visit by Krampus, or in the New World, the Pennsylvania German Belsnickel who acts as a sort of Krampus-combined-with-Santa figure. The Belsnickel will visit local children and is often played by a local teenager dressed in thick furs, a fake beard, and soot on his face carrying a sack of gifts and a buggy whip. He will ask the children to recite a poem or tell them about the chores they've failed to do (after consulting with their parents in advance), then throw candy and treats on the floor and swipe at them with the whip while they dive to pick everything up. Belsnickling—a type of masked procession going from door to door asking for food (later donated to the poor) and strong drink—derives from the Belsnickel tradition, and occurs throughout the winter holiday season.

The Feast of Guadalupe is held on December 12th, and celebrates the miraculous visitation of the Virgin Mary at Tepayac Hill in Mexico. She revealed herself (looking very much like a local Native, and becoming one of the famed "Black Madonnas") to a peasant named Juan Diego, offering him roses that left her image in his *tilma* (cloak), an object that is still on display at the church built for her after the miracle in Mexico City. She is considered the patroness of North America (and likely derives from an Aztec goddess, Tonantzin, worshipped at Tepayac before colonization). Many appeal to her on her feast day for healing, family blessings, and protection from harm. St. Lucia's Day on December 13th is celebrated by people of Scandinavian descent, and involves selecting a young girl to wear a wreath decked with lit candles and wearing a white robe to lead a procession through the community, offering light and guidance to lost souls.

The winter solstice is revered among a number of people, and many Native sites like Cahokia (near modern-day St. Louis) have architectural structures—including one dubbed "Woodhenge"—aligned with the sun or stars on that day. The Blackfeet tribes of the north and northwestern portions of North America held multi-day games and dance celebrations at the solstice. Christmas Eve is rife with lore, including special divination rituals with candle wax or lead (see chapter seven for an example) and a belief that at midnight all animals can speak for a moment. Many people leave out offerings for their house spirits on Christmas Eve, as happens with the Scandinavian *tomte,* who gets a bowl of porridge with a pat of butter on the top.[320] For a long time, the tradition of sharing ghost stories on Christmas made the holiday a little bit spooky, and it's why Charles Dickens made his famous *A Christmas Carol* a tale of hauntings. The period around Christmas also has the famous "Twelve Days" of song fame, involving repeated gift-giving and festive celebrations. Slaves in the antebellum era would receive clothes (often the only ones they received all year) by going to the master's house and shouting "Christmas Gift!"[321] They would also sometimes get the week after Christmas off of work, at least those who were field hands, since household slaves would be forced to do all the holiday cooking and cleaning.

Hanukkah—once considered a somewhat minor holiday in Jewish communities—has become more essential, and the use of lights and candles celebrates a miracle of oil during the Maccabean revolutions (and has come to have significance to Holocaust survivors as well, many of whom would save a bit of the meager butter supply they were given to celebrate the Sabbath). The dreidel—a clay top inscribed with Hebrew letters—acts as a gambling game and occasional fortune-teller. The Hindu festival of Diwali—the festival of lights—happens between October and December, with variable dates. This festival involves lighting candles and setting off fireworks to celebrate the victory of Rama over the tribe of demons. The lights and explosions memorialize the victory and dispel any current evil lingering around. Traditionally, the house is cleaned very thoroughly during this festival to ensure no malignant spirits make a nest in a dirty home, and sweet treats bestow blessings on

320. Raedisch, *The Old Magic of Christmas,* 101–11.

321. Genovese, *Roll, Jordan, Roll,* 580.

those who eat them. Kwanzaa is another light-oriented festival. This holiday was established in 1966 by Maulana Karenga, a Black political activist and later professor of Africana Studies, as a way to celebrate pan-African identity. Candles are lit in the *kinara* to celebrate seven key principles of pan-African values, and music, dance, and gift-giving are part of the ritual as well.

New Year's Eve

Everything comes full circle on the last day of the year. Many clean their homes thoroughly on this day to give themselves a fresh start on the first day of the new year (but don't clean on the day itself because that would mean a year of constant cleaning to follow). Additionally, many people like to ring in the changing year with a good luck kiss at midnight. Scottish tradition says that the "first footing" after midnight is important, too, which means that the first person to cross your threshold after the shift from old year to new should be a tall, dark-haired (or dark-complexioned) man.

These are only a very select few of the days available for celebration and ritual throughout the year. You can likely see that while many of them have religious overlays, they also all have deeply entwined folk practices that create a web of magic and wonder around them. You are likely to find any number of calendar cycles that make sense to you in terms of magic and celebration if you look to the traditions around you just a bit more closely. Holidays are a vital part of our experience, and we love them to be a little bit magical.

Even with all that celebration and enchantment, however, we are human, and we can pick a fight about anything, including holidays.

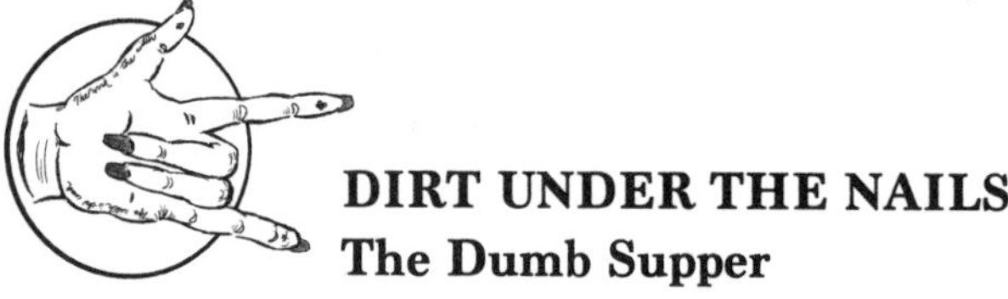

DIRT UNDER THE NAILS
The Dumb Supper

Hosting a dumb supper can be a powerful way to manifest spirits, but be warned that it can also backfire and reveal unwanted things, too. One dumb supper so tormented the spirit of the person conjured that he later killed his wife for summoning him during her youthful game, and some who do this ritual do not see a future spouse but a skull or coffin, indicating they will die young (or at least before they marry). Do this at your own risk!

To conduct a dumb supper you need an odd number of participants and an even number of place settings (one more than the number of participants, so if you do this with nine people you'll set ten places). It can be done on Midsummer Eve, May Day (or May Day Eve/Walpurgisnacht), Halloween, or sometime during the Christmas/New Year cycle. The rules are simple:

1. Prepare all food in silence and add as little salt as possible to the meal. Stir backwards (counterclockwise) and walk backwards as much as possible.
2. Set full place settings for all participants and one extra empty place setting.
3. Leave doors unlocked (or open if you can manage it).
4. Set out each plate full of food, but leave the last one empty. Light a single candle and extinguish all other lights in the room.
5. Everyone should sit and eat, still being silent (not talking—clanking dishes will be hard to avoid).
6. At some point during the meal, an image of the future spouse of one participant (usually the host, but it can be any participant) will appear. In some stories, they appear at the table in an instant, and in others they walk in through the door.
7. Once the meal is done, all plates and dishes are gathered backwards and walked to the sink backward. The doors are closed, and the candle extinguished. The rite is done (and everyone can break into excited chatter about what they have or have not seen).

You can theoretically also use this to call up a spirit to answer a question by asking it aloud before starting to cook the food (or alternately, while lighting the candle, although everything else is done in silence still). Once again, try this rite at your own risk!

Support Your Local Festival

Above, you read that the division between Harvest Home and Thanksgiving was eventually settled in favor of the latter on a national cultural scale. Yet the regional "harvest home" celebration is not entirely gone, and finds occasional footholds through local churches or school festivals. The small and local is intimately tied to the land, to the history and the people who live on that land, to the magic of the peculiar and idiosyncratic that comes through when "little" culture comes through despite "big" culture's lumbering presence.

These little festivals can be a vital way to understand the people and places around us, because they are so often full of rituals and traditions, many of which have magical elements to them. Seeking out a Strawberry Festival in June tells us something about our growing season, but it also shows you how people interact with strawberries, too, as you see them transform them into desserts, art, music, alcohol, and more. You may pick up gardening lore about strawberries, finding that they prefer a certain type of soil, or where to find the best heritage breeds or wild berry patches. You may learn something about the aphrodisiac nature of the strawberry (especially dipped in chocolate) and even hear someone talk about how summer strawberries make springtime babies. You might hear someone tell you about an herbal infusion of strawberry leaves to help "purify the blood" as a tonic. All of this from attending one festival!

You also learn to see the people around you as part of your spiritual landscape, interacting with the same things you do—even strawberries—in ways that you might not but ways that still forge a relationship. Witches are keen observers of people, plants, animals, weather, nature… A witch at a festival is taking in loads of crucial information, and tying herself through the festival to the community around her.

So, if you really want to start building a "wheel" that makes sense for you and where you live, supporting your local festival(s) is a great place to start.

You Are Your Own Holiday

The first spell many of us learn is "blow out the candle and make a wish!" Birthdays are often imbued with a certain magical quality, and we pile on a lot of rituals to make sure that magic is front and center on our annual revolution around the sun. We tie personality traits and behaviors to our astrological signs, usually determined by our birth in Western astrology. We make wishes on candles, eat sweet foods like cake or ice cream as a way to "sweeten" our year to come, and receive spankings or ear-pullings to grant us extra luck (or "one to grow on"). And we are rewarded with gifts, which we hide under bright paper, surprises summoned up by expectant eyes and rabid ripping of ribbons and tissue.

Anniversaries also have a certain amount of magic in them, and we frequently celebrate weddings and other significant dates by doing symbolic rituals with those involved. We may relight a candle used during the original ceremony, or take a piece of (rather stale but likely edible) cake out of the freezer to "resweeten" our connection. We may offer gifts to someone else based on the number of the anniversary, tying symbols of endurance that grow stronger with each year to our anniversary dates.

Our lives fill with holidays of our own making, and building a calendar that means something to us also allows us to use the rites and magic that make the most sense to us (for example, I know plenty of people who would be very happy to drop the birthday spanking ritual entirely for very good reasons).

Some folk beliefs and rituals for birthdays:

- Kentucky superstition says that if you let your birthday pass without thinking of it, you will die before the next birthday.[322]
- One should not celebrate one's birthday before the actual date of one's birth. It will bring bad luck.
- It is bad luck to be wished a happy birthday if one is over the age of forty (instead, many people will have parties on their "name day" instead, which is the feast day of the saint with whom they share a name).
- If you stumble with your right leg, and your birthday is an odd day, it is good luck. If you stumble with the left and your birthday is an even day, it is good luck. But stumbling with the wrong combination (right leg, even day or left leg, odd day) is very bad luck.
- You should always have an odd number of candles on the cake or pie for a birthday, even if you have to add an extra candle.

322. Thomas, *Kentucky Superstitions*, 217.

- Blowing out the candles on a birthday cake will tell you how many years it will be before you are married: (a) by the number of times you have to blow to put them all out, or (b) by the number of candles left lighted after the first blow.
- An Ozark belief states that if you have bad luck on your birthday, even a little bit of it, it means bad luck for the full year to follow.[323]
- On your birthday or anniversary, you can open a book (usually a Bible, but any book will do) to a random passage and put your finger down. Whatever passage you land on is indicative of what your coming year will bring you.
- The best day to start a business is on your birthday.
- If a slice of birthday cake tips over on your plate, you will not marry.
- You should put a pat of butter on your nose on your birthday for good luck.
- A child can be placed in a ring of objects—such as a knife, a coin, a bottle, a deck of cards, etc.—on their first birthday. Whichever object the child reaches for first tells what they will be upon growing up (the knife indicating a soldier, the coin a banker, the cards a gambler, etc. See chapter three for a version of this ritual for adults).

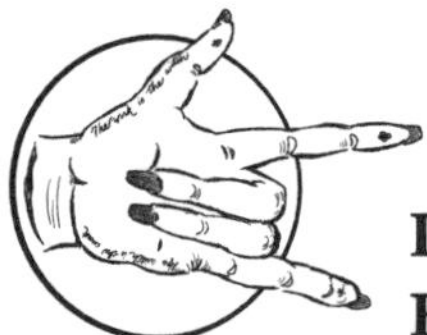

DIRT UNDER THE NAILS
Birthday Bibliomancy

An Ozark ritual says that you can use the Bible to predict future fortunes or marital bliss using your birthday as a guide (similar to astrology).[324] The method is simple: you simply look up the proper verse corresponding to your date of birth in one of two chapters of Proverbs. Proverbs 21 is thought to be the "male" chapter, and Proverbs 31 the "female" one (although I imagine you can try both or either and see what makes sense to you). Each chapter has thirty-one verses, so if you were born on July 20th and identified as male, you would read, "The wise store up choice food and olive oil, but the fools gulp theirs down," implying that acting frugally and carefully

323. Randolph, *Ozark Magic,* 66.

324. Randolph, *Ozark Magic,* 184.

managing one's resources will be important. A female-identifying person born on March 16th would read, "She considers a field and buys it; out of her earnings she plants a vineyard," possibly indicating that she would be very prosperous and good at business.[325]

Consider trying this with other books as well, if there are texts that speak to you more clearly than these do.

THE WORK—Your Year in Magic and Ritual

What cycles do you follow? This is not a question about what cycles you *wish* you followed, or what cycles you plan to start following tomorrow. What cycles do you follow *right now*? Do you celebrate birthdays every year? Whose? Do you do family reunions, or annual vacations? Do you have back-to-school shopping days, winter holidays (even ones where you simply sit cozily by yourself by the fire reading a book—I'm a big fan of the Danish *hygge* phenomenon)? What about things that aren't specific dates, but rather rituals that happen on a regular basis? Is there a day when you *know* fall has begun because you make or eat your first batch of chili? Or do you always rush out for the first snowfall of winter? The first day you can wear shorts or flip-flops in spring or summer?

Take the time to write these things down. Make note of them. Add them to your calendar, mark them in your datebook, do what you need to do to highlight them. Who are you with on these days? If you celebrate birthdays for others, why are they so vital to you, and what can you do to highlight their value beyond the typical card-and-gift combination?

Try turning your own birthday into a folk ritual, too. Give gifts to others, even secretly or surreptitiously (I've done this plenty over the years and you'll be amazed at how rewarding it can be to simply leave a flower on someone's car windshield or doorstep with a note telling them that you value them in your life). Take the day to celebrate your participation in your own annual cycles, turn it into a ritual, and make some magic in the world around you on that day.

325. New International Version (NIV) of the Bible used.

Recommended Reading

All Around the Year: Holidays and Celebrations in American Life, by Jack Santino. Santino is a folklorist and historian focused on American holiday expressions, and I heartily recommend this easy-to-read but highly informative book. It takes the reader through the calendar of American holidays, providing lots of interesting folkloric tidbits along the way, and pointing towards both mass cultural celebrations, pop culture expressions of holiday fun, and unique regional folk traditions.

The Old Magic of Christmas: Yuletide Traditions for the Darkest Days of the Year and *Night of the Witches: Folklore, Traditions, & Recipes for Celebrating Walpurgis Night,* by Linda Raedisch. These two books by Linda Raedisch, a librarian and folklore researcher specializing in the darker side of holidays, provide absolutely loads of great folklore and practical ideas for celebrating both winter and early summer holidays. The lore is largely European, but ventures into the Americas and other places at times as well, and is an invaluable resource to anyone developing magical holiday traditions.

Llewellyn's Witches' Datebook, by various authors. This annual release from Llewellyn Publications is incredibly useful. It frequently has small articles and folkloric morsels about various holidays throughout the year (although it does favor Wiccan "Wheel of the Year" observances, but not exclusively). Additionally, it provides moon phase and astrological information, and leaves you plenty of space to write in your own holiday notes as well.

CHAPTER EIGHTEEN

At Dawn on the First of May—Magic by the Hour

We usually think of fairy tale and folkloric witches as nocturnal creatures, riding broomsticks across the face of the moon and darting between shadows as they speak spells into being over flickering candle flames or by burning bonfires. While this characterization of magic as a nighttime event is the stuff of fiction, the timing of magic in folklore often really does seem to matter to those who practice it. The tenth-century Canon Episcopi, written by the archbishop of Trier, describes "wicked women" who "in the hours of the night… ride on certain animals, together with Diana, the goddess of the pagans, with a numberless multitude of women; and in the silence of the dead of night cross many great lands."[326] The association between witches and the night is long-standing, clearly, and there are reasons for that. The idea that witches work their spells in the unseen hours, under skies with a full moon beaming down upon them, and soaring off to sabbats on certain days (or, rather, nights) of the year lingers in stories, and we still present that image of witches in contemporary times. Think only of the nocturnal machinations of the coven in *Rosemary's Baby* or in the *Paranormal Activity* franchise and the night-working witch is alive and well.

Yet witches and magical folk in general have not been relegated solely to darkness. Hermione Granger and Harry Potter do their magical lessons during school hours.

326. Cohn, Norman, "The Night-Witch in Popular Imagination," 119.

Samantha from *Bewitched* often twitches her nose to make spells spin throughout the course of her busy day. In some American mountain stories, a witch will come borrow something or chase someone away from her land during the daytime hours and they will find they have been cursed by the encounter over the following days or weeks. Dowsers in the Ozarks seldom searched for water in the night, for the simple practical reason that they would likely trip and injure themselves while trying to walk through the dark with their doodlebug rods. The moon certainly plays an important part in the life of a witch, but it is hardly the full moon alone that charges her magical batteries or gives her cause to revel and romp. A witch may be at work at any hour of any day (or night), even right now as you hold this book in your hands.

"Before Sunup" to "The Witching Hour"— Magic Throughout the Day

This chapter looks at the timing of magic from a folk magical perspective. I will not be prescriptive in the sense of advocating a specific ritual calendar, nor stating that a witch or folk magician must particularly follow the examples I present. Instead, these cases will demonstrate just how folk magic gets woven into the fabric of daily living. The moon remains crucial, but the depth of its importance will go beyond simply a full or new phase and into one of the most well-worn and oft-used aspects of the moon in magic: its passage through the zodiac. I don't speak much to the idea of festival and seasonal ritual here, as I cover that more thoroughly in chapter seventeen. Magic always rises to meet a need, and folk magicians have long known how to merge those needs with the places—and times—around them. Performing magic at specific times of day created different results, according to folklore and tradition among a number of magically inclined people.

While determining planetary hours has been a part of ceremonial magic for several hundred years, the effort and detail required to do those calculations often fell into the hands of an elite class. That is not to say that the broader swathes of folk practitioners were incapable of complex calculations. Hardly! As we'll see when we look at the specifics of lunar astrology with relation to all sorts of everyday activities, the regular use of almanacs full of intricately detailed charts and figures frequently factored into the magical worldview. Even as the ability to calculate planetary hours has become more available and sophisticated—it takes only a quick internet search to find a relatively effective calculator now, after all—the exercise of magic associated with specific horary rituals has remained largely within the realms of ceremonial practice. Why? Because folk practitioners were able to get exactly what they needed from their spells, charms, rites, and customs by breaking the day into a few distinct "parts." Going further with those divisions was simply unnecessary in the vast majority of folk magic because the results came along just fine without finding a mathematical-astrological hour of correspondence.

The divisions used in folk magic are deceptively simple, but also involve some notable variations. Largely, the day is divided into the categories of morning, noon, and night. However, for the purposes of magic, additional divisions appear, requiring a spell to be performed "before sunup" or "before dawn," placing it in the liminal space between night and morning. Additionally, night was rife with subdivisions, with sunset, twilight, midnight, and the "witching hour" all earmarked for more specific rituals or magical goings-on.

Dawn/Morning

Magic done in the morning often has to do with new beginnings or the transition from one phase to another, and in that way the hours surrounding sunrise are frequently seen as powerful in North American witchery from a variety of sources. A popular prescription for maintaining a young woman's beauty advised her to rise before the sun on the first day of May and wash her face with the dew she found on the ground (as mentioned in the previous chapter). She was to remain completely silent until after this ritual was completed, and the May Day wash would serve to elevate her youth and charms for another year. While the connection to the first of May is significant, tied as it is to fairy lore and maypole customs, the pre-dawn aspect of the ritual is also a key component. The ritual face-washing empowered the May Day morning dew with supernatural properties of youth and beauty preservation or enhancement. Similarly, magical projects begun at dawn have a potency that spells done at other times can lack. Folklorist Zora Neale Hurston, who documented a number of Hoodoo practices among African Americans in the southern United States during the 1930s, describes a ritual involving a vial of spirit oil poured out by a practitioner on her head while reciting Psalm 23 from the Bible and preparing an offering of cake for a helper spirit, all done before dawn.[327] The connection to beauty rituals is not limited to May, either. One ritual involves going to a cemetery

327. Hurston, "Hoodoo in America," 319–20. In Hurston's specific example, the spirit is unnamed, although it is referred to as an "Uncle Spirit," which makes sense given that the working came out of the Spiritualist Church of Mother Leafy Anderson. In many other local traditions around the New Orleans area where Anderson was located, this spirit would likely be someone like St. Expedite, the apocryphal saint known for granting rapid aid to those who ask for it, and for his fondness for Sara Lee pound cake.

and finding a human bone before sunrise, then rubbing it on the afflicted area of the magician. The ailment being cured? Birthmarks.

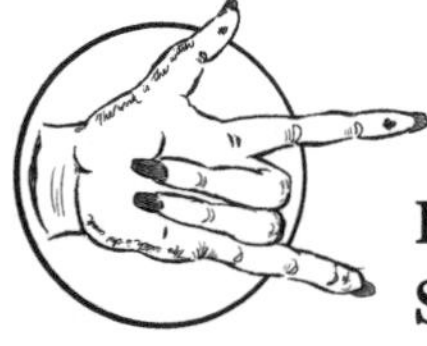

DIRT UNDER THE NAILS
Saints and Spirits Oil

Some formulations of magical oils and mixtures require creation or gathering particular hours of the day as part of their creation. Many grimoires have incredibly detailed ways of determining planetary hours for ceremonial magical ointments and unguents, but folk magic generally works with simplified versions of the hours. One such recipe is the "Saints and Spirits" oil found in several versions of Southern Conjure and Hoodoo. Folklorist Zora Neale Hurston's recipe for spirit oil is given as a combination of "Oil of China" and "Oil of Cedar of Lebanon." These would likely have been a combination of vetiver oil and cedarwood oil, although the exact formula is not clear. The oil was bestowed by the Spiritualist Church upon its members for their use in blessing rituals, along with holy water gathered from a storm before the sun could shine on it and blessed with prayer. In Catholic traditions, olive oil scented with balsam wood is often used this way. Other traditions often use attar of rose or sandalwood in similar ways. If you're looking to make a good, simple spirit oil for use in blessing rituals, this recipe is one that I have used for years that I call "Saints and Spirits."

To a one-quart mason jar, add a palmful each of:

- rose petals
- frankincense gum
- copal resin
- angelica root
- sandalwood or cedarwood

As the sun rises, cover with good olive oil or sweet almond oil and pray your blessing prayer of choice over the jar three times, blowing into it upon each completed iteration of the prayer. Place a lid on the jar and seal it, letting it sit for at least seven days (and preferably twenty-one days), shaking it once per day. Strain off the solids and re-bottle the oil. Store out of sunlight for up to a few months, and use for anointing and blessing work.

The early morning hours are also a time of risk and danger, as evidenced by the number of taboos we see in magical lore associated with the dawn. A person is not supposed to speak or tell a dream before breakfast, for example, or else bad luck will be assured for the day. The first weather of the day also often portends the weather to follow, as indicated by the well-known folk adage:

Red sky at night, sailor's delight,
Red sky at morning, sailors take warning.

In this weather divination, the morning skies foretell the potential for storms at sea. Similar signs are sought in the mornings in the form of "mackerel skies," which look as though they were covered in fish scales. Skies that had such clouds portended high winds and storms. In many cases the weather first encountered in the day would inevitably reverse by the end of the day, and a day that starts with a rain shower is often thought to end with clear skies in folk reckoning.

The morning hours are also an ideal time to dispose of important spells. For example, bath water in Hoodoo washing rituals is often thrown toward the rising sun as a way of dispersing any harmful power that might remain attached to it (especially if the bath was one to clear away a curse or magical work being done against someone). Additionally, the first urine someone made in the morning was thought in many Hoodoo rituals to be incredibly powerful and had additional magical properties of protection or influence.[328]

The potency of the morning in folk magic is rivaled only by the potency of the deep dark night, as we will see, but first we must attend to the often sadly neglected midday hours.

Noon/Midday

The late morning to late afternoon hours are the busy part of the day for many people, and thus the needs of the mundane world take precedence over the experience of the uncanny, mysterious, and magical. That is not to say that the noontide is without its enchantments, however. Several rituals and omens are tied directly to the midday.

328. Hurston, "Hoodoo in America," 395–407; and Hyatt, *Hoodoo-Conjuration-Witchcraft-Rootwork*, 498–508.

Most often, of course, these connections have to do with the solar influences, since the sun is usually brightest and warmest during the hours around noon to three.

Like morning weather, afternoon weather could be used to predict the following day's forecast. Some folklore from Illinois states that if an "afternoon sun draws water" (i.e. if it rains in the afternoon), the following morning will also have rain.[329] A visible halo on the sun, usually called a "sun dog," foretells of heat to follow the next day when seen in the afternoon. Rainbows appearing in the sky at noon mean wet weather ahead, too. Birds sounding off in the afternoon, such as owls or quail, could also be portents of storms to come.

A number of other animal omens are also linked to the noon and afternoon hours. Seeing spiders spin their webs in the afternoon is thought to be a bad sign, although if you only see the spider traveling along its web it indicates travel is in your future. Seeing hens in the afternoon is also a bad sign, especially for egg-laying. A rooster crowing at noon indicates sudden (and often upsetting) news is coming. Even people are marked by noontide associations, as one piece of Rhode Island folklore says children born during the "heat of the day" often have powerful soothsaying abilities and an inherent protection from witchcraft worked against them.[330]

Night/The Witching Hours

The image of the night-working witch has held since at least Antiquity, when Roman descriptions of night-wandering spirits and sorceresses appeared in works by writers like Tacitus, Horace, and Lucian.[331] Often these depictions are incredibly negative, treating those who pursue magic in the dark as sinister and dangerous members of society. At the same time, there are also depictions of witch figures such as Circe or Medea that tap into their sexuality and beauty as a part of their magical nature. The night is the time of both secrecy and sex, and the witch in the popular New World imagination retained these connections, both of which were suspect in North America until well into the twentieth century (and I'm sure some would make a compelling case this trend has never really gone away). I will leave aside the descriptions of nocturnal sex romps for the time being, despite all the fun that line of inquiry prom-

329. Hyatt, *Folklore from Adams County*, 1.

330. See "Ghosts and Witchcraft: A Region in New England Where Superstition Thrives."

331. Stratton and Kalleres, *Daughters of Hecate*, 41–70; and Hutton, *The Witch*, 44–73; and Davies, *Oxford Illustrated History of Witchcraft*, 1–28.

ises. Instead, let's take a look at some of the other activities New World witches were believed to do during the night, according to legend, history, and lore:

- **Night Flight**—Riding poor, beleaguered victims (or, far more often, smarmy and deserving reprobates) as horses using magic bridles, as in the New England tale of Old Betty Booker and the skinflint Skipper Perkins (see chapter nine).
- **Collecting Spell Ingredients**—Some ingredients were believed to bloom best under the moon. Often the ingredients collected were also taken from graves or animals in the form of bones or fat during nocturnal rituals.
- **Meeting with Spirits**—Frequently encounters with familiar spirits, "Black Men" in the woods or at crossroads, or necromantic rituals to raise the dead were conducted in the night. Sometimes these meetings were characterized as meetings among witches, although some New England accounts also claim witches would meet with Native Americans in the woods at night, as many in the Colonial era associated unfriendly tribes with the Devil.
- **Attacking Victims and Targets with Curses**—In the example of the famous "Bell Witch" of Tennessee, the household was most frequently tormented at night, with daughter Betsy pinched, slapped, and tossed about while she was trying to rest in bed. The trend towards nighttime fulfillment of a curse appears in literature of the American Southwest and New England accounts as well.[332]
- **Shape-Shifting**—Witches used the cover of night as an opportunity to slip their skins and travel about during the night. Sometimes that literally meant changing forms, as in the case of Southwestern skinwalkers (see chapters nine and thirteen), although often in lore from places like Appalachia the shape-shifting witch could be spied through her window in bed while her spirit form was out and about.
- **Fire-Based Rituals**—Frequently rituals involving bonfires, oil lamps, candles, or other fiery magic required the cover of night. Many candle-burning manuals from the nineteenth and twentieth centuries recommend doing rites over a series of nights, for example.

Whatever the witch is doing in the dark, most accounts make a point that the hours of midnight to three in the morning are the peak of a witch's power, and that

332. Cave, "Indian Shamans and English Witches"; and Dorson, *Buying the Wind*, 55–64, 436–42.

she must be done with her witchery by dawn. It is worth noting that the hours from midnight to three in the pre-Industrial era were often a time when people would wake up for a brief period and spend some time doing a quiet activity, such as thinking or gently restoking the fire. The absence of light and human predisposition to find faces (a phenomenon known as pareidolia) and meaning in practically everything could well play into the frequent experience of witch visions. Similarly, accounts of "hag riding" often happen during these hours, as they coincide with natural sleep cycles during which a person's body can become rigid or temporarily paralyzed.[333]

At dusk the witch is likely to be getting ready to cavort with her sisters, slip her skin, or dart off to the churchyard for spell components, but her main activities are done in the deepest and darkest hours of the night. The coming of dawn is thought to be an end to her power and a witch still out when the sun rises can be caught in some very unfavorable situations (as in the story of the "Boo Hag" in chapter nine). As we have already seen, of course, dawn was just a time that different magic could be done.

The lore on the timing of witchcraft varies by region and by group, although the association of night with witchcraft and magic does have the firmest footing in most places. Perhaps that connection is so strong because the night is when we see one of the most magical objects in our world: the moon.

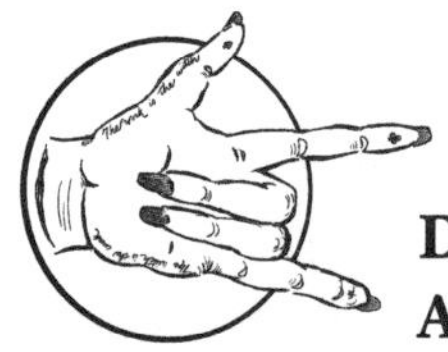

DIRT UNDER THE NAILS
A Multi-Night Candle Spell for Steady Income

Candle-burning rituals often involve multi-night spellwork. Here's an employment spell candle burning adapted from a ritual found in Henri Gamache's popular *Master Book of Candle Burning.* I have used a version of this spell to help get and keep a steady source of income from time to time:

Ingredients:

- A golden or white candle
- Some Crown of Success or Attraction Oil (or a substitute such as olive oil in which you have soaked bay leaves)

333. Multiple accounts and perspectives on hag-riding are found in Hufford, *The Terror that Comes in the Night*; Davis, *The Silver Bullet*; Gainer, *Witches, Ghosts, and Signs*; and Thomas, *Putting the Supernatural in Its Place.*

- Green candles (as many as represent the places of employment you are trying to influence)
- Copies of your résumé, job application, cover letters, etc.
- Tobacco, bay leaves, and allspice (you may also add/substitute bayberry, cinnamon, and/or cinquefoil—I find using just three roots/herbs is best for a spell like this)
- A business card, name paper, or image representing the employer, hiring manager, or place of employment
- Cards from a deck that you are willing to damage/mark: The King of Clubs, the King of Diamonds, and the Eight of Clubs

Starting on a Sunday night, dress the white/gold candle from bottom to top with your chosen oil. Crush your herbs/roots and roll the candle in them. Place the candle in a fire-proof holder. Write your desire (or make a sigil representing it) on each of the documents. On the representation of the employer, write in an unbroken ring around the edges a simple statement of your desire, such as "hire me" (or, again, you can make a sigil for this and mark it on the image). Place the résumé/applications on your working space. Then, on top of the documents place the three cards in a "Y" shape with the two Kings forming the top of the "Y" and the Eight of Clubs forming the bottom branch. Ask the spirits of the cards (or whatever spirits you work with) to help you get the job/jobs you need to maintain a steady income. Put the employer representation on top of the playing cards, and the white/gold candle in its holder on top of the pile of paper and cards (important: make sure your holder will NOT tip over or start a fire!). Around the edges of your working space, place the green candles, naming each one for the potential employer it represents (you can carve the name into the wax, or just whisper the name to each candle before setting it up and lighting it).

Light the candles and use an incantation or charm for success over the working (I like Psalm 65, but feel free to use what works for you). Let the candles burn for at least an hour (do NOT leave them unattended). Put them out, and the next night, move them about an inch closer to the center white/gold candle before relighting all the candles. Repeat your incantation and your request for employment. Perform this ceremony each night for at least seven nights, moving the green candles closer every night until they are surrounding the white/gold one. You can either let them burn down completely on the seventh night, continue working for additional nights until they burn out/you get an offer of employment, or put them out on the seventh night and ritually dispose of them.

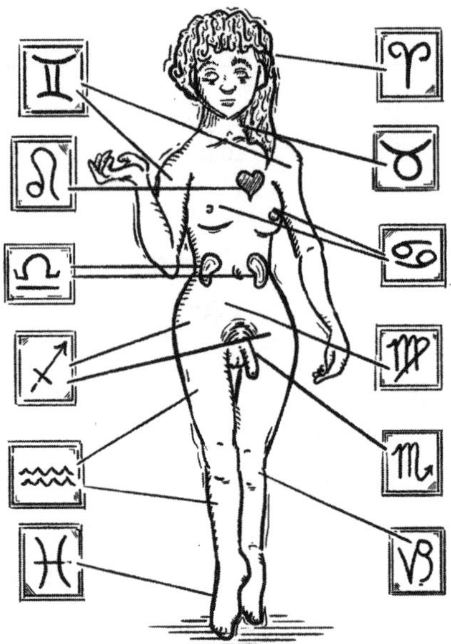

FIG 18-1: The phases of the moon and their progress through the signs of the zodiac are charted onto the human body, with specific signs thought to govern specific body parts.

In the Dark of the Moon: Lunar Movement and Folk Magic

The folk relationship with the moon varies across culture, but there is always *something* connecting people with our satellite neighbor and constant companion. Many cultures depict the moon as female or feminine, although that is hardly universal, as mythologies from places like Japan and the Chehalis tribe in the Pacific Northwest represent the moon with a male deity or spirit. Close links between the moon and water through the movement of tides and a frequent association of the moon with the unseen and uncanny world hidden during the daytime ensure that the moon shows up frequently in magical lore as well.

In virtually every almanac of the past three centuries, there would be an image of a man with his various body parts mapped to the twelve astrological signs, the so-called Zodiac Man who guided the reader through the astrological implications of the coming year for their farms, gardens, and daily life (see figure 18-1). These signs did not focus on the solar placement of the signs, but instead where the moon and the zodiac intersected. While solar signs change roughly once a month, the lunar signs would shift every three days or so, and a farmer would wait until the conditions were right to begin tilling, planting, or harvesting based on those signs. Additionally, the moon's waxing and waning could influence crop growth—underground crops like carrots, turnips, and potatoes would do well planted in the "dark" of the moon while it was a new-to-waxing-crescent, while above-ground plantings did better during the moon's waxing gibbous or full phases, for example.

These signs were thought of in folk terms. A farmer wouldn't say they were waiting for a waxing gibbous moon in the sign of Cancer to plant their lettuce or beans, but instead would wait for something like a "growing moon in the breast" (since the sign of Cancer "ruled" the stomach and breast portion of the torso, minus the heart, which was ruled by Leo). These signs didn't govern only agriculture, but also daily affairs like when to get a haircut (most would avoid cutting hair in a sign like Aries because the sign's dry, hot nature prohibited regrowth), when to can or pickle vegetables (Gemini/the arms), when to set hens for laying eggs (Pisces/the feet or Scorpio/the loins), when to enter business agreements or contracts (Libra/the kidneys), and when to hunt (Aries/the head) or fish (Pisces, of course). Even love affairs were thought to go better when started while the moon waxed or grew full during Leo, the sign of the heart.

Sometimes we can take for granted enchanted associations and correspondences without really thinking about where they come from. Folk who used the moon as a guide, support, or power source for their magic in the past and witches doing so in their backyards, bedrooms, or bathtubs today are linked by moon magic, and the phases the moon passes through shape that magic much the same today as they did for our ancestors.

New Moon

Sometimes the new moon is defined as the time when the moon is fully in shadow and no visible light reflects from her face. Others define the new moon as the night just past the darkest phase, when the moon regains just a faint sliver of her radiance. In either case, new moons are thought to be the time to begin projects and add power for growth and change to existing work. Tasks such as setting new fence posts or making soap were ideally begun in the "dark" of the moon. A simple charm from Kentucky also points to the new moon as a source of divinatory power, especially in love magic:

New moon, new,
Let me see
Who my future husband is to be;
The color of his hair,
The clothes he is to wear,
And the happy day he is to wed me.[334]

Charmers are warned not to make wishes or charms while spying the new moon between the trees, although exactly why the trees present such a hindrance to the magic is unclear. The dark of the moon was also thought to be a perfect time to lay a curse upon an enemy, as the purifying power of light was hidden away. One such curse involves taking a piece of an intended target's old clothing and burying it in the last light of the setting sun as the new moon rises in the sky. As the clothing rots, so will the health and well-being of the victim.[335]

Waxing Moon

This phase is thought to be good for work that expands power or infuses growth, but it can also be a dangerous time because the moon is "traveling" and thus its pull raises up hurtful powers, too. A root doctor in Richmond, Virginia told of the way his veins would bulge during the traveling moon, causing aches and pains. These woes allowed him to make predictions, too, however, related to the weather.[336] The cycle of the waxing moon was thought to affect humans and trees in a similar way, causing their "sap" (or blood) to rise, but also making it an ideal time for purification, as the new lifeblood was replacing the old. The power of the waxing moon on the body can be tamed for benefit, as well. One Southern formula involved taking the "hair of a strong man," some oak bark, a bit of steel wire, and some vinegar, then pounding them all together during the new moon while shouting "Samson!" over

334. Price, "Kentucky Folk-lore," 30–38.

335. Puckett, *Folk Beliefs*, 99; and Hyatt, *Hoodoo-Conjuration-Witchcraft-Rootwork*, 1454–55.

336. Hyatt, *Hoodoo-Conjuration-Witchcraft-Rootwork*, 944.

the pan or bowl, and letting the mixture sit until the full moon (the association with the biblical strongman and his hair is a key part of this spell).[337] The mix can then be rubbed over the body to give a person extra strength when they need it. The rising tide of the moon could also be deployed for love magic. A new moon might help predict a future lover, but the waxing-to-full phase is the time for seduction, and love charms worked during the "growing" moon take control of a target's mind and willpower, making them subject to the desires of the charmer.

Full Moon

The full moon has a cleansing and charging power like the waxing moon, but the effects are more intense, and often rituals of purification begin during the waxing phase and end on the full moon to seal the purge of any curses or illnesses the magician is trying to remove. Of course, it would be absolutely ridiculous not to mention the long-standing folk associations between lunar cycles and menstruation found across several cultures. Some women do, in fact, have lunar-synced menstrual cycles, although many do not. Some rituals are designed to bring about synchronization, including rites of "moon bathing" during the full moon to draw a woman's body into lunar rhythm. Women, then, are often thought to be particularly powerful during a full moon, and their menstrual blood is associated deeply with lunar magic. It can directly influence a man (or anyone, really) to become obedient and docile when used in folk magic (see more on this in chapter six). Men were sometimes believed to sweat more during the full moon, and their sweat sometimes had similar magical properties, but it is never represented as having the same potency as women's bodily fluids do. Shape-shifting, too, is often tied to the full moon, as any werewolf aficionado will know, but in many cultures the nights around the full moon or even the entire waxing phase of the moon could be used for transformation into animal forms. The full moon also reveals hidden secrets and is sometimes thought to be the best time to do treasure hunting because of that connection.

337. Puckett, *Folk Beliefs*, 211–13.

Waning Moon

The same Richmond root doctor mentioned above insisted the waning moon was the ideal time to "take off" curses laid upon a person by baneful witches and conjurers.[338] Especially as the waning moon approaches the new moon, the hex-removal power increases, and often charms laid against a person were vulnerable during this phase. One account notes that sorcery used to "tie a man's nature" (i.e. cause him to have erectile dysfunction) could be removed best on the nights of the waning and dark moon. The waning moon could also be used to work curses, too, with the intention of culminating them on the night of the "dark" moon much as some charms are designed to come to completion on the night of a full moon. A Southern cursing charm involves taking dust gathered from a whirlwind (e.g. either left after a tornado or from the path of a "dust devil") and sprinkle it in a fire while saying the victim's name.[339] This will either drive them away or—in a worst-case scenario—take their life. Iron filings and "anvil dust" (the iron dust left after blacksmithing) could be deployed in a similar way to break up a couple over the course of two months (by burning the dust during the waning phase of both months while saying the targets' names). The waning moon is thought to be the time when ghosts are most active as well, in many places, and often baneful ingredients for cursing spells are gathered when the moon is "shrinking" or "wasting."

One of the most lasting lunar associations in folk magic is the concept of the moon moving through various zodiacal "signs" throughout its waxing and waning phases. Full and new moons often get the strongest associations with the signs, but any phase of the moon can be combined with the signs in the sky to create a particular spell condition. Almanacs throughout North America frequently printed guides to lunar astrology that showed people (and still do to this day) just what sign the moon would be in on any particular day. Some activities, such as planting above-ground crops, are thought to be best done during the waxing moon, but only when the moon is in signs corresponding to parts of the body above the waist (such as Gemini, associated with the arms or shoulders, or Aries, associated with the head). The specifics of these almanacs will be explored more thoroughly in chapter nineteen.

338. Hyatt, *Hoodoo-Conjuration-Witchcraft-Rootwork*, 944–46.

339. Puckett, *Folk Beliefs*, 465.

FIG 18-2: Mother Lane was known as the "New Moon" *curandera* because her powers were centered around the appearance of the new moon.

SINGING BONES
Mother Lane, the New Moon Curandera

Mercedes Peña Lane was born in 1884, the daughter of a Mexican merchant and grocer. She began to exhibit signs of spiritual mediumship and healing abilities after she and her sister contracted an illness that killed her sibling but left Mother Lane alive. Her family moved to the United States in 1898, and Lane experienced strange dreams. In one dream, she was told to leave a pencil and some pink paper on a table. When she awoke, a message had been written on the paper telling her not to fear. She spoke Spanish and English, and her ability to slip into a trance and reveal uncanny truths about her clients earned her a marvelous reputation very quickly. She also had skills as a *sobadora*, or therapeutic masseuse. She claimed to be able to push illnesses and maladies—physical and spiritual—from the bodies of her clients as well as offering them Otherworldly guidance, but interestingly she also claimed her powers only operated during the two weeks following each new moon. Her treatments also earned the ire of professional doctors, and in 1935 she was sued unsuccessfully for practicing medicine without a license. Mother Lane, the *curandera* who inspired a group of followers known as the "New Mooners," died in 1959. She was known to like happy, upbeat music, and clients from both Anglo and Latinx communities remembered her fondly as a powerful woman with a warm heart and a little magic in her.[340]

Hands Rising, Hands Falling: Magic on the Clock

One of the great beauties of folk magic is its flexibility, of course, and understanding how to manipulate a spell to fit a specific time can be the difference between an effective spellcaster and a charmer too tightly tied to a list of correspondences, dates, and hours. Synchronicities and adaptations shape the magical work, leading to new improvisations. As technology changes, folk magic responds, as it has in the case of clocks. In many folk spells found after the early nineteenth centuries, when clocks and watches became more commonplace, the position of analog clock hands determines the type and direction of a spell, with clock hands that are "falling" (i.e. going from the twelve o'clock position to the six o'clock position) used in the same way the waning moon is used, and "rising" hands (the reverse from six to twelve) deployed along the lines of waxing lunar spells. Such changes are not a corruption, but a new thread of magic making effective use of the tools around the magician and the environment in which she finds herself. Similarly, we should not be too quick to judge witches and conjurers in the twenty-first century as they find new ways to adapt their magical timing to correspond with things like a morning commute or engage in "technology cleanses" aligned with lunar phases. I know several people who treat specific hours on a digital clock as special, using them as "wishing" times when the numbers are all the same (as in 2:22 or 11:11) or in a particular sequence (like 12:34). Folk magic, as we are seeing over and over again, changes forms constantly, while the power it taps into remains an active current running through us all, no matter the time of day, month, or year.

DIRT UNDER THE NAILS
The Technology Cleanse

One excellent way to hone your magical connection is to have just such a "technology cleanse" during the new moon, when intuitive powers are often strong and the darkness can inspire us to put away our addictions to screens

340. Hunter, "Mother Lane," 291–325.

and social media. If you've never done it before, use the next new moon to turn off your tech and pull out some tarot cards or a bag of stones and bones. Listen to messages coming from somewhere outside of the digital realm, and see what they say when they have your undivided attention. Similarly, try taking a walk outside in the dark (it's okay to keep a phone on you for safety, just don't use it unless absolutely necessary). Pay attention to the movements of the wind, the stars you can see, the smells and sounds around you. Are there animals or plants you notice differently when you're not thinking about them through the lens of a digital camera? When you've finished this cleanse, take the time to "awaken" your devices again and thank them for the services they provide to you. Doing something like this simple ritual can help you build a respectful relationship with your tech and maybe even tap into its magical potential in ways similar to the first folk magicians to connect the moon and the hands of a clock. You never know!

THE WORK—Observing Daily Cycles

What has learning about these timing systems shown you in terms of your own relationship with folk magic? Do you time rituals or spells, customs or activities, according to a cycle or rhythm? More importantly, do you do so *intentionally*?

Being deliberate in your activities and interpretations is the backbone of this part of folk magic. Go out into the world and start *paying attention* to it. What does the morning look like where you are? Chilly and cool, or touched by the early heat of the day? Are there birds or animals more active in the morning? What does water look like at night where you are? What sounds and smells do you encounter? Log what you observe, and watch as patterns emerge from your observations. If morning is the time when songbirds are most active, what can you do with that magically? If nighttime is peaceful, can you use it to rejuvenate more than just your body? If you get caught in afternoon rush hours, can you use that time to work on magic (or can you begin to "divine" traffic indicators that help you avoid jams and backups more often, much as the shepherds and sailors learned to divine the weather)?

The rituals you develop through this process will speak to you personally, of course, but also to the communities you are a part of. Work and home life have their own rhythms, and learning to read and follow those can allow you to avoid problems and even manipulate the patterns you see to more effectively get what you want—and if that isn't folk magic, I don't know what is.

Recommended Reading

Mules and Men, by Zora Neale Hurston. Hurston gathers a great deal of folklore in this text, and the sections in which she discusses African American Hoodoo include a number of rituals tied to specific times of day or month.

A Witch Alone: Thirteen Moons to Master Natural Magic, by Marian Green. Marian Green's classic introduction to solitary witchcraft practice touches on some folklore elements, but also draws out the connection between the practitioner and the moon in a very practical, grounded way.

In the Light of the Moon: Thirteen Lunar Tales from Around the World Illuminating Life's Mysteries, by Carolyn McVickar Edwards. This is a lovely collection of worldwide folktales that can be useful for tapping into a personal mythos of lunar lore that makes sense for you.

Working the Root: The Conjure Workbook, Volume I, by Starr Casas. Starr's book is largely focused on her version of Southern Conjure practice, and there's a lovely section on "Working by the Clock" which explains the principles of using clock hands as guides to magical timing.

TENTH RITE: WORKING THE CHARM

Or, Folk Magic through Pen, Ink, and Page

"The method of procedure adopted in the following account from Scott County, east Tennessee, has the sanction of a long line of tradition. The narrator, an old white man, said that on one occasion he had stolen and used some white powder which formed part of the stock in trade of a witch. Later he met 'a very small, dark-haired, red-complected man' who said 'You have used some of my material, and now you must put your name in my book.' The trembling mortal wrote his name with his own blood in the stranger's book, but he must have desisted from using the diabolical stuff, for the Devil never came to claim his victim."*

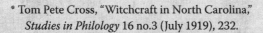

* Tom Pete Cross, "Witchcraft in North Carolina," *Studies in Philology* 16 no.3 (July 1919), 232.

CHAPTER NINETEEN

Devils' Books and Letters from Heaven— The Written Word and Witchcraft

The most popular books printed in the first few centuries of American life were Bibles, prayer books, hymnals, and almanacs. Bibles could be used for bibliomancy (see chapter eight), charming warts and stopping blood (see chapter four), and rituals designed to bring success, purification, love, money, or even vengeance on an enemy. Prayer books and hymnals might also offer the occasional source of magical inspiration, too. Almanacs guided the daily lives of readers through astrological influences, folk cures (with things like a bloodstopping or sprain-healing charm occasionally appearing), and frequently contained advertisements for everything from snake oil and tonics to Hoodoo charms deliverable by post. They also included weather charts—tables predicting likely turns and travails of the atmosphere based on both historical data and a bit of folk prognostication—along with recipes, remedies, local lore, spiritual guidance, and advertisements for all sorts of potentially useful (or at least entertaining) merchandise available for postal order.

Even today you can find many people planting crops based on the advice found in their current almanac. Benjamin Franklin made a name for himself producing just such an almanac (the famed *Poor Richard's Almanack*), and almanac-printing was big business in America from the early Colonial period until well into the nineteenth century. Virtually every local printing press produced their own version of one because it was an almost guaranteed sell-out so long as the information in it was relatively accurate.

Through books and the printed word, magic reached into the homes and lives of thousands upon thousands of people, whether they considered themselves magic-users or not. In some cases, as with bibliomancy and faith healing using Bible verses, that magic was largely accepted or at most treated with indifference or mild disdain. In other situations, a book of magic could be utterly damning.

DIRT UNDER THE NAILS
The Zodiac Garden

Folk astrology can be hard to conceptualize as something in your head alone. I have always found that getting your hands dirty with any kind of magical practice or approach somehow helps me understand the theory better, and what better way to incorporate the hands and the head than with the meditative, body-nourishing (and sometimes body-tiring) practice of gardening?

Below I include a brief outline of a sample planting-and-harvest calendar based on folk astrological methods. This would be the kind of garden that produces food and herbs, but could be easily adapted to other plants as well, such as flowers (in which case the "ground" plants would be things like bulbs and rhizomes and the "flowering" or "leafy" ones are more likely to be annuals and other seeded plants; check your climate map for the most accurate planting guidance). Also note that very little is done on the nights of a full or dark moon, largely because the nights the moon changes phases are considered to be the least lucky for planting and gardening.

Spring

- Waxing Moon in Scorpio, Pisces, Taurus, or Cancer: Plant all aboveground fruiting crops (beans, peas, tomatoes, peppers, etc.).
- Waxing Moon in Libra, Gemini, or Aquarius: Plant all flowering plants or herbs.

- Waxing Moon in Virgo: Plant "bramble" plants like blackberries and raspberries, as well as anything with long vines or stalks and small fruits (but not much else in Virgo, as it is a "barren" sign for most gardening).
- Waning Moon in Capricorn or Pisces: Make root cuttings and trim limbs and vines.
- Waning and Dark Moon in Aries, Leo, Sagittarius: Cultivate and till garden soil for later plantings. Weed and cut back overgrowth.

Summer

- Dark Moon in Virgo, Scorpio, Capricorn, Taurus, or Aquarius: Plant underground crops like potatoes, onions, and carrots.
- Waning Moon in Gemini, Leo, or Virgo: Weed and cut back overgrowth.
- Waxing Moon in Libra, Gemini, Cancer: Plant above-ground grain crops like wheat and corn. Cancer is also good during the waxing moon for cover crops and root crops.
- Waxing Moon in Gemini, Cancer, Scorpio, and Pisces: Plant fruiting crops like squash and melons in early summer months.

Fall

- Waning Moon (not sign-specific): Pick fruits like apples, peaches, and pears to avoid rotting and bruising. Also harvest any crops that need to keep overwinter.
- Waning to New Moon in Capricorn and Pisces: Dig and harvest all root crops.
- Waning Moon in Taurus, Leo, Virgo, or Libra: Harvest final leafy crops and flowers to keep them the longest.

Winter

- Waxing to Full Moon in Aries: Baking is best done during this phase.
- Waxing to Full Moon in Taurus, Cancer, Virgo, or Scorpio: Begin indoor seedlings for transplanting.

Diabolical Knowledge: Reading Forbidden Books

In addition to almanacs, books of magical lore found homes all over North America from the seventeenth century on. These often included early occult chapbooks—short books or pamphlets cheaply produced, widely popular, and generally originating in places like London. They bore titles such as *Dreams & Moles with Their Interpretation and Signification* (London, 1750), *The Fortune Teller & Experienced Farrier* (Exeter, 1794), or the *Spaewife, or Universal Fortune-teller* (Scotland, 1827). They contained advice on interpreting signs, reading palms and other body parts, and performing basic divination such as tasseomancy (tea leaf reading). Some examples of the esoteric knowledge they contained:

- "When a woman dreams she is a man, and is not married, she will have a husband; or if she's without children, she'll have a son, but if married 'twill be ill to have a son; and to a maid-servant, much incumbrance [sic]; 'tis very fortunate to a harlot, because she will forsake her evil ways."[341]
- [On palmistry:] "The liver line, if it be straight and crossed by other lines, shews the person to be of sound judgement."[342]
- "A face naturally pale denotes the person very amorous."[343]

Some of these books gave medical advice as well, and instructions for livestock management. In *The Fortune Teller & Experienced Farrier*, author Ezra Pater tells anyone with a horse suffering from a cough to "take five or six eggs, and lay them in a sharp white-wine vinegar, till the shells be somewhat soft, then fling them down his [the horse's] throat and it will cure forthwith."[344] Such remedies would become standard for magical practitioners in rural locations, and especially in the New World. The reasons for the popularity of such simple guides probably stems from their low cost, but also may have something to do with the rough medicine of frontier life. In many cases, colonizers lived days away from good medical or veterinary care, and so a small practical guide would be indispensable to a rural family. As for magic's entanglement with practical medicine, I can only reiterate that until very recently

341. Anonymous, *Dreams & Moles*, 11.

342. Pater, *The Fortune Teller*, 12.

343. Anonymous, *The Spaewife*, 6.

344. Pater, *Fortune Teller*, 17.

(the mid-to-late twentieth century, really) there was no separation between the two, especially not in rural communities. Not everyone used every remedy, and not everyone used magic, but they were not at odds with each other, either. I find the best analogy here is a cookbook: just because you have one hundred recipes doesn't mean you cook all of them. In most cases, you specialize and repeat the recipes you like or are best at, and those become your signature dishes, but every once in a while, you may stray and try something new with varying degrees of success.

Books also offered information on finding and defeating witches. Naturally, those who feared malefic magic wanted to know how to figure out just who might be bewitching their cattle, stealing their milk, and spoiling their butter (an awful lot of witchcraft seemed to revolve around dairy products), and so they turned to the manuals available at the time, such as the *Malleus Maleficarum* (1486), Reginald Scot's *Discoverie of Witchcraft* (1584), and, crucially, Cotton Mather's *Wonders of the Invisible World* (1693).

These witch-hunting guides were the balance to a whole plethora of texts that made witchcraft and magic readily available to anyone with passing literacy (and in a few cases, even those who did not have full fluency in reading and writing, since the talismans and sigils could simply be copied out of the books). Some of the better-known of these books included *The Sixth and Seventh Books of Moses*, *The Egyptian Secrets of Albertus Magnus*, and *The Black Pullet*. These books often had such a notorious reputation that even owning them could lead to suspicion of nefarious activity and witchcraft. In Pennsylvania Dutch country, manuals that had a reputation for witchcraft, like John George Hohman's *The Long-Lost Friend*, were lightning rods for fear and malice. One of the most infamous incidents of this kind was the "Hex Murder" of 1928, in which a *braucher* (healer) named Nelson Rehmeyer was beaten and burned for owning a reputed book of magic.[345] One key remedy for breaking the spell of any suspected witch involved finding one of their spellbooks or "black Bibles" and looking up the spell used to harm the victim. Then the victim would "read free," or read the spell or passage backwards until the hex was broken.

In rural and farm communities, such as the Pennsylvania Dutch areas of the middle Appalachians and the Ohio Valley, little books like Hohman's *Long-Lost Friend* became household texts. Individual families would also compile their own books,

345. Donmoyer, *Powwowing in Pennsylvania*, 244.

not unlike family recipe books, which might be kept on the same shelf as the family Bible. In many cases, these chapbooks would be the only texts in the home other than the Bible and perhaps a cherished tome or two of literature like Shakespeare. In more urban areas, cheap editions of grimoires found their way into chapbooks, with publishers like Chicago's William Delaurence producing a number of pirated works in reduced pamphlet form, including *The Egyptian Secrets of Albertus Magnus, The Sixth & Seventh Books of Moses,* and *Hindu Magic and Indian Occultism.* In Owen Davies' excellent history of magical books entitled *Grimoires,* he explores the influence of the occult in Chicago, noting that "Rural Pennsylvania may have been the centre [sic] of Pow-wow and New Orleans the home of Hoodoo, but Chicago was the undoubted centre of organized occultism and grimoire publication."[346]

Other cities also began producing quantities of occult chapbooks. Detroit—which had and continues to have a strong tie to Hoodoo—was home to countless candle shops with shelves full of pamphlets on luck, love, and money magic. In Harlem, stores like the Hindu Mysterious Store were selling racks of booklets on occult topics into the mid-to-late twentieth century. Some of the many titles included:

- *Terrors of the Evil Eye Exposed*
- *The Ancient's Book of Magic*
- *The Book of Luck*
- *Sen Chu's Sure Way Number System*
- *The Ancient Book of Formulas*
- *Rajah Rabo's 5-Star Mutuel* [sic] *Dream Book*
- *Aunt Sally's Policy Player's Dream Book*

Books like these, especially the dream books (which purported to interpret dream symbols into lucky numbers to be used in lotteries), were tremendously popular. While the number of shops carrying such literature has diminished recently, the occult pamphlet remains popular and can still be found in many urban magical retailers.

346. Davies, *Grimoires,* 210–11.

Himmelsbriefen: Letters from Heaven

Books are hardly the only printed material with a claim to magical reputation, of course. Sigils, seals, and other forms of occult art have a long history, and the invention of the printing press simply allowed those materials to propagate more quickly than before. A book of magic might also be cumbersome or unnecessary for certain magical functions, while toting around a folded page of printed charms could be a much more manageable way of transporting enchantment from one place to another.

One of the common forms of this printed and portable magic in North American traditions is the *himmelsbrief*, or "heaven letter." These are printed pages, sometimes embellished with religious images, that offered specialized protections for those who had them. These are usually found among Pennsylvania Dutch communities. Some of the best-known examples are the "fire and pestilence" letters, which could be kept on one's person for general protection, or secreted into a space in the upper portion of one's home to prevent against disasters such as a house fire or rampant illness. During both of the World Wars, soldiers from *Deitsch* communities would be sent off to serve with such letters in their pockets, and stories often spread about miraculous saves and wondrous interventions during the heat of battle (there are similar stories about small pocket Bibles stopping bullets, as well).

The origins of these letters are a bit murky, but date back to at least the eighteenth century. The long-standing tradition among the Pennsylvania Dutch is that the original text of these letters appeared in miraculous sheets of paper that would fall down from Heaven in holy places, such as in Koenigsberg (1714) and Madgeburg (1783). Often these missals would include warnings against sin such as "He who labors upon Sunday is damned!," commands against demonic or harmful forces such as fire or sickness, and mentions of biblical or pseudo-biblical personas such as the supposed "Three Kings," Caspar, Melchior, and Balthasar. The letter would then be copied and passed on with instructions to continue its passage and blessing, with a threat of a potential curse against anyone who interrupted the chain of enchanted protection letters. These letters were widespread among the *Deitsch*, appearing in printed broadsides (large newspaper-like publications) to be clipped and carried with the reader. A book about the York "hex" murder of Nelson Rehemeyer (mentioned previously; see also the "Singing

Bones" in this chapter) was printed with a copy of a *himmelsbrief* slipped into each one as late as 1970.[347]

These letters are, of course, connected to—and likely the origin of—a number of other blessing and chain letters, and even the chain "reposts" of social media. The power of these sorts of spellworkings was cumulative, growing stronger with their passage and offering avenues of divine magic and miracles to touch the earthly plane in exponentially more widespread places.

FIG 19-1: The home of Nelson Rehmeyer, known as a Pow-wow, or local healer, in his Pennsylvania German community.

SINGING BONES
Nelson Rehmeyer and John Blymire

Nelson Rehmeyer was a well-known healer in the *braucherei* (or Pow-wow) tradition. He lived near York, Pennsylvania in an old timber home where he provided magical cures. John Blymire, who was a distant relative of Rehmeyer, was also a gifted *braucher*, coming from a multi-generational line of magical healers. Blymire, however, suffered from several mental health issues including an intense paranoia, even receiving institutional evaluation. He blamed Rehmeyer for a decline in his fortunes, and when the local

347. Bilardi, *The Red Church*, 261–322; and Donmoyer, *Powwowing in Pennsylvania* (Exhibit Catalog), 15–22.

"River Witch of Marietta," a woman named Nellie Noll, confirmed that Nelson was at fault, Blymire decided to take matters into his own hands. Initially he and Rehmeyer met on friendly terms in Nelson's home, but after Blymire couldn't find his relative's magic books during a late-night search, he came back another night with teenagers John Curry (who also blamed Rehmeyer for a curse) and Wilbert Hess. The men tied up Rehmeyer and beat him, trying to discover a means to stop the curses they believed they were under, but getting nothing from Nelson they proceeded to kill and burn him, along with part of his house. They fled into the night, but were apprehended and tried for the murder. Hess was given ten years, and Curry and Blymire life sentences, although all would eventually walk free on parole. The case caused a tremendous media stir in the early twentieth century, and became known as the "York Hex Murder" case in both local and national press.[348]

Scraps of Magic: Written Charms

Beyond the professionally printed page, writing itself contains a great deal of magic. In many New World magical practices, the use of written charms creates focused enchantment that can offer protection, target a particular person for a spell's effects, or even be used as a simple way of controlling or hexing someone. There are too many written charms to list them all here, but the following small sampling should give you some idea of just how many traditions emphasize the power of the written word.

Name Papers

Found in Jewish folk magic, Hoodoo, and Southern Conjure traditions, name papers are often substituted for personal items when the spell worker cannot obtain things like hair or clothing. The person's name is written down carefully on a piece of paper, which can then be added to a spell. Some good examples include putting a person's name paper under the lining of the sole of the right shoe to dominate and control them or freezing a name paper in a block of ice to stop them from doing harm or gossiping. One curse involves taking the name paper of a person, chewing bitter herbs or roots such as mustard seed or chicory, and spitting on the paper

348. White, *Witches of Pennsylvania*, 72–76.

while crossing out a letter of the person's name. This is repeated once a day until the name is completely blotted away, at which time the target is expected to be suffering greatly unless they change their behavior and the conjurer stops the hex.

Zauberzetteln

These are derived from Pennsylvania Dutch practice but bear a resemblance to many late medieval charms.[349] They are essentially distilled prayers or blessings in which key letters of a well-known prayer are substituted for the longer version. These are usually done based on the language spoken by the culture using the charm or languages associated with the Church, such as Latin or Greek. Many that survive today are based on German, as well. These may also be text associated with religious language laid out in a specific way on the page, as in the case of the well-known SATOR Square and the INRI Cross (see "Dirt Under the Nails: Door Wards" in this chapter).

Petitions

Petition papers are found in Southern Conjure and Hoodoo practices and have analogs in practices from Appalachia and the Ozarks as well as cunning folk traditions. The primary function of these papers is to contain a complete written spell, customized to a single target, which would then be used in other spell workings. They have specific rules about how they get made, and often involve writing a certain way on the paper. For example, if a spell worker wanted to create a love charm for a client, they would write the client's intended beloved's name three or seven times across the paper, then turn it ninety degrees and write the client's name on top of and across the intended's name. They might then write "He shall love me and only me" in a continuous cursive circle around the crossed names, never lifting the pen from the page until the circle is complete. They would repeat the phrase as often as necessary, dotting "I's" and crossing "T's" once the circle is "closed." A worker would then burn a pink or red candle on top of the petition paper for three or seven nights to finish the spell, or bury it in the front yard of the intended to intensify the charm.

349. Bilardi, *The Red Church*, 269–78.

Sigils and Wards

Sigils appear all over the world, really, but in recent years chaos magicians have been one of the driving forces behind the boom in sigil-crafting. Austin Osman Spare and Peter Carroll have some excellent work on sigil-craft from that vein, and more recently contemporary traditional witch Laura Tempest Zakroff has written an essential guide to effective sigil-crafting that goes beyond the Spare/Carroll methods (*Sigil Witchery*). The chaos method usually involves taking a magical word or phrase (sometimes simply the intended "goal" of the spell) and distilling it to essential letters, then recombining those letters in an artistic way to make an image. The final image is the sigil, and is used to enact whatever changes the spellcrafter desires.

FIG 19-2: The SATOR Square charm.

DIRT UNDER THE NAILS
Door Wards

While some written charms can be extremely involved, often simpler can be better. The above written charm (figure 19-2) is designed to be used to protect your home by writing it on paper and placing it above all your doors (you can do them for windows, too). One of the great things about these is that if you write the charm on slips of paper, you can usually slip it into the frames of the door where it won't be seen at all, and where it will offer a constant stream of protection. Replenish the charm once per year to maintain its effectiveness.

This ward, known as the "Sator Square," is widespread and may or may not directly link to Christian folk magic (some believe that the words are a form of bastardized Latin prayer from the early Church, but others maintain it derives from pre-Christian Roman roots). The Sator Square is often inscribed directly onto a door, but you can also write it on paper and slip it into the doorframe for the same effect.

Living Deliciously: Signing the Devil's Book

Beyond the realm of printed books of magic, almanacs, chapbooks, and written charms and letters, there also existed a mythical book of power that could transform a person into a witch with a few strokes of a pen (or in some cases, a few drops of blood from her finger). This was the notorious "Devil's Book" into which a damned soul might sign her name to offer herself in service to the Devil in exchange for the powers of witchcraft and the opportunity to get whatever she wanted, including unlimited fresh butter or a pretty dress (as seen in the 2015 Robert Eggers film, *The Witch*).

The Devil's Book was frequently thought by Puritan settlers to be the ultimate embodiment of human sin—a willful signing away of one's soul to infernal powers. By simply signing one's name to such a book, a witch gained all her power and lost all her salvation. Some of the key features of a Devil's Book and its accompanying rituals were:

- **The Profaning of the Bible**—The witch would have to stamp upon a Bible or otherwise deface it before being allowed to sign. In some cases, a Bible itself was used to sign the witch into the Devil's service. Several Appalachian tales record instances of witches simply making an "X" in a marred Bible to indicate their pact. In Appalachian lore, witch Rindy Sue Gose performs this sort of ritual to seal her contract with the Devil after cutting her finger and placing a blood mark onto the Bible pages.[350] This action echoes the profaning of the Lord's name or the recitation of a reversed "Our Father" as a way of breaking

350. Davis, *The Silver Bullet*, 16–20.

the bonds of Christianity for a witch. Not that you should read much into that, of course.

- **The Use of Blood as Ink**—When witches made their mark, they often didn't actually sign their name. In a time when general literacy was still low (though it should be noted that literacy among Puritan men was quite high for the era), not everyone would be expected to have a "signature." Instead, they would have a "mark," often an "X" which they used as an indication of their agreement to a contract. To personalize this mark in the rituals of witchcraft, a witch wouldn't simply take an inked quill and make a fancy "X," though. Instead, her blood was an indication that the pact bound her body and soul to the Devil. Puritan minister William Perkins described the process (most business-like) as follows:

> The express and manifest compact is so termed, because it is made by solemn words on both parties. For the satisfying hereof, he [the future witch] gives to the Devil for the present, either his own handwriting, or some part of his blood as a pledge and earnest penny to bind the bargain.[351]

The Devil sometimes used a great iron pen to draw the blood from the witch before having him sign his name, and in cases where the book was not a defaced Bible, the great book contained hundreds of other blood signatures from other witches.

Owen Davies observes in his book, *Grimoires,* that the drawing-up of a pact between a witch or sorcerer and an infernal representative was nothing new—look at the legend of Dr. Faustus, for example. What made these New World magical compacts unique was that the witch did not draw up the document herself, but rather was lured into signing a book which she would never possess. Instead, the book remained in the custody of her magical master. All her magic, then, could be learned without the aid of books, at least in this model of New England Colonial witchcraft. Indeed, the Devil presented himself or his imps to the witch as her means for accomplishing malefic magic rather than gifting her the use of dusty tomes of magical lore and spells. In short, the Devil's Book was merely a roster of the souls won to his service, and possessed little magical power in and of itself, at least superficially. However, a deeper

351. Weisman, *Witchcraft,* p. 36.

reading of the Devil's Book phenomenon reveals that the act of writing in blood on a sacred object in fact demonstrates a type of very old and potent magic. Such a book, if it could be wrested from the Devil, would be very powerful, indeed, perhaps containing the magic of all those who had signed before.

THE WORK–The Commonplace Book

Virtually everyone I know that engages in some sort of magical practice has a secret wish when it comes to magical books. They all want a beautiful, old-looking volume bound in leather or cloth, stuffed with hand-torn pages full of beautifully-designed spells, holiday rituals, magical correspondences, and maybe a few drips of wax or pressed herbs between the pages. In some ways, I blame the 1998 film *Practical Magic*, which showed just such a book and made it all but impossible to have a certain yen for that kind of tome in our magical libraries.

The fact of the matter, however, is that most of the "spellbooks" we have from North American history are not these weighty behemoths of ink and paper, but small, simple journals of everyday recipes and remedies, interspersed with a few magic charms here and there. Some lean more heavily into the magical side of things, as we see in *Joshua Gordon's Commonplace Book*, housed in the archives of the University of South Carolina. Others may be little more than a cheaply-bound and crumbling copy of Hohman's *Long-Lost Friend* or *Dr. Helfenstein's Diverse Proven House-Treasury of Sympathy* (1853) (which sounds like the title for a potentially excellent or disastrous film). Those print copies might have clipped recipes and *himmelsbriefen* broadsides stuffed into the pages with a few handwritten notes.

The point of these books was their everyday use. The magical books of most practitioners do not contain perfectly laid-out designs and/or intricate, sophisticated spells that get performed once and then consigned to one moonlit memory. These are the spells of daily life—treating burns, finding lost goods, warding off harm. They contain recipes for cough syrups and favorite pumpkin pies, or show how to find buried gold while offering a marvelous silver polish made from black walnut hulls. The spells they contain were used over and over again, repeated until they almost became muscle memory. They were not perfect by any means, but they were—and are—useful.

That's not to say you cannot have a beautiful spellbook. If you have the time and inclination, I encourage that. When it comes to an effective spellbook, however,

I invite you to start with a simple blank notebook, or expand upon the notebook I invited you to begin in chapter two. Write down the spells, charms, correspondences, and methods you remember well enough that you don't *need* to look them up, because you've used them that often. Add new spells only when you have tried them half a dozen or more times and found them effective. Include favorite crafts or knitting patterns, songs or song lists that you use to change your moods, scraps of information on remarkable dreams or local lore and legend. Make it personal and make it yours. You might even choose to make it digital, keeping an online document or note file compiling your favorite and most useful spells. The point is to make it part of your everyday life, and see how keeping that record begins to transform your own magical practice.

Recommended Reading

Grimoires: A History of Magic Books, by Owen Davies. Davies' book is scholarly (he is a Professor of History at the University of Hertfordshire in England), but it also relates a lot of wonderfully detailed history about grimoires and magical books. The tour of tomes from the ancient era to the twentieth century covers a lot of ground and shows just how widespread and embedded in print culture our obsession with magic can be.

Making Magic, by Briana Saussy. *Making Magic* is largely an exploration of everyday magic and spiritual engagement, but I include it here because the book offers a way of thinking about enchantment that mirrors what we see in some older commonplace books, albeit in a much more contemporary way. The "Field Notes from Everyday Life" and journal prompts would be a good jumping-off point for developing one's own magical chapbook.

Sigil Witchery, by Laura Tempest Zakroff. This book is one of my favorites published in the past decade, because it pulls from aspects of cultural studies and presents a way of thinking about sigil magic—very much related to written charm-making—that opens up numerous doors for a folk practitioner. The combination of insight, inspiration, and practicality from Zakroff provides excellent guidance for written spellcraft.

ELEVENTH RITE: NECROMANCY

Or, How Witches Make Most Excellent Friends to the Dead

"Patience, good lady; wizards know their times:
Deep night, dark night, the silent of the night,
The time of night when Troy was set on fire;
The time when screech-owls cry and ban-dogs howl,
And spirits walk and ghosts break up their graves,
That time best fits the work we have in hand.
Madam, sit you and fear not: whom we raise,
We will make fast within a hallow'd verge."*

* William Shakespeare, *Henry VI, Act I, Scene 4.*

CHAPTER TWENTY

Those Are My Boys—Friendly Spirits in Folk Magic

During his graduate work studying folk magical traditions throughout the American South, Western Kentucky University librarian and religious historian Jack Montgomery interviewed Lee R. Gandee, a professional *hexenmeister* ("witch master," a term Gandee used as an extension of his *braucherei* Pennsylvania German healing magical practice). Gandee's work often used his "boys," a set of spirits of departed young men who would act on his behalf as sort of spiritual spies and agents. They guided him in his divinatory work, but many who visited Gandee (including Jack), also noted strange things happening whenever Gandee said the boys were present. Small things in the room would move or shift, or strange noises might be heard from outside. Montgomery noted that "Gandee's spirits or boys ... had clearly defined roles. Their most common roles were that of investigator and reporter of activities at a distance. When he needed to know some information not readily available, instead of sending his own consciousness, he sent one of his spirits, who would make the journey and then report back on what had been seen." Or, as Gandee himself explained it, "I'm just getting too old to go myself, and it's a lot easier to send one of the boys."[352]

Gandee surrounded himself with spirits. His "boys" announced their presence to him, and he even kept a coffin handy in his home as a piece of decorative furniture

352. Montgomery, *American Shamans*, 146–152.

(and one that tied him to the world of the spirits). The house he lived in in South Carolina was also the same home once occupied by an accused—and tortured—witch named Mary Ingleman (var. Ingelman and Englemeyer), who was convicted and assaulted in 1798.

"The dead have few friends," says an old English proverb. One of my favorite witchy variants of this proverb adds to that expression: "The Dead have few friends. Be one of them."[353] In recent years, I've also developed my own take on this, and I sometimes note that relationships with the dead are some of the deepest and longest-lasting ones you can have, especially ancestral practices (or, as I put it wryly on a sticker once, "Dead friends are always there for you"). Aligning with the spiritual forces of death and the dead can be a powerful relationship. Necromantic rites of summoning, divinations and séances, even the use of animal bones in spell work—these are all evidence of the close ties between witches and the dead. In North America, this relationship has developed in a few different ways involving both the physical dead and the spiritual dead. In this chapter, we will look into some of those relationships and magical practices a bit further. I focus here on the more "positive" aspects of this work, as we will see the harsher side of necromancy in chapter twenty-one.

If we come to know the dead, to be their friends, we often find they have a lot to offer—sometimes even before they are buried!

Corpse Magic

Earlier in this book we looked at the role of animal bones in magical work (see chapter eleven), but human bodies also have long-standing associations with magic. While they are alive, they produce powerful magical ingredients: hair, nails, blood, tears, sexual fluids, spit, and so forth. When dead, however, they still have some uniquely magical properties, at least according to American folklore.[354] Some groups have very strict rules about the dead, including extreme taboos about touch-

353. The first place I encountered this proverb was on Dawn R. Jackson's now-defunct Hedgewytchery site, but I have seen it circulated widely in the years since then.

354. A word of note: While I will be discussing the uses of human remains as magical components here, please note that there are almost always very strict laws around the disposition of those remains. The examples here are folkloric, not prescriptive. Do not violate local or national laws, please.

ing them or interfering with them in the hours or days after decease. The Hopi and Diné (Navajo) both historically had strongly restrictive practices on bodily disposition. The Diné sometimes abandoned the home of the deceased, leaving the building to act as a burial chamber while the rest of the family relocated. The spirits of the dead are thought to linger for a set period of time after death, frequently around four days, and then to travel to the land of the dead (often represented as a place beneath the waters of the world). In these cultures, contact with the dead could invite serious risk to both the living and the departed. Bad luck or illness might result from improper regard for these rules.[355]

Many other groups do not have these restrictions, however. The Caddo tribes of the Great Plains believe that the recently deceased are in a transitional phase and can actually act as conduits of communication with other ancestors. Relatives and friends would move their hands over the bodies of the dead from feet to head, then repeat the process on themselves while speaking to their ancestors as a way of sharing messages between the worlds.

There are, of course, more gruesome examples of corpse magic, too. Probably one of the most famous and nefarious examples of corpse magic is the Hand of Glory, a special candle made from the severed and pickled hand of an executed criminal which supposedly had intense magical properties. One of its talents was its reputed ability to render anyone in a house near where it was lit unconscious, thus making them easy to rob and explaining why the Hand of Glory might have been sought after by eager thieves. This practice, derived from European (and particularly English) folk magic, required aligning with the proper moon cycle and including "foul-smelling herbs" in the preservation process.[356] Another variation involved filling a human shin bone with tallow rather than the "traditional" mummified hand. The person using the Hand of Glory also had to keep their magical artifact a secret, or else its power might be broken (and there's the whole "Did you know Bill has the pickled hand of a murderer in his fridge?" gossip tree that you don't want to be a part of).

355. Jones and Molyneaux, *Mythology of the American Nations*, 62–63; Erdoes & Ortiz, *American Indian Myths & Legends*, 442–45.

356. Paulson, *Witches, Potions, & Spells*, 40.

In other North American lore, corpses are empowered with crime-detection properties as well. One piece of lore from the Ozarks and Appalachians describes leaving an egg in the hand of a murdered man when he is buried or burning his heart. The murderer will be compelled to some action, depending on the story, ranging from returning to the scene of the crime to confessing guilt to suffering illness and death himself.[357] Sometimes the body will perform its own divination, unaided by other witnesses or participants. A piece of Kentucky lore says, "If a corpse's nose bleeds, it is a sign that the murderer is in the room," for example.[358] A similar piece of African American folklore observes that if a murderer touches a corpse the wounds will begin bleeding, making the corpse a witness to its own murder case.[359] Folklore from throughout the United States holds that at the site of a murder, any bloodstains will become wet again on the anniversary of the murder, a sort of haunted remnant of corpse magic.

Bodies also had curative powers, as well. Ozark folklorist Vance Randolph noted that many in his region believed that rubbing a wart with the finger or hand of a corpse would make it go away (likely using the same rationale as other "rubbing" cures such as those done with potatoes: once the rubbing object is buried, its decay will also decay the wart).[360] Folklore from Illinois says that a similar technique could be used to remove birthmarks, and girls were sometimes advised to run the hand of a deceased relative over a marked part of their body to make it fade or disappear.[361] The corpse could be used to get rid of anything from head lice to bad habits (such as bed-wetting) depending on what you rubbed with it or left in the coffin with it.

Possibly the most widely-known and used variant of corpse magic came once the body was buried. Graveyard dirt acquired (usually "bought"; see the following "Dirt Under the Nails") from a particular grave could spark particular effects, especially in Hoodoo practices, although other traditions have similar variations. Everything from protection to physical pain to curses to legal troubles could be cured with the right graveyard dirt pulled from the right grave.

357. Randolph, *Ozark Magic*, 316.

358. Thomas, *Kentucky Superstitions*, 72.

359. Puckett, *Folk Beliefs*, 88.

360. Randolph, *Ozark Magic*, 131.

361. Hyatt, *Folklore from Adams County*, 64.

Once the dead are buried, however, they do not cease to be helpful—at least not to a witch who knows how to get in touch with them.

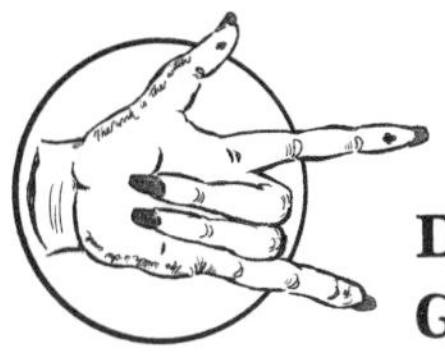

DIRT UNDER THE NAILS
Graveyard Dirt

In both Southern Conjure and Hoodoo, soil taken from a grave can be powerful, a tradition with deep roots in the magical practices of places like Western Africa. Southern Conjure tends to use it as a way of transmitting a certain power of place or to invoke ancestral and spiritual forces—dirt taken from a soldier's grave, for example, might be used to create a protection amulet, which would be additionally powerful if the soldier were also a family relation. Hoodoo expands upon those powers and often uses dirt from particular parts of a grave for particular effects; a handful taken from the "head" area of a judge's grave might be useful in legal case work, for instance. Hoodoo also makes graveyard dirt a key component of the infamous "goopher dust" cursing formula, which mingles the cemetery soil with things like black mustard seeds or other unsavory ingredients to effect physically and spiritually painful results on a target. Goopher dust is usually deployed in a way that requires a victim to walk over it, absorbing its power through the legs (which are then, in turn, frequently the first places pain and suffering manifest). Amulets such as the "Mercury dime" are sometimes warn to deflect these powers (see chapter fifteen).

Gathering graveyard dirt requires "payment" in most traditions. A magical worker will collect a handful or so of dirt from the grave, then offer the spirit of that grave something in turn, such as coins, liquor, tobacco, or even things like toys and flowers. Some workers are elaborate in their gathering rituals, plunging their hands up to the elbow or shoulder into the dirt of a recently dug grave (there were some who speculated that the cursing powers of the dirt came from the diseases in the soil of certain burial plots, especially if those plots belonged to someone with, say, tuberculosis or yellow fever). Other workers bury coins in a "five spot," with one coin at each "corner" of the grave and a final one in the middle above the "heart" of the interred.

While most cemeteries currently have rules (or follow local laws) prohibiting the disturbance of soil or plots, family cemeteries on private lands are often under private control, so you may be able to get permission to gather dirt if you have a family or close personal relationship with a cemetery owner. Similarly, if you volunteer with a cemetery as part of its cleanup crew, you may also be able to gather dust and dirt from around graves when doing things like planting flowers without directly violating any laws or codes.

FIG 20-1: Talking boards, the best known of which is the Ouija board.

Spirits & Séances

In the late 1840s, near Rochester, New York, a pair of sisters began hearing strange knocking sounds in their home. These sisters, Margaret and Kate Fox (aged fourteen and ten years old, respectively) convinced their older sister, Leah (in her thirties at the time) that these were communications from the dead, particularly a spirit known as one "Mr. Splitfoot" (sometimes thought to be a nickname for the Devil). Within a few years, there was an explosion in interest focused on spirit communication that spiraled quickly beyond the Fox sisters and into broader American culture. By the twentieth century, the religious phenomenon of Spiritualism—a term which encompassed a variety of practices including séances, table-tipping, mediumship, and the Foxes' knocking method—had attracted millions of adherents. Spiritualism did not solely burst forth from the parlor games of the Fox sisters, but was a sort of coming together of a variety of practices drawn from multiple New World religious backgrounds. These influences included eighteenth-century Swedenborgianism (practiced by famed frontier-traveler Johnny Appleseed); nineteenth-century movements springing from upstate New York's "burned over district," such as Mormonism; Shaker spirit contact; and Transcendentalism, in addition to what the Fox sisters brought to the table (tilted or not). Additionally, Spiritualism incorporated the slowly surging interest in Eastern lines of thought brought in through the Transcendentalists and the burgeoning Theosophy movement.[362]

Spiritualism offered (and continues to offer, since it hasn't ever really gone away but only diminished in numbers) a direct experience of the spiritual world. A person could communicate directly with their dead relatives, sometimes hearing their voices or getting physical "evidence" of their presence through the projection of ectoplasm or other phenomena. The surge in popularity for Spiritualist séances hit particular heights when the First Lady of the United States, Mary Todd Lincoln, reputedly had them in the White House to communicate with her dead son (husband Abraham was thought to have attended at least one, as well).[363] In a time when thousands of young people were disappearing into the Civil War, lynchings, or onto the terrifyingly unknown and westward-moving frontier, Spiritualism provided comfort to those left behind. It also was one of the first religious movements (along with the aforementioned Shakers) to offer women a central role. While plenty of men and nonbinary people engaged with Spiritualism, a majority of early leaders and adherents were women. Women could act as mediums and facilitate healing and communication in ways that many other churches would not allow.

The methods of Spiritualism have since become standards of spirit communication, and we frequently see them deployed as a part of necromantic rituals in witchcraft now. Following are some of the most common methods and tools still in occasional use by folk practitioners of magic.

Talking Boards

Simply put, these are flat boards with symbols, numbers, or letters on them used to communicate with the dead (hence, allowing them to "talk" through the board).

362. Albanese, *Republic of Mind and Spirit,* 179–89.

363. Horowitz, *Occult America,* 57–62.

The ubiquitous Ouija board, particularly the one marketed by Hasbro (and previously by Parker Brothers), is hardly the only version of the famous "talking board," but it is well-known enough to be iconic (see figure 20-1). Talking boards started off as a dowsing method. The letters, numbers, and a few common answers were written onto a board or surface, and then the medium would ask a question and begin pointing to letters or words in turn. The spirit would "knock" when she reached the appropriate letter and she would start again, continuing until a message was spelled out. The Ouija board simplified the process by adding in the planchette—a small wooden indicator with a magnifying glass or a hole in the center to highlight particular letters. Simple versions of these boards have been made by simply writing letters onto a piece of paper and using an inverted shot glass as a planchette, and one traditional method involves using a pendulum in conjunction with the board to find the letters the departed indicate.

Séances and Mediumship

A large number of Spiritualists and other psychically-inclined people would use themselves as the vessel through which the spirits spoke. Mediums were thought to have a particular link to the other side and could act as literal mouthpieces for the dead, with eerie verisimilar renditions of the voices of the departed emerging from their lips. Mediums might work alone, and they might not be nearly so dramatic as to channel a literal voice, instead conveying general messages from the land of the dead. A medium's power often got a boost from the group séance, a ritual in which a group of people gathered around a table or other space and collectively summoned the dead. Séances also could be done by lay-practitioners without the aid of a specially-empowered medium, and might involve the use of other methods such as knocking, talking boards, or automatic writing. Spirits make themselves known by flickering candles, strange noises and whispers, or even by forming as apparitions of mist or ectoplasm.

Automatic Writing

This method involves using a combination of mediumship and the written word to deliver a message. In some cases, a medium might ask a question, and then begin simply freewriting on a blank page. She would then review the writing when she finished and look for mistakes or strange words that had managed to sneak in, and use those to decipher a message from the dead. Another method involves using a pendulum with a pen or pencil and letting it move freely over a blank sheet of paper in the hopes a word or phrase might become legible. Still another form involved the planchette, used here before it became part of the talking board desk set. The pen or pencil would be loaded into a planchette through a small hole, with the tip just beneath it and able to leave marks on a sheet of paper below. The user or users would then ask a question and place their hands on the planchette, which would move around. After, the planchette was removed and words or even pictures would reveal the message from beyond the grave.

Table Tilting and Knocking

This is really where it all started, and largely has fallen out of fashion. However, there are folkloric accounts of people readily labeled as witches being able to make a table kick or buck like a mule,[364] and frequently these methods are some of the most active. The person making an inquiry would place hands upon the table along with everyone else, and ask yes or no questions. The table would "tilt," meaning it would shift, buck, dance, or otherwise move in response. Alternatively, the spirits would "knock," making rapping or popping noises in response to questions as a way to communicate.

While Spiritualism definitely shaped and influenced the North American spiritual landscape, it was also not without controversies. Ralph Waldo Emerson, for example, called the whole practice "rat-revelation," saying that spirituality should not be based upon strange noises heard from the walls of old buildings.[365] There was also a frequent tendency to fetishize Native Americans or Asians (something that also happened a lot in Theosophy, where founder and Russian émigré Helena Blavatsky called upon the powers of her "Mahatmas" from the East to guide and direct her). At the same time, because the power of Spiritualism, and by extension, talking to the dead, was in the hands of laypeople, the experience of that power very much depended on the person or people involved. It doesn't always work as intended, either. One of my informants told of using a Ouija board in a graveyard to no effect,

364. Dorson, *Buying the Wind*, 57–58.

365. Albanese, *Republic of Mind & Spirit*, 179.

only to later find they had been at the grave of a family friend they didn't know had died![366]

Spiritualism also ran into problems with fraud. The Fox sisters finally fell from grace when Margaret gave a newspaper interview (she was desperate for money and the reporter agreed to pay her) claiming their knocking had been an elaborate hoax done with popping toe joints. She tried to recant that confession later, but the patina of falsehood hung heavy over the sisters. Other mediums were caught faking ectoplasmic projections using technology or trick photography, and any number of television psychics have been shown to use "cold reading," a psychological method of deductive reasoning and sharp guesswork, to simulate messages from the dead. Psychic hotlines from the late twentieth century have gone defunct, with people making jokes about "no one seeing that coming," and so much of this chapter of American history has been put at arm's length as evidence of gullibility. Even the legal precedents used against many practicing "witches" today are known as fraudulent medium acts or statutes. The Catholic Church and other religious groups have done a remarkably effective job getting things like Ouija boards labeled as satanic devices, and horror movie tropes still treat them as gateways to demonic activity (see chapter twenty-two). But for many, and for a very long time, Spiritualism and necromantic communion with the dead was almost commonplace, something perhaps a bit quirky, but not something devious or dangerous.

Today, while Spiritualism has become a much smaller sector of the religious makeup of America, it remains. Spiritualist groups gather and bring messages to one another from dead relatives and friends. It still comforts those who need contact with the other side, and puts the power of the Otherworld in individual hands.

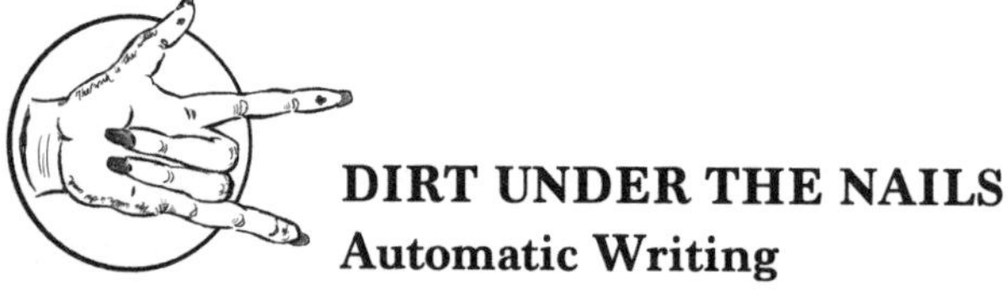

DIRT UNDER THE NAILS
Automatic Writing

Spiritualism left its mark on popular culture through the Ouija board most famously, but automatic writing has also had a profound impact on American literature. Many of the Modern writers, including authors like William

366. A. T., email communication, August 30, 2018.

Faulkner and Eugene O'Neill, used practices like automatic writing to generate some of their ideas, albeit without the spiritual dimension.

The simplest way to practice this sort of mediumship is to simply get a blank notebook and a pen. If you have a specific spiritual aid or ally you work with, you might invoke them or connect with them however you see fit (such as by a short opening prayer to a deity or an ancestor, or the recitation of a particular verse or psalm). If you're trying to answer a specific question, note it at the top of a blank page. Then take a deep breath and begin writing. Write all the way until you get to the bottom of the page, as rapidly as you can without thinking about what you are writing. You can even copy passages out of an encyclopedia (this was one of my mother's favorite punishments, which she took from famous author and Spiritualism enthusiast Sir Arthur Conan Doyle in his Sherlock Holmes story, "The Red-Headed League"). The trick is not to focus on thinking but simply writing. When you finish, look back over what you've written and circle any errors, any misspellings or strange words and phrases. You may need to "unscramble" some letters to have them make sense, or you might use the words with misspellings in them as your clues rather than the letters alone. You may even look at the letters or words at the beginning and end of each line and see if they are offering you some sort of message.

This can take some practice, but it can be a very useful and rewarding experience, especially if you treat the journal you're using as a sort of "workspace" to encounter the dead and receive their messages.

Honoring the Dead

In looking at North American magical practices, one recurring theme seems to be ties to those who have gone before. Virtually all branches of North American magic honor the dead, seek to work with them, or do both. In Appalachian and Ozark traditions, many practitioners seek to identify a spell-casting or fortune-telling relative in the distant past—a "granny" to go with their granny magic. Southern Conjure and Hoodoo place value on things like ancestral memorials, graveside visitation rituals (including a cemetery beautification holiday known as Decoration Day), and the use of ingredients connected with the dead. Curanderismo sprouts from a culture which has enormous festivities honoring the dead every November, which in turn takes its cues from remnants of Aztec ritual and imported European Catholic traditions (see chapter seventeen). Indigenous North American tribes all have different rules about the dead, but many also have specific ways to recognize the visitation of a dead relative in a dream or other liminal space. Some of the ways people practice these sorts of ancestral rites include:

- **Offerings**—Leaving a glass of water, a candle, or a plate of food out for an ancestor seems to be a tried-and-true way of working with the dead. Some traditions might put out a special decoration or a bit of favorite food on a plate to remember someone who has passed. In Chinese American traditions, paper representations of things like money or clothes will be burned as an offering to a departed ancestor to honor them and gain their favor.
- **Major Life Events**—Several traditions will set aside a place at the table, metaphorically or literally, during major life events like weddings or baby showers. Honored ancestors will have an empty seat marked as theirs at these festivities to make sure that the dead are included in the world of the living.
- **Holidays**—Several cultural holidays are specifically oriented toward connecting with the dead. Día de Muertos is one many know (partly thanks to Disney's film *Coco,* which covers some of the basic lore of the holiday quite well). Neopagans have Samhain (roughly pronounced SOW-uhn) as a date for honoring the dead through a "dumb supper" or other memorial feasts, usually around the end of October or beginning of November. In the South, Decoration Day (on or around Memorial Day) is a time to clean up family graves and make them nice, or decorate them.
- **Visitation**—Spending time at a grave site is a wonderful way for people to connect with the dead. Throughout the Victorian period and well into the twentieth century, many people would go on picnics in cemeteries, which doubled as public parks. Taking the time to visit an ancestor on important days like birthdays or death-days is not unusual in the United States, and some families even make regular weekly or monthly visits to family plots.
- **Service**—Giving service to the dead, or in their name, can be another way that people honor the departed. Many Catholics will perform rosaries or hold masses in honor of the dead. Performing work for a charity the departed

enjoyed, or even doing things to repair relationships broken during a person's life, are all established ways of honoring the dead.

- **Naming**—If you've ever been to the So-and-So Memorial wing of a hospital, you've walked right into an ancestral practice. Memorial naming is a common way to help the name of a departed family member or friend live on. Many families do this by naming children after departed relatives as well.

The variety and frequency of ancestral work makes it the most common form of necromancy, even if most who engage in these practices would be scandalized by the idea of calling what they do "necromancy." Yet in keeping the dead alive through relationships and actions, that is very much what happens. The living and the dead need each other, it seems.

THE WORK—Honoring Ancestors

Making a practice of honoring the dead—ancestral reverence—functions as a way of boosting spiritual allies while also creating a space for ourselves on that other side. Many witches work with chthonic spirits or deities (those associated with the Otherworld or Underworld), the dead, or psychopomps (spirits who guide the dead into their next spiritual phase). Why? Because a relationship to the dead is a close relationship with our own mortality and a recognition of a spiritual life alongside our more mundane comings and goings.

"Ancestral reverence" and "honor" are not the words we most associate with necromancy, but I've known enough witches to know that working with the dead opens up new possibilities in magic. That is not to say every witch on record does work with the dead, nor does every witch have an ancestral practice. Those that do, however, seem to get something out of it. I recall that when I was developing my own ancestral practice (built upon some loosely Catholic roots, but with a hefty dose of magic added in), I settled on putting an altar to my departed family members on top of my mother's old writing desk. The very night I set it up, I woke in the night to see the bedroom door had been opened. I felt someone coming down the hall and entering the room, though I could see no one. For a brief moment, I was terrified, but then I felt the brush of a familiar hand on my forehead, pushing my hair from my eyes. It was my mother, who had died a good ten years prior. I knew it was her, and even after that moment faded, I felt that connection lingering on.

Many people do not have that sort of relationship, however. They have dealt with family ties that have been hurtful or cruel, or have lost their longer family line for one reason or another. Just because you cannot work with your blood relatives, however, doesn't mean you don't have ancestors. Turning to teachers, mentors, people who have inspired you—all of those can be ancestors as well. Something as simple as putting up a photograph of astronaut Sally Ride or playing a song that reminds you of someone from your childhood neighborhood can be a gateway into ancestral work that focuses on a relationship of actions or memories. You may find that you are suddenly seeing news from NASA or hearing unexpected songs on the radio in response to these practices, signs the connections are strengthening and expanding. One of my folklore colleagues once told me about a woman she knew who would communicate with her grandfather using the car radio in just that way—asking a question and then seeing what the next full song on the radio gave her as his response!

What would an ancestral practice look like for you? What is the minimum you can commit to? A photo in a wallet or on a wall? A cup of water or coffee left in front of an empty chair? An agreement to whisper the person's name when you think of them, or visit their grave on a birthday or anniversary? Open yourself up to these sorts of workings, and the world of the dead will be something that ceases to scare you. It will be a place with familiar faces, one where people know your name and you know theirs. It will be a home you can one day go to, without fear, ready to be an ancestor yourself.

Recommended Reading

Honoring Your Ancestors, by Mallorie Vaudoise. This may well be the best-written guide on developing a folkloric ancestral practice I've ever read. It covers everything from setting up an altar and making offerings to working with cantankerous and difficult deceased family members. Vaudoise comes from a loosely folk Catholic perspective (which felt very familiar to me), but her text works as a guidebook that could easily bridge to almost any faith tradition.

Lily Dale: The True Story of the Town That Talks to the Dead, by Christine Wicker. Wicker's book takes the reader to the town of Lily Dale, New York, where the Spiritualism movement is still a major part of everyday life. The author goes well beyond the current town, however, and takes the reader on a tour of American Spiritualism in an easy, readable way that doesn't sugar-coat some of the movement's rougher patches. If you want to know more about Spiritualism, this is a wonderful place to start.

CHAPTER TWENTY-ONE

The Witch's Ghost—A Haunted Legacy of Magic

Somewhere in the night, a wail echoes off of the houses near the little canal—a *barranca*—and mothers hold their children a little tighter. The sound is La Llorona, the Weeping Woman, who cries for her dead children, ones she drowned in those same canals. Her reasons for doing so vary from storyteller to storyteller. Sometimes she does it to protect them from exploitation by their father, a Spanish military officer (or government official, again depending on the story). Sometimes it is in a fit of jealousy over the father's decision to marry another woman after throwing La Llorona aside (before she is La Llorona, of course). Sometimes she fears that they will be taken from her and so she drowns them to make them hers forever. This figure sometimes has magical qualities as well—a siren-like call that can lure children to her, or the ability to shapeshift (at least partly) and present the face of a horse rather than her typical mournful expression (although some report her face as completely blank, as well). She is associated with other figures, including the mistress of conquistador Hernán Cortés, who is called La Malinche. She may also derive from the Aztec goddess Cihuacoatl, the Snake Woman, with a half-red, half-black face, who took in the ghosts of those who died in childbirth.[367]

La Llorona is well-known in Mexico, as well as parts of the United States such as Austin or San Antonio, Texas (see figure 21-1). She is a ghost, a revenant, but

367. Ingham, *Mary, Michael, & Lucifer*, 110–12.

also something more. Ghosts may not seem to be exactly magical, but in some tales threads of magic appear. In her story we see similarities with other spurned women, like Medea of Greek myth (notably a witch betrayed by her husband). One of the enduring legacies of many witches appears in the haunted places and people they leave behind. Witches seldom go out without a memorable curse upon those who destroy them, or at least without leaving their mark for others to find later (sometimes literally, as in the case of Moll Dyer/DeGrow's handprints on her Maryland rock—see chapter sixteen).

The relationship between the living and the dead is important in North American witchcraft, but it is not always a mutually beneficial or even positive one. Sometimes the dead are angry, or mean. Sometimes they leave curses, or hauntings, as a way of being remembered. This is especially true when the dead are witches themselves. In the last chapter, we looked at traditions of sharing time and space with the dead in a productive, healthy relationship. In the following pages, we consider what happens on the other side of that coin. What does magic offer when dealing with a witch's ghost or a lingering curse in terms of combatting or reversing it? Are there times when witches avoid the dead? And what can we learn from stories like that of La Llorona about the legacy we choose to leave behind?

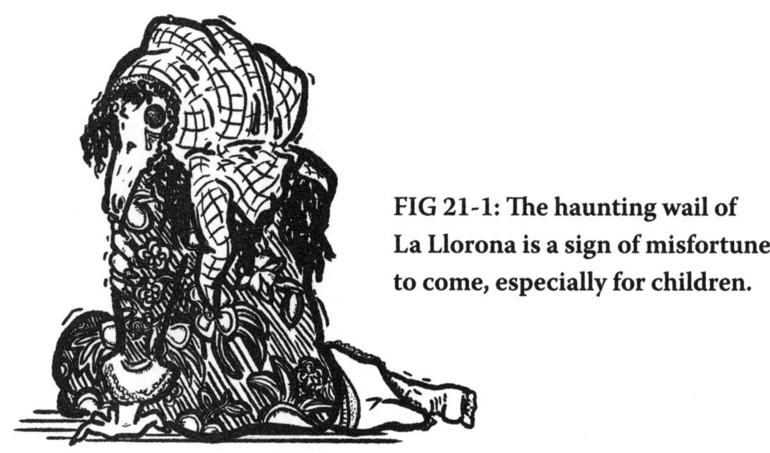

FIG 21-1: The haunting wail of La Llorona is a sign of misfortune to come, especially for children.

Gray Ladies and Wailing Women

Ghosts often tell us about the history of a place. One of the best ways you can get acquainted with local places and tales is to take a ghost tour, which will highlight a number of landmarks and help you connect them with stories. Ghosts often seem to act as spirits of place as well, appearing to interlopers or to locals as a way of claiming a space as "special" or off-limits in some way. Sometimes ghosts are even employed to protect a particular location, as happens with many stories of buried treasure (see chapter eight). Magically speaking, these ghosts are part of an Otherworldly system—a sort of network of beings which traffic in the same sorts of nonrational, unexplainable things that witches do. We also see that a number of ghostly forms are essentially archetypal, with headless horsemen or wailing women showing up in numerous communities. When they do, they almost always take on a bit of local flavor, however, and in that we can see some of the ways that these beings become genii loci as well. Below are some of the ghosts frequently encountered in North American folklore, as well as some ideas about what their lore might tell us about their purpose (and thus magical connection) when they appear.

Gray Ladies

Sometimes also called Women in White, these are usually the ghosts of women seen wearing white dresses, although they often appear somewhat grayish or misty in color, thus lending the name "Gray Ladies" to the stories (and sometimes they appear wearing dark clothing, when they are called, of course, "Women in Black"). Most often these are women who have died in a tragedy of some kind—murdered by a lover or in an accident, although in at least one West Virginia story the reason for her death is a mystery.[368] Sometimes they also seem to be widows who died while waiting for a missing husband to return (especially the wives of sailors). They frequently are seen walking along shorelines or roads, and sometimes are associated with particular houses. One of their most defining features is that they seldom speak. They often represent injustice, a mute witness to a particular area's dark and unspoken past. They can act as protectors of particular places, frightening off those that might be inclined to cause trouble. They can also warn of coming trouble, as in

368. Gainer, *Witches, Ghosts, & Signs*, 88.

one story from Alma, Arkansas, in which a ghostly white woman appeared and was thought to be an omen of an early death coming soon.[369]

Headless Horsemen

If you've ever read Washington Irving's "The Legend of Sleepy Hollow," this ghost is probably very familiar to you. However, the Headless Horseman of Tarrytown is hardly the only specter without a place to hang his hat. In Braxton County, West Virginia, one story tells of a headless ghost riding a horse at high speeds and jumping the lane, frightening those who come across him.[370] These horsemen are often associated with war, having been decapitated in a Civil War battle or Revolutionary-era skirmish, and their appearance is usually frightening but not threatening. They sometimes bring rain or storms with them, as well, and as such may be tied to European figures associated with the Wild Hunt and other spirit-riders. They may also be tied to the fairy realm, as with the *Dullahan* of Irish lore. In some stories the horse becomes a car or a stagecoach, and the driver is headless (although in at least one version of this variant from Pennsylvania, a group of Civil War soldiers in a coach and their driver all keep their heads).[371] Another tale from North Carolina features a headless ghost who acts not as a harbinger of storms or war, but who acts as a treasure guardian (and, remarkably for a headless ghost, speaks!).[372]

Wailing Women

Like La Llorona, other wailing women are often seeking something they've lost—children or a husband. They are sometimes not seen, but only heard (which is often the case in tales of the Irish *bean sidhe* or "banshee" in Anglicized form). Wailing women seem to work as boogeymen (or boogeywomen) for children, preventing them from sneaking out of the house at night, but can also act much like the "boo hag" in African American folklore and point out the abuses of menfolk in the community (see chapter nine).

369. Randolph, *Ozark Magic*, 224–25.

370. Gainer, *Witches, Ghosts, & Signs*, 89–90.

371. Schlosser, *Spooky Pennsylvania*, 85–91.

372. Schlosser, *Spooky South*, 32–38.

Restless Souls

This is the *anima sola,* the Lonely Soul often pictured in Purgatory—not quite damned enough for Hell nor holy enough for Heaven. Sometimes these spirits are travelers who never quite get the chance to rest, a frequent motif in tales of the "Wandering Jew" of European lore who has also appeared in places like the Mormon cultural region of the United States.[373] Frequently these ghosts need someone to make something right for them—a reburial of their bones, as in the story of a peddler's ghost from Missouri,[374] although in some cases they may simply be doomed to walk the earth until the end of time or Judgement Day. If you've ever heard the story of Jack O' Lantern, you know that the reason we put lights in pumpkins (or more traditionally, turnips) is to imitate one such condemned soul, who used an ember of Hell to light his way in the world. Sometimes these figures are also somewhat monstrous, as in some Utah tales where the wanderer is something of a mix between Bigfoot and the biblical Cain or in an East Tennessee tale where a man runs into a big, hairy creature stopped by a roadside ditch for a drink of water and offers it a ride to the next town.[375] Magically, these spirits act as bargaining partners, and they may offer gifts or service in exchange for momentary rest or offerings (like water). These figures can act as harbingers of change coming to a community, but often also connect to a bigger mythology about generational curses and making things right while people are still alive.

Vanishing Hitchhikers

Like the Restless Souls, Vanishing Hitchhikers move around, but the difference is that they frequent the same stretch of road or general location over a long period of time, rather than moving on to other places. Likely the most famous version of this story involves a young man offering a ride to a young woman on a lonely back road. She looks cold so he offers her his jacket or sweater, then when they arrive at the destination, she is gone. He knocks on the door only to find that the girl was the family's daughter, now dead for several years. When the boy goes to visit the girl's

373. Dorson, *Buying the Wind*, 507–508.

374. Randolph, *Ozark Magic*, 219.

375. Wigginton, *Foxfire 2*, 336–37.

grave, his jacket is hanging on her tombstone, of course.[376] These hitchhiking spirits can represent both the fear of strangers (hence their sudden popularity when hitchhiking-related disappearances or murders began appearing in national news stories) and also a desire for the dead to be remembered.

Native or Indian Spirits

This troubling category of spirit is almost always shared by non-Natives. Usually a "Native" spirit is simply a way of labeling a ghost that seems to conform to certain Native stereotypes, but there are occasions when spirits of particular Native Americans have been reported (such as Geronimo or those who died in the Wounded Knee massacre). Many tales associate Indian spirits with guardianship of a particular place, especially if that place houses a treasure of some kind. It's not much of a stretch to see the connection between guilt about taking land and prosperity from Indigenous peoples and these sorts of spirits.

Ghost Children

Sometimes the most terrifying ghosts are the most innocent ones. Ghostly children appear in places where there have been tragedies, especially places that have experienced things like fires or floods in which many children died. There are also more particular examples, such as bridges where a baby can be heard wailing somewhere nearby, usually associated with stories of a mother abandoning her child (or dying herself). Ghost children frighten away unwanted visitors and, like Wailing Women, seem to speak to a past with secrets and dark deeds. In contemporary legends, we also have the "Black Eyed Kids," who are similarly eerie but somehow more nefarious. They come knocking, bringing terror to your doorstep, and may represent the intrusion of the Otherworld into our own in times of crisis.

Ghost Lights

A number of places have stories of will-o-the-wisps, ghost lights, or "corpse candles" floating in the dark and leading travelers astray. In Pottsville, Pennsylvania, some have seen a procession of shadowy figures going through the graveyard car-

376. See Brunvand, *The Vanishing Hitchhiker: American Urban Legends & Their Meanings.*

rying lit candles,[377] while in parts of the Ozarks this "foxfire" appears starting in the graveyard and then traveling down the road as a pale blue light.[378] There's some science to this phenomenon as a certain type of fungus gives off a faint bioluminescent glow in swamps or other rural areas, and it can very much look like a pale blue fire. These tales are sometimes linked to the Wandering Spirit tales, too (such as Jack O'Lantern) and these spirits seem to be tricksy ones that want to lure humans among them (and in that way rather resemble some aspects of fairy lore).

Spirit Hounds

Human spirits should hardly have all the fun. One of the most common figures in ghost-lore is that of the black dog who mysteriously appears by the roadside or in front of a traveler (see figure 21-2). In most cases these dogs act as guides or protectors for the travelers, although most who see them are also somewhat terrified of their large, hulking appearance and their frequently red eyes. Sometimes these dogs are not black, but white. Many times people try to shoot these dogs, but quickly discover they cannot. Why they do this is a mystery, as in most North American stories ghost dogs seem benevolent. One tale from the South tells of a white dog who chased a man who'd been hitting the bottle a bit too much all the way home, only to then disappear. His wife then told him that there had been an arrest of a pair of robbers who were waiting to waylay him on his typical route home, which he only changed because of the dog.[379] Similar tales of ghost foxes and dogs show up throughout the Appalachians and Ozarks, and in Mexican lore the Xolo dog also acts as a protector for travelers wandering the roads between the living and the dead.

377. Schlosser, *Spooky Pennsylvania*, 158–61.

378. Randolph, *Ozark Magic*, 334–35.

379. Schlosser, *Spooky South*, 77–82.

FIG 21-2: Spectral dogs and spirit hounds romp through many American stories.

Of course, there are many ghosts that don't fit so neatly into boxes, and each ghost's local lore varies significantly. Understanding how these sorts of spirits fit into not only a broad category but the specific local landscape is key to unlocking the ways in which they act as "guides" to the local rules of the Otherworld. For example, running into a black dog and hearing tales of a wailing woman or ghost child near a local river bridge might tell you that there are dangers in that part of your county or town and that you should bring something protective with you when wandering the same roads as the spirits at night. A tale of a vanishing hitchhiker might inspire more visits to a local graveyard and some cemetery upkeep, while you might use the appearance of a headless horseman to predict a coming storm. Understanding spirits and their relationships to both us and our surroundings can be just as valuable as being able to correctly read the almanac for moon signs or know which herbs grow wild in your area for a practicing witch.

Then again, there are also situations in which you *don't* want spirits lingering around—particularly spirits with intent more sinister than leading someone off of a path or warning them about a rain shower on the way.

Get Out—Dealing with Angry Spirits

The spiritual world can be very appealing, especially to those with magical inclinations. In folklore, however, we also see that it has any number of risks: fairy abductions, physical torments by poltergeists, or even unwanted possession (please note that I say "unwanted," as there are instances in folk magic and folk religion where possession is very much wanted).

So what do witches do when they are confronted with these sorts of beings? After all, a witch is supposed to be able to have a good rapport with those on the other side, right? And what about curses left behind by witches themselves?

There are numerous spells in folklore that deal with quieting intranquil spirits and angry haints. Some examples include:

- **Reuniting Remains**—Often a ghost lingering in a particular area simply wants a proper burial, one that they were denied upon their death. Finding separated bones or a body that didn't get a ceremonial send-off and providing a grave or funeral often quiets these sorts of spirits. Sometimes finding a spirit's hidden cache of money or goods will also settle them (plus, bonus: treasure!).
- **House Cleansings**—A particular house (or sometimes person) can be "cleansed" of an unwanted ghost or ghosts, usually by a professional spiritual worker. Sometimes this involves bringing a priest or preacher for a house blessing, and sometimes someone with magical abilities—like a witch—is asked to perform a ritual banishing harmful haints from a home. Sometimes incenses ranging from the pleasant (juniper berries or frankincense) to the noxious (garlic or asafetida) are incorporated to "smoke" the spirit out. Windows should be left open to give the spirit somewhere to flee (and any queasy humans, as well).
- **Spirit Traps**—Some witches use specific bottle spells or sigils as "spirit traps," often made with particular woods like rowan or juniper included to stymie the spirit once it's caught and keep it too weak to do any further harm. Another spirit trap involves coaxing a ghost or spirit into a mirror with a candle and prayer, then covering the mirror with black cloth and burying or destroying it. This relates to both the Southern practice of covering mirrors during periods of mourning following a death and some children's occult games like "Bloody Mary."
- **Noise**—Many spirits like to be the scariest, loudest thing in the room, so getting rid of them can be as simple as being more obnoxious than they are. You can use bells or even just bang pots and pans together while telling a ghost to leave you alone. As with the incense method, windows are usually left open to give spirits a place to exit (although it will likely make it easier for angry neighbors to yell at you).
- **Pets**—Animals seem to have a knack for seeing and experiencing things that humans don't. Black cats are sometimes thought to be particularly good at

chasing away ghosts. Other pets may at least be able to see or hear ghosts when we don't, as a number of ghost stories mention pets reacting strangely before a ghost appears. This is more of an early-warning system than an eviction notice, but might be a useful tool nonetheless.

- **Iron or Steel**—Keeping iron or steel around has a long association with warding off unwanted spiritual beings (such as we find in some European fairy lore). Rural traditions from the South and Midwest of the United States describe keeping a steel pocket knife and a Bible under or by the bed (or even under the pillow) to prevent harassment by ghosts.
- **Mustard Seeds**—One interesting custom from Illinois folklore (likely derived from African American Southern lore) says that putting mustard seeds in the four corners of a room will prevent ghosts from bothering you.[380] This is likely related to other magical protection methods involving small, countable objects, also used to keep away witches.
- **Flowers**—Strange as it may seem, keeping flowers (especially fresh ones) in a home is one way to bring quiet and peace. Perhaps this is related to the idea of leaving flowers at grave sites as well. Some of the flowers frequently associated with clearing the spiritual air are carnations, gardenias, lilies, roses, and sweet peas.[381]

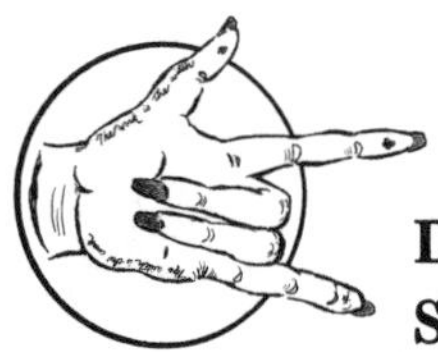

DIRT UNDER THE NAILS
Setting Lights (A House Cleansing)

Sometimes witches are happy to welcome the dead or other spirits into their homes, and sometimes a witch needs to firmly-but-politely ask for some space. Intranquil spirits and haints (a Southern word for a type of frustratingly tenacious spirit) occasionally need to be asked to pack their ghostly bags and go. The following method is one I've adapted from a few different sources, not the least of which is Draja Mickaharic's *Spiritual Cleansing* (Weiser Books, 2012). This is not an exorcism rite designed to

380. Hyatt, *Folklore from Adams County*, 399.

381. Mickaharic, *Spiritual Cleansing*, 95–96.

remove a particular spirit, but one designed to clear the spiritual forces in a space while leaving room for good ones to return.

You will need:

- A white candle (one you can carry)
- A cleansing incense such as sage, rosemary, juniper, or sandalwood
- A favorite holy text or prayer (you can even use a poem if you are not inclined towards any denominational text)
- A bowl of water (holy water or salt-infused is good for this)
- A bell or other chiming instrument (if you have to you can use a ceramic bowl and a wooden spoon to get the right sound)

Begin by actually cleaning your house as best you can. Sweep and mop and vacuum. Get rid of any clutter. Open the windows (even just a bit, but all the way if possible). Wash surfaces and get the house really clean. Then, begin in the bottom-most floor in the room farthest from the front door. Enter each room and put your materials down in the center. Ring the bell three times.

Light your candle and let it burn, then your incense. Sprinkle water in each of the corners of the room while reciting your chosen verse, prayer, or incantation. Then, walk in a clockwise path around the room three times with the incense, creating a ring of smoke. Repeat with the candle (make sure to have a heat-proof plate or tray to set these down on when not holding them). Finish in the center of the room and ring the bell three more times and close any windows or doors you've left open. Move on to the next room and repeat, working your way in as much of a clockwise pattern around each floor of your house as you can. Finish the bottom floor, then move up a level (if you have a multi-level home, obviously). When you have completely cleansed each room of your house, go to the front door and repeat the cleansing there. Toss the rest of the water over the front threshold if you can (or at least sprinkle it there), extinguish the incense and candle, and close the door, blessing it as you do.

A Good, Old-Fashioned Curse

One final way that witches and the dead get tied together is the concept of the curse. Of course, many stories tell of curses placed by living witches on particular individuals, but there are also plenty of stories about witches leaving curses behind them to torment a group of people or an entire community. One such example is Moll DeGrow (sometimes a variant like "Dyer" or "Rowe" is used) from Maryland. Her story states that after being driven out of her village Moll died in the woods, leaving her handprints on a rock (which is still present near the town of Woodside—see chapter six for a fuller version of her tale). Other versions of the tale say that the mob came to burn her but found her dead already, sitting in a rocking chair with a grin on her face. In most accounts of her story, she is blamed for ill happenings in her area that she may or may not have had anything to do with, but her spirit lives on after her. She causes fires or makes it impossible for anything to grow near the remains of her cabin, and even gets blamed for missing children or injuries and deaths anywhere near her land.[382]

Other, similar curses linger on in other parts of North America as well. A Pennsylvania legend tells of a witch named Aunt Sally Hillock who was attacked by a man's dogs and later stabbed by his wife. Her curse lingered on and drove the man to flee from his home and join the army, but still he was pursued by her vengeful spirit. Finally, he hung himself, setting off a great storm and linking bad weather to Aunt Sally in the popular mind for years to come.[383] A legend from Columbia, Missouri tells of a group of witches who tried to entrap one of their neighbors, but when he refused to join them, they ran him out of town. The witches then disappeared, but the hill where they had worked was known as "The Devil's Garden," and nothing but sage-grass would ever grow on it.[384]

Perhaps the most famous of these witch curses is the Bell Witch of Adams, Tennessee, a legend I grew up hearing as I lived close by. She is often reputed to be a woman named Kate Batts in stories, although there are also those who think the spirit haunting the Bell family was simply using Kate's name as a way to mislead her

382. Purcell, "DeGrow, Moll," in *American Myths, Legends, & Tall Tales*, 299–302; Carey, *Maryland Folklore*, 50–52.

383. Botkin, *Treasury of American Folklore*, 690–92.

384. Botkin, *Treasury of Southern Folklore*, 541–43.

victims. The torments of the Bells involved pinches and slaps against the children, especially the teenage daughters in the household, as well as strange laughter and voices, bedclothes suddenly yanked off, and a number of other dastardly doings. The final attack was fatal, causing the family father, John Bell, to become ill and slowly waste away to death.

In all of these stories, the curse lingers on as a legacy of the witch's presence. The lore of magic passing through a family line also involves a type of legacy. What witches choose to leave behind them varies. In some cases, like Moll DeGrow's, a curse is a form of accountability or a demand for justice which might have been denied in life. In others, such as the tale from Missouri, the curse is a marker of witchcraft's presence in the landscape. The long-running trope of the "cursed Indian burial ground" has some shared DNA with these sorts of stories, too, in that it demonstrates a need to deal with the sins of the past, even if that disrupts the present. Witchcraft is rather good at disruption, and so a witch's curse is her insurance policy that magic lives on after her, even if it causes a little chaos in her wake.

THE WORK—Your Magical Last Testament

Given the option to leave a magical legacy, why do some witches choose the cursing route? We may not have any choice in whether we become Gray Ladies or Headless Horsemen in some sense, but we do get to make choices about the legacy we leave behind, even in our magic.

One thing that comes up often in folklore and discussions of magic is the "generational curse," the sense that a person feels like there is a curse hanging not only over themselves, but over their entire family line. There are plenty of unscrupulous magic workers who have perpetuated that story, as well, because it offers the opportunity for long-time repeat customers looking to ease the burden of the curse. In most cases, however, such generational curses are unlikely, or could be counteracted simply by finding a way to make peace or amends to an angry spirit or deceased witch. Even more helpful is if witches leave behind some indication of just *how* conditions like that could be met, or how they wish to be remembered.

Throughout this book, I have had you negotiate your "contract" several times. In chapter four, I had you draw up the terms of your own "deal with the Devil" (although it is truly a deal with yourself). In chapter fourteen I asked you to revise that contract even further, thinking about it as a living document and one that would change and grow with your magical practice. You have set the terms of your own initiation, and you have set the challenges and goals that will guide your path. You should continue to change and update that contract and renew your magical work, but at some point you also must consider what will happen when your "term" is up. What will you be leaving behind to those who inherit magic from you? What will you offer them to put them on their own path, while still helping to guide them with the lessons you've learned?

Why not draw up a document that outlines these points? A sort of magical last testament? Think of it as a sort of testament to your own magical life, what is sometimes called the "ethical will" of a person who has passed on. Write of your own life walking with witchcraft. If you are choosing to leave curses or blessings, explain them; let those who will be living with those consequences know why you are doing what you do. More importantly, figure out who will be the right person to find and inherit this magical legacy (someone always does, and in folklore it can't hurt to set the "conditions" for your intended heir to inherit the tremendous gift you are offering). Think about the world you will leave behind, and the magic you want to put into it. And think about how you can use this document, too, to help set your own goals while you're living.

Recommended Reading

The Encyclopedia of Ghosts & Spirits, by Rosemary Ellen Guiley. Guiley's books (I also recommend her encyclopedias on demons and witches) are always crammed with fun, brief entries that lead to rabbit holes of learning. You can discover a number of good stories in their pages that will guide you to new spirits, beasties, demons, and magical folk while also giving you a bit of background on each one. Plus, it's helpful to know your boggarts from your Black Shucks, and Guiley's book is great for that.

The *Spooky* Series, by S. E. Schlosser. This series, collected by an amateur folklore storyteller with lots of excellent illustrations and maps locating each tale in a specific place, documents a number of stories from around the United States and even parts of Canada and Mexico. It deals largely with ghost lore, although there are cyptids, demons, and witches in many of the stories, too, and it offers good insight into the many types of spirits discussed in this (and several other) chapters.

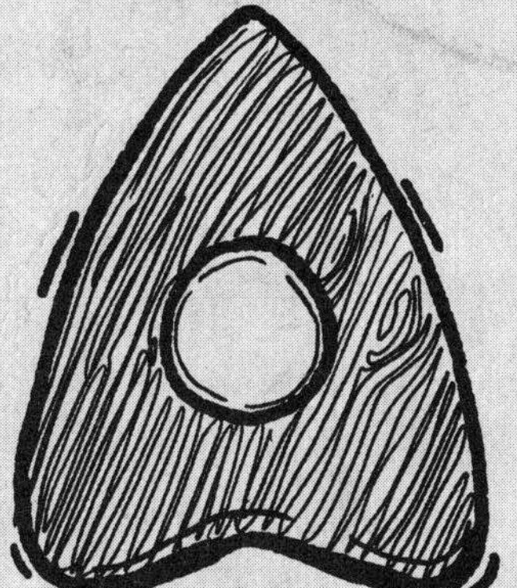

TWELFTH RITE: INVISIBILITY

Or, Secret Witcheries in the Modern World

"[M]uch like religious rituals allow people to tap into a larger mythical realm, by traveling to and entering a legendary or supernatural landscape participants ritually transform themselves into story characters and then wander around in a performative supernatural realm … Collective narrative becomes embodied, lived experience, not so much because legend has been transformed into fact but because the participants have become storied."*

* Gabbert, "Legend Quests and the Curious Case of the St. Ann's Retreat," 164.

CHAPTER TWENTY-TWO

Dangerous Games—Folk Magic in Contemporary Times

A group of teenagers pile into a car and head off into the night to visit an abandoned house, reputed to have belonged to Satanists practicing sacrifices and dark rituals an unknown number of years ago. Simultaneously, a group of young women in middle school stay up late at a Friday night sleepover, fueled by questions about their unknown futures and whether they will live in a mansion, alley, shack, or house (they may also be fueled by pizza and soda in their quest). Another group of college freshmen gather in their dorm's common lounge and pile papers with stat sheets, pencils, multi-sided dice, a handful of small pewter figurines, all while a smirking young woman settles in with a large folder and a thick book to guide them through an adventure with wizards, monsters, spells, weapons, curses, and treasure (they may be fueled by pizza and soda, too).

Tweens and teens playing levitation games in dark bedrooms, summoning ghosts in bathroom mirrors, driving out to sites of local legends to meet strange things in the dark, or even just sitting down to play a game of swords and sorcery—these are the secret rites of adolescence for many in North America. Contemporary kids and young adults are not alone. Games like this have been played for centuries: experimentations with unknown forces through Ouija boards, "Light as a feather, stiff as a board" incantations, an egg cracked into a glass of water or a meal served "backwards" in silence. All of these are a part of the deeply twined roots of folk magic here. While we frequently think of witchcraft as the provenance of a gifted few, the reality—one that I hope this book has opened up thus far—is that people are engaged with folk magic at various levels all the time. This chapter will explore a slightly different side of folk magic—folk magic that slips and slides around the public mind, folk magic that engages with the law of the land (for better or worse) or shapes the way we raise our children and offers them a space to play with divination, conjuration, and other sorceries.

We know that experimentation with occult forces touches any number of lives, even those lives that have strict prohibitions about magic, such as those from religiously conservative backgrounds. We also know that there are many who are uncomfortable with just how "occult" we can get.

Occult Experiments—Satanic Panics of Yesterday and Today

A young boy from a good, churchgoing family suddenly goes missing. When no one can find him, the local authorities turn their attention on a sect of a fringe religious cult in the community, one that wears strange costumes and chants in ancient tongues during its nighttime ceremonies. As the town sheriff investigates, he discovers some evidence that seems—to him—to point to the cult's ongoing diabolical activity. Rumors circulate that they desecrate churches and crosses, steal the blood of children to mix with their ceremonial wine, or even murder babies while masquerading as midwives so that they can later dig up the unbaptized infants for use in their hellish rites. Soon, the town is in an uproar, and members of the cult are brought in for questioning. The boy's body is then discovered, and many blame the cult, accusing them of the same sorts of satanic activity they've been circulating for years.

You can probably guess how a story like this would end, not least because it's a very old story. In Geoffrey Chaucer's "The Prioress' Tale," local Jews are quartered by horses and hung after the boy's body is discovered (a body that, in the story, continues to sing even after death because of a miracle wrought by the Virgin Mary).

Stories like the one from the *Canterbury Tales* are still in circulation, and still aimed at the stranger in the midst of a community, or sometimes even a longtime member who falls outside of everyone else's "normal." When touched by even a hint of the occult, in the case of three teenagers from West Memphis, Arkansas, it resulted in eighteen years of jail time (and an unfulfilled death sentence for a teenager).[385] In the case of the owners of the McMartin Pre-School, the school was shut down and the family who owned it went through a five-year, multi-million dollar trial to eventually prove their innocence.[386]

Stories of ritual murder and abuse are nothing new. The Chaucer tale dates to the fourteenth century, and has roots much older than that. Ironically, the genre of "blood libel" legends that erupted during medieval Christianity as a reaction to the presence of "satanic" Jews in their culture was the same sort of legend that was directed against early Christians in Ancient Rome.[387] By the time we reached the late twentieth century, that legend had become the spark that ignited a cultural phenomenon known as the "Satanic Panic." From the 1970s to the 1990s, rumors of ritual abuse—usually involving children—circulated among Christian religious communities, fueling a powerful resistance to anything perceived as "occult." The appearance of first-hand accounts of Satanic Ritual Abuse (SRA for short, because it was really that commonly reported) like *Michelle Remembers,* by Michelle Smith and her psychiatrist Lawrence Pazder, fueled the fires and led to a determined mob mentality that attacked people, usually older teenagers, who engaged in any sort of fringe cultural activity such as listening to heavy metal music, using Ouija boards, or playing Dungeons & Dragons games. Talk shows like *Geraldo* and celebrity psychiatrists like Pazder depended upon a steady stream of people being prompted to recall incidents in which they watched animals brutally slaughtered prior to or during pedophilic orgies (Geraldo Rivera later apologized for his involvement and for helping spread the rumors). Later revelations that many of the children who reported SRA were coached and rewarded for their sensational accounts, and that very few of the children showed any medical evidence of abuse, helped to uncover the phenomenon of False Memory Syndrome. Having those memories fed to them frequently did plenty of harm to the kids, even when there had been no physical abuse by those accused of it.[388]

385. See Berlinger and Sinofsky, *Paradise Lost: The Child Murders at Robin Hood Hills.*

386. See Robinson, "The McMartin Ritual Abuse Cases in Manhattan Beach, CA."

387. McGowan, "Eating People," 413–42.

388. See Bor, "One Family's Tragedy Spawns National Group."

The whole Satanic Panic period of recent history feels like an open wound. Those who practice occultism of any kind, from the gentlest version of New Age nature-veneration to those practicing Satanism in an avowedly anti-authoritarian and politically assertive way (but crucially a non-abusive way), all get tarred with the brush of Satanic Ritual Abuse. Have there been instances in which children (and adults, as not all rumors are about children) have been abused by Neopagans, witches, and occultists? Of course. There have been people in the magical community arrested for murder (even using ritual objects like athames) or caught in cases of sexual abuse, just as there have been in Christian, Jewish, Muslim, Buddhist, and other religious communities. In some cases, as in the sex abuse scandal with the Catholic Church which surfaced during the early twenty-first century, the religious group in question undoubtedly has some involvement, but by and large if a member of a faith community commits some sort of an atrocious abuse, they do so individually and not as part of a broader conspiracy or organization.

People in the late twentieth century were ready and willing to believe, though, that pretending to fight Demogorgons in a role-playing game or wearing black nail polish somehow indicated a conspiracy of abusive occultists. But there was never an organized occult group behind any of it, despite all the rumors, and that's important to remember.

Why, then, was it so easy to link the occult to abuse? Why did the occult even attract that kind of attention, given just how much of a fringe movement and personal path it was during most of the latter twentieth century? My suspicion, and one borne out by other scholars like Joshua Gunn, is that "occult" ideas work somewhat against themselves in the public mind.[389] Because they are intentionally hidden away or secretive, certain groups and practices become appealing as a form of cipher for other issues, such as patriarchal abuses within religious settings. It's worth noting, of course, that there absolutely were children being sexually abused by religious authority figures during the Satanic Panic, but almost entirely by ostensibly Christian priests and youth group leaders (which is not to say all abuse only happens in religious frameworks, either, as we know that youth sports camps at places like Penn State became epicenters of assault). Abusers coax or demand secrecy, and secrecy is

389. Gunn, *Modern Occult Rhetoric*, 171–203.

a term that maps easily onto "occult," and so we have the roots of a panic waiting to happen. Add to this the factional and political in-fighting among religious groups or hokey psychologists trying to get rich quick off of a false-memory phenomenon and those engaged in personally fulfilling occult practices suddenly wind up in the crosshairs of major news outlets and public outcry.[390]

The remarkable thing about all of this is just how backwards the assignment of blame winds up being. Most of the things that are "occult" in these accusations are things done openly—listening to heavy metal music is hardly a quiet activity, and you need a good-sized group of friends to launch any sort of decent Dungeons & Dragons campaign. Occult experimentation is often a part of typical rites of adolescence, too, as I mentioned at the beginning of the chapter. Folklore scholar Bill Ellis has even pointed out that many teenagers playing with Ouija boards come from conservative religious backgrounds and their experiments become part of their confirmation of their religious systems, thus actually *boosting* participation in the religion of their upbringing.[391] This book has largely been built upon the reality that magic is incredibly present in North America, surrounding us and informing many of our everyday practices, even if we don't consider ourselves "witches," necessarily. Those of us who do claim that term seem to have a lot more fun with the occult side of things, but that is not the point.

Magic is everywhere, and yet it still raises eyebrows and suspicions. Surges of interest in witchcraft and magic often seem to weave into a culture that treats spells and sorcery as either aesthetic or dangerous, and so we are not likely to see future panics and witch hunts go away. Magic is often both aesthetic *and* dangerous. It does us no good to live in fear, although we may try to pull on a cloak of invisibility from time to time.

390. Ellis, *Raising the Devil,* 87–119.

391. See Ellis, ibid.

FIG 22-1: The set-up for the Three Kings ritual.

DIRT UNDER THE NAILS
The Three Kings Rite

Rituals of divination are nothing new (see chapter seven), but that doesn't mean we aren't constantly inventing new ones anyway. The following ritual is called the "Three Kings Rite," and derives from folklore circulated on internet forums such as those featuring Creepypasta or the Reddit "NoSleep" board.

A word of warning: There are plenty of people who have performed this rite. Most seem to report being very shaken up by it, but also getting interesting experiences. Perform at your own risk.

You need:

- A candle
- Three chairs
- Two mirrors (that will fit in the chairs)
- A cell phone
- A good friend or significant other
- A cup (or bucket) of water
- An object of personal protection (such as a talisman you can wear)

You begin by setting up the room, usually around midnight before the ritual. You want a dark room with no windows, if possible (such as a basement), or with the windows blacked out or covered completely. Put the chairs into a triangle arrangement with one chair facing north. On the other two chairs put the mirrors. Sit down and make sure you can see both mirrors in your peripheral vision, but that you can also look directly ahead without staring straight into either one. Place the cup of water in the center of the chair triangle, but out of easy reach of anyone. Some versions of this also call for you to have a fan behind the north-facing chair (your "throne"). Leave the room dark and the door open, and go to bed, setting your alarm for 3:30 a.m. Make sure your partner/friend sets their alarm, too.

When you wake at 3:30 a.m., light your candle and go to the dark room. If, for any reason, your candle won't light or your alarm fails to wake you or the room is closed when you left it open—if anything seems "off"—leave the house with your friend and don't come back until after dawn. If all is well, take a seat in your throne and hold the candle in front of you. Do not let it go out for any reason. If it does, hold onto your object of protection and exit the premises with your friend in tow.

Say something to the effect of "Three Kings meet at the crossroads. Come King, Come Fool, Come Queen," three times. Eventually you should perceive figures or shapes from your peripheral vision in the other two chairs. One of you is now the King, one the Queen, and one the Fool. The Fool may try to lie or trick you, and the Queen may offer you good advice. You should assume you are the King, but know that from their perspective you are either the Fool or the Queen. You may ask questions or sit quietly and listen, but keep the candle lit and stay calm.

At 4:34 a.m. you should put out the candle and quietly leave the room. If you do not leave the room at this time, your friend should enter the room and call your name (hopefully breaking any trance you might have). They may also call you or douse your candle (or you) with the water, but they should not touch you until you have left the room and closed the door.

This ritual is essentially no different than grimoire spirit conjurings, but it is a decidedly modern take on the rites of summoning. As with most such rituals, keeping yourself protected and safe is frequently emphasized when this ritual is shared online. And, of course, it has now become a very popular sleepover game/experiment, and is exactly the sort of thing that will attract accusations of the kind during the Satanic Panic. On all fronts, as I've said before, you perform this at your own risk.

Hiding Your Imps—Witches and the Law

Legally, witchcraft also has dubious standing. Of course, when most people think about witchcraft and courts, they immediately turn to the Salem trials, but those were hardly the first or only prosecutions of witchcraft—and broader forms of magic—within American courts. Even the Salem trials were not particularly distinct at first, and some of those accused, such as Dorcas Hoar, had existing criminal records of practicing occult arts. Hoar famously performed divination and landed in court in 1678 on burglary charges with testimony that also touched on her work as a fortune-teller.[392] The introduction of the court of Oyer and Terminer ("to hear and determine") and the inclusion of "spectral evidence" (including the nightmarish visions and shrieking reactions of accusers in the presence of the accused) set those trials apart and became a source of immense regret to all involved, not least those who were eventually condemned to death (Hoar was so condemned but escaped after a last-minute confession and a commutation of her sentence that let her evade punishment).[393]

Trials for witchcraft began to shift after Salem, although the tide of change moved slowly in some places. By the 1830s, however, most accusations of evil magic were not taken seriously by courts east of the Mississippi, and even the religious court systems found in Spanish-held territories seldom pursued capital punishments for malefic sorcery. The exception became cases of fraud involving magic, which would downplay magical results in favor of holding professed occultists accountable for any claims they made and could not readily substantiate or replicate. In a time of snake oil salesmen, mesmerism, animal magnetism, Spiritualism, and other burgeoning new movements mingling the supernatural and the medical, application of laws was often uneven or biased but also sometimes necessary. People poisoned by foul concoctions made by unscrupulous men could use these laws to get some measure of justice, and fortune-tellers often got caught up in the dragnet of such accusations when their predictions either fizzled out or foretold unfavorable outcomes. Worse, some fortune-tellers would exploit their clients by convincing them that an ever-more expensive series of divinations and spells was needed to address a longstanding "curse" on them or their families.

392. Norton, *In the Devil's Snare*, 113; Karlsen, *Devil in the Shape of a Woman*, 38.

393. Howe, *Penguin Book of Witches*, 184–85.

Those substituting magic for medical treatments also ran afoul of these laws. Even into the twentieth century, the Pennsylvania Dutch community often relied on *brauchers* and hex-doctors to treat diseases that were beyond the known purview of medical science, such as infants who were "liver-grown" (*Aagewaxe*) or who showed signs of rashes and fever known as wild-fire (erysipelas, as contemporary medicine would have it). Such reliance could sometimes lead to misdiagnoses of other illnesses or a delay in medical treatment, and in 1909 one coroner reported six infant deaths brought to him on a single day after failed *braucherei* treatments, a problem that provoked Pennsylvania to pass the Medical Practices Act in 1911.[394]

Sensationalist cases also sometimes brought magic to public attention, although frequently in ways that showed the tidal shift from a pre-Industrial belief in witchcraft and magic to a much more skeptical perspective that mocked such beliefs. The 1928 murder of Pow-wow practitioner Nelson Rehmeyer in Pennsylvania caused a stir both inside and outside the Pennsylvania Dutch community because, to many, it seemed unbearably embarrassing. Rehmeyer's magical work went afoul of one of his neighbors, John Blymyer, who believed that Rehmeyer had cursed him. Blymyer then led two friends to break into Rehmeyer's home, bind him, and torture him to discover the location of his magic books as a way to break the hex (see chapter nineteen for a fuller version of the story). Rehmeyer was killed and the invaders tried to burn the home, but were caught and a trial ensued which garnered attention from papers in New York and even overseas. Locals felt ashamed that the spotlight was on them and that they were being mocked for still having such "backwards" beliefs among them.[395]

In 1975, Dianic Wiccan Zsuzsanna or "Z." Budapest (a pseudonym adopted upon her immigration to the United States) was arrested for fortune-telling at her San Francisco storefront under the aegis of a fraudulent mediums statute. The case eventually became an argument over religious freedom, as Budapest argued that her divinatory practices constituted religious rituals, and the California State Supreme Court agreed with her.[396] While this case opened up religious protections for Neopagan diviners, many also see it as a fine line being walked by those who

394. Davies, *America Bewitched*, 150–53.

395. See Davies, ibid.; See also Kriebel, *Powwowing Among the Pennsylvania Dutch*.

396. See Davis, *The Visionary State*, 210–12. See also Adler, *Drawing Down the Moon*.

charge money in any way for divinatory services, which is why some readers will suggest a "donation" rather than charging a fee or will specify that their fortune-telling services are "for entertainment purposes only."

Today, witchcraft and magic still operate under the strange umbrella of religion and entertainment, no matter how seriously practitioners take what they do or how little they see magic as a specifically religious practice. No one questions a teenager levitating their friend at a slumber party as to whether their magic is part of a sincerely held belief, of course, and plenty of those who practice magic balk at the commercialization of it as a sort of corruption of religious purity. Folk magic, however, has always been comfortable in those in-between spaces—divinations as party games or spells involving burying jars with psalms in them can be magical, entertaining, and religious simultaneously. Small and intimate magic never really goes away, it seems, even if we sometimes blush a bit as our little daily spells and weekly rituals accidentally meet the eyes of outsiders.

The transition from everyday belief in magic to a perspective that treats magic as something laughable, foolish, or ridiculous did not happen overnight, and there's nothing to say it will remain that way forever. Still, if you ask someone about what magic they do today, you likely will get a mocking laugh or a look of genuine surprise. Occasionally, though, you may find someone who tells you a bit about a candle they lit for a daughter's exam, or a crystal they carry to keep them calm and centered. Or someone who recoils in genuine horror, a valid reaction given some of the things magic seems to do for (and to) people. Magic is very good at hiding when it needs to, but remaining within reach in contemporary North America. And, of course, I don't think we'll ever lose the magic we find in the dark, after bedtime, when we stay up with a group of our friends, and someone says, "You know, I heard about this game..."

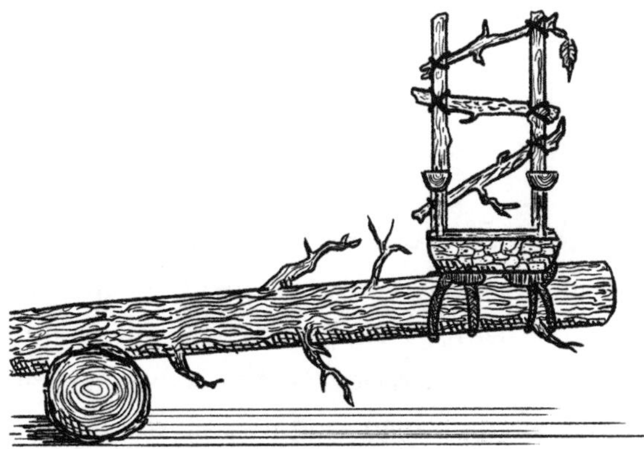

FIG 22-2: A ducking stool, used to prove one was not a witch.

SINGING BONES
Grace Sherwood

Grace Sherwood, the "Witch of Pungo," clearly had a temper. She had a bad reputation among her Virginia neighbors, a witch's reputation, although she was also quite clearly not well-treated by those around her. Grace, to her credit, fought back when accused of witchcraft, suing those who spoke ill of her for slander in court and usually winning her cases (as she did in 1689 and 1704). She seems to have dealt in herbal cures and other folk remedies, but her neighbors also claimed she would appear as a black cat and ride them, a charge that resulted in neighbor Elizabeth Hill physically attacking and beating Grace. Grace, of course, sued, but after winning her case Hill countersued and charges of witchcraft were formally drawn up again. This time, however, she took a very unorthodox approach to her trial. She agreed that she should be "ducked" or "swam" to prove that she was not, in fact, a malefic witch. The court was flummoxed, as the Salem trials were recent history and no one wanted to repeat that embarrassment. Yet, since Grace consented, the court agreed but insisted that the court have "care of her life to preserve her from drowning," after which she would be searched for witch's marks. The marks were, of course, found since any abnormal marking like a mole could be thus labeled. Grace floated during the trial, proving to the court she was, in fact, a witch. She was arrested and held for trial, but in the end we do not know if charges were dropped or if she simply served her time. We do know she lived on for a further three decades, thus escaping the fate of many of those accused in Salem.[397]

Hiding in Plain Sight—Obvious Invisibility

As you look, listen, or feel around you, hopefully you sense plenty of things that remind you of magic. There may be doors that have a bit of salt across their threshold or a jar of pebbles nearby to ward off unwanted nasties. A broom may be leaning against a wall, reminding you of stories of witch flight and emancipation. Perhaps something is baking in the oven, and the scent reminds you of a spell you've read in these pages or inspires thoughts of a new spell you want to write, one that you might pass down someday.

We come full circle here to the idea of "hiding in plain sight." Magic is all around us, practically all the time. New World Witchery is simply the folk magic that those of us in North America weave into our daily lives or pull out when the occasion calls for a solution that can't be met with non-magical means. It ties us to the past, of course. We have seen in this book that there have been people practicing magic in these lands for thousands of years, and we have only scratched the surface of the magic available here. It also leads us into the future, to magic we have not yet discovered or tried and magic that we may one day be handing down to someone else. We know that we have to hide magic sometimes—in a way, that may be part of magic's power, its ability to operate unseen. We also know that when magic does bubble up, we are not alone in sensing it, wanting it, and using it.

There will always be those who condemn magic or hate those who practice it. I can tell you, though, that they have not yet defeated the spell magic casts over us, nor have they ever been able to erase the fingerprints of magic from the world around us. Look around you and you will see magic in some of the most unexpected places: a necklace around a store clerk's throat that you know protects her from the evil eye, a spritz of urban graffiti in the shape of an empowerment sigil, or the laughter from a child's room where she and her friends have suddenly scared one another and broken into giggles after standing in front of a bathroom mirror with a candle.

397. Howe, *The Penguin Book of Witches*, 214–19; Illes, *The Encyclopedia of Witchcraft*, 780–81.

Magic is everywhere. It is yours, and mine, and ours. Go and work your spell, and carry with you the blessings of all who have come before you, weaving their magic into your story.

THE WORK—Share Your Magic

If you are coming to this section, then there is a good chance you have had a chance to absorb and transform the spells and folkloric workings of many magicians who came before you. You may have tried a few things picked up in the previous pages, or modified them to fit your own world a bit better.

An early section of this book begins with the concept of initiation, but that really comes down to the idea that you should share the witchery you do with others. For some, that involves a formal ritual to bless and guide a newcomer on a path of magical action. For others, though, initiation is simpler, a passing of a few words or a cherished object to someone else, giving them the gift of power and enchantment.

That is what I will ask of you in this work. Share your magic. Initiate someone else into the spells and enchantments you know. That does not have to involve anything overt or formal—magic operates in the hidden and unseen as easily as the bright light of day. You don't even have to call it magic, or tell someone exactly what you're doing. Perhaps you will be having coffee with a friend, or eating a family meal, and you pass on a bit of something you learned in these pages. Maybe you'll make a little gift for someone, an evil eye bead or a silver Mercury dime on a red string, and say nothing of the magic behind it (but protecting them from harm nonetheless). Perhaps that will start a conversation, one in which the magic they live gets passed to you, too. Or perhaps it will just be one of your own magical fingerprints left in the world, carrying a piece of you to someplace new.

Share your witchery, and see what happens.

Recommended Reading

America Bewitched: The Story of Witchcraft after Salem, by Owen Davies. If you are looking for a good deep-dive into the legal history of witchcraft in the United States, Davies has written the book for you. His historical method may be a bit dry for some, but the rewards of reading his work are plentiful, as you see just how frequently aspects of magic and witchcraft seem to show up in American history.

Raising the Devil: Satanism, New Religions, & the Media, by Bill Ellis. I have to admit that reading Bill Ellis is a treat for me. He writes in a combination of scholarly contemplation and enthusiastic, almost adolescent excitement. Given that several of his books deal with rumors and legends, that makes his work all the more enjoyable. In *Raising the Devil*, Ellis addresses the appeal of the occult in popular culture, as well as the ways it sometimes plays out in unexpected ways in the media. It's got some good contact points for those who want to know more about the Satanic Panic, as well.

Magickal Faerytales: An Enchanted Collection of Retold Tales, by Lucy Cavendish. If we're thinking about passing on magical knowledge, what better way than with a story? I've often thought fairy tales hold a number of magical secrets that we can discover, and while I do not get into that as much in this book (focusing instead on folktales and folklore in other forms), Cavendish's book does a marvelous job of connecting the old stories with potions, charms, and enchantments galore. The beautiful artwork by Jasmine Becket-Griffith enhances what is already a delightful book.

CODA
Or, the Value of a Witch Hidden in Plain Sight

"And so. All of this widespread bewitchment begs the question: Who gets to use the word *witch*? Well, as we've seen thus far, the short answer is: anyone who wants to."*

* Grossman, *Waking the Witch,* 256.

CODA—THE THIRTEENTH RITE

Witches in the Popular Imagination, for Better or Worse

Witches have never really gone away. Even when they have been forced into invisibility, or mastered invisibility to protect themselves, witches have remained a part of the nearly-everyday experience of most people in North America. They may not consciously be thinking of witches, witchcraft, or magic, but they permeate our culture too deeply for them to disappear. Even when people think of them as "fairy tales" or "just stories," witches linger at the edges of our consciousness, ready to don red caps and fly up our chimneys. We see them at Halloween, and read about them in books. They fill our screens: on television (think *Bewitched, Sabrina the Teenage Witch*, or its more recent incarnation *The Chilling Adventures of Sabrina*), in films (*The Wizard of Oz* or *Harry Potter*, anyone?), and even in popular apps like Bubble Witch.

In fact, witches seem to be having something of a renaissance. They are part of our popular culture, of course, with shows like *Little Witch Academia, Vampire Diaries, True Blood*, and others pouring out witchcraft by the cauldron-full (although I will always be partial to Willow Rosenberg on *Buffy the Vampire Slayer*). Witches and witchcraft are also experiencing ascendance in other places as well. Politically active women are embracing the archetype of the witch, and even discovering witchcraft as a practice through that process, especially in the era of #MeToo. Feminist scholars like Kristen J. Solleé see the witch as a transgressive figure for combatting the patriarchy that has dominated North American history for centuries.[398] People of Color, especially Women of Color, are also finding power through witchcraft, elevating and celebrating a long-slanderous term through the #bruja movement on social media platforms like Instagram and Twitter, which intertwines with other movements like Black Lives Matter. As of the writing of this book, for example, Witch of Color Bri Luna (a.k.a The Hoodwitch) has nearly half-a-million followers on Instagram, where she shares rituals, inspirational images, and witchy aesthetics.[399] Other marginalized groups, such as those in the LGBTQ+ community, are also embracing witchcraft as a source of reclaimed power. Political protest happens through spellwork, as seen in the famed "Trump Hex" initiated by Michael M. Hughes, author of *Magic for the Resistance: Rituals and Spells for Change.* Major news outlets send reporters to cover assemblies of African American women who practice magic (even if the coverage is somewhat flawed).[400] As Pam Grossman, author of *Waking the Witch: Reflections on Women, Magic, & Power,* says, "The witch is the ultimate feminist icon because she is a fully rounded symbol of female oppression *and* liberation. She shows us how to tap into our own might and magic, despite the many who try to strip us of our power. We need her now more than ever."[401]

This is not necessarily new. Witches have been embedded with transgressive culture for a long time. As Salem scholar Carol F. Karlsen notes, "New England witches were women who resisted the new truths, either symbolically or in fact. In doing so, they were visible—and profoundly disturbing—reminders of the potential resistance of all women."[402] When the Quakers were rejected by their Puritan neighbors, it was often under the aegis of "practicing witchcraft."[403] The Pueblo Revolt in New Mexico of 1680, led by a Native "sorcerer" named Popé, was thought to be the result of witchcraft and diabolism by the local Catholic authorities.[404] During the late 1960s,

398. See Solleé, *Witches, Sluts, & Feminists: Conjuring the Sex Positive.*

399. See Luna, "thehoodwitch."

400. See Sigal, "The Witches of Baltimore: Young Black Women Are Leaving Christianity and Embracing African Witchcraft in Digital Covens."

401. Grossman, *Waking the Witch,* 9.

402. Karlsen, *Devil in the Shape of a Woman,* 180–81.

403. Karlsen, *Devil in the Shape of a Woman,* 122–25.

404. Games, *Witchcraft in North America,* loc. 2827–2907.

a group of countercultural youths gathered outside the Pentagon in an effort to levitate, or "raise," it as a way to stop overseas military conflicts through magical ritual.[405] At the same time, a radical feminist group calling itself W.I.T.C.H. (sometimes said to stand for the "Women's International Terrorist Conspiracy from Hell") used the image of the witch as a way to reject patriarchal expectations and put forth feminist political and social campaigns.[406] Much of this activity paved the way for feminist Dianic covens during the 1970s and 1980s, as well.

FIG 23-1: Astrology, tarot, and other occult apps put modern witchcraft literally at our fingertips.

But what about folk magic? Where is folk magic in all of this? Once again, we come around to the nebulous term "witch," and its utility as so many things to so many different people. The witches we see on our screens and in our feeds often emphasize the power of the witch and her ability to shake up authority and stagnation. The magical side of the witch sometimes gets left behind for ritual, performance, aesthetic, or politics. Political hexes are important to those participating and those incensed by them, but folk magic is usually more intimate and direct, as we have seen in these pages. We can get very drawn into the aesthetics of witchcraft, because they are quite frankly pretty awesome. Who doesn't want to bedeck themselves in black and silver and bones and fill their house with candles, incense, and stones? That aesthetic, however, is only a surface one, something those who practice

405. See Buck, "The Plan to Levitate the Pentagon Was the Perfect Absurdly Inspiring Protest for the Time."

406. Clifton, *Her Hidden Children*, 119–20; Adler, *Drawing Down the Moon*, 207–208.

witchcraft have reclaimed from pop culture in many ways (and an aesthetic that continues to inspire even in recent years, offering us a potent commentary on what we find powerful in our contemporary world). The physical manifestations of magical practice are oh-so-frequently a well-stocked spice cabinet, a well-worn and marked family Bible, a drawer full of pins and bent nails or old wishbones or loose change, and a broom turned up behind a doorway.

And, if I'm being honest, a library a little overburdened with books of folklore. Perhaps that's just me, though.

Thankfully, folk magic also never really goes away. It continues to flourish in and among the everyday lives of those who use it and those who pass by it unaware. A penny picked up for luck or a slap of the car roof when passing under a yellow light send a little shiver of magic through the world. Astrology has undergone a boom in the early twenty-first century, with many people following YouTubers who provide regular astrological breakdowns and virtually everyone on Instagram or Snapchat knowing just when a Mercury retrograde happens. People maintain Facebook pages for departed loved ones like digital altars, with birthdays or death anniversaries receiving dozens of votary "likes" of remembrance. Children make paper fortune-tellers or play on apps that let them determine whether they will live in a mansion, alley, shack, or house.

Folk magic meets the needs of those who use it, and sometimes it hides in sneaky places to do so. As we reach the end of our journey here, I invite you to take a look at the rising popularity of the witch in a different way: she is hiding something. She is glamorous and beautiful, bold and unapologetic, standing up for rights and demonstrating ferocity to all who see her. And in between all of that, she may light a candle or turn over some cards to see what part of the future she can change. She works her spells, sometimes making them beautiful for her followers, but meeting her needs under the sparkling veil that the witch wears now. The rite of glamor, of hiding in plain sight, covers her. In the film version of *The Wizard of Oz,* no one questions why Dorothy has the power to go home all along, because the shoes are so beautiful that of course they must be magic. But Glinda doesn't say it's the shoes doing the work, does she? The shoes hide where the magic is really happening, in the new "witch" of Oz, Dorothy.

Witches ascend into glamor or descend into infamy as with the tides, but the witch always finds a place here. New World Witchery continues to be practical, wondrous, and traditional. We meet our needs with it, experience a world inhabited by enchantment through it, and pass it along to those who need it next.

In writing this book, I sincerely hope that I have passed some of that magic on to you.

Thank you for reading.

Be well.

Bibliography

Adler, Margot. *Drawing Down the Moon: Witches, Druids, Goddess-Worshippers and Other Pagans in America*. Revised edition. New York: Penguin Books, 2006.

Albanese, Catherine L. *A Republic of Mind and Spirit: A Cultural History of American Metaphysical Religion*. London: Yale University Press, 2008.

Ancelet, Barry Jean. *Cajun and Creole Folktales: The French Oral Tradition of South Louisiana*. New York: Garland Publishing, 1994.

Anderson, Jeffrey A. *Hoodoo, Voodoo, and Conjure: A Handbook*. Westport, CT: Greenwood, 2008.

Anonymous. *The Black Pullet*. New York: Red Wheel/Weiser, 2007.

Anonymous. *Dreams & Moles with their Interpretation and Signification*. London: London & Middlesex Printing Office, 1750.

Anonymous. *The Magical Powers of the Holy Death: Practical Spellbook*. S.M. Editorial, 2008.

Anonymous. *The Spaewife, or Universal Fortune Teller*. Kilmarnock: H. Crawford, Bookseller, 1827.

arrowclaire. "Keys to the Hidden Door: Part 1." Wandering Arrow. Last updated November 21, 2020. https://wanderingarrow.wordpress.com/2010/11/21/keys-to-the-hidden-door-part-i/.

Avila, Elena. *Woman Who Glows in the Dark: A Curandera Reveals Traditional Aztec Secrets of Physical and Spiritual Health.* New York: Tarcher Perigee, 2000.

Baker, Jim. *The Cunning Man's Handbook: The Practice of English Folk Magic, 1550–1900.* London: Avolonia, 2013.

Baring-Gould, Sabine. *Curious Myths of the Middle Ages.* London: Rivingtons, 1877.

Baudelaire, Charles. "The Generous Gambler," in *Paris Spleen.* New York: New Directions, 1970.

Beck, Horace P. *The Folklore of Maine.* Philadelphia: Lippincott, 1957.

Bell, Charles Bailey, and Harriet Parks Miller. *The Bell Witch of Tennessee.* Nashville: Charles Elder Publishers, 1972.

Berlinger, Joe, and Bruce Sinofsky, dirs. *Paradise Lost: The Child Murders at Robin Hood Hills.* 1996, HBO. Documentary, 90 minutes.

Bilardi, Chris. *The Red Church, or the Art of Pennsylvania German Braucherei.* Los Angeles: Pendraig Publishing, 2009.

"Black Sesame Seeds/Hei Zi Ma." Me & Qi. Accessed 2019. https://www.meandqi.com/herb-database/black-sesame-seeds.

Bledsoe, J. *Carolina Curiosities.* Charlotte: Fast & Macmillan, 1984.

Bliss, William Root. *The Old Colony and Other Sketches.* Boston: Houghton Mifflin Co, 1893.

Bolton, Henry Carrington. "Fortune Telling in America To-Day: A Study of Advertisements." *Journal of American Folklore* 8, no. 31 (Oct.-Dec., 1895): 299–307.

Booss, Claire, ed. *A Treasury of Irish Myth, Legend, and Folklore.* New York: Crown Publishers, 1986.

Bor, Jonathan. "One Family's Tragedy Spawns National Group." *The Baltimore Sun,* December 9, 1994. https://www.baltimoresun.com/news/bs-xpm-1994-12-09-1994343022-story.html.

Botkin, Benjamin, ed. *A Treasury of American Folklore.* New York: Crown Publishers, 1944.

Botkin, Benjamin, ed. *A Treasury of New England Folklore.* New York: Crown Publishers, 1947.

Botkin, Benjamin, ed. *A Treasury of Southern Folklore.* New York: Crown Publishers, 1949.

Bowles, David. *Border Lore: Folktales and Legends of South Texas*. Beaumont, TX: Lamar University Press, 2016. Kindle.

Bowles, David. *Feathered Serpent, Dark Heart of Sky*. El Paso: Cinco Puntos Press, 2018. Kindle.

Boyer, Paul, and Stephen Nissenbaum. *Salem Possessed: The Social Origins of Witchcraft*. Cambridge, MA: Harvard University Press, 1974.

Brandes, Stanley. "The Day of the Dead, Halloween, and the Quest for Mexican National Identity." *Journal of American Folklore* 111, no. 442 (Autumn 1998): 359–80.

Breslaw, Elaine G. *Tituba, Reluctant Witch of Salem: Devilish Indians and Puritan Fantasies*. New York: NYU Press, 1997.

Breslaw, Elaine, ed. *Witches of the Atlantic World: A Historic Reader & Primary Sourcebook*. New York: NYU Press, 2000.

Bronner, Simon J., and Joshua R. Brown, eds. *Pennsylvania Germans: An Interpretive Encyclopedia*. Baltimore: Johns Hopkins University Press, 2017.

Brooke, John L. *The Refiner's Fire: The Making of Mormon Cosmology, 1644–1844*. Cambridge: Cambridge University Press, 1994.

Brown, Dee. *Bury My Heart at Wounded Knee: An Indian History of the American West*. New York: Holt, Rinehart, & Winston, 1970.

Brunvand, Jan Harold. *American Folklore: An Encyclopedia*. New York: Garland Publishing, Inc., 1996.

Brunvand, Jan Harold. *The Vanishing Hitchhiker: American Urban Legends & Their Meanings*. New York: W.W. Norton, 1981.

Buck, Stephanie. "The Plan to Levitate the Pentagon Was the Perfect Absurdly Inspiring Protest for the Time." *Timeline*, February 26, 2017. https://timeline.com/pentagon-exorcism-ae0aad1b55c5.

Buenaflor, Erika. *Cleansing Rites of Curanderismo*. Rochester, VT: Bear & Company, 2018.

Burns, William E. *Witch Hunts in Europe & America: An Encyclopedia*. Westport, CT: Greenwood, 2003.

Burriss, Eli Edward. *Taboo, Magic, Spirits: A Study of Primitive Elements in Roman Religion*. London: Macmillan Co., 1931.

Bushman, Richard. *Mormonism: A Very Short Introduction*. New York: Oxford University Press, 2008.

Calef, Robert. *More Wonders of the Invisible World*. London: Nath. Hillar, 1700.

Carey, George C. *Maryland Folklore*. Centreville, MD: Tidewater Publishers, 1989.

Casas, Starr. *Working the Root: The Conjure Workbook, Volume One*. Los Angeles: Pendraig Publishing, 2013.

Cashdan, Sheldon. *The Witch Must Die!: The Hidden Meaning of Fairy Tales*. New York: Basic Books, 1999.

Cave, Alfred A. "Indian Shamans and English Witches," in *Witches of the Atlantic World: A Historic Reader & Primary Sourcebook*. Edited by Elaine G. Breslaw. New York: NYU Press, 2000.

Cavendar, Anthony. *Folk Medicine in Southern Appalachia*. Chapel Hill, NC: University of North Carolina Press, 2003.

Chase, Richard. *The Jack Tales: Folktales from the Southern Appalachians*. Boston: Houghton Mifflin Harcourt, 2003.

Cherry, Fannye N. "The Sources of Hawthorne's 'Young Goodman Brown.'" *American Literature* 5, no. 4 (January 1934): 342–48.

Chireau, Yvonne P. *Black Magic: Religion and the African American Conjuring Tradition*. Berkeley: University of California Press, 2003.

Clifton, Chas S. *Her Hidden Children: The Rise of Paganism and Wicca in America*. Lanham, MD: AltaMira Press, 2006.

Cohn, Norman. "The Night-Watch in Popular Imagination," in *Witches of the Atlantic World: A Historic Reader & Primary Sourcebook*. Edited by Elaine G. Breslaw. New York: NYU Press, 2000.

Cox, John H. "The Witch Bridle," in *Southern Folklore Quarterly* 7 (1943): 203–209.

Cummins, Antony. *The Dark Side of Japan: Ancient Black Magic, Folklore, Ritual*. Gloucestershire, UK: Amberly, 2017.

Cunningham, Scott. *Earth Power*. Woodbury, MN: Llewellyn Publications, 1997 (1983).

Cunningham, Scott. (1983) 1997. *Earth, Air, Fire, & Water*. Reprint, Woodbury, MN: Llewellyn Publications.

Cunningham, Scott. *Cunningham's Encyclopedia of Magical Herbs.* Woodbury, MN: Llewellyn Publications, 1998.

Curious Curandera. "The Basic Egg Limpia." Accessed October 7, 2009. www.curiouscurandera.com.

Curious Curandera. "Herbs Used in Spellwork." Accessed September 27, 2011. www.curiouscurandera.com.

Curious Curandera. "Spiritual Cleansing Six-Week Course." Accessed December 8, 2009. www.curiouscurandera.com.

Daigle, Ellen M. "Traiteurs and their Power of Healing: The Story of Doris Bergeron." *Louisiana Folklore Miscellany* VI, no. 4 (1991): 43–48.

Davies, Owen. *Popular Magic: Cunning-folk in English History.* London: Hambledon Continuum, 2007.

Davies, Owen. *Grimoires: A History of Magic Books.* New York: Oxford University Press, 2010.

Davies, Owen. *America Bewitched: The Story of Witchcraft After Salem.* New York: Oxford University Press, 2013.

Davies, Owen, ed. *The Oxford Illustrated History of Witchcraft and Magic.* New York: Oxford University Press, 2018.

Davis, Erik. *The Visionary State: A Journey through California's Spiritual Landscape.* San Francisco: Chronicle Books, 2006.

Davis, Hubert J. *The Silver Bullet, and Other American Witch Stories.* Middle Village, NY: Jonathan David Publishing, 1975.

Davis, Wade. *The Serpent and the Rainbow.* New York: Simon & Schuster, 1985.

Deren, Maya. *Divine Horsemen: The Living Gods of Haiti.* New York: McPherson Publishing, 1983.

Dillard, Tom. *Statesmen, Scoundrels, & Eccentrics: A Gallery of Amazing Arkansans.* Fayetteville, AR: University of Arkansas Press, 2010.

Donmoyer, Patrick. *Hex Signs: Sacred & Celestial Symbolism in Pennsylvania Dutch Barn Stars* (Exhibit Catalog). Kutztown, PA: Pennsylvania German Cultural Heritage Center, 2019.

Donmoyer, Patrick. *Powwowing in Pennsylvania: Healing Rituals of the Dutch Country* (Exhibit Catalog). Kutztown, PA: Pennsylvania German Cultural Heritage Center, 2015.

Donmoyer, Patrick. *Powwowing in Pennsylvania: Healing, Cosmology, & Tradition in the Dutch Country* (Exhibit Catalog). Kutztown, PA: Pennsylvania German Cultural Heritage Center, 2016.

Donmoyer, Patrick. *Powwowing in Pennsylvania: Braucherei & the Ritual of Everyday Life*. Kutztown, PA: Pennsylvania German Cultural Heritage Center, 2018.

Dorson, Richard M. *Buying the Wind*. Chicago: University of Chicago Press, 1974.

Dorson, Richard M. *Bloodstoppers & Bearwalkers*. Cambridge, MA: Harvard University Press, 1972.

Dr. E. "Making Doll Babies for Spiritual Use," in *The Black Folder: Personal Communications on the Mastery of Hoodoo*. Edited by Catherine Yronwode. Forestville, CA: Missionary Independent Spiritual Church, 2013.

Duncan, Hannibal Gerald, and Winnie Leach Duncan. "Superstitions and Sayings among the Southern Highlanders." *Journal of American Folklore* 42, no.165 (1929): 233–37.

Dundes, Alan. *The Meaning of Folklore: The Analytical Essays of Alan Dundes*. Boulder, CO: University of Colorado Press, 2007.

Eliason, Eric A. "Seer Stones, Salamanders, and Early Mormon 'Folk Magic' in the Light of Folklore Studies and Bible Scholarship," in *BYU Studies Quarterly* 55, no.1, (2016): 73–93.

Ellis, Bill. *Lucifer Ascending: The Occult in Folklore and Popular Culture*. Lexington, KY: University Press of Kentucky, 2004.

Ellis, Bill. *Raising the Devil: Satanism, New Religions, and the Media*. Lexington, KY: University Press of Kentucky, 2000.

Ellis, Bill. *Aliens, Ghosts, & Cults: Legends We Live*. Jackson: University Press of Mississippi, 2003.

Emery, George Alexander. *The Ancient City of Georgiana and the Modern Town of York (Maine) from Its Earliest Settlement to the Present Time*. Boston: G.A. Emery and Hervert M. Sylvester, 1909.

Emery, George Alexander. *Maine Pioneer Settlements: Old York.* Boston: W.B. Clarke Co., 1873.

Erdoes, Richard, and Alfonso Ortiz, eds. *American Indian Myths & Legends.* New York: Pantheon Books, 1984.

Fadiman, Anne. *The Spirit Catches You and You Fall Down.* New York: Farrar, Straus and Giroux, 1998.

Falassi, Alessandro. *Time Out of Time: Essays on the Festival.* Albuquerque: University of New Mexico Press, 1987.

Fee, Christopher R. and Jeffrey B. Webb, eds. *American Myths, Legends, & Tall Tales: An Encyclopedia of American Folklore.* 3 volumes. Santa Barbara, CA: ABC-CLIO, 2016.

Forester, Sibelan. *Baba Yaga: The Wild Witch of the East in Russian Fairy Tales.* Jackson, MS: University Press of Mississippi, 2013.

Frazer, James. (1890) 2009. *The Golden Bough: A Study of Magic & Religion.* Reprint. New York: Oxford University Press.

Gabbert, Lisa. "Legend Quests and the Curious Case of the St. Ann's Retreat," in *Putting the Supernatural in Its Place.* Edited by Jeannie Banks Thomas. Salt Lake City: University of Utah Press, 2015.

Gainer, Patrick W. *Witches, Ghosts, & Signs: Folklore of the Southern Appalachians.* Morgantown, WV: West Virginia University Press, 2008.

Games, Alison. *Witchcraft in Early North America.* Lanham, MD: Rowman & Littlefield, 2012. Kindle.

Gandee, Lee R. *Strange Experience: The Secrets of a Hexenmeister.* Englewood Cliffs, NJ: Prentice-Hall, 1971.

García, Nasario. *Brujerias: Stories of Witchcraft and the Supernatural in the American Southwest and Beyond.* Texas Tech University Press, 2007.

Gardbäck, Johannes. "Nordic Bread Spells," in *The Black Folder: Personal Communications on the Mastery of Hoodoo.* Edited by Catherine Yronwode. Forestville, CA: Missionary Independent Spiritual Church, 2013.

Gates, Jr., Henry Louis, and Maria Tatar, eds. *The Annotated African American Folktales.* New York: W.W. Norton & Co., 2018.

Genovese, Eugene. *Roll, Jordan, Roll: The World the Slaves Made.* New York: Penguin Random House, 1972.

"Ghosts and Witchcraft: A Region in New England Where Superstition Thrives." *The New York Times,* April 6, 1889.

Ginzburg, Carlo F. *The Night Battles: Witchcraft & Agrarian Cults in the 16th & 17th Centuries.* Baltimore: Johns Hopkins University Press, 2013.

Ginzburg, Carlo. *Ecstasies: Deciphering the Witches' Sabbath.* Chicago: University of Chicago Press, 2004.

Grossman, Pam. *Waking the Witch: Reflections on Women, Magic, & Power.* New York: Gallery Books, 2019.

Guiley, Rosemary Ellen. *The Encyclopedia of Witches & Witchcraft,* 2nd Ed. New York: Checkmark Books, 1999.

Gutiérrez, Ramón, S. Scalora, D. Salvo, and W.H. Beezley. *Home Altars of Mexico.* Albuquerque: University of New Mexico Press, 1997.

Gunn, Joshua. *Modern Occult Rhetoric: Mass Media and the Drama of Secrecy in the Twentieth Century.* Tuscaloosa, AL: Alabama University Press, 2005.

Hall, David D. *Worlds of Wonder, Days of Judgment: Popular Religious Belief in Early New England.* Cambridge, MA: Harvard University Press, 1989.

Hammond, Joyce D. "The Tourist Folklore of Pele: Encounters with the Other," in *Out of the Ordinary: Folklore & the Supernatural.* Edited by Barbara Walker. Logan, UT: Utah State University Press, 1995, 159–79.

Hand, Wayland D., ed. "Folk Medicine in French Louisiana," in *American Folk Medicine.* Berkeley: University of California Press, 1976. 215–234.

Hand, Wayland D., ed. *The Frank C. Brown Collection of North Carolina Folklore,* Vol. VI. Durham, NC: Duke University Press, 1961.

Hand, Wayland D., ed. *The Frank C. Brown Collection of North Carolina Folklore,* Vol. VII. Durham, NC: Duke University Press, 1961.

Harden, John. *The Devil's Tramping Ground and Other North Carolina Mystery Stories.* Chapel Hill: University of North Carolina Press, 1949.

Hardy, Rodger L. "Shhh … Do You Hear Someone Weeping?" *Deseret News.* Last updated October 18, 2005. https://www.deseret.com/2005/10/18/19917855/shhh-do-you-hear-someone-weeping.

Haskins, Jim. *Voodoo & Hoodoo: The Craft as Revealed by Traditional Practitioners.* Chelsea, MI: Scarborough House, 1990.

Hawthorne, Nathaniel. *Twice-told Tales,* Volume 1. Boston: American Stationers' Company. 1851.

Hawthorne, Nathaniel. "Young Goodman Brown," in *Mosses from an Old Manse* 1. Boston: American Stationers Company. 1846.

Hazzard-Donald, Katrina. *Mojo Workin': The Old African American Hoodoo System.* Champaign, IL: University of Illinois Press, 2012.

Henderson, Raechel. *Sew Witchy: Tools, Techniques, & Practices of Sewing Magic.* Woodbury, MN: Llewellyn Publications, 2019.

"History of Attacks against Persons with Albinism." *Under the Same Sun.* Accessed-July 15, 2013. http://www.underthesamesun.com/sites/default/files/History%20of%20Attacks%20against%20PWA.pdf.

Hohman, John George. *The Long-Lost Friend: A 19th-Century American Grimoire.* Daniel Harms, ed. Woodbury, MN: Llewellyn Publications, 2012.

Horowitz, Mitch. *Occult America: White House Seances, Ouija Circles, Masons, & the Secret Mystic History of Our Nation.* London: Bantam, 2010.

Howe, Katherine, ed. *The Penguin Book of Witches.* New York: Penguin, 2016.

Hufford, David J. *The Terror that Comes in the Night: An Experience-Centered Study of Supernatural Assault Traditions.* Philadelphia: University of Pennsylvania Press, 1989.

Hunter, Leslie Gene, and Cecilia Aros Hunter. "'Mother Lane' and the 'New Mooners': An Expression of 'Curanderismo.'" *The Southwest Historical Quarterly* 99, no. 3 (1996): 291–325.

Hurley, Gerald T. "Buried Treasure Tales in America." *Western Folklore* (Summer, 1951): 197–216.

Hurston, Zora Neale. (1942) 2006. *Dust Tracks on a Road: An Autobiography.* Reprint. New York: Harper Perennial Modern Classics.

Hurston, Zora Neale. *Every Tongue Got to Confess: Negro Folk-tales from the Gulf States.* New York: Harper Collins, 2001.

Hurston, Zora Neale. "Hoodoo in America." *The Journal of American Folklore* 44, no. 174 (1931): 317–417.

Hurston, Zora Neale. (1935) 2008. *Mules and Men*. Reprint. New York: Harper Perennial Modern Classics.

Hurston, Zora Neale. (1938) 2008. *Tell My Horse: Voodoo and Life in Haiti and Jamaica*. Reprint. New York: Harper Perennial Modern Classics.

Hutcheson, Cory Thomas. *54 Devils: The Art and Folklore of Fortune-Telling with Playing Cards*. CreateSpace Independent Publishing, 2013.

Hutcheson, Cory Thomas. "Aunt Caroline Dye: Sunbeam of the World," in *The Cauldron*, no.142 (November 2011): 29–35.

Hutcheson, Cory Thomas. "Home and Vehicle," in the *Oxford Handbook of American Folklore and Folklife Studies*. New York: Oxford University Press, 2019. 625-642.

Hutcheson, Cory Thomas. "Old Betty Booker." *American Myths, Legends, and Tall Tales*. Vol. II. Santa Barbara, CA: ABC-CLIO, LLC, 2016: 734–35.

Hutcheson, Cory Thomas. "Old Granny Tucker." *American Myths, Legends, and Tall Tales*. Vol. II. Santa Barbara, CA: ABC-CLIO, LLC, 2016: 735–36.

Hutton, Ronald. *The Stations of the Sun: A History of the Ritual Year in Britain*. New York: Oxford University Press, 1996.

Hutton, Ronald. *The Triumph of the Moon: A History of Modern Pagan Witchcraft*. New York: Oxford University Press, 2001.

Hutton, Ronald. *The Witch: A History of Fear from Ancient Times to the Present*. London: Yale University Press, 2017.

Hyatt, Henry M. *Folklore from Adams County, Illinois*. Alma Egan Hyatt Foundation, 193.

Hyatt, Harry M. *Hoodoo-Conjuration-Witchcraft-Rootwork Volume 2*. Cambridge, MD: Western Publishing, Inc., 1970.

"Ifa divination system." UNESCO Cultural Heritage. 2008. https://ich.unesco.org/en/RL/ifa-divination-system-00146.

Illes, Judika. *The Encyclopedia of 5,000 Spells*. New York: HarperOne, 2009.

Illes, Judika. *The Encylopedia of Mystics, Saints, & Sages*. New York: HarperOne, 2011.

Illes, Judika. *The Encyclopedia of Spirits*. New York: HarperOne, 2009.

Illes, Judika. *The Element Encyclopedia of Witchcraft*. New York: Harper Element, 2005.

Ingham, John M. *Mary, Michael, & Lucifer: Folk Catholicism in Central Mexico*. Austin: University of Texas Press, 1986.

Ingham, John M. "On Mexican Folk Medicine." *American Anthropologist* 72, no. 1 (Feb. 1970): 76–87.

Jones, David M, and Brian L. Molyneaux. *Mythology of the American Nations*. London: Hermes House, 2001.

Junker, Kristine. *Afro-Cuban Religious Arts: Popular Expressions of Cultural Inheritance in Espiritismo and Santería*. Gainesville, FL: University Press of Florida, 2014.

Kail, Tony. *A Secret History of Memphis Hoodoo*. Charleston, SC: The History Press, 2017.

Karlsen, Carol F. *The Devil in the Shape of a Woman: Witchcraft in Colonial New England*. New York: W.W. Norton & Co., 1998.

Kerr, Breena. "Tarot Is Trending, and Dior Predicted This Months Ago." *The New York Times*, October 25 2017. https://www.nytimes.com/2017/10/25/style/tarot-cards-dior.html.

Koch, Stephen, and Max Brantley. "Aunt Caroline Dye: 'The Worst Woman in the World?'" *Arkansongs/Arkansas Times*, January 2000.

Kreibel, David W. *Powwowing Among the Pennsylvania Dutch*. Philadelphia: Pennsylvania State University Press, 2007.

Lawless, Sarah Anne. "What Makes One a Witch." Last modified March 28, 2010. http://sarahannelawless.com/2010/03/28/what-makes-one-a-witch/.

Lecouteux, Claude. *The Tradition of Household Spirits: Ancestral Lore and Practices*. Rochester, VY: Inner Traditions, 2000.

Lee, Jonathan H. X., and Kathleen M. Nadeau, eds. *Encyclopedia of Asian American Folklore and Folklife*. Vol. 3 (ABC-CLIO, 2011).

Leeming, David, and Jake Page. *Myths, Legends, & Folktales of America: An Anthology*. New York: Oxford University Press, 2000.

Leland, Charles G. (1899) 2010. *Aradia: Gospel of the Witches*. Reprint. Newport, RI: The Witches' Almanac.

Long, Carolyn Morrow. *Spiritual Merchants: Religion, Magic, & Commerce.* Knoxville: University of Tennessee Press, 2001.

Looking Horse, Chief Arvol. "Concerning the Deaths in Sedona." *Indian Country Today*, October 16, 2009.

López, Celia. "Santa Fe, New Mexico," in *Brujerías: Stories of Witchcraft and the Supernatural in the American Southwest and Beyond*, by Nasario García. Lubbock, TX: Texas Tech University Press, 2007.

Luna, Bri. "thehoodwitch." Instagram account. https://instagram.com/thehoodwitch.

Madsen, William and Claudia. *A Guide to Mexican Witchcraft.* Insurgentes Centro, Mexico: Minutiae Mexicana, 1972.

Malotki, Ekkehart, and Ken Gary. *Hopi Stories of Witchcraft, Shamanism, and Magic.* Lincoln, NE: University of Nebraska Press, 2001.

Mann, Charles C. *1491: New Revelations of the Americas before Columbus.* New York: Vintage Books, 2006.

Mather, Increase. *An Essay for the Recording of Illustrious Providences.* Samuel Green Publishers of Boston, 1684.

McAtee, W. L. "Odds and Ends of North American Folklore on Birds." *Midwest Folklore* 5, no.3 (1955): 169–83.

McGowan, Andrew. "Eating People: Accusations of Cannibalism Against Christians in the Second Century." *Journal of Early Christian Studies* 2, no.4 (1994): 413–42.

McMillan, Timothy. "Black Magic: Witchcraft, Race, & Resistance in Colonial New England." *Journal of Black Studies* (Sept. 1994): 99–117.

McRobbie, Linda Rodriguez. "The Strange and Mysterious History of the Ouija Board." *Smithsonian Magazine* (Online Ed.). October 27, 2013. https://www.smithsonianmag.com/history/the-strange-and-mysterious-history-of-the-ouija-board-5860627/.

Meley, Patricia. "Adolescent Legend Trips as Teenage Cultural Response: A Study of Lore in Context." *Children's Folklore Review* 14, no. 1 (1991): 5–24.

Mickaharic, Draja. *Magic Spells of the Minor Prophets.* Lulu, Inc. 2007.

Mickaharic, Draja. *Spiritual Cleansing.* Newburyport, MA: Red Wheel/Weiser Books, 2012.

Miller, Jason. *Protection and Reversal Magick*. Newburyport, MA: Red Wheel/ Weiser Books, 2006.

Milnes, Gerald C. *Signs, Cures, & Witchery*. Knoxville, TN: University of Tennessee Press, 2007.

Montell, William Lynwood. *Upper Cumberland County (Folklife in the South)*. University Press of Mississippi, 1993.

Montgomery, Jack. *American Shamans: Journeys with Traditional Healers*. Ithaca, NY: Busca, Inc., 2008.

MormonThink. "Bigfoot." Accessed October 21, 2020. http://www.mormonthink.com/glossary/bigfoot.htm

Muise, Peter. "The Witch Bridle: Ride 'Em Cowgirl!" New England Folklore Blog. April 10, 2010.

Mullen, Patrick B. "The Folk Idea of Unlimited Good in American Buried Treasure Legends." *Journal of the Folklore Institute* (Fall, 1978).

"Native History: A Non-Traditional Sweat Leads to Three Deaths." *Indian Country Today*, October 8, 2013.

New World Witchery. "Episode 126—Magic and the Great Lakes." Podcast, 1:35:29. April 26, 2018. https://newworldwitchery.com/2018/04/26/episode-126-magic-and-the-great-lakes/.

Neighbors, Keith. "Mexican-American Folk Diseases." *Western Folklore* 28, no. 4, (1969): 249–59.

Nissenbaum, Stephen. *The Battle for Christmas: A Social and Cultural History of Our Most Cherished Holiday*. New York: Vintage Books, 2010.

Norton, Mary Beth. *In the Devil's Snare: The Salem Witchcraft Crisis of 1692*. New York: Vintage Press, 2003.

Oberon, Aaron. *Southern Cunning: Folkloric Witchcraft in the American South*. Alresford Hampshire, UK: Moon Books, 2019.

Opie, Iona, and Moira Tatem. *A Dictionary of Superstitions*. New York: Barnes & Noble Books, 1989.

Orapello, Christopher, and Tara-Love Maguire. *Besom, Stang, & Sword*. Newburyport, MA: Red Wheel/Weiser Books, 2018.

Orth, Richard L. T. *Folk Religion of the Pennsylvania Dutch: Witchcraft, Faith Healing, and Related Practices.* Jefferson, NC: McFarland & Co., 2018.

Paredes, Americo. *Folktales of Mexico.* Chicago: University of Chicago Press, 1970.

Paddon, Peter. *Visceral Magic.* Green Valley Lake, CA: Pendraig, 2011.

Parker, Mary Ann. "The Hoo Doo Woman of Arkansas." Last updated March 2016. Ozark Mountain Region Website—A division of the Arkansas Parks Department. http://www.ozarkmountainregion.com/node/2673.

Parton, Dolly. "These Old Bones." *Horns & Halos.* Sugar Hill Records, 2002.

Pater, Ezra. *The Fortune Teller & Experienced Farrier.* Exeter: Herald Printing Office, 1794.

Paulson, Kathryn. *Witches, Potions, & Spells.* Mt. Vernon, NY: Peter Pauper Press, 1971.

Phoenix, Robert. *The Pow-Wow Grimoire.* CreateSpace Independent Publishing, 2014.

Pieper, Jim. *Guatemala's Folk Saints.* Los Angeles: Pieper & Associates, 2002.

Pinckney, Roger. *Blue Roots: African-American Folk Magic of the Gullah People.* Orangeburg, SC: Sandlapper Publishing, 2003.

Pitt Rivers Museum Collection. "Caul: A Sailor's Charm." http://england.prm.ox.ac.uk/englishness-sailors-charm.html.

Potts, Albert M. *The World's Eye.* Lexington, KY: University of Kentucky Press, 1982.

Powwowing in Pennsylvania (Exhibit Catalog). Schwenkfelder Library & Heritage Center and Pennsylvania German Cultural Heritage Center at Kutztown University, July 19, 2015-January 31, 2016.

Price, Sadie F. "Kentucky Folk-lore." *The Journal of American Folklore* 14, no. 52 (Jan.-Mar. 1901): 30–38.

Probert, Thomas. *Lost Mines and Buried Treasures of the West.* Berkeley: University of California Press, 1977.

Puckett, Newbell Niles. (1926) 2017. *Folk Beliefs of the Southern Negro.* Reprint. Chapel Hill, NC: UNC Press.

Purcell, Ryan Donovan. "DeGrow, Moll," in *American Myths, Legends, & Tall Tales: An Encyclopedia of American Folklore.* Edited by Christopher R. Fee and Jeffrey B. Webb. Santa Barbara, CA: ABC-CLIO, 2016.

Raboteau, Albert J. *Slave Religion: The 'Invisible Institution' in the Antebellum South.* New York: Oxford Univ. Press, 2004.

Raedisch, Linda. *Night of the Witches: Folklore, Traditions, & Recipes for Celebrating Walpurgis Night.* Woodbury, MN: Llewellyn Publications, 2011.

Raedisch, Linda. *The Old Magic of Christmas: Yuletide Traditions for the Darkest Days of the Year.* Woodbury, MN: Llewellyn Publications, 2013.

Randolph, Vance. *Ozark Magic and Folklore.* Minneola, NY: Dover Publications, 1964.

Richards, Jake. *Backwoods Witchcraft: Conjure & Folk Magic from Appalachia.* Newburyport, MA: Red Wheel/Weiser, 2019.

Richards, Jake. "Grave Traditions: the Southern Mourning Jug." *Holy Stones and Iron Bones Blog.* Last updated May 27, 2019. https://littlechicagoconjure13.wordpress.com/2019/05/27/grave-traditions-the-southern-mourning-jug/?fbclid.

Richards, Jake. "When the Bones are Calling." *Holy Stones & Iron Bones Blog.* Last modified June 28, 2017. https://littlechicagoconjure13.wordpress.com/2017/06/28/when-the-bones-are-calling/.

Roberts, Hilda. "Louisiana Superstitions." *Journal of American Folklore* 40, no. 156 (1927): 144–208.

Robinson, B.A. "The McMartin Ritual Abuse Cases in Manhattan Beach, CA." ReligiousTolerance.org. Last updated March 17, 2016. http://www.religioustolerance.org/ra_mcmar.htm.

Russell, Jeffrey Burton. *Witchcraft in the Middle Ages.* Ithaca, NY: Cornell University Press, 1972.

Russell, Randy, and Janet Barnett. *The Granny Curse, and Other Ghosts and Legends from East Tennessee.* Durham, NC: John F. Blair Publisher, 1999.

Saussy, Briana. *Making Magic: Weaving Together the Everyday and the Extraordinary.* Boulder, CO: Sounds True, 2019.

Schlosser, S.E. (2004) 2020. *Spooky Maryland.* Reprint. Guilford, CT: Globe Pequot Press.

Schlosser, S.E. *Spooky New Jersey.* Guilford, CT: Globe Pequot Press, 2006.

Schlosser, S.E. *Spooky New York.* Guilford, CT: Globe Pequot Press, 2005.

Schlosser, S.E. *Spooky Pennsylvania.* Guilford, CT: Globe Pequot Press, 2006.

Schlosser, S.E. *Spooky South.* Guilford, CT: Globe Pequot Press, 2004.

Schlosser, S. E. *Spooky Southwest: Tales of Hauntings, Strange Happenings, & Other Local Lore.* Guilford, CT: Globe Pequot Press, 2004.

Schmidt, Leigh Eric. *Consumer Rites: The Buying and Selling of American Holidays.* Princeton: Princeton University Press, 1997.

Schreiwer, Robert L. *The First Book of Urglaawe Myths.* Bristol, PA: Distelfink Sippschaft, 2014.

Schreiwer, Robert L. "Requirements for Butzemann Construction." Distelfink Sippschaft of Urglaawe Website. Last updated January 2016. http://site.distelfink.org/Resources.html.

Schwartz, Howard. *Lilith's Cave: Jewish Tales of the Supernatural.* New York: Harper & Row, 1988.

Sigal, Samuel. "The Witches of Baltimore: Young Black Women Are Leaving Christianity and Embracing African Witchcraft in Digital Covens." *The Atlantic,* November 5, 2018. https://www.theatlantic.com/international/archive/2018/11/black-millennials-african-witchcraft-christianity/574393/.

Simmons, Marc. *Witchcraft in the Southwest: Spanish & Indian Supernaturalism on the Rio Grande.* Lincoln, NE: Bison Books, 1980.

Simmons, Marc. "Pueblo Witchcraft," in *Witches of the Atlantic World: A Historic Reader & Primary Sourcebook.* Edited by Elaine G. Breslaw. New York: NYU Press, 2000.

Slade, Paddy. *Magic: Diary of a Village Witch.* Milverton, UK: Capall Bann Pub., 2001.

Solleé, Kristen J. *Witches, Sluts, & Feminists: Conjuring the Sex Positive.* Berkeley: ThreeL Media, 2017.

Stough, Mulford. "The Yellow Fever in Philadelphia 1793." *Pennsylvania History* 6, no. 1 (January 1939): 6–13.

Stratton, Kimberly, and Dayna Kalleres, eds. *Daughters of Hecate: Women and Magic in the Ancient World.* New York: Oxford University Press, 2014.

Taliman, Valerie. "Selling the Sacred." *Indian Country Today,* October 13, 2009.

The Talking Board Historical Society. tbhs.org.

Tallant, Robert. *Voodoo in New Orleans*. Gretna, LA: Pelican, 1983.

Taylor, Alan. "The Early Republic's Supernatural Economy: Treasure Seeking in the American Northeast, 1780–1830." *American Quarterly* (Spring 1986): 6–34.

Taylor, Nicole. "Hot Links and Red Drinks: The Rich Food Traditions of Juneteenth." *The New York Times*. June 13, 2017. https://www.nytimes.com/2017/06/13/dining/juneteenth-food-slavery-abolition.html.

Thomas, Daniel & Lindsey. *Kentucky Superstitions*. Princeton: Princeton University Press, 1920.

Thomas, Jeannie Banks. *Putting the Supernatural in Its Place: Folklore, the Hypermodern, and the Ethereal*. Salt Lake City: University of Utah Press, 2015.

Thomas, Keith. *Religion and the Decline of Magic*. London: Penguin UK, 2003.

Torres, Eliseo "Cheo." *Curandero: A Life in Mexican Folk Healing*. Albuquerque: University of New Mexico Press, 2005.

Turner, Kay. "The Witch in Flight: AFS Presidential Address." Presented at Annual Meeting of the American Folklore Society, October 2017. Video. https://www.youtube.com/watch?v=ALw2Zw_4hyI.

Ulrich, Laurel Thatcher. *A Midwife's Tale: The Life of Martha Ballard, Based on Her Diary, 1785–1812*. New York: Vintage, 1991.

Vang, Christopher Theo. *Hmong Refugees in the New World: Culture, Community, & Opportunity*. Jefferson, NC: McFarland & Co., 2016.

Virginia Historical Society. "Grace Sherwood: The 'Witch of Pungo.'" Virginia History Explorer.

Wachter, Aidan. *Six Ways: Approaches & Entries for Practical Magic*. Red Temple Press, 2018.

Washington, Glynn. "The Curse." *Snap Judgement Presents: Spooked*. September 21, 2017. Podcast, 22:33. https://www.wnycstudios.org/podcasts/spooked/episodes/the-curse.

Watts, Linda S. *The Encyclopedia of American Folklore*. Infobase Publishing, 2007.

Weisman, Richard. *Witchcraft, Magic, and Religion in Seventeenth-Century Massachusetts*. Amherst, MA: University of Massachusetts Press, 1985.

White, Sam. "'Shewing the difference between their conjuration, and our invocation on the name of God for rayne': Weather, Prayer, and Magic in Early American Encounters." *The William and Mary Quarterly* 72, no. 1 (January 2015): 33–56.

White, Thomas. *Witches of Pennsylvania*. Charleston, SC: The History Press, 2013.

Wigginton, Eliot, ed. *The Foxfire Book*. New York: Anchor Press, 1972.

Wigginton, Eliot, ed. *Foxfire 2 (Foxfire Series)*. New York: Anchor Press, 1973.

Wigginton, Eliot, ed. *Foxfire 3 (Foxfire Series)*. New York: Anchor Press, 1975.

Wilby, Emma. *Cunning Folk & Familiar Spirits*. Chicago: Sussex Academic Press, 2005.

Wolf, John Quincy. "Aunt Caroline Dye: The Gypsy in the 'St. Louis Blues.'" *Southern Folklore Quarterly* 33 (1969): 339–46.

Yeats, William Butler, and Lady Gregory. *A Treasury of Irish Myth, Legend, & Folklore: Fairy & Folk Tales of the Irish Peasantry*. New York: Avenel Books, 1988.

Yoder, Don. *Discovering American Folklife: Essays on Folk Culture & the Pennsylvania Dutch*. Mechanicsburg, PA: Stackpole Books, 2000.

Yronwode, Catherine, ed. *The Black Folder: Personal Communications on the Mastery of Hoodoo*. Forestville, CA: Missionary Independent Spiritual Church, 2013.

Yronwode, Catherine. *Hoodoo Herb & Root Magic*. Forestville, CA: Lucky Mojo Press, 2002.

Yronwode, Catherine. *Throwing the Bones: How to Foretell the Future with Bones, Shells, and Nuts*. Forestville, CA: Lucky Mojo Curio Company, 2012.

Zakroff, Laura Tempest. *The Witch's Cauldron*. Woodbury, MN: Llewellyn Publishing, 2017.

Index

G

N

Q

R

To Write to the Author

If you wish to contact the author or would like more information about this book, please write to the author in care of Llewellyn Worldwide Ltd. and we will forward your request. Both the author and the publisher appreciate hearing from you and learning of your enjoyment of this book and how it has helped you. Llewellyn Worldwide Ltd. cannot guarantee that every letter written to the author can be answered, but all will be forwarded. Please write to:

Cory Thomas Hutcheson
℅ Llewellyn Worldwide
2143 Wooddale Drive
Woodbury, MN 55125-2989

Please enclose a self-addressed stamped envelope for reply, or $1.00 to cover costs. If outside the U.S.A., enclose an international postal reply coupon.

Many of Llewellyn's authors have websites with additional information and resources. For more information, please visit our website at http://www.llewellyn.com

Notes

Notes

Notes

Notes

Notes

Notes

Notes

Notes

Notes

Notes

Notes